With best wishes

Marcus Braybrooke

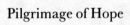

Pilgrimage of Hope

Marcus Braybrooke

Pilgrimage of Hope

One Hundred Years of
Global Interfaith Dialogue

Crossroad · New York

1992
The Crossroad Publishing Company
370 Lexington Avenue, New York, NY 10017

Printed in Great Britain
Library of Congress Cataloging-in-Publication Data
Braybrooke, Marcus
    Pilgrimage of hope : one hundred years of global
        interfaith dialogue.
    Marcus Braybrooke.
        p.   ca.
    Includes index.
    ISBN 0–8245-0949-8
    1. Religions—Relations—History.   I. Title
BL410.B72   1991b
291.1'72—dc20   91–35765
                                                  CIP

To Mary

*'A Devoted Companion and Unfailing Support
in this Pilgrimage'*

Contents

Preface

This book is primarily a tribute to the many people in different countries, who, through various organizations have worked for inter-religious co-operation. I am grateful to all who have been or are active in the interfaith movement. Without them, I would have had nothing to write about! There are many colleagues with whom I have worked closely and rereading reports and correspondence has brought back vivid memories. Some colleagues have become close friends and one of the joys of interfaith work is to have friends in each religion – even if it sometimes means that you have enemies in your own!

I am especially grateful to a number of people who have helped me with this book and who have provided me with material, answered my questions, or read the draft of one or other chapter. Amongst them, I mention by name Rev. Dr Wesley Ariarajah, Dr John Berthrong, Dr Francis Clark, Fr M. Fitzgerald, Rev. Diether Gehrmann, Rev. Peter Godfrey, Dr Homer A. Jack, Maria Joyce, Dr Frank Kaufmann, Dr Peter Laurence, Mrs Heather McConnell, Mr Brian Pearce, Sally Richmond, Richard Richmond, Rev. Dr Christoph Schmauch, Mr William Stansmore, Mr Peter Stewart, Mr David and Mrs Celia Storey, Dr John Taylor, Mrs Ruth Weyl, Dr Michael Pye and Dr Jacques Fisher. My thanks also go to Rev. Andrew Hill for his help in obtaining the cover photograph. Again I am grateful to my family for their support: to Mary, to whom this book is dedicated, to Jeremy Braybrooke and to Rachel and Peter Hobin. I am also grateful again to the help and encouragement of Rev. Dr John Bowden and other members of SCM Press as well as Werner Mark Linz of the Crossroad Publishing Company.

Some of the material is drawn from my *Interfaith Organizations, 1893–1979: An Historical Directory*, published by The Edwin Mellen Press. Much has happened in the last ten years and I have reworked all the earlier material, having had access to more sources. The plan of the book also is different. This book is intended to be a history. For a directory of organizations the reader would do well to consult the *Interfaith Directory* edited by Dr Francis Clark, although addresses of major organizations are given in the notes.

A history of necessity is selective, whereas a directory tries to be comprehensive. In this history the primary emphasis is on the four international interfaith organizations, namely, the International Association for Religious Freedom, the Temple of Understanding, the World Congress of Faiths and the World Conference on Religion and Peace. Their work, however, can only be understood in context, so, besides an account of the 1893 World's Parliament of Religions, I sketch the development of bilateral conversations, of the initiatives in dialogue now being taken by religions themselves and the growth of the academic study of world religions, both in universities and schools. There is some unavoidable overlap and repetition.

The need for all who are concerned for interfaith understanding to share their resources so that their efforts are more effective has seemed to me, for some time, to be obvious and urgent. The book ends with an account of attempts to encourage this co-operation, of which one fruit is the widespread agreement to mark 1993 as A Year of Inter-religious Understanding and Co-operation.

I am conscious of my Christian and European perspective. Certainly Christians and Europeans or Americans have often taken the initiative in interfaith work, but the interfaith movement is now very much an inter-religious and international effort, to which people of many faiths and countries are contributing. I have not been able to acquire as much detailed information about Asian, and especially about Japanese initiatives, as I would have wished. Little of the information is available in English. I apologise to those whose work has not been mentioned. One of my dreams is the establishment of an International Interfaith Centre, where information on the many interfaith organizations would be documented and recorded.

My hope is that this book will make more widely known what has been achieved in one hundred years of the interfaith movement, so that people are better prepared to mark 1993 as a Year of Inter-religious Understanding and Co-operation. May the Year live up to its name and more people share in the pilgrimage of the interfaith movement which offers hope both to individuals, to our national communities and to our world society.

August 1991

Marcus Braybrooke

Introduction

In 1993 the Interfaith Movement will celebrate its one hundredth birthday. This will come as a surprise to those who speak of interfaith dialogue as being still 'in its babyhood' or 'not yet come of age'.

Although isolated figures like the Buddhist Emperor Asoka or the Moghul Emperor Akbar or the mediaeval Cardinal Nicholas of Cusa advocated religious tolerance, the beginnings of the interfaith movement are usually traced to the World's Parliament of Religions, which was held in Chicago in 1893.

The distinctive feature of the interfaith movement is the effort to ensure that the relationships of religious people are respectful and co-operative rather than competitive. The history of religions has been marked, on the whole, by hostility and rivalry. Religions and indeed rival groups within religions have claimed possession of the truth. Those who disagreed with them were wrong and to be refuted and perhaps physically repressed and persecuted.

Such attitudes still persist. In many parts of the world, religious rivalries enflame existing bitterness and conflict. Yet increasingly members of all religions are recognizing that such hostility betrays the true spirit and teaching of their faith.

How to relate to those of other faiths, however, remains a problem. Indeed it is one of the continuing themes of this book. There are those who actively seek the creation of one world religion. Some who hold this view have participated in the interfaith movement, but the great majority of those involved in interfaith organizations recognize the distinctiveness and differences between religions. Even so, they have sought a basis for coming together, perhaps in the search for peace and human rights, perhaps in the hope of a coming convergence of religions. For some believers, such a coming together seems to threaten traditional claims to possess the final or unique revelation of God. The interfaith movement has, therefore, challenged members of the great religions to rethink their theological understanding of other religions.

It is impossible to give a complete picture of the interfaith movement. It is essentialy a meeting of people, whose lives have been changed and enriched. Many could speak of the friendships which they have made and the new awareness of God which they have discovered. Here it is only the growth of organizations and the multiplication of conferences that can be chronicled. The external history can be told, not the inner adventure of the Spirit.

The story begins with the World's Parliament of Religions in Chicago in 1893. It was shaped by Christian and American presuppositions, but gave a first platform in the West for some Asian religious leaders. Rather than initiating the meeting of religions it was a focus for various developments then taking place. Nor did the Parliament initiate a continuing organization, although several bodies look back to it for inspiration.

The first surviving interfaith body to emerge was what is now known as The International Association for Religious Freedom, although it is only in recent years that it has become increasingly an interfaith rather than a Unitarian organization. The World Congress of Faiths, inspired by Sir Francis Younghusband, was formed in 1936 and the Temple of Understanding, the dream of Judith Hollister, was founded in 1960. All three, whilst taking seriously the distinctiveness of religious traditions and whilst repudiating syncretism, have looked for an underlying or emerging unity.

Those whose approach to inter-religious co-operation has arisen from their work for peace have been more ready to recognize the differences of religions and have avoided theological and philosophical discussion. Their work has been more practical. The World Conference on Religion and Peace has brought together leaders of many religions in the search for peace. Increasingly, religious leaders are conferring together about issues of human rights and the threats to the environment.

Such practical co-operation has only been made possible by the work of other interfaith bodies in removing suspicion and prejudice and in encouraging members of one religion to meet, in good conscience, with members of another religion. In this task, the representative religious bodies have played an increasing part. They have encouraged their members to meet people of other faiths and have produced theological justification of this. The lead was taken by the Vatican and the World Council of Churches, but other religious bodies now share in this work.

If the distinctiveness of each religion is recognized, it follows that the conversation between particular religions will have its special character. In recent years, the number of bilateral conversations has increased rapidly. In some cases, particularly in the field of Jewish-Christian relations, international organizations have developed to encourage these exchanges. As yet, one party to most of the bilateral conversations are Christians.

The interest in other religions has both stimulated, and been stimulated by academic study. Slowly the teaching of world religions has spread to many schools and colleges.

The growth of international inter-religious dialogue and co-operation has been accompanied by similar growth in many countries and localities. In some areas, Networks have emerged to stimulate such developments.

In terms of activity, it is clear that inter-religious dialogue has spread to many parts of the world and involves people at many levels of society. Yet religious intolerance and extremism persists – indeed, in many places, it seems to be on the increase. Religions have, on the whole, been powerless to stop conflict and may well embitter it. The conviction, however, voiced recently by Professor Hans Küng, that there will be no world peace without peace between religions echoes the dream of those who promoted the World's Parliament of Religions. It is a hope that has inspired the interfaith movement and gives to it continuing urgency today. Indeed there are those who believe religions' ability to contribute to world peace and justice will be the test of religions' future credibility.

Yet the practical urgency of religious co-operation should not hide the search for truth which is at the heart of inter-religious dialogue. The expectation is that as we come closer to each other we shall also come closer to the Divine Source of Light and Life and Love.

Inter-religious dialogue may be a pilgrimage of hope if it helps to unite people of many faiths in awareness of their unity as members of the one human family and in their concern for each other and if it helps to deepen them in communion with the Eternal.

PART I

The World's Parliament of Religions

'When the religious faiths recognize each other as brothers, children of one Father . . . then . . . will the nations of the earth yield to the Spirit of concord and learn war no more.'

· 1 ·

The World's Parliament
of Religions I

Two days before the end of the World Columbian Exposition, of which the World's Parliament of Religions was part, the Mayor of Chicago was assassinated. This led to the cancellation of the elaborate closing ceremonies which had been planned. Instead, the flags hung at half mast during a simple benediction. Then, less than three months later, fire swept through the White City which had housed the Exhibition.[1]

Looking back after a century which has seen the bloodiest of wars and the resurgence of religious extremism and intolerance, it may seem that the dreams of the Chicago World's Parliament of Religions were as short lived as the euphoria and the buildings of the exposition. Had the White City, asked Rabbi Emil Hirsch of Chicago, been just 'a dream, unreal, destined to vanish into thin air?' 'No', was his answer. Hirsch compared the Exposition to an oriental flower that, although withered, continued to exude a powerful aroma or to a star, that although dead, continued to send its 'light and cheer and glory' to distant planets.[2] Certainly, although the Parliament left no continuing body, its ideals have continued to inspire those who seek understanding between religions and their co-operation for peace. Max Müller, a pioneer of the comparative study of religions, predicted that the Parliament would 'take its place as one of the most memorable events in the history of the world'. He predicted that 'it will be remembered, aye, will bear fruit, when everything else of the mighty Columbian Exhibition has long been swept away from the memory of man'.[3] Charles W. Wendte, who did so much to create what is known now as the International Association for Religious Freedom, called the Parliament 'one of the landmarks of human history'.[4]

Although flawed in several ways as a model of interfaith co-operation, the World's Parliament of Religions, held at Chicago in 1893, has come to mark the beginning of what is now known as 'the interfaith movement'. Acknowledgment was made, at the time, to the efforts of the Indian Buddhist Emperor Asoka and of the Moghul Emperor Akbar. On a much smaller scale there had been some previous inter-religious meetings, but the World's Parliament was unprecedented. It issued invitations to participants from all over the globe and its doors were open to the general public.

It is difficult for us today to recapture the enthusiasm and self confidence of late nineteenth-century America. An evolutionary optimism was in the air. To understand the Parliament, it is helpful to appreciate the context – or rather the contexts. First, the physical location was significant. Secondly, the Parliament's relation to the Congresses and the Exposition helped to make it possible. Thirdly, it took place at a transitional period in American life. The Exposition has been said to mark America's development from a rural to an industrial and urban economy and to signal the USA's emergence as a world power. Further, in terms of American religious life, the Parliament took place when the USA was ceasing to be just a Protestant Christian nation. Indeed, the Parliament symbolized the coming change to a religiously plural society.

The White City

The US Congress agreed in 1890 that Chicago should be the venue for a World Exposition to mark Christopher Columbus' 'discovery' of America. It was in October 1492 that Columbus reached the island of San Salvador and neither then nor in three subsequent trips did he set foot on the mainland. Nor was he the first European to reach America, which in any case had its native population. But this was irrelevant in 1893, as the Exposition assumed the ascendancy of Western powers who then dominated the entire world politically, economically and culturally.

The Exposition although originally planned for 1892, did not in fact take place until the following year. The reason given was that this allowed for local celebrations and was for the convenience of foreign exhibitors, although it was probably the organizers who needed more time. Other cities, including New York, St Louis and Washington had vied to host the exposition, but it was Chicago – the city with 'go' in it – which won.[5]

The World Fair was one in a series of such extravaganzas. 'The self-confidence of the nineteenth-century West', writes Professor Joseph Kitagawa, who was for a time Dean of the Divinity School at Chicago, 'was extravagantly displayed in a series of large-scale exhibits and fairs held in Europe and America, starting with the 1851 exhibition at the Crystal Palace in Hyde Park, London. The nineteenth century also witnessed the emergence of the United States onto the world stage as a new Western power, whereby eager Americans sponsored their own Crystal Palace exposition in New York', on the site of the present Bryant's Park, in 1853. A more successful international exhibition was held in Fairmount Park, Philadelphia, the first capital, in 1876, to mark the one hundredth birthyear of the nation. 'This event was followed by the Paris Exhibition of 1889, which lured the curious multitudes to the newly built Eiffel Tower. Then, in 1893, the Columbian exposition, the last major exhibition of the nineteenth century, was held in Chicago as the crowning symbol of the achievement of Western civilization during the great century.'[6]

The site chosen was a seven hundred acre piece of undeveloped land on the shore of Lake Michigan, several miles south of Chicago's downtown. It is now the campus of the University of Chicago. The completed exposition was composed of three distinct parts, linked together with promenades and avenues and enclosed within the tracks of a winding, elevated electric train, reputed to be the first of its kind in the world. The most popular and entertaining section was the Midway Plaisance, a mile-long avenue of amusements, commercial stands and ethnological exhibitions. A second section, laid out semi-formally in the wooded area around the Serpentine Lagoon, was adjacent to the main Exposition and included the national and state buildings and the palace of Fine Arts. The third area, which was the White City proper, was the austere, symmetrical and formal Court of Honour. The triumphal arch was inscribed with mottoes reiterating America's traditional commitment to the ideals of tolerance, freedom of religion and truth. 'The United States both as the New Rome and as a modern technological marvel', writes Richard Seager in his study of the Parliament, 'was explicit in the exposition's design, but America's traditional self-identification as the New Jerusalem was equally reaffirmed. America's aspiration to be the millennial nation was a leitmotif that appeared repeatedly in the rites, rhetoric and pageants held in the course of the quadricentennial summer'.[7] It is important to be aware of this self-confident uncritical sense that God had blessed America and that she had a civilizing mission to the world in judging the Christian assumptions which underlay the Parliament. The ethnic exhibitions on the Midway Plaisance confirmed to Americans how advanced they had become. 'Dazzled by their own accomplishments and charmed by their own magic, Americans were primed to encounter the Asians at the World's Parliament of Religions not in "real" time, but in the realm of America's messianic myth', writes Dr Seager. It is still a frequent temptation to try to fit other people and cultures into a pre-existing myth or theological scheme.[8]

The Congresses

The US Congress, in the act that created the exposition, said it was to be an international display of the 'arts, industries, manufactures and the products of the soil, mine and sea'.[9] In 1889, however, whilst debate still raged about the venue, Charles Caroll Bonney, a prominent lawyer from Illinois, published his opinion that the 'crowning glory' of any exposition should be not 'the material triumphs, industrial achievements, and mechanical victories of man, however magnificent that display may be. Something higher and nobler is demanded by the enlightened and progressive spirit of the present age'. Bonney suggested 'A World's Congress at the World's Fair' of 'statesmen, jurists, financiers, scientists, literati, teachers and theologians'.[10] The Chicago Provisional Committee for the Fair at once welcomed the suggestion and appointed a committee, called the World's Congress Committee for 1892, to implement the proposal. Bonney was asked to become chairman. The committee met for the first time on 15 October 1889. It quickly issued a circular suggesting a 'series of World's Congresses'. Soon backing was received from the US State Department and publicity sent out across the world.

Within a year, the World's Congress Auxiliary became an official and integral part of the World's Columbian Exposition. Bonney, who had been talked about for a vacancy on the US Supreme Court and had gained public attention for his advocacy of a permanent international court of justice, became president of the auxiliary. Eventually twenty distinct congresses were held, including Medicine and Surgery, Music, Woman's Progress, Engineering and Education. The congresses ran concurrently with the exposition and some were counterparts of departments of the fair. Yet to differentiate the intellectual achievements of mankind from the display of material progress, the World's Congress Auxiliary met some miles away at what is now the Art Institute of Chicago, a building near the lakefront in downtown Chicago. The Art Institute had some thirty-three halls and in addition there were two temporary halls – the Hall of Columbus and the Hall of Washington, each with a seating capacity of over 3,000. During the religious congress 'the building was found inadequate to the demands'.[11]

The initial circular included a reference to theologians, but the question of whether there should be a religious congress caused some doubts lest it should prove divisive. Clearly the holding of a religious congress was Bonney's chief hope. As Seager says, 'If it had been left to ecclesiastical authorities to call a Parliament, the encounter between East and West would not have happened in quite the way it did'.[12] It is doubtful whether it would have happened at all. Often subsequent interfaith initiatives have been taken by lay people with a vision.

In 1891 Bonney, appointed a general Committee on Religious Congresses to discuss the possibilities. The Committee was varied in its composition. It included The Most Rev. P. A. Feehan, the Roman Catholic Archbishop, Dr William McLaren, the Protestant Episcopal Bishop of Chicago, members of the larger Protestant Churches, a Unitarian, a Quaker, a Universalist and a member of the New (Swedenborgian) Church as well as Dr E. G. Hirsch, a Reform Rabbi, who was Minister of Sinai Temple and Professor of Rabbinic Literature. Rev. J. H. Barrows, Pastor of the First Presbyterian Church of Chicago, was chosen as chairman.[13]

The Preliminary Address

Although so predominantly Christian, the Committee soon decided that the Congress should try to represent the many religions of the world, not just one or two. In June 1891, therefore, the General Committee sent out a preliminary address, explaining the proposed purpose of the Congress. Calling attention to the importance of religion as a factor in human development, the address expressed the hope that all the great historic faiths would co-operate. The committee believed that the time was ripe for a new manifestation of human fraternity and noted that the sacred scriptures were increasingly studied in a spirit of candour and brotherhood. There was no desire to create a mood of indifferentism. Rather the hope was that a friendly conference of eminent men, strong in their personal conviction, would show what are the supreme truths and the light that religion could throw on the great problems of the time.[14]

More than three thousand copies of the preliminary address were sent to religious leaders across the world. There was a considerable welcome for the suggestions. Those, like Max Müller, who were working in the field of the comparative study of religion, hoped the conference would increase interest in their subject. Others hoped it would provide an opportunity to show the superiority and sufficiency of their particular form of Christianity. Others who felt that their religion had been misunderstood saw the Parliament as a chance to correct these misconceptions. Some hoped that the conference would draw Christians closer to each other, whilst the more progressive and broad-minded 'championed the Parliament from the feeling that they, as Christians, might wisely and rightly show a more brotherly spirit towards representatives of other faiths'(p.15).

There was some opposition. William Gladstone, a former Prime Minister of Britain, whilst wishing the Parliament well, wrote, 'I am one of those who look more to improved tempers and conceptions in the individual, than to the adoption of formulated plans for the promotion of religious unity'(p.10). The Sultan of Turkey also opposed the idea and this was one reason why so few Muslims were present. It was the opposition of the Presbyterian Church in the USA – Barrows' own church – and of the Archbishop of Canterbury which caused most disappointment.

In 1892 the General Assembly of the Presbyterian Church in the USA, at Portland, passed a resolution expressing strong disapproval. The resolution was passed hurriedly at the end of a session, without a debate. Yet it was a blow to Henry Barrows and seems to have made some of his statements about the Parliament more defensive. In fact, Presbyterian opinion was divided. Several Presbyterian journals gave support and some Presbyterians accepted appointments on the Advisory Council. The church's Board of Foreign Missions also gave general approval (p.19).

The Archbishop of Canterbury, E. W. Benson, said that his difficulties rested 'on the fact that the Christian religion is the one religion. I do not understand how that religion can be regarded as a member of a Parliament of Religions, without assuming the equality of other intended members and the parity of their position and claims'. He then objected to the assumption that the Church of Rome was the Catholic Church and the implication that the Church of England was outside the Catholic Church. He also raised the question of how those outside a tradition could come to appreciate its inner life of devotion. 'While I quite understand how the Christian religion might produce its evidences before any assembly, a "presentation" of that religion must go far beyond the question of evidences, and must subject to public discussion that faith and devotion which are its characteristics, and which belong to a region too sacred for such treatment' (p.21–2).

It is interesting to note the reply, which was sent, on behalf of the committee, to *The Review of the Churches* by the Rev. F. Herbert Stead. He said that the treatment of Christianity would be fraternal, devotional and courteous. Calling churches by the name which they themselves chose was a matter of courtesy. No one, Stead continued, would 'be expected to regard all other faiths as equal to his own'. The Archbishop's opposition, nevertheless, continued. This did not, however, stop some members of the Church of England serving on the Advisory Council. Further, the Bishops of the Protestant Episcopal Church were, on the whole, in favour of the Parliament (p.22–5).

Bonney and Barrows

The three prime movers of the World's Parliament of Religions were Charles Carroll Bonney, Rev. John Henry Barrows and Rev. Jenkin Lloyd Jones.

The idea of the Parliament and its inspiration came from Bonney. He was born in 1831 and was educated in Hamilton, New York. He became a prominent lawyer in Illinois, where he took a leading part in establishing the educational system. In 1860, he moved to Chicago. From 1885 to 1890 he was President of the Citizens' Law and Order League of the US. He was a member of the Swedenborgians, whose church is sometimes called the New Church or the New Jerusalem Church.[15] Bonney said that the 'whole plan of the religious congresses' rested upon the fundamental truths that he had learned in the New Jerusalem Church and that these truths made the Parliament of Religions possible.[16]

Emanuel Swedenborg (1688–1772), the eighteenth-century Swedish scientist, philosopher and theologian, did not himself found a church, but remained a Lutheran, although his theology was very different from that of the Lutheran Church. Soon after his death, a group in England established a separate church. The first building for New Church worship was opened in Great East Cheap, London, in 1788. In the USA, the first society was organized in Baltimore in 1792 and the first American ministers were ordained in 1798. The General Convention of the New Jerusalem Church in the USA was founded in 1817 in Philadelphia.

Swedenborg devoted the latter part of his life to extensive writing on the Bible, relating this to what he had heard and seen in the world of spirits and angels. From 1749 to 1771 he published some thirty volumes. He summarized much of his thinking in *Vera Christiana Religio* (1771) (*The True Christian Religion*, 1781), written when he was 83. The being of the Lord, he said, cannot be described, but his essence can be understood in two of its primary qualities, love and wisdom. The Lord has also manifested himself in other forms, above all in his Word. Such an approach suggested a mystical truth beyond creedal formulae and, as Bonney said, implied that 'every nation has some religion' and that there are 'common essentials of all religions, by which every one may be saved'.[17] Swedenborg believed that the ultimate end of creation can only be achieved through humans – giving a certain optimism to his thought.

For Bonney, the object of the Congress, was 'to unite all Religion against all irreligion; to make the Golden Rule the basis of this union; (and) to present to the world . . . the substantial unity of many religions in the good deeds of the religious life'.[18] In his opening address to the Congress, he defined 'religion' in this way. 'In this Congress the word "religion" means the love and worship of God and love and service of man' (p.68). He further voiced his hope that 'when the religious faiths of the world recognize each other as brothers, children of one Father, whom all profess to love and serve, then, and not till then, will the nations of the earth yield to the Spirit of concord and learn war no more' (p.67). His belief that divine light could be found in all religions and his hope that all religions could work together for human welfare are shown in the last three (of twenty one) themes that he suggested for the religious congresses:

s.   The coming unity of mankind in the service of God and man.
t.   That there is an influx from God into the mind of every man, teaching that there is a God and that he should be worshipped and obeyed; and that as the light of the sun is differently received by different objects, so the light of divine revelation is differently received by different minds, and hence arise varieties in the forms of religion.
u.   That those who believe in these things may work together for the welfare of mankind, notwithstanding they may differ in the opinions they hold respecting God, His revelation and manifestation, and that such fraternity does not require the surrender of the points of difference. The Christian believing in the supreme divinity of Christ, may so unite with the Jew who devoutly believes in the Jehovah of Israel; the Quaker with the High Church Episcopalian; the Catholic with the Methodist; the Baptist with the Unitarian, etc.[19]

This last point was one that he emphasized in his opening address. Delegates were asked to meet in a spirit of mutual respect, but no one was asked to compromise his or her individual convictions (p.68).

Bonney said that he approached the first meeting of the committee on religious congresses with 'much anxiety'. He was relieved and delighted, therefore, to discover the group was in basic accord with his views, which themselves reflect the influence of Swedenborg.[20]

'If it was Bonney's inspiration to hold the religious congresses', writes Kenten Druyvesteyn, 'it was Barrows energy and single-minded determination that made the idea a reality'.[21]

John Henry Barrows, who was born in 1847, was at the time of the Parliament, pastor of the First Presbyterian Church in Chicago. A graduate of Olivet College, Yale University, Union Seminary and Andover Seminary, Barrows had had pastorates in Kansas, Massachusetts and Paris. He was a relative newcomer to Chicago. He liked the city, which was then rebuilding from the devastation of the Great Fire. He soon made the aquaintance of civic leaders, many of whom supported the Parliament and the new University of Chicago. He was a great admirer of William Rainey Harper, the energetic first president of the University of Chicago, who had a vision of the 'second reformation' of Christianity through scholarship. He was a self-confessed Liberal Christian. It was reported that over one thousand members were added to Barrow's church during the first two years of his pastorate.

'Both as an American and as a Christian', writes Professor Joseph Kitagawa, 'Barrows shared the optimism of his generation. He lived at a time when America was internally recovering from the effects of the Civil War and externally emerging as a new world power. His was also the time when many idealistic young men and women took up evangelistic, educational and philanthropic activities in far-off lands. Their vision was exemplified by the motto of the Student Volunteer Movement, 'The evangelization of the world in this generation'.[22]

Barrows made clear his Christian commitment and was sensitive to criticisms that the Parliament was damaging to Christianity. Indeed, Dr Seager says, Barrows 'more than anyone else epitomized the peculiar combination of generosity and arrogance in American Christian cosmopolitanism'.[23] This comes out in the 'Review and Summary' with which Barrow ends his two volume record of the Parliament. Besides strengthening religion, 'it is clarifying many minds in regard to the nature of non-Christian faiths; it is deepening the general Christian interest in non-Christian nations; and it will bring before millions in Oriental lands the more truthful and beautiful aspects of Christianity (p.1569) . . . The idea of evolving a cosmic or universal faith out of the Parliament was not present in the minds of its chief promoters. They believed that the elements of such religion are already contained in the Christian ideal and the Christian scriptures' (p.1572). Participation in the Parliament did not, Barrows claimed, compromise a speaker's belief in the supremacy and universality of the Gospel. 'The Parliament', he wrote, 'has shown that Christianity is still the great quickener of humanity, and thus it is now educating those who do not accept its doctrines, that there is no teacher to be compared with Christ, and no Saviour excepting Christ . . . The non-Christian world may give us valuable criticism and confirm scriptural truths and make excellent suggestions as to Christian improvement, but it has nothing to add to the Christian creed. It is with the belief, expressed by many a Christian missionary, that the Parliament marks a new era of Christian triumph that the editor closes these volumes' (p.1581).

This position is reiterated in the Barrows lectures, endowed by Mrs Caroline Haskell, which Henry Barrows gave in Asia in 1896. Cast in the mould of a comparative study, the lectures explain why Christianity was destined to become the universal religion of the entire world. He based his argument on an evolutionary theory of religion, whereby 'lower' forms of religion are absorbed into a 'higher' religion. Eventually these 'higher' religions will be assimilated to the religion of Christ. Christianity, he claimed, was 'a celestial seed capable of indefinite expansion and wide variation'. Christianity was the 'universal religion', the Bible the 'universal book' and Jesus Christ the 'universal man and saviour'.[24]

Barrows lectured in China, Japan and Ceylon, but spent most time in India, which, as for so many, was a culture shock. Benares, the holy city, was, he said, 'an endless succession of scenes weird, beautiful and disgusting'.[25] Back in the USA, Barrows delivered a series of lectures which were published in 1899 under the title *The Christian Conquest of Asia*. Whilst sympathetic to Hindus, he is contemptuous of Hinduism. Even a fairminded observer, he wrote, felt 'the hopelessness of raising the people out of the bottomless depths of moral rottenness'.[26] Christianity could, however, assimilate and transform all that was sacred in Hinduism. His approach was similar to that to be made widely known, a few years later, by J. N. Farquhar in his book *The Crown of Hinduism*, namely that Christ fulfils all that is good and true in other religions.[27] Such a view replaced hostility to other religions with sympathy, but, influenced by ideas of evolution, assumed that a Christianity, broadened and deepened by contact with other faiths, would absorb into itself all that was good in other religious traditions.

Barrow, as Kitagawa said, 'did not see any fundamental tension between being both a seeker of universal religious truth and a Christian'.[28] He sincerely believed that in an evolving Christianity all could be at home. Whilst, therefore, as in his closing words to the Parliament, he affirmed what he owed to Jesus Christ, he was unfailingly sympathetic and respectful to all the delegates. His geniality, his learning, his rhetorical gifts and his sense of humour won the admiration of participants and of the press. He was universally proclaimed by the Asians as a liberal, congenial spirit. Anagarika Dharmapala from Ceylon spoke of him as 'The American Asoka'.[29]

Barrows perceived the Parliament in terms of three concentric circles. At the centre was the Christian assembly – the first modern Parliament of Christendom. In this, the whole-hearted Roman Catholic participation was particularly significant. Secondly, there was the American religious assembly, in which Jews played an important part. What has become a common ecumenical pattern in the USA of Catholic, Protestant and Jewish co-operation was beginning to take shape. Thirdly there was the outer circle of all religions, in which 'Christianity was one among many faiths competing for the conquest of mankind'.[30] Barrows found the plurality of religions a genuine mystery, but believed that the God whom Jews and Christians worshipped was deeply concerned for members of other religions. He argued that Christians should be glad to learn what 'God has wrought through Buddha and Zoroaster – through the sages of China, and the prophets of India and the prophet of Islam'.[31] As Kitagawa points out, Barrows in his search for 'a spiritual root of all human progress' turned not to theology but to comparative religion and expressed his great admiration for Max Müller.

It is interesting to compare Barrow's conviction that Christianity would become the universal religion with the views of the Unitarian Rev. Jenkin Lloyd Jones. In an obituary, John Haynes Holmes said of him that 'no man was more largely responsible for the World's Parliament of Religions . . . than he: and no man did more in ways of practical labour for the success of that epoch-making assembly'.[32] This view has been widespread amongst Unitarian historians. Yet in the proceedings there is very little mention of Jones.

Jones had entered Meadville Seminary, a small Unitarian College in Western Pennsylvania, in 1866. There, in 1868, he attended classes on world religions. This was only the second such course to be offered on the subject in North America and was modelled on the pioneering course that George Freeman Clarke had introduced at Harvard the previous year. After college, he became the Unitarian minister in Janesville, Wisconsin. There, dissatisfied with the heavily Bible-centred Sunday school programme, he produced some modern courses including scientific material and lessons dealing with the founders of the world religions.

In 1884 he moved to Chicago and resuscitated the Fourth Unitarian Church there, which was renamed All Souls Church. He was to be pastor there for thirty-four years. All were welcome at his church. 'Into our fellowship no one will ever be prevented to come by doctrinal bar; here at least let no man be a stranger, who chooses to stand within our gates, let him be Jew, Gentile or Agnostic, Mohammedan or Buddhist, Infidel or Atheist so long as he desires to share with us the burden bearing, the life helping, the love extending duties he is welcome'.[33] Jones also became Editor of the Western Unitarian newspaper, *Unity*, and regularly included articles about world religions.

Jones was involved in plans for the Parliament from the beginning. Bonney's law office was in the same building as the editorial offices of *Unity*. Bonney and Jones knew each other and shared a concern for inter-religious understanding. The plan for a Parliament of the World's Religions was leaked in *Unity* some weeks before its publication in *The Statesman*. Jones was invited to serve on the General Committee for the Parliament and was elected secretary. Somewhat to his surprise, however, Barrows, as chairman took control. Aware of hostility to the project amongst some Christians, Barrows may not have wanted a Unitarian to assume too great prominence. Jones, for example, drafted the original programme (which was reshaped by Bishop Keane), but it was presented anonymously. It seems also that Jones was in the habit of taking on more than he could accomplish. At the time he was involved in arguments within the Western Unitarian Conference and *Unity* was in financial difficulties. Barrows once described Jones as 'our humanitarian cyclone'.[34] Jones did produce a hymnal for the Parliament, but it was not used, although Jones used it at his All Souls Church. It seems that Barrows relied on him for a great deal of detailed work. In a letter written to Jones in early 1894, Barrows spoke of 'the stigmata of that great movement and meeting you and I must bear as long as we live'.[35]

Jones was not just concerned with the Parliament. The Congress of the Religious Association, the Congress of the Ethical Culture Society and the Congress on Evolution were all the results of his efforts.[36] Afterwards, it was Jones, who at the end of the Parliament, proposed that the next Parliament should be in Benares in 1900. He struggled to keep going a continuing 'Congress of Religions', which later linked to the International Association for Religious Freedom.

After the Parliament, Jones criticized Barrow's official record because of what he claimed was its 'doctrinal basis'. Barrows, Jones said, made the Parliament appear 'Christo-centric' instead of 'homo-centric'. 'Not the supernatural Christ, but the natural soul of man was the centre round which the Parliament moved'.[37] Jones looked forward to a new religion having 'open temples of reason, holy shrines of helpfulness and confessionals where the soul will not be afraid to confess its ignorance'. Its platform would embrace Christians, Buddhists, Agnostics and Brahmans; its Deity would be neither 'unifold' nor 'trifold' but 'manifold'. It would be a temple of universal religion dedicated to progress. 'Let us', he wrote after the Parliament, 'build a temple of universal religion dedicated to the inquiring spirit of progress, to the helpful service of love'.[38]

A minority in the interfaith movement have re-echoed this hope in subsequent years, but the majority view has been to respect the identity of the world religions. The issue has therefore been how to relate their competing claims. This issue, as we shall see, was a major subject of debate at the Parliament itself.

· 2 ·

The World's Parliament
of Religions II

The Opening

When the Parliament opened on 11 September 1893, more than four thousand people crowded into the Hall of Columbus. At ten o'clock, representatives of a dozen faiths marched down the aisle, arm in arm. On the platform the central position was taken by Cardinal Gibbons, 'clad in scarlet robes' (p.64). At a recent conference some monks felt they were only there to adorn the photographs with their bright costumes. There were no colour photographs at Chicago, but certainly the multi-coloured robes dazzled the audience. Henry Barrows describes those seated next to the Cardinal. 'On either side of him were grouped the Oriental delegates, whose many coloured raiment vied with his own in brilliancy. Conspicuous among these followers of Brahma and Buddha and Mohammed was the eloquent monk Vivekananda of Bombay, clad in gorgeous red apparel, his bronze face surmounted with a huge turban of yellow. Beside him in orange and white, sat B. B. Nagarkar of the Brahmo-Samaj and Dharmapala from Ceylon (p.64). There were some sixty people on the platform, of whom ten per cent were female (later conferences were to have target percentages of women and young people!). One can sense the organizers' excitement, which still marks the beginning of a large international conference, that, after all the time and correspondence, people from around the world had assembled in Chicago. Names on paper had begun to become friends. As Barrows said in his opening address, 'When, a few days ago, I met for the first time the delegates who have come to us from Japan, and shortly after the delegates who have come to us from India, I felt that the arms of human brotherhood had reached almost around the globe' (p.79).

Although care had been taken to ensure that the platform party was widely representative, the pervasive Christian ethos of the Parliament was soon revealed. A few voices, with the organ accompanying them, began singing a paraphrase of the hundredth Psalm, to which the crowd added the Trinitarian doxology. (In the 1970s I was at what had been advertised as an 'All Faiths Service' and was sitting next to a rabbi. The service turned out to be Anglican Evensong. At one point we were all asked to say the Apostles' Creed. 'A bit difficult for some of us', muttered the rabbi).

After the psalm, Cardinal Gibbons asked everyone to say the Lord's Prayer. Charles Bonney, the Chairman of the World's Congress Auxiliary, then gave an opening address. This carefully avoided reference to any specific religion and any obvious Christian bias. His hope was that 'when the religious faiths of the world recognize each other as brothers, children of one Father, whom all profess to love and serve, then, and not till then, will the nations of the earth yield to the spirit of concord and learn war no more' (p.67). Nearly one hundred years later the title of a major talk by Professor Hans Küng, the Catholic theologian, to a big interfaith conference was 'No Peace in the World without Peace Between Religions'.[1] Bonney explained that in the Congress 'religion' meant 'love and worship of God and love and service of man' (p.68). God, he said, had made himself known in every nation. Because of human differences, these revelations were not identical. Yet they should not be a cause of discord, 'but rather incentives to deeper interest and examination'. 'The religious faiths of the world', he continued, 'have most seriously misunderstood and misjudged each other from the use of words in meanings radically different from those which they were intended to bear and from a disregard of the distinctions between appearances and facts'. Subsequent dialogue has shown how often we fail to understand other's real meaning. Participants, Bonney emphasized, must assume that others hold their beliefs as sincerely as they hold their own. Whilst ecclesiastical rank would be respected, all members of the Congress, Bonney said, 'meet, as men, on a common ground of perfect equality'. People might make claims to the superiority of their faith, but they were, to use a phrase which later became fashionable, to accord each other 'parity of esteem'.[2] The hope was that the Congress could demonstrate to the world the brotherhood of religions.

John Henry Barrows, Chairman of the General Committee, spoke self-consciously as a Christian and was in large part concerned to answer Christian critics of the Parliament. The glory, he said, was wholly due to Him who taught 'the blessed truths of divine Fatherhood and human brotherhood' (p.73). He stressed that it was representatives of the Christian faith, 'which we believe has in it such elements and divine forces that it is fitted to the needs of all men' who had arranged the Parliament –

although he acknowledged the help of Jews, 'Old Testament Christians' who had worked with 'New Testament Jews'. He affirmed his confidence in Christian America, 'which we love to contemplate as the land of earth's brightest future' (p.72), and which, he claimed, was 'in a true and noble sense a Christian nation', although church and state were separated (p.74). Barrows affirmed that the Spirit of God had not left himself without witness in 'non-Christian nations'. 'There is a divine light enlightening every man' (p.74). The loving thoughts of all people should be cherished. 'The Parliament', he said, 'is likely to prove a blessing to many Christians by marking the time when they shall cease thinking that the verities and virtues of other religions discredit the claims of Christianity or bar its progress . . . Why should not Christians be glad to learn what God has wrought through Buddha and Zoroaster – through the sage of China, and the prophets of India and the prophet of Islam' (p.75).

Barrows insisted that people were not there to speak for a particular religion or denomination, but 'as members of a Parliament of Religions, over which flies no sectarian flag' (p.75). They were not there to criticize each other, but frankly to express their own convictions. He explained that there would be social gatherings so that people could get to know each other better and there would be smaller meetings for friendly question and answer. Scholarly essays had been prepared. There was also to be attention to practical issues. 'How can we make this suffering and needy world less a home of grief and strife and far more a commonwealth of love, a kingdom of heaven? How can we abridge the chasms of altercation which have kept good men from co-operating?' (p.76). Barrows was concerned too to encourage Christian unity as well as inter-religious understanding.

Even if the Parliament had been confined to one day, 'the truthful historian', Barrows claimed, 'would say that the idea which has inspired and led this movement, the idea whose beauty and force have drawn you through these many thousand miles of travel, that this idea has been so flashed before the eyes of men that they will not forget it, and that our meeting this morning has become a new, great fact in the historic evolution of the race which will not be obliterated' (p.73).

Speeches were then given by The Catholic Archbishop of Chicago, Archbishop Feehan, and by Cardinal Gibbons of Baltimore. Clearly the high level of Catholic representation paid off in terms of the star-billing they were given. Archbishop Feehan, whilst recognizing that no one would surrender an atom of what they believed, affirmed that all could meet on the basis of their 'common humanity' (p.80) – a phrase that was to recur in World Council of Churches' circles in the seventies, when some felt that there was no special religious basis for interfaith co-operation.[3] Cardinal Gibbons underlined this. 'Thanks be to God there is one platform on which we all stand united. It is the platform of charity, humanity, and of benevolence' (p.80).

The contribution of women to organizing the congresses was then acknowledged by asking the Chairman of the Women's Committee of Organization, Rev. Augusta Chapin, to speak. She mentioned that it was only the marvels of modern travel and communication that had made possible the Congresses. She spoke too of the new opportunities for women to contribute to the religious life of the world. The President of the World's Columbian Exposition, H. N. Higinbotham, also spoke and Rev. Alexander M'Kenzie on behalf of New England Puritanism. Responses were given by The Archbishop of Zante in Greece, by P. C. Mozoomdar of the Brahmo Samaj in Calcutta, by Hon Pung Kwang Yu, First Secretary of the Chinese Delegation in Washington, by Prince Serge Wolkonsky, who was there in his own right and not as a representative of Russia, by Rt Rev. Reuchi Shibata of the Shinto religion, by Count A. Bernstorff, an Evangelical Protestant from Germany, who said that 'an honest fight with spiritual weapons need not estrange the combatants' (p.93), and by Archbishop Redwood, a Catholic from New Zealand, and by the Buddhist H. Dharmapala from Ceylon, who recalled the example of the Buddhist Emperor Asoka.

Subsequent conferences have not avoided the temptation to have too many speeches – religious dignitaries are not noted for a humility that forbears the opportunity to utter on a public platform. Dr Momerie of Kings College, London, however, who spoke in the afternoon, quoted the words of the American humourist, Artemus Ward, 'I am always happiest when I am silent'. In explaining that not all in the Church of England agreed with the Archbishop of Canterbury's opposition, he rejected a narrow Christian triumphalism. 'It cannot be that the New Commandment was inspired when uttered by Christ and was not inspired when uttered, as it was uttered, by Confucius and by Hillel. The fact is, all religions are fundamentally more or less true and all religions are superficially more or less false' (p.100–1). Other speeches after lunch came from Virchand Gandhi, a Jain from Bombay, from Professor Tcheraz, an Armenian Christian, from Professor C. N. Chakravati, a theosophist from Allahabad, and from Swami Vivekananda whose opening words 'Sisters and Brothers of America' were greeted by a prolonged burst of applause. Principal Grant from Canada, Mr Nagarkar and Miss Sorabji, a Christian convert from Zoroastrianism, both from Bombay also spoke as well as Bishop Benjamin W. Arnett, of the African Methodist Episcopal Church, who had been asked 'to give colour' to the Parliament. He represented both Africa and Africans in America.

An Account of the Parliament

The intention, according to the 'Second Report', was to have a particular theme for each of the sixteen days. The topics listed were: God, Man, Religion Essentially characteristic of Humanity, Systems of Religion, Sacred Books of the World, Religion and the Family, The Religious Leaders of Mankind, Religion in its Relations to the Natural Sciences and to Arts and Letters, Religion in its Relation to Morals, Religion and Social problems, Religion and Civil Society, Religion and the Love of Mankind, The Present religious Condition of Christendom, Religious Reunion of Christendom, The Religious Union of the Whole Human Family and Elements of Perfect Religion. As Kenten Druyvesteyn says, 'The mark of Christianity is readily apparent in the topics that were chosen for discussion before the Parliament. The themes reflected centuries of thought and concern about the relationship of Christianity to morality, learning, society and the world . . . A striking example of the Christian imprint on the proceedings in this regard is evident in the advance questions put to Manilal N. D'vivedi who addressed the Parliament on the second day on Hinduism. The questions were "intended to cover points of principal interest to the Western mind"'.[4]

In fact, it proved impossible to keep to this scheme. The general themes were retained, but usually at most only half the papers presented were on the theme for the day. Lewis P. Mercer, a member of the planning committee, deplored the unsystematic approach, which made 'arrangement of opinion on the great subjects of religion a work of toil, even for an expert. Each man speaks as if he had the whole field before him, and therefore of many things which throw no light upon the specific system of thought which he represents' – and it is still not easy to persuade speakers to stick to the point and be relevant! Mercer further complained that 'the interest centred in great men rather than in great subjects'.[5] Yet one can sympathize with the difficulties of the organizers. As Barrows commented afterwards, 'the elements [were] too various, the presence of speakers not always assured' (p.1558). The organizers did manage to restrict speakers to half an hour.

Even so, most of the suggested topics were covered. This shows the enormous range of material presented. There were papers on theological and philosophical topics, there were presentations of a religion's belief and there were comparative presentations. On the second day for example, talks included arguments for the existence of God, a theology of Judaism, a paper on Hinduism, a paper on 'The Harmonies and Distinctions in the Theistic Teaching of the Various Historic Faiths' and a description of 'Idealism, the New Religion' (p.112–3) – for new and minority groups were given the opportunity to present their views. There was also discussion of practical topics, such as 'The Religious Training of Children', 'The Weekly Rest-day', 'Social Reform in India', 'What Judaism has Done for Women' and 'Crime and its Remedy'. There were also papers about the Reunion of the Christian Church, the relation of Christianity to other world religions, the purpose and place of Christian missionary endeavour, and about hopes of religious brotherhood.

Besides the World's Parliament of Religions itself, there were a large number of other religious congresses. One section was labelled 'Scientific'. This was arranged partly to accommodate the crowd. The main sessions of the Parliament were normally held in the Hall of Columbus, which, although it could seat three thousand people with another one thousand standing, was not big enough. At the scientific section papers of a 'more scientific and less popular character were read', often followed by open, informal   discussion   or   conferences   (p.116   and   pp.152–4   and pp.1347–1381). Amongst the papers were ones on less well known religions such as Zoroastrianism, Taoism and Shintoism.

There were also denominational congresses. These were mostly held at the same time as the Parliament, although the Jewish, Lutheran, Catholic and Congregational congresses were held before 11 September.[6] The denominational congresses were related to the Parliament, but were deliberately kept separate from it. At the Parliament, the intention was to stress the unifying points of the various religions. The congresses included those of the Anglican Church, and of the main Protestant Churches, as well as congresses of Theosophists, Unitarians and Universalists. There were some interdenominational congresses as well as a congress of Sunday Rest and of Missions (pp.1383–1555).

Other Meetings

Barrows records that 'very much of the best life of this first great convention of the world's religions was lived outside the daily meetings in the Hall of Columbus. The friendships which were formed, and the social intercourse enjoyed will be a part of the Parliament's contribution to that true charity in which, as Lord Bacon said, "there is no excess"' (p.154) – and often the warmest memories people take away from a big conference are of new friendships made. On the evening of the opening day the Chairman gave a reception at the elegant home of Mr and Mrs A. C. Bartlett on Prairie Avenue. On the second evening a public reception was given by Charles Bonney. Other social occasions were arranged.

There were also some devotional gatherings in the early morning arranged by Mr Theodore F. Seward, the founder of the Brotherhood of Christian Unity.

The Closing Session

More than seven thousand people crowded into the Washington and Columbus Halls for the final session. There was even a black market in tickets. On the stage, beneath the flags of all nations were the representatives of the religions of the world. Twice during the evening, Barrows records, flash-light photographs were taken of the platform party.

The evening began with the singing by the Apollo Club of Handel's 'Lift Up Your Heads, O Ye Gates'. Then after a silent invocation, the choir sang 'Lead, Kindly Light'. There followed numerous speeches, rightly full of praise for the organizers and especially for Dr Barrows, by Dr Momerie, P. C. Mozoomdar, Prince Serge Wolkonsky, Mr Hirai, Hon Pung Kwang Yu, Rt Rev. R. Shibata, Rev. George Candlin, H. Dhamapala, Swami Vivekananda, who included criticism of Christian triumphalism, Mr Ghandi, Prince Momolu Masaquoi from Africa, and, of course Charles Bonney, who asked various Americans to convey their messages in two-minute addresses. These included Rev. George Dana Boardman of Philadelphia, Rabbi Hirsch, Dr F. Bristol for the Methodists, Rev. Jenkin Lloyd Jones, Secretary of the Parliament, who suggested that the next Parliament to usher in the twentieth century, should be held 'on the banks of the Ganges in the ancient city of Benares' (p.177), Pastor Fliedner of Spain, Mrs Charles Henrotin, Vice-President of the Woman's Branch of the Auxiliary and Rev. Augusta Chapin, Chairman of the Woman's Committee. Charles Bonney then introduced Mrs Julia Ward Howe of Boston, the author of the 'Battle Hymn of the Republic', who read a few lines about a dream she had had:

> Before, I saw the hand divine
>   Outstretched for human weal,
> Its judgments stern in righteousness,
>   Its mercy swift to heal;
> And as I looked with hand to help
>   The golden net outspread,
> To gather all we deem alive,
>   And all we mourn as dead;
> And as I mused a voice did say:
>   'Ah not a single mesh;
> This binds in harmony divine
>   All spirit and all flesh.' (p.179)

Bishop Arnett of the African Methodist Episcopal Church then spoke and was followed by the Catholic Bishop Keane with a passionate plea for unity.

The final speaker was, appropriately, Henry Barrows. He said that the highest hopes for the Parliament had been realized. People had expressed their views without compromise but without criticism of others. 'We have learned that truth is large and that there are more ways than one in God's providence by which men emerge out of darkness into heavenly light' (p.183). He hoped that Christians had gained a new sympathy and understanding for other faiths. He asked those of other faith to 'tell the men of the Orient that we have no sympathy with the abominations which falsely-named Christians have practised'. He hoped too that through the written record of the Parliament they would in some measure 'discover what has been the source and strength of that faith in divine fatherhood and human brotherhood which, embodied in an Asiatic Peasant who was the Son of God and made divinely potent through him, is clasping the globe with hands of heavenly light'. His last words were to speak 'the name of Him to whom I owe life and truth and hope and all things, who reconciles all contradictions, pacifies all antagonisms, and who from the throne of His heavenly kingdom directs the serene and unwearied omnipotence of redeeming love – Jesus Christ, the Saviour of the world' (p.184).

Charles Bonney, as President of the World's Congress, then spoke the closing words. He affirmed that the Parliament's influence would affect all people and that although external creeds might not change, they would be pervaded by a new spirit of light and peace. He concluded, 'Henceforth the religions of the world will make war, not on each other, but on the giant evils that afflict mankind. Henceforth let all throughout the world, who worship God and love their fellow men, join in the anthem of the angels:

"Glory to God in the highest
Peace on earth, good will among men"' (p.186)

The assembly then joined Rabbi Dr Hirsch in saying the Lord's Prayer and Bishop Keane gave a prayer of benediction. Finally, the audience joined with the Apollo Club in singing 'America'. Meanwhile Dr Barrows went to the Hall of Washington to deliver his address again there and then adjourned the World's first Parliament of Religions *sine die* (p.187).

· 3 ·

The World's Parliament
of Religions III

Both in the numbers who attended and in its length the World's
Parliament has had few, if any, equals. The most important issue was the
relation of religions to each other, although this was often discussed as the
relation of Christianity to other religions.

In approaching the issues, it may be helpful to consider who participated. The Parliament was dominated by English-speaking Christianity.
Seventy-eight per cent of the one hundred and ninety-four papers were
delivered by those who belonged to the Christian tradition. Of the one
hundred and fifty-two Christians present, seventy three per cent came
from the USA. A further forty were from Britain, Canada and continental
Europe. The other eleven Christians were either converts from South Asia
or members of the Orthodox churches. Although the majority were
American Protestants, non-evangelicals were in a slight majority. Richard
Seager uses the work of a church historian called Robert Baird, who
distinguished between evangelical and non-evangelical religion in
America, to classify participants. A total of seventy-nine out of the one
hundred and ninety-four people who presented papers were clearly
outside the evangelical mainstream. Add to this the Swedenborgians,
members of Eastern Orthodoxy, Armenians, Universalists, African
Methodist Episcopalians, Christian Scientists, Quakers, Shakers and one
member of the Salvation Army, then the total of non-evangelicals comes to
one hundred and two.[1] It is not surprising that some evangelical
Christians viewed the Parliament with alarm. Those who took part tended
to love the sinner and hate the sin. They affirmed their brotherly feeling for
the Asians, but condemned other religions as they did not offer salvation.
Christianity, said James Dennis, a historian of Christian missions, must
'be uncompromising because it is true' (p.1254). Joseph Cook, a Boston

evangelist, compared Asian religions to a shattered Greek torso, unspeakably beautiful, but only partial. Referring to Lady Macbeth, Cook asked, 'I turn to Mohammedanism. Can you wash our red, right hand? I turn to Confucianism and Buddhism and Brahmanism. Can you wash our red right hand?' (p.538).

The Parliament has been described as the most important Christian ecumenical event of the nineteenth century. Indeed, one participant, said that it, rather than the Council of Nicaea, deserved to be called the first universal council. This was partly because the Roman Catholic Church, although an outsider to the American evangelical tradition, lent its weight to the Parliament. A widely respected evangelical leader, Philip Schaff recognized that the unity he looked for would have to centre on the Greek or Roman church (p.1195). He suggested that the Pope 'should infallibly declare his fallibility in all matters outside his own communion' (p.1196).

Roman Catholics

Official Catholic participation was limited to the Columbian Catholic Congress, the extensive Catholic Educational Exhibit in the Palace of Manufactures and Liberal Arts and to the World's Parliament of Religions. Individual Catholics also participated in many other dimensions of the Exposition. It is fair to say, as Seager does, that the liberal Catholic response was 'enthusiastic but cautious',[2] although the more traditional neo-Scholastics, such as Thomas Dwight, the Parkman Professor of Anatomy at Harvard and Fr D. J. Kennedy, Professor of Theology at St Joseph's College, Ohio, were hesitant. Amongst the progressives, P. J. Muldoon, Chancellor of Chicago Archdiocese, wanted to show that Catholicism was part of Chicago life. 'The aroma of Catholic life', he said, 'was clearly discernible in the replica of the Santa Maria with the Immaculate Virgin on its prow, in the Liberal Arts building with the Catholic Education exhibit, in the Women's Building where Catholic women played a prominent role, and even in the Third World and ethnic villages of the Midway Plaisance'.[3] Cardinal Gibbons, in his opening words at the Catholic Congress, showed a similar enthusiasm by christening Chicago, 'Thaumatopolis', 'the city of wonders, the city of miracles'.[4] He cautioned his followers to be charitable in their approach to others, recalling the words of St Vincent Lerins, 'in essentials, unity; in doubtful things, liberty; in all things, charity'. There was, he said, a 'vast field of free discussion' between 'the calm and luminous region of faith and the dark and chaotic region of error'.[5]

At the Parliament, Gibbons restricted his remarks to Catholic charities and social concerns. Bishop John Keane, who was Rector of the Catholic University and who had master minded the Catholic participation, was forthright in support of progressive views. 'The chief characteristic and chief instrumentality of human progress must be progress in religion', he said (p.1332). His secretary, Merwin-Marie Snell, said, that by the laws of evolution, all aspects of church life must be expected to advance. The religion of the future, Snell said, 'will be universal, it will establish on earth a heavenly order' (p.1327). Afterwards, Keane said, that the Parliament had been a magnificent opportunity to compare the Catholic Church with various stages of Asian 'arrested development', which served as stepping stones to Christianity. It had also been helpful to observe Protestant denominations at close quarters. The comparison showed more clearly than ever that the Roman Church is 'the one universal church as her name, Catholic, implies'.[6] Liberal Catholics saw in the Exposition a great opportunity to show they were patriotic and progressive. They were careful not to antagonise Protestants who were alarmed over Catholic parochial education and the increasing number of Catholic immigrants from Southern Europe. They also sought to avoid conflict with conservative Catholics and with Rome.

Reaction soon after the Congress became hostile. The *American Ecclesiastical Review* and the *Western Watchman* of St Louis were critical. By August 1894, German-American delegates to the Katholikentag in Cologne condemned the liberal tendencies of Catholicism in the US. They cited as a chief example the 'unholy memory' of the Parliament. Soon there was to be censure from Rome. In 1895, in a letter to Archbishop Francis Satolli, the Apostolic Delegate to the US, Pope Leo XIII officially censured Catholic participation in any 'future promiscuous conventions'. The following year, John Keane was dismissed as rector of the Catholic University.[7]

Jews

Jews officially participated through involvement in the Jewish Religious Congress, the Jewish Women's Congress and the World's Parliament of Religions. There was little internal controversy about this. The Chicago *Reform Advocate*, warned that many of the people likely to attend the Jewish Congress would not be Jews but Christians who regarded Jews 'as a curiosity, a freak, or an archaeological specimen'. These Christians loved Jews, but 'would have Israel at last accept its true glory, now stubbornly rejected'.[8]

Orthodox Judaism was presented by Rabbi Henry Pereira Mendes, a Sephardic rabbi from New York. He argued that distinctiveness, separation and protestation for righteousness must remain the hallmark of the Jews. He also argued that the attitude of historical Judaism towards the other religions was one of spiritual co-operation (p.1150).

Reform Jews were enthusiastic about the Exposition. Rabbi Hecht saw the displays of music, sculpture and painting as allies for religion. Rabbi Hirsch saw man's Promethean spirit at last manifesting itself. Jews were thus able to include themselves as sharers of classically-inspired ideals of beauty, inspiration and art. Both Rabbis Kaufmann Kohler and Emil Hirsch expressed pluralistic and affirmative attitudes towards other religions. The latter's address was entitled 'Elements of Universal religion'. He believed that the great faiths would be eclipsed in a universal religion, 'The all-embracing temple of humanity' (p.1308). One day, creeds would become outdated and in the universal church, the distinction between sacred and profane would be done away (p.1306).

Just as Catholics by the level of their representation gained a high profile at the Parliament, so Jews by their ready participation helped to form what was to become the characteristic American ecumenical alliance of Catholics, Protestants and Jews.

American Blacks

American blacks held no position of authority on any of the Exposition's many committees. Frederick Douglas, representing Haiti, declared that for black Americans the White City was a 'whitened sepulchre'.[9] They were present, but equated with the Midway, with heathenism, and low culture. They were disqualified from 'real partnership in the august ideals of the Court of Honour'.[10]

The Participation of Other Faiths

Although Christians were in a strong majority, the representatives of other faiths were of high calibre and gave to the Parliament its distinctiveness.

Buddhists

There were twelve Buddhists, who came from Siam, Ceylon and Japan. Most of their papers were presented by translators and were largely descriptive of Theravada or Mahayana Buddhism. Few of the papers were interpretative. The Buddhist layman, Kinza Riugi M. Hirai, startled the gathering by his attack on the unfair way in which the West had treated Japan (pp.444–50). Horin Toki, a Shingnon Buddhist, also attacked western prejudice. Sumangala Nayaka Thera wrote from Ceylon to criticize the anti-Buddhist bias of the educational system there. Anagrika Dharmapala, however, spoke English and gave the most vivid account of his tradition. Dharmapala was an advocate of the importance of the

Buddhist heritage and of Buddhist education, and particularly of the Singhalese language and culture. Two years before the Parliament, in 1891, he founded the Bodhgaya Mahabodhi Society in Colombo, which later became known as the Maha Bodhi Society, with branches in many parts of the world. He was given considerable help by the Buddhist Theosophical Society, which had been founded in Ceylon by Colonel Henry Steel Olcott and Madame Blavatsky of the Theosophical Society. At the Parliament, with an ancient statue of the Buddha on the platform, Dharmapala gave two long addresses, explaining the Four Noble Truths and the law of karma. Aware of the appeal of theosophy to some in a Western audience, he also stressed the appeal to those of a scientific disposition of Buddhism's non-theistic world view and its emphasis on psychological disciplines. 'Buddhism', he said, 'is a scientific religion, inasmuch as it earnestly enjoins that nothing whatever be accepted on faith' (p.878). He also gave advice to Christian missionaries. 'If you want to establish Christianity in the East, it can only be done on the principles of Christ's love and meekness. Let the missionaries study all the religions; let them be a type of meekness and lowliness and they will find a welcome in all lands' (p.1093).

Shaku Soyen was another remarkable leader, although he is mostly remembered in the West as being the person who brought D.T. Suzuki to the West. He was born shortly after Japan had been forcibly opened up to the West by Commodore Perry's expeditions. During his childhood, the feudal regime was declining and the Meiji (1868–1912) emperors began to reign. With their pro-Shinto policy, Buddhism lost many of its traditional privileges. At the same time, Buddhism had to cope with the impact of Western civilization and Christian missionaries. Morale was at a low point, but a few Buddhists, including Soyen's own master, Imagita Kosen (1816–1892) were determined to reform Buddhism. Soyen studied for a time at Keio Gijuku, the centre of the Japanese enlightenment movement. He also spent two years in Ceylon, with visits to Thailand and China. In 1892, at the age of 33, Soyen became chief abbot of the prestigious Engaku-ji monastery at Kamakura and attracted many seriously minded lay disciples, including D. T. Suzuki. At the Parliament he pleaded for world peace and mutual assistance. 'Let us', he said, 'the true followers of Buddha, the true followers of Jesus Christ, the true followers of Confucius and the followers of truth, unite ourselves for the sake of helping the helpless and living glorious lives of brotherhood under the control of truth' (p.1285). After the Parliament, he returned twice to the West, accompanied by D. T. Suzuki. In Japan, despite strong opposition from both sides, he organized, in 1896, a Buddhist-Christian conference, known as the 'Little Parliament of Religions'. At its second meeting in 1897, Henry Barrows was the main speaker.[11]

Hindus

It was the Hindus who made the greatest impact on the American audience, especially Swami Vivekananda and P. C. Mozoomdar. Other Hindus of the eight who presented papers included Manilal N. D'vivedi, a high caste Brahmin, Lakshmi Narain from Lahore, S.Parthacarathy Arjangar and Nara Sima Charyar, both Vaishnavites (one of the Hindu theistic traditions) and Mohun Dev, a devotee of Mahamaniya Pujniyabar Sattyanand Agnihotori who, in 1887, having become disillusioned with the Brahmo Samaj had founded his own Dev Dharm.

Vivekananda (1863–1902) was the most colourful character and made the greatest impact. It is said that to retain a satisfactory audience for a particular session, the chairman's secret was to announce Vivekananda as the final speaker.[12] He had studied law at Calcutta University so was thoroughly at home in English language and culture. As he was about to sail for England for further study, he was persuaded to visit Sri Ramakrishna (1836–86), the saintly mystic. The meeting changed his life. He devoted the rest of his life to translating Ramakrishna's teaching into concrete efforts towards the revitalization of Hinduism. He also became the best known early advocate of Hinduism in the West.

His arrival in Chicago itself was remarkable. He arrived late at night by train. He had lost the address of the Parliament and receiving no help at the station, he slept the night there in a large empty box. Next morning, he called at a number of houses asking in vain for assistance. He decided to sit down and wait for help. It came quickly. A woman looking out from her window in North Dearborn Avenue, noticed his strange appearance. She asked if he were a delegate to the Parliament. She then invited him in and took him to meet Mrs Hale, one of her personal friends, who was the President of the Parliament.

This was in July and Vivekananda soon discovered that the Parliament did not start until September. He was fascinated by the World's Fair, but his money was beginning to run out. He was advised that he would be able to live more cheaply in Boston, so he made his way there. On the train he met a wealthy woman, Kate Sanborn, who offered him somewhere to stay and introduced him to some of her influential friends. One of these was J. H. Wright, Professor at Harvard. He was appalled to learn that Vivekananda had no credentials to speak at the Parliament. 'To ask for your credentials', Wright said, 'is like asking the sun to state its right to shine'.[13] He wrote, in rather extravagant terms, to the Chairman and this, with Mrs Hale's introduction, ensured that when Vivekananda returned to Chicago for the Parliament, he was welcomed as a participant.

Vivekananda separated what he regarded as the essential principle of

Hinduism from its philosophical and ritualistic expressions. The message that the soul is eternal and capable of becoming divine was a universal message at the heart of all religions. 'Do not care for doctrines, do not care for dogmas or sects or churches or temples; they count for little compared with the essence of existence in each man which is spirituality.'[14] Yet in extending his tolerance to all religious practices, he undercut his programme to reform Hinduism, which he had been advocating in India. 'All religions', he said, 'from the lowest fetishism to the highest absolutism' are so many attempts of the human soul to grasp and realize the Infinite, 'as determined by the condition of birth and association' (p.977). The varieties of religion were adapted to the varieties of human personality and development. He quoted the words of the Bhagavad-gita where Lord Krishna says, 'I am in every religion as the thread through a string of pearls' (p.977). With an appeal to evolution, he affirmed 'Every religion is only an evolving of God out of material man. The same God is the inspirer of all' (p.977). He thus answered the missionary challenge by suggesting that missionaries were intolerant and immature. Their call for conversions was irrelevant and narrow-minded.[15] In his reply to the welcome, he declared 'I am proud to belong to a religion which has taught the world both tolerance and universal acceptance. We believe not only in universal toleration, but we accept all religions as true. I am proud to belong to a nation which has sheltered the persecuted and the refugees of all religions and all nations of the earth' (p.102). Such tolerance, however, had to be applied to practices that in another context he would like to have seen changed.[16]

Vivekananda stayed on in America after the Parliament and set off on a nation-wide lecture tour. Except for a brief visit to Britain, he stayed in the USA for three years and in 1896 founded the Vedanta Society. On his return to India he founded the Ramakrishna Mission Association. He returned to USA in 1899 and during this visit founded the Vedanta Society of California.[17]

Two members of The Brahmo-Samaj, a Hindu Reform movement, participated. One was B. B. Nagarkar, who was born in 1860, of a very high caste family. He was educated at a Christian Mission school. Nagarkar spoke of the cost and benefits of British rule and, in a second paper, laid out the progressive and universalist ideals of the Brahmo-Samaj, which was committed to the harmonization of all the prophets. Protap Chunder Mozoomdar, presented a progressive version of Hinduism. Mozoomdar was already known to Americans through his book *The Oriental Christ*. In this he argued that Asians were best able to understand the true message of Christ, because Christ was an Asian. At the Parliament, in one paper, he reviewed the life and teaching of

Rammohan Roy, the founder of the Brahmo Samaj. In another his defence
of the eastern tradition drew from the Methodist commentator, Charles
Little, the observation that his words 'fell upon the startled listeners like
flakes of biting flame'.[18] He hoped that in due course East and West 'might
combine to support each other's strengths and supply each other's
deficiencies' (p.1092). His respect for Christ was apparent, but also his
rejection of the traditional exclusivist claims of Christians. 'Along with
Nagarkar, Vivekananda, Dharmapala, and the Asian scholars,' writes
Seager, 'he dealt a heavy blow against the arrogance of those who claimed
the exclusive possession of Christ and those who presumed that western
Christianity was a superior religious tradition. Together with the minority
report of the American liberals and the theories of scholars in the discipline
of comparative religion, the presentations of the Asians created a powerful
corrective to the majority report of the Christian triumphalism on the
Parliament floor'.[19]

Muslims

The chief exponent of Islam at the Parliament was an American convert,
Mohammed Alexander Russell Webb. He made clear that Muslims
expected their religion to become the universal religion. This statement
and his reference to polygamy were greeted by cries of 'Shame'. Some
Christian scholars also gave papers on Islam, but it must be said that the
representation of Islam at the Parliament did not do justice to that
religion.

Other Religions

Shintoism, Confucianism, Jainism, Zoroastrianism were all represented,
and a reference made to the Bahá'i religion.[20] A number of papers were
presented by leading scholars in the science of religions. Those by
C. P. Tiele of Leiden, by Albert and Jean Reville of the Sorbonne and
F. Max Müller and J. Estlin Carpenter of Oxford were read for them, as
they were not able to attend. It is noteworthy that no distinguished
European theologian took an active interest. Some 'scientific' papers were
presented by the Asians present and some 'comparative' papers by
Christian missionary scholars.

The Asian Impact

The Asians, although few in number, made a major impact. They gave
credible and persuasive presentations of their religions. They drew

attention to unfair pressure and behaviour by missionaries and they questioned the 'Christian universalism', which was the prevailing sentiment of the organizers. 'As a rite of passage', writes Richard Seager, 'the Parliament resembled what the anthropologist Victor Turner called the liminal state, a state of transition charged with a dangerous but fascinating ambiguity in which all things seemed possible. Before the American public and press, the Parliament crested in a flood of spontaneous universalistic hopes for a global spiritual community; all the religions of the world seemed to fold, one upon the other, into a single vision of the future progress of the race. The Father seemed to be in it, Christ was written all over it; the Spirit seemed to be moving throughout it, together with Krishna, Confucius and the Buddha too. The nineteenth century, nay the ages, seemed to have found their spiritual fulfilment in a universal Pentecost as Christian America processed towards a new and even grander century'.[21] Kenten Druyvesteyn writes in a similar way that 'probably the most sensational effect of the Parliament was the direct introduction it made of non-Christian, and especially non-Western, religions to the American people. Not only was unprecedented public attention centred on the non-Christian religions but representatives of these religions actually set foot on American soil, toured the country and journeyed to the heartland of the nation'.[22]

The psychological impact of the Parliament needs to be measured as well as the intellectual content of the papers. The key issue was the relation of religions to each other – usually formulated in terms of the relation of Christianity to other religions. The balance of the intellectual arguments do not entirely square with the emotional and psychological impact and although it is fair to describe the Parliament as a Christian assembly to which guests of other faiths were invited, it has come to symbolize something more.

The Relation of Religions

Professor Bishop[23] distinguishes three ways of describing the relation of religions to each other: Exclusion, inclusion and pluralism. Exclusion implies that one religion is eventually to dominate the world. 'Christianity is to conquer and supplant all the other religions of the world', said a writer in the *American Advocate of Peace*.[24] 'There is not a Mussulman on earth who does not believe that ultimately Islam will be the universal faith' (p.989), said Mohammed Alexander Russell Webb. 'The attitude of Christianity', said William Wilkinson, towards religions other than itself is an attitude of universal, absolute, eternal, unappeasable hostility', however sympathetic it may be to the followers of those religions (p.1249). 'Only Christianity has power to save' (p.1247). For George Pentecost 'Jesus stands without peer among men or gods . . . Jesus will never be surpassed' (p.1167). Others pointed to the good that Christianity does. America was, for David Burrell, the advertisement for the Gospel. 'The world will ultimately believe in the religion that produces the highest type of government and the best average man . . . The history of America gives proof on every page that the Gospel of the crucified Nazarene is interwoven with our entire national fabric' (p.1157).

Others responded to the longing for a universal faith by claiming that Christianity could fit the bill – perhaps with some growth or adaptation. Many affirmed that evidence of God's activity could be seen in all religions. 'In all religions', said the Roman Catholic Archbishop Redwood of New Zealand, 'there is a vast element of truth' (p.441). The Presbyterian journalist, Rev. Henry M. Field claimed that he had every-where in his travels across the world seen 'evidence of God's presence' 'I have found that "God has not left himself without witness" in any of the dark climes or in any of the dark religions of this world' (p.127). T. E. Slater, in arguments that anticipated Farquhar's *Crown of Hinduism* claimed that Christianity fulfilled the aspirations of other religions. A comparison of the Bible with other scriptures, 'establishes Christianity's *satisfying* character in distinction from the *seeking* spirit of other faiths. The Bible shows God in quest of man rather than man in quest of God. It meets the questions raised in the philosophies of the East and supplies their only true solution' (p.459). Some Christians made a distinction between Christ and Christianity. 'It is not Christianity that we want to tell our brethren across the sea about, it is Christ' (p.300), said Rev. Lyman Abbott. Others said there was something to learn from other religions.

Many suggested that the universal religion of the future would be a developed Christianity. One achievement remained, declared Rev. A. Gmeiner, 'to crown the work of the unification of the human family with the heaven-given blessing of religious unity'. The day would come, he predicted, when all would recognize as their true home under God what by its 'providentially given and preserved name, known all over the world, [is called] "the Holy Catholic Church"' (p.1266). For some, such as Professor Valentine, it was Christianity's faith in a personal God that fitted it for a universal role (p.285). Others pointed to the perversions in other religions. 'It is a notable fact that there has been a deterioration in the sacred books of the ethnic religions, and not, as is the case of the Hebrew, an evolution toward greater light and truth', said Rev. T. J. Scott in a paper generally marked by great openness and longing for a more universal religion (p.925). In a somewhat similar way, without recourse to the divine character of Christianity, Dr Gracey of Rochester, New York, argued that

Christianity held the seeds of all human belief and was most fitted successfully to meet the religious needs of all people. 'Christianity is to become the religion of Men' (p.1330).

The inclusivists in Bishop's classification were those who held that one universal religion would emerge, but it was not yet in existence. It was not the case, therefore, that one religion would triumph or absorb all others into itself. What would happen, this group claimed, was that something new would emerge. The process of smaller religions being absorbed into greater religions would not, according to the Free Religious Association of America, end with Christianity. That religion too would be absorbed in something grander. 'The history of man is not Christo-centric, but cosmo-centric'.[25] Rabbi Dr Hirsch, as we have seen,[26] spoke about the elements of a universal religion, (p.1305) and Mozoomdar said, 'the Hebrew, the Hindu, the Mongolian, the Christian are ever at one, for that Wisdom is no part of themselves but the self-revelation of God' (p.1087). J. Estlin Carpenter of Manchester New College spoke of God's continual self-revelation which could not be confined to a particular tradition and Colonel T. W. Higginson of the USA said that it was a matter of birth which religion people adopted but he hoped that 'all will come at last upon the broad ground of God's providing, which bears no name' (p.782).

The pluralists were those who did not envisage the emergence of one more universal religion, but expected that the great religions would retain their distinct identity, although they hoped the relations between them would reflect brotherhood and charity. At times Mozoomdar seemed to adopt this rather than an inclusivist position. Rt Rev. Reuchi Shibata, a Shintoist, said it was impracticable to combine all religions into one. The variety met different human needs. They should, however, conquer hostile feelings and work together for peace (p.454). This was similar to the view voiced by Bonney in his opening address 'For when the religious faiths of the world recognize each other as brothers, children of one Father, whom all profess to love and serve, then, and not till then, will the nations of the earth yield to the spirit of concord and learn war no more' (p.67).

The debate about the relation of religions to each other is still by no means resolved. The various positions adopted at Chicago have been repeated in subsequent years. There are those who believe that their religion is true and that all others are false. They adopt a missionary stance and have little use for dialogue or interfaith activity. Others, equally sure that theirs is the true religion will allow for God's activity in other religious traditions and make some place in their theologies for other religions. They may be willing for inter-religious dialogue, but mainly for peace and on questions of human rights and on social issues. They maintain the right to witness to the truth claims of their tradition. Others believe that no religion can claim finality and that out of dialogue and interfaith co-operation a more universal religion may emerge. Some hope for, even anticipate, a new universal religion, whereas others look for a growing assimilation of religions to each other or stress a 'mystical unity' that transcends particular traditions. Others take a more pluralist view. Whilst affirming loyalty to their tradition, they do not assert its supremacy over others nor do they assume an underlying unity. Rather, they recognize the distinctiveness of the great faiths, but believe that by their co-operation all people are enriched. This latter view has perhaps predominated in the interfaith movement, setting it apart from a unitive view, perhaps more associated with the Theosophical movement and those who speak of a 'perennial religion', and from the stance of official religious bodies, who usually maintain the supremacy of their religion.

The debate begun at Chicago has continued and often, as with the key organizers of the World's Parliament, leading members of the same organization are inspired by rather different visions of religious co-operation.

· 4 ·

The World's Parliament
of Religions: Conclusions

The proceedings of the Parliament were quickly published. What other legacy did it leave? There was some talk at the Parliament of arranging a similar gathering in the future but no plans were made for this. A continuing body was talked about and Rev. Jenkin Lloyd Jones became secretary of the Congress of Religions. This, however, was never an effective body and eventually it was subsumed by the International Association for Religious Freedom. Also active in The International Association for Religious Freedom in its early years was Rev. Jabez Sunderland, who had attended the 1893 Parliament. In 1933, The World Fellowship of Faiths was to call its gathering in Chicago a Second World Parliament of Religions.

The Parliament failed to establish an effective continuing organization. In part this was because of the particular combination of circumstances that made the Parliament possible – 'its timeliness', to use Henry Barrows' words (p.1568). The Parliament was possible, he said, because it was part of an international exposition 'under no ecclesiastical dictation' (p.1568). 'The world needed to wait till English had become an Asiatic as well as an European and American language' (p.1569).

In assessing 'the extraordinary success of the Parliament' (p.1568), Barrows said 'It has shown that mankind is drifting toward religion and not away from it; it has widened the bounds of human fraternity, it is giving a strong impetus to the study of comparative religion; it is fortifying timid souls in regard to the right and wisdom of liberty in thought and expresssion; it is clarifying many minds in regard to the nature of non-Christian faiths; it is deepening the general Christian interest in non-Christian nations; and it will bring before millions in Oriental lands the more truthful and beautiful aspects of Christianity' (p.1569). Barrows hoped the Parliament would give an impetus to the reunion of Christendom (p.1573). He went on once more to disown any idea of evolving 'a cosmic or universal faith' (p.1572). 'The best religion must come to the front' (p.1572). For Barrows, that religion was clearly Christianity, 'the great quickener of humanity' (p.1581). 'The non-Christian world may give us valuable criticism and confirm scriptural truths and make excellent suggestions as to Christian improvement, but it has nothing to add to the Christian creed' (p.1581).

Kenten Druyvesteyn dismisses the enthusiasm and florid rhetoric of Barrows as 'naive, at times even pathetic'.[1] Some of Barrows' more general claims are impossible to assess. In Europe, mankind has drifted away from religion, but in other parts of the globe there has been religious growth. Liberty of thought and tolerance have grown, but so also has fanaticism. International organizations have increased, but narrow nationalism seems as strong as ever.

The Parliament did give an impetus to the comparative study of religion. As Kitagawa points out, the Parliament did not initiate the study of comparative religion in USA, but it did provide a strong stimulus. More specifically, Barrows' enthusiasm prompted Mrs Caroline Haskell to endow both the Haskell Lectureship in Comparative Religion at the infant University of Chicago and the Barrows lectureship, through which a number of distinguished scholars, such as Charles Gilkey and James Gustafson have lectured in India. Mrs Haskell also endowed a lectureship at Oberlin College, which brought Rudolf Otto, Adolf Deissman, Gunther Bornkamm and other scholars to the USA. Soon after the Parliament, a group of scholars on the East coast formed the American Committee for Lectures on the History of Religions. This arranged for T. W. Rhys Davies, Franz Cumont and other well known scholars to lecture in the USA. In 1937 the lectureship was taken over by the American Council of Learned Societies and has come to be known as the ACLS Lectures on History of Religions.[2]

The Parliament as we have seen gave a prominent role to Roman Catholic leaders and to Jewish rabbis. It demonstrated what was to become the characteristic American ecumenical alliance of Protestants, Catholics and Jews.[3]

Most important was the impact of Asian religious leaders. Clay Lancaster draws a parallel between 'What Louis Sullivan said about the preponderance of Classic architecture at the Columbian Exposition and the paramount orthodoxy of faith that was meted out at the World's Parliament of Religions. Sullivan's comment was that the retarded style would delay the progress of architecture in this country fifty years. The overwhelming enthusiasm over an archaic religion impeded any advance toward spiritual truths in like measure'.[4] Yet even if the hopes of Barrows and others were that the Parliament would demonstrate the superiority of Christianity, in fact, it presented Asian religions to the American public as alternatives to be seriously considered. Ignorance about Asian faiths was widespread. At one of the meetings, Dharmapala inquired how many people had read the life of Buddha, to which only five people responded affirmatively. 'Five only!', said Dharmapala, 'four hundred and seventy-five millions of people accept our religion of love and hope. You call yourselves a nation – a great nation – and yet you do not know the history of this great teacher'.[5]

The Chicago *Tribune*, after only a week of the Parliament, had a heading 'Wells of Truth Outside'.[6] In its editorial at the end of the Parliament, the *Tribune* said that while different religions had different understandings of truth, they were engaged together in a common search. Christianity had learned at the Parliament that 'there are no longer pagans and heathens'; Christians, Buddhists, Confucians, Hindus and others all stood together 'upon the same plane of morality and humanity'.[7] America was made publicly aware of Asian religions and soon those same religions were to become part of the American scene. Vivekananda stayed on and visited several American cities, in some of which Vedanta groups were formed. Dharmapala made two return visits to the USA.

The Parliament has been called by Sidney Ahlstrom[8] a watershed in American life – marking the change from the dominance of Anglo-Saxon Protestantism to the start of a multi-religious society. Henry Nash described the entire exposition as 'something like a mark of punctuation in American cultural history'.[9] Richard Seager concludes his study in a similar way, 'As far as religious pluralism in America is concerned a strict construction of the issue would seem to suggest that after the Parliament, there were many ways to be religious. One could be saved or self-realized or grow in God consciousness or be self-emptied. And as America itself continued to pursue its messianic mission, it was a nation under a changed God. Krishna, Vishnu, the Buddha (technically a not-God), the Divine Mother, and other deities had been tucked up in the nation's sacred canopy, where they joined the Christian Father and Son, Jehovah, Nature's God, and Apollo and his Muses. America had gone into the parliament claiming to be a cosmopolitan nation and had come out having to live up to the claim. There was no going back'.[10]

Ken Druyvesteyn, however, warns that the wateshed metaphor is an artificial means of establishing chronology. 'It bears the same relationship to history as a mark of punctuation does to a sentence. It does not create the meaning of a sentence. It is not even the reason for writing the sentence. Rather it aids in making the message of the sentence clearer and more understandable. So also with the Parliament. As an episode of a larger drama it is of only minor significance. But as a symbol of its age it reveals once again the intensity of the crisis that American Christianity was experiencing at this time'.[11] The crisis included the challenges of urbanism, industrialism, Darwinism, naturalism, and biblical criticism. The Parliament did not of itself destroy the Protestant hegemony, but contributed to this by symbolizing the changes taking place.

In Asia, as Kitagawa points out, Vivekananda, Dharmapala and Shaku Soyen returned with an adaptation of the 'fulfilment' theory of religions. Instead of suggesting that Christianity was wrong, they embraced it in a larger framework, which was determined by their religious views.[12] They provided Asian religions with an apologetic to resist Christian missionary pressure and indeed to suggest that the wisdom of the East is superior to Christianity. 'In retrospect', writes Kitagawa, 'it becomes clear that what the Parliament contributed to Eastern religions was not comparative religion as such. Rather, Barrows and his colleagues should receive credit for initiating what we call today the "dialogue among various religions", in which each religious claim for ultimacy is acknowledged'.[13]

It is the symbolism of the World's Parliament of Religions which has perhaps given it a continuing significance. It seems doubtful that it altered the movement of history, although it may have given a boost to some developments. It embodied, however, the aspirations of those who believed that religions should be friendly and co-operative to each other and work together for human welfare and peace. Those aspirations have often been reiterated by members of interfaith organizations. Whilst they do not wish to imitate the programme and style of the 1893 Parliament, they see it as marking the start of what has become known as the 'interfaith movement'.

· PART II ·

Yearning for Unity

'An underlying and overarching harmony'

· 5 ·

Is There a Unity of Faiths?

All the interfaith organizations disavow any attempt to create a single world religion. They recognize the distinctiveness of world religions and see in their variety an enrichment of the human spirit. Yet, although they may not agree how, members of these organizations sense or hope for an underlying unity or future convergence of religions. This approach has been particularly associated with the International Association for Religious Freedom, the World Congress of Faiths and, more recently, the Temple of Understanding.

The claim was made by the nineteenth-century Hindu leader, Sri Ramakrishna, that he had discovered that the mystical experience at the heart of every religious discipline was essentially the same.[1] On this claim, Swami Vivekananda based his call for tolerance at the World Parliament of Religions.[2] If the essential religious experience is similar, the differences, which in his view were caused by theological and cultural conditioning, become inessential. Instead of competing, religions should, therefore, co-operate. It has also been felt that this was timely, at a moment in history when modern communications were making the world one.

These views have been eloquently expounded by Dr S Radhakrishnan, who spoke at early gatherings of the World Congress of Faiths and later became its Patron. He also became a supporter of the Temple of Understanding. In the Preface to his *Eastern Religions and Western Thought*, he revealed his universal interest. Because there is a growing world consciousness, he saw a new humanism on the horizon, embracing the whole of humankind. The supreme task of our generation is to give a world soul to this growing world consciousness. 'Should we not', he asks, 'give a spiritual basis to the world which is now being mechanically made to feel its oneness by modern scientific inventions?'[3] In his opinion, a world community, of which the various nations are the units, and universal religion, of which the various historical religions are the branches, should arise as the social and spiritual counterparts of the scientific progress of this century. International contacts through improved means of communications and the growth of commerce are only the body of the new world. A feeling of brotherhood among all nations, a spirit of co-operation in the pursuit of common peaceful aims, international fellowship and universal toleration – these should form the soul of that world. In his *Kamala Lectures*, he argued that through the influence of science and trade a world culture is shaping itself and that as religions adapt to this new world and express themselves in a new idiom so they are 'approximating to one another'. The universal elements in them will be emphasized and the 'gradual assimilation of religions will function as a world faith'.[4] 'The time has come', he wrote in his book *Religion in a Changing World*, 'for us to join in unity of spirit'.[5] His view rests on two premises. First, that the underlying mystical experience of the great religious leaders is closely related. 'The seers describe their experiences with an impressive unanimity. They are near to one another on mountains farthest apart'.[6] The second premise is that each individual must discover the truth for himself and that it will differ as each individual's development differs. This allows for the acceptance of variety and of different views of truth.

Today leading members of interfaith organizations would usually wish to give more importance to the distinctiveness of the different religions, which enrich the human spirit. They would not necessarily share Radhakrishnan's view. Indeed the nature of the relationship of religions is still a subject of much debate. They retain the belief, however, that the great religions share a vision of life which is significant for all people and the hope that together people of all faiths can contribute to a happier future for humankind.

· 6 ·

The International Association for Religious Freedom I

Beginnings

The name of the International Association for Religious Freedom is rather misleading and has been changed on more than one occasion. It is in origin a grouping of those committed to 'free' or liberal religious values, rather than a body campaigning for religious liberty and the rights of the individual's conscience, although today there is more emphasis on this.

The movement dates back to 1900, when on 25 May the 'International Council of Unitarian and other Liberal Religious Thinkers and Workers' was founded. Indeed, the origins are even earlier. From about 1870, Rev. Dr Charles W. Wendte began trying to build up a sense of fellowship among the scattered liberals of the world. He made numerous journeys to help establish links between the American Unitarian Association and the German *Protestantenverein* (Free or Liberal Protestant Union).

Charles Wendte

Charles William Wendte was born in 1844 in Boston. His parents had come to America on their honeymoon. Life in Boston at first was difficult for them. One day they went to a church of which they knew nothing. Afterwards, Wendte's father commented. 'That was real common sense. Fancy hearing something sensible from a preacher!'[1] The church was Unitarian. Wendte's parents became Unitarians. When Charles was born, his proud father declared, 'We want him to become a Unitarian minister'.[2] Towards the end of his life, Charles voiced his gratitude to his parents. 'I am more grateful than words can express that I grew up under free Christian influences. From the start I was encouraged to think about religious and moral problems in full freedom and to put my faith in the eternal goodness which lives in all things'.[3]

As a young man, he had a serious illness. Soon afterwards, he joined a Unitarian Young Men's club and started to become interested in religious and social matters. His doctor advised that California would provide a better climate for him, so he moved there with his mother and brother – his father had died when he was only four years old. He came under the influence of the distinguished Unitarian minister, Thomas Starr King, and of Professor Charles Miel, who for a time had been a Catholic priest. After a period, Wendte decided to become a Unitarian minister, although he said that at that time his interest in religion was mainly intellectual and that he did not possess 'the consciousness of his presence and closeness . . . which are the secret sources of inspiration for the real servants of God on earth'.[4] Such a turning point occurred just before he started his theological training at Meadville (1866–7) and Harvard (1867–9). In his studies, he was particularly interested in comparative religion. In 1869, he read about the Free Protestant Union (*Protestantenverein*), which had recently been formed in Europe, and he translated the article for the *Christian Register*.

Wendte became a keen member of the Free Religious Association of America. In 1869 he was asked to form the fourth Unitarian church in Chicago. In 1871 his church became a centre for relief work, following the great fire of Chicago. He described a delightful scene of a Rabbi, to help the hungry, slicing a joint of bacon which was held by a Catholic priest. This convinced him that all were part of one human family, children of the Father of the Universe.[5]

In 1874 he had to take sick leave and travelled, with his mother, to Europe, where he made some contact with the Free Protestant Union. He returned to Chicago for a time, but in 1875 moved to Cincinatti. Then, from 1886–1898, he did missionary work on the West coast, where in 1887, he was joined by Samuel A. Eliot, with whom he was to work closely for the rest of his life. In 1896, he married Abbie Louise Grant. In 1889, he made his fifth journey to Europe and was asked by Eliot, who was then Secretary of the American Unitarian Association to invite some Europeans to the celebration of the Association's seventy fifth anniversary. When Eliot became President of the Association, he asked Wendte to take responsibility for their foreign affairs (on a part-time basis, as well as looking after a congregation in Brighton, Mass). In large measure he fulfilled this responsibility through his enormous work for the International Council, although he was never paid by this body. His salary came from the American Unitarian Association and his congregational work. He was well suited for his international work. As one of his friends said, 'How your

German-American, East-Westerly cosmopolitanism has trained you' for the work.[6]

Some of the participants in the inaugural meeting in Boston in 1900 of International Council of Unitarian and other Liberal Religious Thinkers and Workers had been at the 1893 Chicago World's Parliament of Religions. Others were British Unitarians. There were also members of the Romanian and Hungarian Unitarian churches, which dated back to the sixteenth century. Other European and Free Christian churches were also represented. People from several countries were appointed to the Executive Committee and Dr Wendte was chosen to be secretary. By his travels and voluminous correspondence he built up contacts with liberal groups in various parts of the world.

The founding meeting was followed by Congresses in London (1901), Amsterdam (1903), Geneva (1905), Boston (1907), Berlin (1910) and Paris (1913). In London, the opening address was given by Rev. Dr J. Estlin Carpenter, the Principal of Manchester New College at Oxford, who was a distinguished Sanskrit scholar. In Geneva, the Congress opened with a service at the Cathedral of St Pierre. The 1907 Boston Congress was the largest of these early gatherings. It had 2391 members, of sixteen nationalities, coming from eighty-eight groups, among which were liberal Muslims and some liberal Jews and Catholics, as well as members of the Brahmo Samaj, a Hindu Reform movement, which had had links with the Unitarian Church from early in the nineteenth century. Formal invitations were sent to the Universalist body of churches, which, at the time, surprisingly did not have particularly close relations with the Unitarian churches, to the Liberal Friends, sometimes called Hicksites, to the Free Religious Association and to the Congress of Religions, whose central figure was Jenkin Lloyd Jones, who had been secretary of the 1893 World's Parliament of Religions.

The Berlin Congress in 1910 also attracted nearly two thousand participants, at a time when liberal theology was in the ascendant. There was some press criticism of the Congress for questioning the uniqueness of Christianity and the Crown Prince of Prussia warned against the spread of internationalist sentiment. There were addresses by some outstanding scholars, including Adolf Harnack, Wilhelm Bousset, Walter Rauschenbusch and Ernst Troeltsch. The Liberal Jewish scholar Claude Montefiore said that the hopes of each religion that it would dominate the world were unrealizable and undesirable. If there were to be a single religion, this would be an impoverishment. Quoting Goethe, he said tolerance was only a beginning, it should lead to appreciation. Rabbi Hirsch of Chicago and two Hindus also spoke. One of the sections was devoted to 'Religion and the Woman Question'. Another concentrated on

'International Peace and Amity'. It called in a strongly worded resolution for 'a patriotism worldwide in its scope'.[7]

There were many scholarly papers at the Paris Congress in 1913. Dr Wendte in his report of the 1913 Paris Congress, was full of optimism, when he wrote, 'Everywhere we find the same issues: a passionate search for truth, aroused consciences, abandonment or modification of antiquated dogmas, re-wording of the principles of religious belief and enlarged comprehension of the universality of religious inspiration'.[8]

At that time ambitious plans were nearing their fulfilment to hold a series of congresses, beginning in Europe and extending through Asia. A small core group would attend all the gatherings. Charles Wendte took responsibility for those in America and the Near East and Rev. Jabez Sunderland, for some years Editor of the *Unitarian*, who had attended the 1893 World's Parliament of Religions, was in charge of plans for those in the Orient. By travel and correspondence, he built up an impressive range of contacts. It was hoped that by the autumn of 1914 all the preliminary work would have been completed and the congresses could begin. But then, World War I broke out and, although the various local committees remained in contact for some time, the plans came to nothing. 'The moral foundations of the world had been so badly broken up', wrote Jabez Sunderland later, 'and all nations had been so filled with hate of one another, that there seemed no place left for faith, or trust, or friendship, or brotherhood of any kind'.[9] His hopes, however, were renewed by the World Fellowship of Faiths and their second World Parliament of Religions in Chicago in 1933.

What's in a Name?

The name adopted in 1900, as we have seen, was 'The International Council of Unitarian and other Liberal Religious Thinkers and Workers'. There had been considerable discussion on the advisability of using either 'Christian' or 'Unitarian' in the title. Wendte clearly wanted the fellowship to be as inclusive as possible. In his view, 'Unitarian' was 'justified by the circumstances under which the Council at first functioned': but he stressed, however, that the agreed purpose was 'to open communication with those in all lands who are striving to unite pure religion with perfect liberty, and to increase fellowship and co-operation among them'.[10] By 1907, he and some others argued that the Congress had outgrown 'the swaddling bands of its infancy'.[11] This view predominated and the word 'Unitarian' was dropped. The gathering was called the 'Congress of Religious Liberals'. At Berlin, however, in 1910 the congress was called 'The International Congress of Free Christians and other

Religious Liberals'. Wendte wrote that 'I fought hard for the name we had given our Boston meetings as the broader and more inclusive term. It was felt, however, by some of the more timorous spirits that the title chosen would subject the German clergy and educators participating to less hostile criticism by the State Church and authorities'.[12]

In 1932 at the St Gall Congress, the name was changed to 'The International Association for Liberal Christianity and Religious Freedom'. In 1934 the Americans tried to get 'Liberal Christian' dropped from the title. The matter was raised again at the meeting in Chicago in 1958 and at successive meetings in Davos (1961), Scheveningen, near the Hague (1964) and London (1966). At Boston in 1969, the term was dropped and the organization became the 'International Association for Religious Freedom' (IARF) – established at that time at the Hague to continue as 'Het Internationaal Verbond voor Geloofsvrijheid'. This, wrote Dr June Bell soon after the Congress, at last opened the way to 'liberals of other-than-Christian persuasion to feel entirely free to join a world wide religious movement which now offers no suggestion of specialization'.[13]

Between the Wars

Between the World Wars, the main activity was the triennial congress. The first Congress after World War One was held in 1922, at Leiden. Only twelve countries were represented – all except for USA, being European. Europeans, scarred by war, were sometimes irritated by the naive utopianism of the Americans. A youth organization was established at the congress. The 1925 Congress, planned for Germany, had to be cancelled because of political and economic problems. The 1927 Congress was in Prague. Again the attendance was mostly European and American, with only one Indian present. There were three people from Palestine and two from South Africa. Just over one third of the participants were women. The Congress attracted a lot of local interest so that attendance at some sessions reached two thousand.

Before the 1930 Congress at Arnhem, W. H. Drummond had resigned as General Secretary, so the Congress was organized by The Central Committee of the Free Protestants in the Netherlands. The next Congress, held in 1932 at St Gall was, for the first time, preceded by a Theologians' Conference and this became customary for some years. The 1934 Copenhagen Congress pleaded for a separation of religion and politics. The emphasis was on the 'spiritual community'. In 1937, the congress was at Oxford, but war came before another congress could be held, although there was a theological conference in the Netherlands in 1938.

Increasingly Interfaith

There has always been some dispute whether it is appropriate to call Unitarians 'Christians'. Some members of 'main-line' churches object and some Unitarians prefer to think of themselves as 'universalists'. From the beginning the IARF included groups which were not of Christian/Western origin. The Brahmo Samaj Movement, based in Calcutta, has been a member from the beginning. The Japan Free Religious Association, a movement based in Tokyo, joined IARF in 1923. It was led by Dr Shinichiro Imaoka, who had met Charles Wendte in 1915 and who at the age of 102 was present at the Tokyo IARF Congress.[14] At Boston in 1969, Rissho Kosei Kai, a large lay Buddhist movement in Japan, led by Rev. Nikkyo Niwano, became a full member as did The International Religious Fellowship, which from the 1920s had been the youth association for liberal religion and religious freedom. Four new groups were admitted to Associate Membership.[15]

IARF has thus become an increasingly interfaith organization. Elke Schlinck-Lazarraga, at one time the international affairs secretary of the German Unitarians, in her history of IARF, distinguishes three phases. The first, under American leadership, lasted from 1900 to 1930 and had a 'broad Unitarian/liberal religious vision'. This was narrowed down in the second phase to a 'liberal Christian outlook'. The third phase, from the 1969 Boston Conference, she sees as a return to the original vision. Diether Gehrmann, however, who was the energetic and far-sighted General Secretary from 1972–1990 sees the third phase as progression to an 'interfaith vision'. Writing in 1984, Diether Gehrmann said, 'The IARF's history is characterized by continuity and a steadily advancing openness to interfaith insight and co-operation on the level that truly puts such ideals to the test, namely, corporate endorsement by religious denominations and at the grassroots level of the local religious community. Since 1900 the name, structure, priorities and centre of initiative of the IARF have changed. Having first been primarily a sequence of congresses, the IARF attained greater institutional stability through adopting a constitution and by establishing a secretariat . . . What began as an initiative of liberal Christianity came to include liberal and reform movements of all faiths, developed into an interfaith coalition for social justice and world peace that is transcending the division between "liberal" and "conservative", and is entering the phase of an ecumenism of world religious communities. Consequently, in the year of the Congress in Japan (1984), the IARF is composed of fifty member groups in twenty-one countries, on all continents. Its spiritual horizon includes liberal Christians and Unitarians, mostly from Europe and North America, and Buddhists,

Shintoists, Hindus, Sikhs and Muslims from Asia.' The perspective of tribal socio-religious communities is represented through the Seng Khasi of India.[16]

Gehrmann recalled that Charles Wendte as early as the 1903 Amsterdam meeting had said, 'It is one of our cherished hopes that this council shall yet hold a session in the Valley of the Ganges and the Land of the Rising Sun, if only to vindicate the great central doctrine of our faith, that while religions are many, religion itself is one'.[17]

This underlying perception of the relationship of religions is echoed by Diether Gehrmann in this article. 'The spiritual basis of the IARF is the insight that there are many manifestations in this world of what we perceive as the Divine or Eternal or Creative Spirit. It is the insight that more than one path leads to this ultimate Reality, that as religious people we can partake of this Spirit, that we all care about suffering and hope for fulfilment'.[18] Reverend Nikkyo Niwano echoed this when he said, 'The time has come when we must, while paying ample respect to each other's faith, search out the true religion that underlies all our beliefs'.[19]

Europeans and Americans

This is a view that perhaps echoes the American Unitarian-Universalist contribution to IARF. For many Europeans, free Christianity has to be understood in the context of the dominance of state-churches. In most European countries religious liberals 'have been non-conformist in matters of dogma, of church-order, of traditional morality, of social outlook'.[20] After the Reformation, in the sixteenth and seventeenth centuries, non-conformists were often thrown out of the state-church and suffered discrimination and the loss of civil rights. For much of the nineteenth century, they were concerned to get such discrimination removed. They were also more welcoming to new thought, such as ideas about evolution, biblical criticism and knowledge of Eastern religions than their orthodox contemporaries. Essentially, however, they have remained minority churches and in this century many Europeans who have become disillusioned with traditional orthodox churches have seen no need to belong to any religious community. Only a minority of the disillusioned have become members of free Christian churches, of the Society of Friends or of Buddhist or Hindu groups. Others have put their energies into social causes or work for peace. In the USA, partly for social reasons, church membership, including that of the Unitarian Universalist Association, has remained higher.

As has been mentioned, at times the American influence has been stronger, at other times the European. Initially the headquarters were in

USA, they then moved to London, then to the Netherlands and in 1974 to Frankfurt, where an office, with professional staff was set up. The differences were highlighted at the Boston Congress of IARF in 1969, which was combined with the Unitarian Universalist Association's annual convention. The combination of the two events was not entirely satisfactory and the IARF meeting seems to have been overshadowed by the UUA gathering.

Diether Gehrmann

The two traditions came together in the person of the Rev. Diether Gehrmann, who was General Secretary from 1972 to 1990. His father was a Roman Catholic priest, who became a Unitarian minister, and who then served the Free Religious (Unitarian) Church at Offenbach, near Frankfurt in West Germany for nearly thirty years. Diether's first charge was at the same church, but then from 1967–72, he served in the USA as minister at Philadelphia Unitarian Church and then at the Unitarian Church at Pomona, near New York. His ministerial education had also been in both Germany, at Mainz and Frankfurt Universities, and in the USA, at Meadville Theological Seminary, Chicago and at Starr King School for the Ministry, Berkeley. Whilst in America, he was active in the interdenominational coalition against the Vietnam War, having as a boy experienced the horrors of World War II in Germany.

· 7 ·

The International Association for Religious Freedom II

After the Second World War

Just as IARF's membership has broadened, so its activities have increased. After the war, contact between members in different countries was slowly resumed. Some thirty members gathered in Cambridge in July 1946. They agreed that the secretariat should remain in the Netherlands. Preparations were made for the first post-war congress, which was held in Amsterdam in 1949. At this Congress the distinguished British Unitarian Rev. Stewart Henry Carter succeeded the American Dr John Howland Lathrop as President. There were three hundred and forty-five participants, who came from fifteen countries. There were no Asians. One of the speakers was the British politician, Mr Chuter Ede. Much of the work was done in four groups. One was on social issues, another on theology, the third on religious education and the fourth on world religions. In the latter there was debate as to whether Christianity is the final revelation. Many claimed that Love, which is the highest religion, underlies all religions. This love, it was said, was not only for human beings but for the earth and the plants – indeed for the whole cosmos (ecological concerns are not new!)[1]

Subsequent congresses were held at Oxford (1952), Belfast (1955), Chicago (1958), Davos (1961), The Hague (1964) and London (1966). In Oxford, a fifth group on 'Religion and Science' was added to the other four groups. At Belfast, participants divided into three groups on theological matters, on 'Church, Family and Home' and on 'How to bring the spirit of Free religion to a rising generation'. The second group was led by Rev. Arthur Peacock, who was later to become Secretary of the World Congress of Faiths. The Chicago Congress was well attended, with over seven hundred participants. More attention was given to other world religions besides Christianity. Sir Zafrullah Khan, who for a time was Pakistan's representative at the United Nations and who became a President of the International Court of Justice at the Hague and who was later to attend meetings of both WCF and the Temple of Understanding, was one of the speakers. Dr Kalidas Nag, from West Bengal, Thado Maha Thray Sitha U Chan Hoon, a Buddhist from Burma, Rabbi Dr N. Solomon from Britain, and Dr B. Freehof from Chicago also spoke. Amongst speakers at Davos, was the distinguished scholar Friedrich Heiler, whilst Sir Alister Hardy, a marine biologist who became famous for his studies of human religious experiences, was a speaker at The Hague Congress.

Speakers at the London Congress in 1966 included the Jewish scholar Samuel Sandmel, who lectured on 'Jesus in World History'. Soon afterwards, he preached at the first WCF 'All Faiths Service' to be held in a synagogue. Another speaker was Dr Dana McLean Greeley, then President of the American Unitarians, who was to play a leading role in both IARF and WCRP. He talked about the situation in Vietnam.

At the London congress it was agreed to set up three commissions to carry on the work of IARF between congresses. A fourth commission was added at Boston. The First Commission was on 'The Christian in the World Today', the second on 'The Religious Approach to the modern world', the third on 'The Dialogue of World Religions' and the fourth on 'Justice, Peace and Human Rights'. Initially, it was felt that the commissions were rather abstract and detached from the members. Increasingly, instead of dealing with religious and moral questions in the abstract, IARF has sought to develop its intercultural and inter-religious encounters into a living dialogue deepened by personal experiences. In 1970, a gathering was held in Japan for the first time and then in 1973 there was a first meeting in Africa. At the Boston Congress, speakers included the American Professor Martin Marty and the distinguished Israeli scholar Zwi Werblowsky.

From its busy office in Frankfurt, in partnership with member organizations, meetings and conferences have been arranged regularly in many parts of the world. In the fifteen years from 1972 to 1987, the budget rose from $60,000 to $600,000.

Social Service Network

In 1979, Lucie Meijer, from the Netherlands, joined the staff of IARF. Already from 1972–6, she had been a member of the IARF Council. Soon afterwards the IARF Social Service Network was established, to which she has given special care. Previously, IARF had arranged emergency relief for member groups in disaster areas. Through the Network, the IARF Secretariat was able to assess on the spot the needs and conditions for social service projects run by local IARF member groups and then make known these needs to the wider IARF membership and channel their help to the project.

One of the earliest projects was support for a Mothers' and Toddlers' Club in strife-torn Belfast. Help has been channelled to several schemes. In the remote hills of Meghalaya and Assam, at the foot of the Himalayas in North East India, help was given to the Khasi Village Education Project. Teachers were appointed, in conjunction with the local Unitarian church, to run a number of non-sectarian kindergartens and primary schools for the people of the area who are poor and who often suffer from discrimination. In Lagos, Nigeria, Sister Talabi, a trained nurse, who had attended the 1981 and 1984 IARF Congresses, started a course in home nursing. Soon she was asked to give sewing and cooking classes. The Social Service Network has been able to provide her with necessary equipment, such as a cooker, mixer and meat grinder. In 1989, for example, support was given to a literacy centre in India, to relief work in Eastern Europe and to a training scheme in the Philippines. All the schemes offer help to their communities, 'irrespective of caste or creed' and, wherever possible, are inter-religious in character. Certainly in terms of support, the projects allow Buddhists to help Unitarians, Christians to support members of the Brahmo Samaj or Universalists to support Muslims.[2]

Recent Congresses

Recent Congresses have been held in Montreal in 1975, in Oxford in 1978, in Holland in 1981, in Tokyo in 1984, at Stamford University, California in 1987 and at Hamburg in 1990.

At Montreal, a Manifesto on World Community was adopted. The Manifesto, produced after extensive discussion, outlines basic principles and methods and then offers a vision of positive possibilities for world community and suggests the contribution that IARF can make to this. Interestingly, the inspiration of other documents is acknowledged, showing thereby the overlap and mutual influence of groups which together belong to 'the interfaith movement'. Specific reference is made to WCRP's Louvain Declaration, the New Delhi Declaration of the World Federalists and to the Humanist Manifesto. Indebtedness to Lester Brown's *World Without Borders*, Mihajlo Mesarovic's *Mankind at the Turning Point*, Barbara Ward's *Only One Earth* and to Richard Falk's *A Study of Future Worlds* is also recorded.

The Basic Principles of the Manifesto are:

1. We believe in the inherent worth and dignity of all human beings. This means that, in formulating goals and policies, we give all people equal consideration and equal preference.
2. We believe that political power on all levels – international, national and local – must be considered as held in trust for the benefit of those whom it affects and that it must be regularly accountable to them.
3. We believe that all of the resources of the earth are the common heritage of the human family, to be used for the benefit of all. Those who possess such resources are, like those with political power, trustees for humankind.[3]

The Long-Term Goals relate to Peace, Economic well-being for all people, Freedom from oppression, Ecological integrity, World governance. The strong warning about the threats to the environment and the clear support for the UN are noticeable.

At Oxford, the theme was 'The Limits of Toleration Today'. The Declaration points to various barriers which need to be overcome if tolerance is to increase, but it also recognizes social injustices which should not be tolerated. Perhaps surprisingly there is no discussion of the relationship of traditional religions to new religions, but there is particular attention to dialogue between religions and Marxism and humanism. At Oxford, Dr Carolyn Howlett was elected as the first woman president.

The 1981 Congress, held at the Leeuwenhorst Congress Centre near Leiden, was attended by nearly five hundred participants.[4] The Declaration voiced alarm at 'the demonic tide threatening humankind',[5] mentioning particularly the arms race, the growing gap between rich and poor nations, the threats to the environment and the abuses of human rights. Rev. Nikkyo Niwano, President of Rissho Kosei Kai, who had received the Templeton Award in 1979, was elected President – the first Asian to hold the office.

Tokyo

The Tokyo Congress was the first time that IARF had met in Asia. There were nearly eight hundred full-time participants from twenty-two countries and huge crowds of Japanese joined for the opening ceremony and the Congress service. The lavish hospitality of Rissho Kosei Kai was particularly memorable and delegates were invited into Japanese homes. Great attention was given to the worship as well as to the cultural programme and there were creativity workshops. This meant that the conference avoided being as cerebral as many such gatherings. The theme was 'Eastern Initiative and Western Response', but it became clear that it was too simple to think of the East as 'spiritual' and the West as 'technological and scientific'. As the conference was held in the only country that had suffered a nuclear attack – and some survivors of Hiroshima were present – peace was a dominant theme. Peace was seen to be an inner spiritual state as well as an external social condition, the latter being dependent on the former. 'Spiritual peace is the foundation for peace in the world.'[6] It was recognized that religious differences often aggravated other differences. People of all religions were urged to struggle together for peace and justice. The call for action invited support for the International Year of Peace.

Another feature of the congress was the participation of a number of young people, who produced their own declaration. The number of women participating has steadily increased at recent gatherings.

Stanford

The Congress at Stanford University was the first to be held on the Pacific coast of America. Preparatory conferences had been held in France, India, Denmark and Japan. In addition to the main week there were, as usual, other conferences, tours, home visits and intercultural encounters, as well as events for youth and for women. There were eight hundred and eleven registered participants and they were joined by numerous day visitors. The theme was 'World Religions Face the Twenty-first Century'.[7] There were five working groups and also thirty-five 'circle groups', which allowed for close personal interchange and helped to prevent the feeling that some delegates have of being 'lost' at an enormous conference.

The declaration reaffirmed the importance of dialogue and religious co-operation and called upon IARF to involve itself in plans to mark the centennial of the 1893 World's Parliament of Religions. 'Only an acceptance of the variety of traditions and cultures as a source of mutual enrichment, rather than any attempt to impose conformity to one idea and practice, however loftily conceived, can lead us forward in hope . . . We affirm that all religious traditions express universal human experiences and aspirations, which are expresssed in a great variety of particular manifestations according to local history and culture. While each of us is dedicated to one particular path, we see in this a manifestation of what is universal and timeless.'[8] This is a statement true to the IARF tradition. Dr William Schulz in the Congress sermon said that all were agreed on the conviction that 'there is wisdom to be found in traditions other than our own',[9] but it sharply raises the continuing question of whether those who make monopolistic claims for their religion can play a full part in the interfaith movement.

At Stanford, the General Assembly adopted a 'Statement of Purposes'. 'IARF is an inter-religious, international, intercultural organization. It advocates religious freedom in the sense of:

(*a*) free, critical and honest affirmation of one's own religious tradition;
(*b*) religion which liberates and does not oppress;
(*c*) the defence of freedom of conscience and the free exercise of religion in all nations.

IARF advances understanding, dialogue and readiness to learn and promotes sympathy and harmony among the different religious traditions. It is dedicated to a global community of mutual co-operation among religious communities and adherents of different religions. It strives for an attitude of openness to truth, to love and to justice.'

The statement then speaks of encouraging religious and cultural exchange and scholarly study, and of IARF's social responsibility and educational work.[10]

Hamburg

IARF's work has continued to expand since the Stanford Congress. The leadership's commitment to the interfaith composition of IARF is clear. At the Hamburg Congress, however, American members of the Universalist/Unitarian church and Unitarians from Europe were the largest groupings. For some, IARF serves as the Unitarian world body and this is not entirely compatible with its interfaith purposes.

The Congress was particularly excited by the presence of several delegates from Eastern Europe who were able to talk about the changes there. The changes in South Africa were also welcomed. The key note address was given by Professor Hans Küng on 'No peace among nations, without peace among religions'. The Zen Buddhist monk, Rev. Eshin Nishimura shared his experiences of staying in Christian monasteries. The attention given to the worship services ensured that they were of a remarkably high standard.

Much of the time was spent in study groups and workshops. The Congress agreed that IARF should develop a role of 'advocacy of human rights', concentrating especially on 'issues of religious freedom'.[11] This would give a further meaning to the title of the organization.

The Congress marked the end of Rev. Diether Gehrmann's eighteen years as General secretary. He was awarded an honorary doctorate from Lombard Meadville College in recognition of his work. His successor, Dr Robert Traer, a Presbyterian from USA, spoke of his hopes for the future of the IARF. 'First we must broaden our participation to include more persons from the religious traditions not well represented. We must welcome Jews and Muslims and Christians from mainline denominations and others . . . Second, we must deepen our faith within our own religious traditions . . . Third, we must with renewed vigour reach out to those with needs greater than our own. We must share more of our resources with the poor and the disadvantaged, in programmes which help them help themselves. And we must stand in solidarity with those who are denied the religious liberty which we cherish'.[12]

Dr Traer ended with these words, 'My friends, it is up to us. All we need do is love our children and our grandchildren, and then live so that they may live. All we need do is love the flowers and the birds and cherish their beauty and their music, and then live so that they may live. All we need do is love our religious and cultural traditions, our hymns and our chants, our prayers and our precepts, our scriptures and our sutras, our rituals and our rites, and then live so that we all may live. All we need do is love our God and our world, the heavens and the earth, the seas and the soil, and then live so that all life may live.'[13]

In the declaration, IARF renewed its opposition 'to racism, sexism, apartheid, anti-semitism and all other forms of racial or religious prejudice'.[14] It committed itself to share fully in the plans to mark 1993 as a Year of Inter-religious Understanding and Co-operation. As major celebrations are to be held in India, it was fitting that Punyabrata Roy Choudry, was elected President. He is the first Indian to hold this office.

Conclusion

Each of the interfaith organizations has its own distinct character. IARF is based on its member organizations. Initially most of these were Unitarian or Free Christian. From the beginning there were member groups which were not of Christian origin and the number of these has now increased considerably. IARF is now fully interfaith, but the member organizations, because of the nature of the Association, are mostly liberal in their outlook. This gives a unity to the organization, but it means that some more orthodox groupings in the religions are not participants. IARF, therefore, is not representative of the whole spectrum of religious life nor does it seek to be so. There is also at this time no Jewish member group. Participation in a Congress is open to those who wish to attend. People are not 'representatives' of the world religions, although attempts are made to attract as widespread and balanced participation as possible. There is great emphasis on personal meeting and encounter across the divides of religion and culture. As Diether Gehrmann has said, An essential element of IARF is 'the emphasis on illuminating personal experiences as the foremost motivational and educational factor in religious life'.[15] This gives a particular dynamic to the congresses which centre on human interaction more than on agendas and discussion of resolutions. Many participants in the Tokyo Congress spoke of it as 'a life time experience' and it is experience that often changes attitudes. Besides, it is changed people who change the world.

· 8 ·

The World Congress of Faiths:
The Beginnings

Sir Francis Younghusband

It was his own mystical experience that led Francis Younghusband to work for interfaith fellowship.

Francis' father was Major-General J. W. Younghusband and his mother was Clara Jane Shaw, who was the sister of Robert Shaw, an explorer of Central Asia. Francis, their second son, was born at a hill station on the North-West Frontier on 31 May 1863. At the age of seven months, he was taken home to Britain by his mother to her mother. It seems that the grandmother, who lived in Bath, then provided a home for them. After the grandmother's death, the family returned to India. When Francis was six, he was sent back to England for his schooling. In 1876, he started at Clifton College, Bristol, and was expected to conform to the rather conventional public school version of Christianity. Yet already at his confirmation he was thinking for himself. He had some doubts about the virgin birth and the physical resurrection and ascension of Jesus. During this time, he paid a visit to the Alps, which he said, 'did far more for me than all the sermons I had ever heard'.[1]

In 1881 he entered Sandhurst. The following year he set sail for India. His choice of reading for the journey showed that already he had considerable interest in religion. Amongst many biographies, lives of Christ were prominent. He had time to think and determined that in the future he would take nothing on authority. Ritual and dogma were unimportant. He came to think of Jesus Christ as a real man, with all the frailties of men, who became great because of indomitable courage. Already his basic convictions were largely fixed. These were to develop in two main ways: in greater experience of the mystery of the universe and in broadening sympathy with, and understanding of people of other faiths.

The highlights of the next few years of military service were his journeys of exploration to Manchuria and across the Gobi Desert. In 1888 he was granted a short leave, so that he could lecture about his travels to the Royal Geographical Society. He tried, unsuccessfully, to communicate to his parents his new sense of spiritual values. He had met and spoken with Christians of many denominations and with both educated and simple adherents of other faiths. He did not think one religion alone could be true and all others false. In the Gobi Desert, he had studied Darwin's work. He had found confirmation for his views on the gospels in Renan's *Life of Jesus* and Seeley's *Ecce Homo*. The book that had impressed him most was Tolstoy's *The Kingdom of God is Within You*. For him, at the time, the essence of Christianity was that the divine Spirit, which in Christ was a living flame, was latent in all men. All therefore were children of the same Father and should seek to develop the divine Spirit. Thus by 1889, he had made his own religion for himself.[2]

On his return to India, after a time of 'arid and meaningless' soldiery, he was asked to explore all the Himalayan passes from the north. He was in his element as an explorer, but even so, during his leave in England in 1891, he again discussed with his father his project to leave the service and devote his life to the conduct of a spiritual campaign. This would not have been as an official of any church, but in some undefined way. Events on the frontier, however, demanded his immediate return to duty. In 1903, he was asked by Lord Curzon, the Viceroy of India, to lead a mission to Tibet. This was a difficult and dangerous undertaking. At Lhasa, where he met the Dalai Lama, he successfully signed a treaty, but his work was repudiated by the politicians. It was as he was leaving Lhasa that he had a decisive spiritual experience which largely determined his future life. He described it in his book *Vital Religion*:

The day after leaving Lhasa I went off alone to the mountainside, and there gave myself up to all the emotions of this eventful time. Every anxiety was over – I was full of good-will as my former foes were converted into stalwart friends. But now there grew up in me something infinitely greater than mere elation and good-will. Elation grew to exultation, exultation to an exaltation which thrilled through me with overpowering intensity. I was beside myself with untellable joy. The whole world was ablaze with the same ineffable bliss that was burning within me. I felt in touch with the flaming heart of the world. What was glowing in all creation and in every single human being was a joy far beyond mere goodness as the glory of the sun is beyond the glow of a candle. A mighty joy-giving Power was at work in the world – at work in all about me and at work in every living thing. So it was revealed.

Never again could I think evil. Never again could I bear enmity. Joy had begotten love.[3]

Already for some fifteen years, religion had been Francis Younghusband's primary interest. He was aware of the Higher-Critical study of the scriptures and of scientific advance. As a result he was dissatisfied with the conventional religion in which he had been brought up. 'I had visions of a far greater religion yet to be, and of a God as much greater than our English God as a Himalayan giant is greater than an English hill'.[4]

Already he wished to communicate this 'greater religion' but he knew that first he had to clarify the intellectual framework of his conception of the universe. Convinced that the universe was governed by its own laws and not by external interference, he continued his study of science and came, for a while, under the influence of Herbert Spencer. Yet, a variety of experiences and his reading of nature-mystics, such as Blake and Wordsworth, made him dissatisfied with Spencer's 'petty-minded hatred of religion'.[5] A study of McTaggart's *Some Dogmas of Religion and Studies in Hegelian Cosmology* led him to seek the author's acquaintance, which issued in a close friendship.

Having tested his faith against intellectual criticism, he set to work to give it shape and definition in a book to be called *The Inherent Impulse*. As the work was nearing completion, he met, whilst in Belgium, with an accident, which was followed by prolonged illness. This experience led him to revise his book, which, eventually, was published in the autumn of 1912, with the title *Within*. This was the first of several books in which he described his religious views.[6]

His basic conviction was that joy was the ground and crown of all religion.[7] Joy, he claimed, was at the heart of Christ's message. Hindu, Buddhist and Muslim saints had also declared the same; and the Psalms were full of its expression. Although love was usually regarded as more fundamental, he held that joy was both deeper and higher.[8] This emphasis did not mean that he disregarded evil and suffering. He believed, however, that the joy of life not merely counterbalanced the suffering and wickedness but could transform it into good.[9]

It is important to recognize that his conception of a fellowship of faiths sprang from a mystical sense of the unity of all people. The 'brotherhood of man' was for Sir Francis not a religious slogan but a truth realized in religious experience. In such an experience, a person is 'lifted right out of himself and wafted up to unbelievable heights. He seems to expand to infinite distance and embrace the whole world'.[10]

In his later working for the World Congress of Faiths, Sir Francis made it clear that there was no intention of formulating another eclectic religion. It was rather to help members of all faiths to become aware of the universal experience which had been his. The Congress, he hoped, 'would awaken a wider consciousness and afford men a vision of a happier world-order in which the roots of fellowship would strike down deep to the Central Source of all spiritual loveliness till what had begun as human would flower as divine'.[11] The human fellowship that he sought to promote was inextricably linked to communion with the divine. The Congress, therefore, was an attempt to give practical expression to the mystic's vision of unity.

The World Congress of Faiths 1936

In 1924, Sir Francis Younghusband played an active part in the Religions of Empire Conference. Although the intention of the conference was that it should only present information, Sir Francis, in his opening address, made clear that he saw in it an expression of the fundamental unity of religion. He asserted that religion was the ultimate basis on which the Empire must stand and that the conference was against exclusive views. 'We may each of us hold that our own religion is more completely perfect than any other. But even then we may recognize that God reveals himself in many ways, and that to the followers of other religions than our own may have been revealed much that may be of value to us. And we may hope to seize from each some of that Divine Spirit which inspires every religion in diverse ways.'

Besides recognizing that God reveals himself through the various religions, Sir Francis was also suggesting that members of one faith might learn from the revelation given in other faiths. Recognizing the significance of the difference between religions, Younghusband went on to say, 'We need never lose our faith that all the time there may be an underlying and overarching harmony which may reconcile them all, if only we could reach it.'[12]

There was no direct follow-up to this conference, but some of those responsible for it helped to establish the Society for the Study of Religions, which arranged and published lectures. Sir Francis became chairman of the Society's committee. After the Second World War, this society merged with the World Congress of Faiths. Sir Francis also supported the Inter-Religious Fellowship, which was organized by Rev. Leslie Belton, who was at that time the editor of *The Inquirer*, a Unitarian paper.[13]

In 1933, Sir Francis attended the World Fellowship of Faiths conference held in Chicago in 'conscious imitation' of the 1893 World Parliament of Religions.[14] He also took part in similar gatherings held in New York and other American cities in 1934. He was in touch, too, with the attempt to arrange an Inter-Religious Peace conference.[15] The organizers of both these efforts urged him to inaugurate an Inter-Faith Congress in London, and by the time he returned to England in 1934, he felt that the moment was ripe for such an initiative.

He therefore invited a number of people to a meeting on 12 November 1934, at which it was agreed to establish a British National Council of the World Fellowship of Faiths. H. H. Maharaja Gaekwar of Baroda became president and Sir Francis was elected chairman and organizer of the British National Council. Soon afterwards, Sir Francis published his Chairman's proposals for the Congress, stressing that the aim was not to formulate a new synthetic faith, but to provide a meeting ground for followers of different religions.

The Congress itself was held at University College, London, from July 3rd to 18th, 1936. Sir Francis succeeded in getting outstanding members of the main traditions to speak. He believed that they would then influence their followers. Participants included Yusuf Ali, known for his carefully annotated translation of the Qur'an, the Russian theologian Nicolas Berdiaeff, Dr Surendranath Dasgupta, author of a massive History of Indian Philosophy, the philosopher C. E. M. Joad, Dr G. P. Malalasekara from Ceylon, Dr Joseph Needham, a historian of China, Dr Radhakrishnan, Sir Herbert Samuel, a leader of the Jewish Community who later became Lord Samuel and the Buddhist scholar, Dr Suzuki.

A wide range of views was represented. Besides representatives of the main traditions, there were speakers from the Church of the Latter Day Saints, from Caodia or Renovated Buddhism, 'a new faith' which claimed one million adherents, from Jainism and from the Baha'i faith. An Abyssinian priest and a humanist also spoke.

The Congress was not residential and this restricted the social intercourse between participants. Yet, for the first time at an inter-religious gathering, discussion was encouraged and was carried on in good humour. The chairmen and leaders of debate were carefully chosen.

Many of the published papers are of a high quality. Of greatest interest, perhaps, is the different attitudes which they display towards the relationship of religions. On the one hand, Rev. P. T. R. Kirk claimed that Christianity must be accepted by the whole of mankind and Mr Moulvri A. R. Dard made a similar claim for the Ahmadiyya community. By contrast, the paper prepared by Professor Haldane, who had died shortly before the conference, included this passage: 'Many Christians entertain the ideal of converting non-Christian peoples to Christianity. I think that a much higher ideal is to understand and enter into sympathy with the religions which exist in other countries and to use this understanding and sympathy as a basis for higher religion.'[16] Several speakers, such as the Chief Rabbi and Canon Barry, stressed the difference between religions, whereas Ranjee G. Shani said the differences were trivial. 'Jesus and Buddha, Shakespeare and Ramakrishna – are in essence "members one of another".'[17]

In general it was agreed that the aim of the Congress was not to create one new synthetic religion, but to generate understanding and a sense of unity between the religions of the world. Rabbi Dr Israel Mattuck, Chairman of the Executive of the World Union for Progressive Judaism, put it like this: 'I am not pleading for one religion to include all men. I like diversity. I should no more want a world with one religion than I should want only one coloured rose in my garden. But we can have diversity without enmity and when we do this, I believe, the world will be more ready to receive our message about human unity and human peace.'[18]

Several speakers hoped that the world religions could together work for peace and spiritual uplift. Professor Marcault, a French Professor of Psychology, highlighted the important question of what in practice religions can actually do together. It is not easy to find areas of practical co-operation in which to give concrete expression to the desire to work together. 'Peace and fellowship', he said, 'can only be constructive if they are incarnated in some positive religious aim in whose realization all faiths can agree to co-operate, and whose universality maintains them united.'[19]

In his foreword to the published papers, *Faiths and Fellowship*, Sir Francis Younghusband stressed again that the one aim of the Congress was to promote the spirit of fellowship. He ruled out certain misunderstandings. There was no intention of formulating another eclectic religion, nor of seeking the lowest common denominator, nor of appraising the value of existing religions and discussing respective merits and defects. It was not maintained that all religions are the same, nor equally true, nor as good as one another. The hope was to 'intensify that sense of community which is latent in all men' and to awaken a livelier world-consciousness. Sir Francis mentioned that through discussion and reflection, the conception of God grew greater and that by coming closer to each other, members of different religions deepened their own spiritual communion.[20]

In estimating the value of the Congress, the question that has to be asked, as it has to be of the subsequent life of the World Congress of Faiths, is, whether, however worthy, the aims are sufficiently precise. The question of the relation to each other of the world religions is still much debated. The position of the Congress rules out the view that any one religion has a monopoly of truth. It assumes that despite differences, the world religions have an affinity, and share a recognition of spiritual reality and of ethical values. It is hardly surprising that adherents of missionary religions have opposed and still take issue with the Congress, claiming that their particular religion is the true one. Often, they are reluctant to grant even limited validity to other religions. On the other hand, the Congress rules out the attempt to create a new synthetic religion. It insists that differences are important and must be respected. It is therefore criticized both by those who advocate a new unified religion and by those who hold that differences are only external and irrelevant.

Is, then, the promotion of a spirit of fellowship and world loyalty a sufficient aim to engender enthusiasm? Clearly it is for some, but the number of people, even including religious leaders, with a world consciousness and interest, is small.

How fellowship is understood may vary considerably. It should imply learning to appreciate others whose values and ways of life are different. In a world of prejudice, this is important, but somewhat negative. Fellowship may be concerned with the discovery of areas of ethical agreement and perhaps with taking common action on certain moral issues.

At its deepest level, the search for fellowship becomes a search for truth and flows from communion with the divine. Here it is assumed that the truth is greater than the understanding of any individual or of any one religion and that by sharing together with members of other faiths, each individual will be deepened in his knowledge of truth and usually in his appreciation of his own religious tradition. It seems that Sir Francis Younghusband saw the development of all these aspects of fellowship as part of the work of the Congress, although he was aware of the difficulty of conveying exactly what he meant by fellowship. He perhaps came nearest to expressing his understanding in a talk given soon after the outbreak of war. 'When I speak of fellowship', he said, 'I have found subtler and deeper meanings emerge as I study the idea more closely. It is not exactly either friendship, or companionship, or neighbourliness, or co-operation, though these may develop from it. And the sentiment from which it springs is something more than compassion, for compassion concerns itself with unhappiness alone rather than with both happiness and unhappiness. Even sympathy is associated rather with suffering than with enjoyment. At its intensest and highest, fellowship seems to be a communion of spirit greater, deeper, higher, wider, more universal, more fundamental than any of these – than even love.'[21]

· 9 ·

The History of
the World Congress of Faiths

A Continuing Body

On the morning after the first Congress ended, it was unanimously agreed
to set up a continuation committee, of which Sir Francis was elected
chairman. It was decided that activities would continue under the
auspices of the World Congress of Faiths (Continuation Movement) and
that individual membership would be invited. This was an important
decision, as it gave the Congress its own independent life. The executive
Committee is answerable to the members, and whilst this may mean that
there is an imbalance of the religions represented, it allows the Congress
freedom of activity. To have sought official representation from religious
groups – even had it been forthcoming – might have gained wider support
for the Congress, but would have restricted its freedom.

This committee soon arranged another congress, which was held at
Oxford in 1937. This was residential. In the next year, one was held at
Cambridge, and, in 1939, in Paris.[1] The latter conference helped to sow
the seeds of a French group, 'L'Union des Croyants'.

The outbreak of war severely restricted the work of the Congress.
Communications with friends abroad became difficult and international
congresses impossible. Sir Francis, like many others, thought the war
would not last long and was concerned that the world religions should be
ready to share in the post-war task of reconstruction. Inviting members to
a meeting, he wrote: 'A new world order is now the dream of men, but for
this a new spirit will be needed. This is the special concern of men of
religion, in this case men of all religions – non-Christians as well as
Christians – all combined to create a world loyalty, and a sense of world

fellowship and to provide the spiritual impetus, the dynamic and the direction to the statesmen and economists, whose business is to give it bodily expression'.[2] Again when the Atlantic Charter was proclaimed, he at once arranged a series of meetings on an inter-religious foundation for the Atlantic Charter, saying that 'of all the forces which are to be marshalled behind the Charter, the force which may be engendered by all the religions working together in unison will be incontestably the most potent'.[3]

To maintain communications with the scattered membership, a 'Chairman's Circular Letter' was started. By 1941 this had developed from a typewritten sheet to a four-page printed pamphlet. In one, Sir Francis urged members to meet together locally. As a result, at Bournemouth, Madeleine Lady Lees took the initiative in forming a local group.

In 1942, despite many difficulties a congress was held in Birmingham. At it, Sir Francis was taken ill and he died soon afterwards at the home, in Dorset, of Lady Lees. A memorial service was held at St Martin-in-the-Fields, London, on 10 August 1942. Appropriately, the service included short lessons from the sacred scriptures of the world.

The death of Sir Francis was a heavy blow to the Congress, because it depended so much on his inspiration and effort and because no plans had been prepared for this possibility. Many, too, had taken part out of personal regard for Sir Francis. Lord Samuel, temporarily, became chairman. Soon Baron Erik Palmstierna took his place.

Sir Francis' Successors

Baron Erik Palmstierna was for a short while Foreign Minister of Sweden and from 1920 to 1937 he was Swedish Ambassador in London. After his retirement he settled in England. His two books, *Horizons of Immortality* and *Widening Horizons*, show his concern for spiritualism. He found Sir Francis a kindred spirit and took a leading part in the 1939 conference. Like Sir Francis he, too, believed in an essential mystical unity of religions. In his book, *The World: Crisis and Faith*, he wrote that 'a striking congruity of views and aims occurs among Saints and Mystics belonging to races which were alien to each other'.[4] Of the Congress, he said, 'We are not looking for any super-world religion which ought to replace existing historical institutions and dogmas – but we search for organic elements of religious experience'.[5] The Baron's five-year chairmanship was marked by important international contacts and he gave much attention to *The Three-Faith Declaration on World Peace*. In a speech in the House of Lords, Dr Bell, the Bishop of Chichester, suggested that an international authority, backed by the monotheistic faiths, might secure the rule of law in international affairs. The Baron contacted the Bishop, and a small committee met to explore the suggestion. It was decided initially to see what support existed for the *Three-Faith Declaration on World Peace* that had been issued in America in October 1943.[6] There was an encouraging response from all, except the Christian churches. Without their support, the idea came to nothing, but it is evidence of a hope, often repeated in the history of the Congress, that religions together might be able to exert an influence for peace and world order.

The Baron was succeeded by Sir John Stewart Wallace, who had been Chief Registrar for England and Wales. He was particularly keen to encourage 'seekers' – those without a definite religious commitment but who were interested in spiritual matters – to join the Congress. This move met with some opposition, but Sir Francis in choosing the title Congress of Faiths rather than Congress of Religions had hoped that such seekers might join the movement. Sir John also tried to introduce a deeper spirit of devotion into the Congress by encouraging All Faiths Services and also meditation meetings, which were led by Rev. R. G. Coulson, Bhikkhu Thittila, and Swami Avyaktananda. Conferences again began to be held, but on a smaller scale than before the war.

After Sir John Stewart Wallace's resignation because of illness, Baroness Ravensdale, daughter of Lord Curzon, took the chair and the day-to-day running of the Society was in the hands of Rev. Arthur Peacock, who became Hon. Secretary. Arthur Peacock had become a minister of the Universalist Church in 1937. With the decline of Universalism, he decided, in 1951, to become a Unitarian minister. His motto was a verse of Elizabeth Barrett-Browning's:

> Universalism – universe religion – the unity
>   of all things,
> Why it's the greatest word in our language.

An energetic secretary, he helped to develop the work of the Congress. The predominance, however, of Universalist Unitarian and neo-Hindu views tended to discourage those with more orthodox religious views, especially Christians, from participating in the Congress. WCF was regarded in some quarters as 'syncretistic', although the Congress repudiated this charge. Syncretism, a term originally used by Plutarch of the fusion of religious cults which occurred in the Graeco-Roman world, is usually used in a pejorative sense of an artificial mixing of religions. Christians, many of whom at the period were deeply influenced by the theology of Barth and Kraemer, who stressed that the Gospel was discontinuous from world religions, were suspicious of any such mixing of religions.[7]

Reg Sorensen

In 1959 the Rev. Reginald Sorensen MP, who in 1964 was created a baron, became chairman and retained the office until his death in 1970. A tireless worker for numerous causes, he and his wife Muriel brought to the Congress their gift of friendship and concern for individuals of all races and conditions. He was a Unitarian and his interest was especially in seeking the common moral values contained in the teachings of the world religions. The emphasis shifted, therefore, away from the mystical.

Conscious of the obscurantist and reactionary character of so much religion, he had a love-hate relationship with organized religion. In his book, *I Believe in Man*, he criticized religion's opposition to new knowledge, to scientific advance and to social progress. He disliked all intolerance and found orthodox Christianity too rigid and dogmatic. Yet he never doubted that the human spirit could commune with the divine and sought to commend a 'modern faith'.[8] 'I affirm that we should not be seduced into thinking that the only reality is the tangible and the sensuous, but that reality is vaster and more permeative of our material environment that we can neatly tie up with intellectual string.'[9]

With his belief in a divine spirit, went a deep and optimistic belief in the human spirit and in man's ability eventually to overcome evil and suffering in the world. He held that this belief was enshrined in all the great religious traditions and hoped that the Congress could help the religions emphasize the ethical values which they held in common. Impatient with doctrinal debate or theological dialogue – despite his questioning mind – in his addresses, again and again Reg Sorensen came back to matters of ethical and moral concern.

He was well aware of the endless variations of moral patterns or 'mores', but held that there could be found in the world religions an essential moral content beyond transient communal codes.[10] 'It is necessary', he said at a conference service, 'to distinguish between paramount moral values and what I term "moral patterns".'[11] 'Moral patterns vary considerably, but penetrating, yet transcending those variables are moral values, that, with degrees of priority and emphasis, exist within all faiths and religions. Among these are justice, mercy, compassion, integrity, courage, sacrifice, fidelity and fraternity. Here is where all can meet on common ground.'[12] He believed that despite differences of metaphysics and custom, all religions could agree on these moral values and that such agreement was vital for the world. 'I would claim that only a measure of inter-religious, international and inter-racial agreement on essential moral values can enable mankind to dwell on this earth in co-operation, amity and peace.'[13] During the sixties, one of the honorary secretaries was the very remarkable

Levantine priest, Fr Lev Gillet, whose wide-ranging reading made him a source of knowledge on an amazing range of topics. The devoted office secretary for many years was Olive Dearlove, a Unitarian.

The Seventies

Whilst the Congress has continued to seek for common moral values and to work for international peace and the development of a world community, in recent years there has been a deepening of interfaith dialogue within the Congress. Committed members of world religions have taken a more active part. The Rev. Dr Edward Carpenter, who was a Canon and then Dean of Westminster, has been active in WCF for many years and has been President for more than twenty years. He and his wife Lilian have given a lifetime of support to interfaith and peace organizations. At Westminster Abbey, he liked to stress the theme 'One People'. Rt Rev. George Appleton, whose ministry has taken him to many parts of the world and who was for five years Anglican Archbishop of Jerusalem, was, for a time, chairman of WCF. A vice-chairman for many years has been Rabbi Hugo Gryn, who is the Rabbi of an important Reform Synagogue in London. Leading members of all the faith communities in Britain have served on the Executive Committee.

For some years the enthusiastic and energetic secretary was Kathleen Richards, who took a very personal interest in all the members. She was followed by the Buddhist, Rev. Jack Austin, who sought to increase the influence of WCF and make it a source of information on interfaith relationships.

By the seventies the mood in Britain had changed. The presence in Britain, through immigration of sizeable Muslim, Hindu and Sikh communities, has given new importance to interfaith relations. The attitude of Christians has become more open and interfaith dialogue is widely encouraged. The teaching of world religions has also been a major development in religious education and there is an interest in world religions amongst a wider public, shown, for example, by the number of programmes on the subject shown on Television.

Yet whilst interfaith dialogue is now more common, there remains a particular emphasis to the work of the World Congress of Faiths. Much dialogue is at the level of seeking to understand what others believe and practise, in the hope that this will promote tolerance and goodwill. The Congress goes beyond this and sees dialogue as a 'truth-seeking' exercise. The assumption is often voiced that there is a truth which transcends any one world religion, and that the coming together of religions is mutually enriching.

This was voiced by Bishop George Appleton, in a lecture at the Fortieth Anniversary Conference of the Congress, in Canterbury, in 1976. He distinguished certain stages in the meeting of religions.

'There is first of all the stage of self-affirmation, in which adherents of any particular faith feel the need to proclaim and propagate their own faith'.[14] Then comes a period of self-criticism. 'Finally there should be a stage of renewal and a deepened sense of vocation and mission. I believe that each religion may have a mission, which in theistic terms might be spoken of as God's mission to the world through Hinduism, Buddhism, Judaism and Islam, while our Baha'i brethen may with some justice claim that they were an early ecumenical movement among the world religions. So each religion has a mission, a gospel, a central affirmation. Each of us needs to enlarge on the gospel which he has received, without wanting to demolish the gospel of others. In this deeper fellowship of spirit we can understand the way of salvation perceived and sometimes enjoyed by others – the "moksha" or liberation of the Hindu, the enlightenment or "satori" of the Buddhist, the rule of God as accepted by the Jew or the Muslim, the reconciliation of sinful man through the Cross. Inevitably when we learn about the discoveries and insights of other Faiths, we relate them to our own and assess them by our own basic convictions. So we can enlarge and deepen our initial and basic faith by the experience and insights of people from other religions and cultures without disloyalty to our own commitment.'[15]

Edward Carpenter has suggested that the recovery of belief requires the coming together of the insights of many faith traditions.[16] Similarly, Yehudi Menuhin, one of the Patrons, in a message to the 1976 conference said, 'Until you transform your various weaknesses into a single strength, into an evolved conception of life and eternity, into a unified force, you will carry no weight with the behaviour of man'.[17] The emphasis is therefore on the mutual enrichment that may come from the meeting of people of various faiths.

The Eighties

During my chairmanship, 1978–1983, considerable efforts were made to build up personal fellowship at the conferences. Use was made of art and music and drama to escape from the emphasis on words that is so frequent at inter-religious conferences. In the well-attended annual interfaith services, also, experiments were made to discover universal symbols. This was part of the recognition that dialogue is more than an intellectual task. The attempt was also made to enter into one another's spirituality by arranging a number of small meditation weekends. These were held at the Ammerdown Conference Centre, near Bath. Leaders belonging to different faiths were invited to share their spiritual path and to explore each other's spiritual disciplines. Swami Bhavyananda of the Ramakrishna Mission and Bishop George Appleton were regular participants and with others, such as Professor Hasan Askari, they encouraged a deep meeting in times of meditation and silence.

This emphasis, whilst it re-echoes the sense of the mystical unity of religions which is to be found in the writings of Sir Francis Younghusband, is rather richer and deeper than the 'universalism' of the nineteen-fifties. Instead of stressing only what is common, it sees the great religions as complementary – each with particular insights and treasures to share with others. Such an approach does justice to the variety and actuality of the world religions and at the same time suggests that their coming together may be mutually beneficial. This view was persuasively argued by Dr Ursula King in her Younghusband Lecture.[18]

Although many members of WCF have sensed an underlying unity of faiths or have hoped for a future convergence, WCF as an organization has never espoused any one view of the relationship of religions to each other. It has expressly rejected syncretism or the attempt to create a single new world religion. Since its beginnings, WCF, in the words of Raimon Panikkar 'has sensed that the solution (to the relationship of religions) lies not in eliminating differences or in debunking faith altogether, but precisely in building up a Congress, "A walking together", where religious identity is not lost and underlying fellowship not destroyed'.[19]

The secretary was the dynamic Anglican deacon, Sister Theresa, an American, who combined her efficient work at WCF with many other interests. She was succeeded by Patricia Morrison, a New Zealander, who had worked with YWCA. Her experience and her international contacts did much to increase the reputation of WCF. She was followed by Tom Gulliver, a member of the Society of Friends, who had worked with Toc H. His organizational interest helped WCF to address questions about its role in the future and to adjust its constitution. After much discussion it was agreed to appoint an Executive Director (albeit part-time, because of lack of finance).

The first Executive Director is Lesley Mathias, who has brought to the work her experience as a teacher and her active role in the local interfaith group at Peterborough. 'I see WCF', she writes, 'as an organization which cherishes and values different religious traditions and seeks only to promote understanding between them. It does not seek "common ground" or to syncretize but to affirm the identity of each religious tradition as it is, upon its own terms.'[20] The hope, she says, is to establish a national interfaith youth forum and to strengthen links with local interfaith groups. WCF will also play an important part in stimulating observance in Britain of 1993 as a Year of Inter-religious Understanding and Co-operation'.

In recent years, an academic rigour has been added to the conferences by chairmen Viscount Combermere (1983–1988), who is Senior Lecturer in Religious Studies at the Extra Mural Department of London University and Professor Keith Ward (from 1988), who was Professor of Theology at King's College, London and is now Regius Professor at Oxford. As, in the eighties, the involvement in dialogue has increased and the membership of WCF has broadened, a greater variety of views about the nature of religions' relationships to each other has been expressed. One speaker, Dr Yaqub Zaki, said, 'Dialogue, I grow ever more convinced, is an exercise in futility . . . Any religion taking a linear view of history assumes its own finality . . . Islam, as a post-Christian religious system, is from a Christian perspective ipso facto false, and Christianity in Muslim eyes can never be more than a superseded religion'.[21] Raimon Panikkar, in his Younghusband Lecture, argued for a Pluralism of Truth that is beyond unity and plurality. 'Pluralism affirms neither that truth is one, nor that it is many'.[22] Whilst the commitment to dialogue and the fellowship of faiths remains, there is greater emphasis on the distinctive identity of each faith and a reluctance to blur the differences.

Younghusband Lectures

The ethos of the Congress is well reflected in the series of Younghusband Lectures, in which scholars of different faiths were asked to outline the attitude of their religion to other religions. Each lecturer affirmed the distinct identity of religions and his or her own particular commitment, but in a way which was not exclusive.

Professor Seshagiri Rao used his lecture in 1982 to expound the views of Mahatma Gandhi on the relation of religions. 'Gandhi's inter-religious dialogue authentically represents the Indian attitude of respect for all religions. The idea that "Truth is one: sages call it by different names" has been alive since the time of the *Rgveda* (the earliest Hindu scriptures) . . . To ignore any of the religions meant to ignore God's infinite richness and to impoverish human spirituality. He wanted all

religions to revive their pristine past and develop their traditions. "I ask
no Hindu or Mussalman to surrender an iota of his religious principle.
Only let him be sure that it is religion" . . . Gandhi advocated harmony
among the world's religions instead of playing down the importance of
any of them . . . Each religion must bring its individual contribution to
humanity's understanding of the spiritual world and not quarrel about
the superiority of one religion over another. For God's love embraces
the whole world. He believed that all the world religions are God-given
and that they serve the people to whom they are revealed. They are
allies in the common cause of the moral and spiritual uplift of humanity. In the context of the emerging world community, all the great
religions are useful, necessary, and complementary to one another as
revealing different facets of the one Truth.'[23]

Dr Zaki Badawi, in his 1984 lecture, started with the assumption that
each religion sees its beliefs as final. 'No religious community can allow
itself to float in the empty space of uncertainty.'[24] He outlined Islam's
view of other religions and suggested that the initial classification of
Hinduism as paganism was regrettable. He ended with these words:
'The Muslim accepts differences of belief as a fulfilment of the will of
Allah. "If He so willed He would have made you unto one religious
community". He sees in them a manifestation in mankind of the deep
feelings of the Eternal. To quote a Sufi poet whom I often quote – who
once said addressing the Creator, "On my way to the Mosque, Oh
Lord, I passed the Magian in front of his flame, deep in thought, and a
little further I heard a rabbi reciting his holy book in the synagogue,
and then I came upon the church where the hymns sung gently in my
ears and finally I came into the mosque and watched the worshippers
immersed in their experience and I pondered how many are the different ways to You – the one God".'[25]

Rabbi Dr Norman Solomon, in his 1985 lecture, suggested that the
dialogue of faiths was a natural outgrowth of the mission of Judaism.
'The "covenant of Noah" offers a pattern for us to seek from others not
necessarily conversion to Judaism, but rather faithfulness to the highest
principles of justice and morality which we perceive as the essence of
revealed religion.'[26] 'I cannot', he said, 'set the bounds of truth, I want
to listen and to learn, to grow in experience and forge language, to be
open to the world around me and its many people and ways, and to
reread and reinterpret my scriptures and the words of the sages con-
stantly, critically, in response to what I learn each day. Only by
exposing oneself to such a process can one hope to meet Truth revealed,
no granite statue but a living, dynamic force.'[27]

Dr Robert Runcie, the Archbishop of Canterbury, in the 1986 lecture, given to mark the fiftieth anniversary of the Congress, expressed very well the hopes of WCF. Dialogue, he said, 'can help us to recognize that other faiths than our own are genuine mansions of the Spirit with many rooms to be discovered, rather than solitary fortresses to be attacked'.[28] Whilst theology is talk about God, we must recognize 'that no words, no thoughts, no symbols can encompass the richness of this reality, nor the richness of its disclosure in different lives, communities and traditions. Signs of divine life and grace, of the outpouring of the spirit on earth can be seen in myriad forms in human history and consciousness. From the perspective of *faith*, different world religions can be seen as different gifts of the spirit to humanity. Without losing our respective identities and the precious heritage and roots of our own faith, we can learn to see in a new way the message and insights of our faith in the light of that of others. By relating our respective visions of the Divine to each other, we can discover a still greater splendour of divine life and grace'.[29] 'For Christians', he affirmed, 'the person of Jesus Christ, his life and suffering, his death and resurrection, will always remain the primary source of knowledge and truth about God.'[30] 'I am not advocating', he said, 'a single-minded, and synthetic model of world religion. Nor was Sir Francis Younghusband. What I want is for each tradition, and especially my own, "to break through its own particularity", as Paul Tillich put it . . . The way to achieve this, he says, "is not to relinquish one's religious tradition for the sake of a universal concept which would be nothing but a concept. The way is to penetrate into the depths of one's own religion, in devotion, thought and action. In the depth of every living religion there is a point at which religion itself loses its importance, and that to which it points breaks through its particularity, elevating it to spiritual freedom and to a vision of the spiritual presence in other expressions of the ultimate meaning of man's existence".'[31]

The Buddhist scholar Ven. Pandith M. Vajiragnana in his response to Professor Hans Küng at the 1988 WCF Conference said, 'Buddhists are not looking for a convergence of religions'. Quoting the well known edict of the Buddhist Emperor Asoka, Ven Vajiragnana continued, 'Let us be prepared to accept our crucial differences without trying to throw a threadbare rope between them. Rather let us build bridges of better understanding, tolerance for diverse views, plus encouragement for morality and ethical culture. This is where harmony is to be found.'[32]

It may be seen that whilst all speakers affirm the importance of understanding and mutual respect, their view as to the relationship of religions may differ. To some the mystery of the Divine transcends all human language, for others it is shared ethical imperatives which are vital. These differences are reflected in the varying motivation of members of the Congress. Indeed they stimulate the continuing debate about the relationship of religions to each other to which WCF has made a significant contribution.

· 10 ·

The Work of
the World Congress of Faiths

The work of the Congress has been primarily educational. It has helped to remove the prejudice and ignorance that has often existed between members of different religions and encouraged them as they became friends together to seek for deeper truth. The annual conferences have been important in drawing members together. Much of the work, especially in earlier years, was to provide accurate information about the world religions. This was done by talks, by information sheets and by answering a wide range of queries, received at the office. The emphasis on personal meeting has characterized the conferences and lectures, which have been held in London, provincial centres and on the continent of Europe, arranged by the overseas groups.

Conferences

Conferences have been of three main types. Large conferences with a high level of intellectual content; quiet smaller conferences of a retreat character for spiritual sharing; and conferences to meet with members of different faith communities. The large conferences have attracted well known speakers. Ven. Thich Nhat Hahn, Professor Harbans Singh, Bishop George Appleton, Dr Ezra Spicehandler and The Lord Abbot Kosho Ohtani were among the speakers of the Fortieth Anniversary Conference at Canterbury in 1976.[1] One of the best conferences was on 'Creative Responses to Suffering' at which the speakers were Professor Donald Nicholl, Ven. Sumedho, Rabbi Hugo Gryn, Dr Frank Chandra and Fr Benedict Ramsden.[2] The previous year Professor Maurice Wiles and Dr Al Faruqi spoke on 'The Language of Faith'.[3] In 1987, a rather similar subject was discussed when the main speaker was Professor

Wilfred Cantwell Smith.[4] Responses on 'The Language of Dialogue' were made by Professor G. S. Mansukhani, Ven. Dr M. Vajiragnana and Professor Seshagiri Rao, Professor Keith Ward, Rabbi Dr Norman Solomon and Dr Zaki Badawi.[5] In 1989 the main speaker was Professor Hans Küng on 'No World Peace without Peace between Religions'.[6] Responses were made by two Buddhists, Dr Paul Williams and Ven. Dr M. Vajiragnana,[7] by two Muslims, Dr Muhammad Mashuq Ibn Ally and Dr Yaqub Zaki,[8] and by the Hindu scholar, Professor Seshagiri Rao.[9] Other speakers have included Dr Ursula King, now of Bristol University, on 'Mysticism and Feminism',[10] Dr Frank Lake, founder of Clinical Theology, at a conference on 'Wholeness and Healing',[11] Professor Zaehner, former Spalding Professor at Oxford on the 'Dangers of Mysticism'[12] and Dr Martin Israel, a well known author and mystic, on 'The Scientific View and the Mystical Vision'.[13]

The retreat conferences, usually held at the Ammerdown Centre, near Bath, have been designed to encourage personal spiritual growth and appreciation of the inner meaning of religions. A similar emphasis characterized the St Alban's Congresses, led by Rev. Peter Dewey and arranged by the Interfaith Association.[14]

The encounter weekends have been held in centres where there is a wide variety of religions, such as Birmingham (1983) or Wolverhampton (1989).[15] In 1990, an imaginative interfaith pilgrimage was held from Derby to Iona. This involved links with many local interfaith groups and stressed both fellowship and the shared spiritual search.[16]

The Journal

Through its journal WCF has sought to disseminate the lectures given to it and the papers presented at conferences to a wider audience. During the Second World War, Sir Francis Younghusband himself, as we have seen, started a 'Chairman's Circular Letter', which was carried on by Baron Palmstierna. It was designed to maintain contact between the scattered members of WCF. By 1941, this had developed from a type-written sheet to a four page printed pamphlet. In 1949, Sir John Stewart Wallace persuaded a then young member, Heather McConnell, who was just back from the Far East, to launch a journal for the WCF. This was named *Forum* and became a journal with reprinted talks, especially commissioned articles, book reviews and Editor's Notes, which gave news of WCF activities. Until his death, Baron Palmstierna contributed a regular, inspirational column. The aim has been to address a non-specialist serious audience, helping them to learn about the religions of the world and to consider how the relationship between them can be more creative and harmonious.

In 1961 the journal was renamed *World Faiths*, with Heather McConnell, who has given a lifetime of service to WCF, still as Editor. In 1976, I succeeded Heather McConnell as editor. After some negotiation, in 1980 it was agreed to merge the WCF journal with the journal *Insight*, which had been produced from 1976 by the Temple of Understanding. The merged journal was called *World Faiths Insight* and Professor Seshagiri Rao, of the University of Virginia at Charlottesville, and I became co-editors. This increased the breadth of contributions and has given an international flavour to the journal. News of major interfaith conferences and events is given, besides articles and reviews. Although the circulation is not large, the journal goes to many parts of the world – often to libraries. It has been one of the ways by which WCF has tried to offer a service to the world rather than just to Britain. In 1991 a new editorial board took responsibility for the journal with Rev. Alan Race as co-editor with Professor Rao. The hope is to improve the format and attract more readers.

In the early eighties, WCF approached other bodies to discuss the publication of a news-sheet of interfaith activities, to keep pace with the proliferation of interfaith activities in Britain. WCRP (UK), the Week of Prayer for World Peace, the Committee for Relations with People of Other Faiths of the British Council of Churches and, recently, the Inter Faith Network for the United Kingdom sponsor this publication. The first editor was Geoffrey Bold and the present editor is Dr Paul Weller. *Interfaith News* gives a lively account of activities and future events and has helped to ensure that those working in this field, for various national and local organizations, keep in touch.

Interfaith Worship

The World Congress of Faiths has been a pioneer of interfaith worship. Sir Francis wished that the Religions of Empire Conference (1924) had included times of devotion, but this was not possible, although the Reverend Tyssul Davies arranged an interfaith gathering at the Theistic Church. At the 1936 conference, there were some readings from the sacred scriptures and members of the conference attended Anglican services at St Paul's and Canterbury Cathedral. It is, however, only since the second World War that attempts have been made to develop interfaith worship. This goes beyond the attendance of members of one faith at the worship of another to the attempt to arrange a joint service in which members of several faiths can share.

One of the first services in which people of several faiths took part was the memorial service for Sir Francis Younghusband at St Martin-in-the-Fields, London, in 1942. In 1946 an 'All Faiths' service was arranged during the Annual Conference at the Institut Francais. In 1949, the Rev. Will Hayes, who for some years had been experimenting with universalist worship, compiled and conducted a service for the World Congress of Faiths, called 'Every Nation Kneeling'.[17] On the occasion of the Coronation of Queen Elizabeth II, inspired by her request that people of all religions should pray for her, the Congress organized a special service, at the Memorial Hall, Farringdon Street, London. About six hundred people attended and this success led the Executive Committee to decide on an annual service. At the first of these, held at the King's Weigh House, Oxford Street, the preacher was Dr Edward Carpenter. Subsequent services have been held at churches of several denominations, including Roman Catholic, Anglican, Baptist and Unitarian. They have also been held at Reform and Liberal synagogues. Until recently, other faiths have not possessed large enough buildings in central London for the Annual Service.

Amongst the most memorable services was that held at the West London Synagogue in 1973, when the speaker was His Holiness the Dalai Lama, who said he was deeply moved by the collection of prayer readings from different religious groups.[18] The following year saw the introduction, at the conclusion of the service, of a religious dance-mime, which vividly expressed the search for unity. A problem of interfaith services is to ensure real participation without asking those present to compromise their particular beliefs. Hymns have therefore to be chosen with great care and it was some time before there was sufficient trust to join together in prayer and affirmation.

A number of Christians expressed their disapproval of interfaith services – indeed, there was some picketting of them. Dr Carpenter, as President, therefore gathered together a small group of Christians, of several denominations, to consider the theological rationale for such services. The report of the group [19] suggests that those taking part believed that members of all faiths worshipped the same God, the Creator of all, and that such services witnessed to the ethical values upheld in every faith. The group rejected the view that attendance at such services implied disloyalty to Jesus Christ. Although the discussion centres on questions of Christian theology, the report contains comments from members of many religions. Subsequently, the Anglican Consultants on Interfaith Affairs to the Archbishops and the Committee for Relations with People of Other Faiths of the British Council of Churches have produced reports on this subject.[20]

In recent years the number of interfaith services has been increasing. In 1966 a Multi-Faith Act of Witness was held on Commonwealth Day for the first time and similar ceremonies have been held in subsequent years.[21]

The Week of Prayer for World Peace has been marked by interfaith services. Because an inaugural service is held in connection with this week, usually in London, it was decided in the early eighties by WCF to discontinue their Annual Service for People of All Faiths. This, with hindsight, I feel was a mistake. The Week of Prayer Services, in fact, proved to be rather different. They usually consisted of a service by the host community, followed by prayers for peace by representatives of all religions. They were not designed as a unity. The WCF service was a focus for members and expressed symbolically the WCF's hope that, whilst respecting their distinct traditions, people of faith could meet together in the presence of the One Divine Reality. Although WCF has not held a large public service for some years, it has continued to develop patterns of praying together at its conferences. Some of these, which have included a flower communion, whereby each participant is given a flower, have been imaginative and moving.

Several local groups of the United Nations Association and some councils for community relations have held similar services. It seems clear that in the religiously plural situation in Great Britain, the need for interfaith worship will continue to grow. Indeed the psychologist, Professor Thouless, told the 1952 conference that such services might well be the best way of forwarding the aims of the Congress.[22]

At the Annual Conferences, members of different faiths are asked to lead times of devotion. Another area of growth has been the desire to learn from each other about prayer and meditation. This was evident during the festival 'Ways of the Spirit', held in London in 1975, with which the Congress co-operated and which prompted plans for some small devotional conferences.[23]

As yet, little thought has been given to more personal situations, such as a wedding where bride and groom belong to different faiths but wish for a religious ceremony. Quite a lot of thought, however, has been given to school assemblies and the possibility of children of different faiths worshipping together.[24]

Religious Education

For many years an important concern of the Congress has been religious education. It was one of the first bodies to advocate the teaching of world religions and to express concern about provision for the religious education of children of minority faiths. An article in *World Faiths*, in March 1961, said there was a need for an 'Advisory Council for Inter-Faith Understanding in Education', 'on which would be representatives of the teachers' bodies, local education authorities, teachers' training colleges, the churches and such organizations as the WCF and the Council of Christians and Jews'.[25] On more than one occasion, Lord Sorensen raised the matter in Parliament.[26] In 1965 Bernard Cousins, a member of the Congress, published a booklet giving examples of his own efforts to introduce world religions into the classroom. 'The study of one faith in isolation', he wrote, 'with scarcely any reference to the greatness of others can produce a narrowness of outlook, an arrogance and exclusiveness which give rise to suspicion, contempt and dislike for the unfamiliar'.[27] In the same year, Rev. John Rowland compiled an All Faiths Order of Service for World Childrens' Day, which was distributed through UNICEF.[28]

In 1969 the Congress convened an Education Advisory Committee. At that time it was thought that a new Education Act was being prepared, so the Committee's first task was to draw up a statement, issued in July 1970, about the provision of Religious Education in local authority schools 'with particular reference to the teaching of world religions and the needs of all children in a plural society'.[29] The Committee, on which all major religions were represented, argued that religious education should have a place in schools, primarily on educational grounds. 'We believe that religious education should have a continuing place in our schools. The primary reason for this is educational. A knowledge of man's religious history is essential to an understanding of our culture and our fellow beings. The spiritual dimension is a part of human experience and pupils should be given the opportunity to understand and assess religious claims. As people of faith we believe that individuals and society need a spiritual basis. Moral values, too, although they may be independent, are often closely related to religious faith.'[30] In calling for the teaching of other religions, besides Christianity, the group said that what was needed was 'the imaginative sympathy that enables a child to appreciate what living by another faith means to its followers'.[31] The committee suggested that assemblies might sometimes be interfaith in character. Subsequently the committee discussed assemblies in greater detail.[32] It also considered the misunderstandings that religious communities have about each other.

The resources available to the Congress have been very limited and, whilst continuing to answer queries and provide information, it largely withdrew from this area of work. The leadership in this field has been taken by the SHAP Working Party, which has encouraged a wide range of publications and organized many valuable conferences for educationalists, and by the Standing Conference on Inter-Faith Dialogue in Education, formed in 1973 and originally sponsored by WCF, which has held a series of conferences. The Religious Education Council, although its scope is wider, has also been concerned about the teaching of world religions.[33] Recent rather restrictive legislation has somewhat checked progress in this field.[34]

Interreligio

The provision of information on a wide variety of religious subjects has been an important task of the Congress. This work was especially developed in the Netherlands by Interreligio.

Interreligio, founded in 1947 and then called *Wereldgesprek der Godsdiensten*, has been one of the most successful of WCF groups outside Britain. The sixties and seventies saw a considerable change in the population of the Netherlands, which is now a plural society. Interreligio, devotedly led by Dr Rudolph Boeke, whose doctoral thesis was on Rudolf Otto, attracted many who were not in contact with the main religious bodies but who were concerned for spiritual values and religious experience. It dealt with inquiries about the specific practices of the world religions and with requests for educational material, for speakers, and for information on new religious developments. It maintained contact with similar centres abroad, especially through the newsletter *Lifesign*, which went to about five hundred people or institutions overseas. When it had a centre in Rotterdam it provided help for teachers of world religions and arranged exhibitions. It started meetings for those working for the media, to encourage more responsible reporting of religious matters. The society also took the initiative in efforts to establish a Council on Religions, on which the main religious groups in the Netherlands would be represented.[35] Recently Interreligio has been less active.

France, Belgium and India

For some years *L'Union des Croyants*, led by Comtesse de Pange and which had been supported in its formative years in the forties by Teilhard de Chardin, arranged programmes of scholarly lectures, but its activities seem now to be only occasional.[36] The Faculty for the Comparative Study of Religion at Antwerp University, developed under the inspiration of Rev. Christiaan Vonck, drew initial support from the World Congress of Faiths. It has grown steadily to become an important centre of study.[37] In south India, based on the ancient city of Madurai, Dr Ahamed Kaber, who is a poet and the author of *The Beacon Light to the World*, founded a branch in 1950. As Founder-President of the South Asiatic Zone of WCF, he has arranged regular lectures and meetings.

WCF Tours

The WCF Tours pioneered the idea of travel as a way of inter-religious meeting. Each included visits to a variety of religious communities. On the first WCF Tour to India we were very hospitably received when we visited Madurai.[38] On the Second India Tour, the group was warmly welcomed by the Guru Nanak Foundation in New Delhi and welcomed to the Golden Temple at Amritsar, where the Treasury of Jewels was specially opened. The Tour to Israel, which I led with Rabbi Hugo Gryn, included Jews, Christians, Hindus and Buddhists.[39]

In recent years, WCF has tried to discharge its international role by building up links with other interfaith bodies in different parts of the world and particularly by initiating the conferences for international interfaith organizations which have been held at Ammerdown. This has led to the plans, described in the final chapter, to mark 1993 as a Year of Inter-religious Understanding and Co-operation.

The Interfaith Network

Rather than try to become a large 'multinational' organization, WCF has encouraged others to develop appropriate interfaith work. As we have seen, WCF has been pleased that other bodies, with more resources, have taken on the work of encouraging the teaching of world religions. Other groups too have taken on arranging interfaith services. Many WCF members supported the development of the Week of Prayer for World Peace.

It was in keeping with this style of growth, that WCF supported the establishment of the Interfaith Network of the United Kingdom to link together the various religious organizations and communities in Britain. The initiative was taken by Brian Pearce, an active member of WCF.

In 1965 besides the WCF, only the Council of Christians and Jews and the London Society for Jews and Christians were already active. Since then, both organizations have expanded their work and influence. Whilst Christian-Jewish dialogue retains its specific character, it has become more related to wider interfaith dialogue. In 1977, The British Council of Churches Committee for Relations with People of Other Faiths was formed, with Rev. Kenneth Cracknell as first full-time secretary, now succeeded by Rev. Dr Clinton Bennett. Several denominations now have special committees for interfaith reflection and dialogue, some with, at least, part time officers. Meanwhile, other faith communities have become better organized and there is, for example, a National Council of Hindu Temples and two Councils of Mosques.

There has also been a considerable growth in the number of local interfaith groups and of voluntary groupings, such as the Interfaith Association and SHARIFH. The Interfaith Association was primarily concerned to help Christians become aware of the importance of interfaith

dialogue. Led by Rev. Peter Dewey, it arranged several large conferences at St Alban's and elsewhere. It has now merged with WCF.
SHARIFH (Sharing the Future in Hope) was organized by Dr Brian
Pamplin, who lived in Bath, and gave special attention to the relationship of religion to science. The group is now known as the Bath Interfaith Group.

There are some thirty local groups, each with their own fascinating
story, of which Wolverhampton, led by Mrs Ivy Gutteridge, Leeds
Concord Group, inspired by Dr Peter Bell and Glasgow, stimulated by
the unforgettable Deaconess Stella Reekie, are best known. Interfaith
gatherings are held quite widely, especially in connection with the Week
of Prayer for World Peace. There are study centres, particularly in
Birmingham with its MultiFaith Centre (MUFU), The Centre for the
Study of Islam and Christian-Muslim Relations and the Centre for the
Study of Judaism and Jewish-Christian Relations. Several conference
centres, such as Ammerdown or, until its recent closure, Spode House,
include interfaith conferences and retreats in their programme.

In 1977–8 Canon Peter Schneider, Rev. Jack Austin and I, with some
others, made tentative moves to explore forming a 'Consultative Interfaith Council'. In a Memorandum, Canon Peter Schneider, outlined the
possibilities. On the projected Council, compared to the BCC Committee on Relations with People of Other Faiths, 'members of various
Faith Communities would meet and discuss as equal partners. All are
hosts and none are guests'. Compared to WCF, which was based on
individual enthusiasts, the council 'would consciously relate to the various Faith Communities as a whole and seek to provide a structured
forum of meeting and discussion'. 'The aims of this Council can be seen
as facilitating a more comprehensive meeting and acquaintance and
knowledge of different Faiths than is at present the case. Further its
purpose would be that issues of common interest and concern could be
discussed and, if it seemed proper, decisions reached. In times of crisis
the Council would be the obvious framework for urgent consultation
and possible united decision, provided this had the support of the Faith
Communities represented in the Council.'[40] Nothing came of these
moves, partly because of the untimely death of Peter Schneider and
because of lack of support from the religious communities.

Recently, after much patient and energetic work by Brian Pearce,
many of the British groupings have come together in the Inter Faith
Network. Formally established in 1987, the Inter Faith Network links
over sixty existing organizations and groups including representative
bodies from within different faith communities, existing countrywide
organizations, local interfaith groups and bodies concerned with relig-

ious education on a multifaith basis and related academic institutions and study centres. At the inaugural meeting, this resolution was adopted:

> We meet today as children of many traditions, inheritors of shared wisdom and of tragic misunderstandings. We recognize our shared humanity and we respect each other's differences. With the agreed purpose and hope of promoting greater understanding between the members of the different faith communities to which we belong and of encouraging the growth of relationships of respect and trust and mutual enrichment in our life together, we hereby jointly resolve: that the Inter Faith Network for the United Kingdom should now be established.[41]

The constitution sets out the aim of the Network as being 'to advance public knowledge and mutual understanding of the teachings, traditions, and practices of the different faith communities in Britain including an awareness both of their distinctive features and of their common ground and to promote good relations between persons of different religious faiths'.[42] To fulfil this, the Network, under the joint chairmanship of The Rt Rev. Jim Thompson, Bishop of Stepney and Rabbi Hugo Gryn, promotes dialogue between members of different faith traditions, encourages local interfaith initiatives, provides information and facilitates communication. The Network is only for organizations and is not open to individual membership.

Already the Network has done much to improve communication between groups and has arranged important meetings, for example, about the role of the media in relation to the faith communities or, following the publication of Salman Rushdie's *The Satanic Verses*, about blasphemy in a multifaith society.[43]

Achievements

It is hard to estimate what has been achieved by the World Congress of Faiths. Indeed it is always difficult to assess the results of bodies concerned to change attitudes by the long-term education of the public.

The Congress has over the years suffered from a persistent underfunding and lack of staff. Most of the work has been on a voluntary or semi-voluntary basis, although now a paid part-time Executive Director and a secretary have been appointed. The various General Secretaries whom I have known, Miss Olive Dearlove, a Unitarian, Miss Kathleen Richards, an Anglican, Rev. Jack Austin, a Buddhist, The Rev. Sister

Theresa, a member of an Anglican religious order, Miss Pat Morrison, an Anglican from New Zealand and Tom Gulliver, a Quaker, have all given sacrificially of their time and service. The same is true of the honorary officers and other members of the Executive, although all, because of other commitments have had limited time for WCF. The failure to attract funding is partly the failure of WCF to project a higher profile, but it also reflects the reluctance of any of the faith communities in Britain to make resources available for interfaith work, of which there is still in many quarters some suspicion.

Certainly the relationship of religions to each other in Britain is now more open than it was fifty-five years ago. There are many reasons for this. The number of adherents of religions other than Christianity has increased significantly. Christianity's position in society has declined and is less dominant. The theological mood is more open and sympathetic to dialogue. The existence of the Congress, however, although numerically and financially a very weak organization, has, at times when the climate of British opinion was less sympathetic to religions other than Christianity, served to witness to the possibility of another view. Some of its members have been influential in public life and others have been strengthened to find they were not alone in their views.

More recently, Muslim, Hindu and Sikh communities have become settled and organized. The need for good community relations has been widely recognized. In the sixties and seventies the theological mood of the Christian churches, still the dominant religious grouping in Britain, became more open – even if the mood has rather changed in the late eighties.

'Interfaith dialogue', it has been said, has become 'a concern for the many rather than a dream of a few'.[44] Interfaith organizations and groups have mushroomed, so that it has become common to speak of the 'interfaith movement' just as people speak of the 'peace movement' or 'green movement' as shorthand for a wide range of concerns and activities. As with these movements, most of the work has been the voluntary, sacrificial work of dedicated pioneers.

Now, as interfaith dialogue becomes more popular and is given a fresh urgency by the desire for good community relations, the Congress can contribute by its experience and by concentrating on the 'truth-seeking' dialogue which is its *metier*. Whilst such 'truth-seeking' dialogue may be discursive or theological, it should also deepen into the interior dialogue which is the common exploration of spirituality. It needs to express itself in a common concern for world community. If the Congress concentrates on 'truth-seeking' dialogue, in its various aspects, it can make others aware how easily, now that dialogue is fashionable, it can be perverted for political, polemical or proselytizing purposes. Dialogue's true purpose remains 'the deepening of spiritual life' and the task of the Congress continues to be to encourage the growth of a spirit of fellowship amongst all believers.[45]

The Temple of Understanding I

Beginnings

The story begins in the sunporch of a house on Maher Avenue, Greenwich, Connecticut. One October afternoon in 1959, Mrs Judith Hollister was talking to a friend, Virginia Pronut. Discussing the world situation over a lunch of peanut butter sandwiches, they came up with the idea of gathering together in one building the great religions of the world. 'We spend hours at the conference table – but no time at all in trying to understand what is going on in the other man's mind.'[1] Impelled by that thought, Mrs Hollister contacted the Ford Foundation and spoke to William Nims. At first Mr Nims was reluctant, saying that the Ford Foundation rarely touched on religious endeavours. But as Mrs Hollister further explained the idea of a centre for the general public that would focus on the study of world religions, he changed his mind. She had initiated the conversation by saying that there was a small committee in Greenwich interested in the idea. Now Mr Nims suggested she bring the committee in to see him to explain it further.

Excited by this open door, Mrs Hollister called her friend Virginia that afternoon and between them they endeavoured to create a committee. The names of some outstanding leaders were suggested, such as historian Arnold Toynbee, theologian Paul Tillich, recently retired President Dwight Eisenhower and Dr Albert Schweitzer. There was, however, little response and her friends were sceptical of the idea.

Yet Mrs Hollister persisted. Since the age of eighteen she had been fascinated by the study of the world's religions. As a lay person, she had taken courses on the topic at Union Theological Seminary and at Columbia University. She had had the chance to meet a number of Eastern religious leaders. Her husband, Dickerman Hollister, a lawyer who was more conservative in thought and action, became convinced that the plan was more than a passing enthusiasm. He suggested that she should discuss the project with Eleanor Roosevelt.

Mrs Hollister hesitated to approach Mrs Roosevelt, but it so happened that ten days after her husband had made his suggestion, Judith Hollister found herself at a dinner party sitting next to Eleanor Roosevelt's cousin, who suggested that they both have tea with his famous relative the following week. This was an opportunity, but Mrs Hollister had nothing to show Mrs Roosevelt. She contacted her architect friend, Lathrop Douglass, and by tea time the next week he had sketched a plan of the proposed building.

When Mrs Hollister arrived for tea she was taken aback to find the room crowded with what turned out to be Eleanor Roosevelt's friends from the United Nations and from Washington DC, who had gathered for the weekly salon. She wondered if there would be any chance to share her dream with Mrs Roosevelt. After a time, Mrs Roosevelt leaned across the table and asked, 'My dear Mrs Hollister, is there anything in particular that you wish to discuss with me?' Soon Lathrop Douglass' plans of the building were unrolled on the hastily cleared tea table. Everyone gathered around to look at the beautiful architectural rendering of a sun bursting with light. The light radiated from the centre into six rays – one for each of the major world religions – Hinduism, Buddhism, Christianity, Islam, Judaism and Confucianism. The whole edifice was centred on a flame, held in a lotus flower in a pool of water. The outer periphery of the design was also circumscribed by water. For a few moments no one spoke. Mrs Roosevelt broke the silence by saying, 'This is very beautiful – a sort of spiritual United Nations. My dear, how can I help you with your dream?'[2]

Six weeks later, at Mrs Roosevelt's suggestion and with letters of introduction from her, Mrs Hollister, accompanied by her eleven-year-old redheaded son, Dickerman Jr, set out to meet international religious leaders to discover if there were support for the scheme. They went first to Rome, where they met Pope John XXIII, who gave no official blessing but promised to pray for the project. From there they went to India to meet with Prime Minister Jawaharlal Nehru and Vice-President Sarvapali Radhakrishnan, then on to Cairo to see Anwar el-Sadat, who was then Secretary General of the Islamic Congress. The results were encouraging.

In 1964 Judith spent a week in Lambarene with Albert Schweitzer and gained his interest and support. He wrote in her booklet of supporters, 'The Spirit burns in many flames'. Later, in 1967, Mrs Hollister was received in a special audience at the Vatican by Pope Paul VI, who promised to pray for 'il Tempio della Comprehensione.' In the same year an International Committee was formed under the chairmanship of Mrs

Basant Kumar Birla of Calcutta, India. In 1968 after Spiritual Summit Conference I, Mrs Hollister and her husband Dickerman travelled to Dharmsala to visit His Holiness the Dalai Lama, who expressed great interest in the project. He had been following each day of the Spiritual Summit conference by short wave radio. He immediately joined the new International Committee and has remained a member and a close friend since that time.

At the time of her initial trip in 1960 the project had no official name, but when Mrs Hollister visited India to see the Prime Minister she was also invited to the home of the American Ambassador, Ellsworth Bunker. Over tea in the garden alone with Mrs Bunker, Mrs Hollister was asked the name of this new project, to which she replied, 'The name has yet to be determined – perhaps "A Centre for World Religions"?' Mrs Bunker said, 'What you are trying to do, my dear, is really to create a sort of Temple of Understanding, isn't it? A Temple of Understanding,' she went on to say, 'would be understood by followers of religion around the world. Another "Institute for the Study of . . . " or another "Centre for . . . " sounds so Western. You want, I believe, to bring together the Asian and Western worlds, right? The word "temple" is a common denominator for all religions – think about it.' The suggestion excited Mrs Hollister and the name 'Temple of Understanding' was adopted.

When Mrs Hollister returned home in the summer of 1960, the Voice of America invited her to record a fifteen-minute tape to be translated into thirty-two languages and spun around the world. Down in Washington to make the tape, not knowing what to say, the name was used for the first time and the dream described. There purposely was no solicitation for funds – just a suggestion that if this concept of a spiritual United Nations had meaning for you, you could write to Judith Hollister's home in Connecticut. After making it, Mrs Hollister forgot about the tape, doubting that there would be any reply. A few weeks later, Sam, their friendly mailman, came up the front walk looking like Santa Claus on Christmas eve. 'Mrs Hollister, why are you all of a sudden receiving all of this?' He pointed to the bulging mail bag slung over his back. 'Haven't the foggiest idea,' she replied, 'but bring it into the kitchen, Sam, and let's dump it on the table and see.'

An unbelievable assortment of letters greeted their eyes. After Sam departed Mrs Hollister began to open them. They were from Nigeria, Yugoslavia, Italy, the Galapagos, Hong Kong, Singapore, ships at sea – sixty-seven different countries! And amazingly almost all the letters in different languages (later translated) reiterated the same theme – 'We have long had the same dream. We understand. We share your vision.' And enclosed came money in all forms – yen, Hong Kong dollars, rupees, drachma, money orders. This avalanche of mail continued for about six weeks. The local bank helped out by providing a free room in the bank and an experienced teller who knew world currency. The Temple of Understanding was officially born then and there.

Having no paid staff and not wanting to send form letters in reply to the tender avalanche, Greenwich High School students were asked to volunteer to help answer the mail. A month later, U Thant, then Secretary-General of the United Nations, heard of the idea and became a great supporter. Mrs Hollister was invited to make more tapes to be sent out by the UN. More mail!

Now interest was expressed by Henry Luce of Time-Life, Inc., and he assigned Robert Wallace to do an in-depth story of the Temple of Understanding for *Life* magazine, which appeared in both national and international editions on 12 December 1962. The response world-wide was so overwhelming that the Hollister telephone had to be taken off the hook for three weeks, and the mail, again with wide variety of the world's currency freely donated, resumed its avalanche.

By now the Temple of Understanding had well outgrown Mrs Hollister's kitchen, and, with assorted funds at last in the bank, an office was opened in the town of Greenwich. Marion Taylor was employed as a secretary to Mrs Hollister, with the rest of the staff working as volunteers. In 1965, with continued expansion, the office was moved to Washington DC, with Mr Finley Peter Dunne as Executive Director.[3]

At that point the Board of Directors numbered about twenty religious representatives as well as a lawyer and a banker and a few friends. The search for land began. After much thoughtful discussion it was determined that the best location for the Temple of Understanding would be in the nation's capital, to symbolize the insistence on religious freedom that was such a major part of the founding of the United States. It needed to be enough land for the visiting public to bring their children and expose them to the profound truths embedded in the great religious traditions – to emphasize the differences as well as the similarities – to implant new ideas in the minds of the young – to have picnics and fun while learning and absorbing. All this needed to be done with the funds in hand.

Peter Dunne scoured the surrounding countryside with the help of Mrs Hollister and other Directors, and one day an eighteen acre site was found in Prince George's County, Maryland, just over the line from Washington. Overlooking the Potomac River, with the famous Washington Monument in sight, the site seemed ideal – easy for tourists to reach, a half hour's drive from the White House, and room for picnics and play.

On 12 October 1966, a formal dedication ceremony was held there with ambassadors and press attending. Appropriate trees were planted to represent the six major world religions. The local press reported, 'Spiritual United Nations to be built in Nation's Capital.' At the time of writing the land is there – waiting.[4]

Spiritual Summit Conferences

In 1968 two important conferences were held. The First Washington Conference on Inter-Religious Understanding took place in January at Georgetown University and the First Spiritual Summit Conference met in Calcutta in October. The Washington conference was a one-day meeting. A panel of speakers talked on 'The Validity Which Each of the Religions Accords to Other Religions'. What emerged most distinctly from the day was a ringing affirmation, phrased in as many kinds of theological terminology as there are religions, that the great faiths of the world do possess the capacity and the will to join hands for the common good, and that none of them considers that this would call for any compromise of their essential doctrines or rituals.[5] This was the first time a Roman Catholic University had held such a conference. Credit is due to the combined efforts of Dr Lowell Ditzen, Director of the National Presbyterian Center in Washington DC, and Finley Peter Dunne, Executive Director of the Temple of Understanding.

Spiritual Summit I, Calcutta

Even before the Washington meeting, preparations were in hand for the First Spiritual Summit Conference on 'The Relevance of Religion in the Modern World' which was held in Calcutta from 22 to 26 October 1968. That conference brought together fifty religious leaders from ten religions, members of the Board and Friends of the Temple, a few scholars, and a few representatives of youth. The public was invited to some sessions. On Friday the 25th, the entire conference crossed the Ganges River by steamboat to the Calcutta Botanical Gardens to join in prayer for peace and the salvation of humankind.

An illustrious array of famous speakers included Professor Huston Smith, a distinguished scholar of world religions, Fr Pierre Fallon SJ, who had a deep knowledge of Hinduism, Princess Poon, a Buddhist leader from Thailand, Dr Syed Vahiduddin, a Muslim scholar from India, Fr Thomas Merton, a well known monk and writer on the contemplative life, Swami Chinmayananda, a Hindu leader, Dr Ezra Spicehandler, Head of the Hebrew Union College in Jerusalem, Dr Seyyed Hossein Nasr, a leading Muslim philosopher, and Rev. Toshio Miyake from Japan, who has played an active part in worldwide interfaith movements.

The declaration, agreed by participants, said that the Conference had demonstrated that 'inter-religious communication is possible' and said that the time had come for religions to speak to each other and to the total human community.[6]

Spiritual Summit II, Geneva

The Second Spiritual Conference, which was my first introduction to the Temple, was held in Geneva, Switzerland, from 31 March to 4 April 1970, on the theme, 'Practical Measures for World Peace'. The main subjects of the conference were 'The Population Problem', 'The Role of World Business', and 'The Role of Women in Peace'. The opening address was given by Dr Eugene Carson Blake, the General Secretary of the World Council of Churches, on 'The Ambiguous Role of Religions in Relation to World Peace'. He reminded his audience that religion often does not make for peace. He warned against trying to create any sort of super-authority and any tendency towards syncretism. Speakers included Dr Ernst Benz from Marburg University, Professor Amiya Chakravarty, a disciple of Tagore, Dr Mohamed Kamel Hussein of Cairo, author of *City of Wrong*, Swami Ranganathananda of the Ramakrishna Mission, and Dr James Deotis Roberts, who was then at Howard University in Washington DC.

In an effort to carry forward the spirit of the conference it was decided to create the 'Continuing Conference on World Religions', 'To promote understanding and enduring appreciation of the different faiths, and to bring to bear all the resources at our disposal towards the solution of human problems, both personal and social.'[7] In fact, the continuing work was carried out by the Temple of Understanding itself.

Some forty-four leaders and sixty others took part in the Second Spiritual Summit conference. Christians were in the majority (twenty-seven) with seven Buddhists and Muslims, but only a couple of Hindus. Nearly all religions had at least one representative. There was a Jain, a Sikh, a Zoroastrian, but no member of the Baha'i faith. A number of special advisors added their expertise to the discussions, which in general were well informed and of a high quality, bringing together religious leaders and experts on the matters discussed.

The final session ended with some young people symbolically binding together the delegates with strands of silk. The conference concluded with a significant ceremony in the thirteenth-century Cathedral of St Pierre. In the church where John Calvin had once preached, representatives of the religions present prayed in their own sacred languages. Pastor Henry Babel of the Cathedral, who had faced some opposition in agreeing to the ceremony, read from the Bible and the writings of Calvin, and the sermon was preached by Dr Lowell Ditzen, Director of the National Presbyterian

Centre in Washington DC. At the conclusion, all delegates said the Lord's Prayer. Media coverage, mainly in the local press, headlined, 'Unprecedented Event Takes Place in Cathedral of St Pierre'. An unprecedented event it was indeed! A month prior to this Temple of Understanding conference Pope Paul had visited Geneva and had asked to pray in the Cathedral, but the conservative church elders would not permit him entry! It was in the same cathedral, however, that sixty-five years earlier members of the IARF Geneva conference had been welcomed and that prayer from different religious traditions had been offered.

Spiritual Summit III, Harvard

The next Spiritual Summit was held at Harvard Divinity School in October 1971, and began the useful pattern of arranging such conferences in conjunction with an educational institution. It was intended to demonstrate in America 'that the religions of the world do know how to collaborate, and that understanding, as we mean it in the Temple of Understanding, can become a great source of hope for mankind in this doubting and pragmatic century'.[8] The subject of this conference was 'Religion in the Seventies'. The opening address was given by Professor Krister Stendahl, while Professor Harvey Cox, author of *The Secular City*, was another speaker. The challenge of science and technology to religion was considered and also the questioning of traditional religions by young people – a discussion which was enlivened by the presence of a good number of local students and some 'hippies' from California, who demonstrated their alternative life-style. In the words of Fr Masson, who represented the Vatican, 'More serious than their sometime bizarre costumes would have led one to believe, they demonstrated by their presence and their questions that there exists in America another youth culture than that of sex and LSD'.[9] There was some feeling that religions need to free themselves from inherited cultic and cultural patterns. The Harvard conference was followed by gatherings at Princeton University, Sarah Lawrence College, Manhattanville College, and Wainwright House in Rye, New York.

Spiritual Summit IV, Cornell

The next year a weekend symposium was held at Cornell University in Ithaca, New York, at the invitation of Rev. Robert Beggs, and in 1973 a weekend colloquium was arranged at Yale University. This was on the topic of meditation and consisted of meditation sessions as well as talk about it. The leaders included Brother David Steindl-Rast, OSB, of Mt. Savious Monastery, Shimano Eido Roshi, Abbot of the New York Zendo, and Srimata Gayatri Devi, founder of two Vedanta Centres in America.[10]

In May 1974 another, larger gathering was held again at Cornell, on the theme, 'Toward World Community'. The conference explored various means, such as publications and education, through which a sense of world community could be fostered, and coincided with the opening of a Centre for World Community at Cornell. Amongst those taking part were Ven. Maha Thera Piyananda, of the Washington Buddhist Vihara, Swami Adiswarananda, of the Ramakrishna-Vivekananda Centre in New York, Rabbi Samuel Silver of Stamford, Connecticut, and Rabbi Herbert Weiner of South Orange, New Jersey, author of *9 1/2 Mystics*, Fr Masson from the Vatican, Archbishop George Appleton, Chairman of the World Congress of Faiths and former Anglican Archbishop in Jerusalem, Sir Zafrulla Khan, a former President of the International Court of Justice, Munishri Chitrabhanu, a Jain who was President of the Divine Knowledge Society, Rev. Toshio Miyake, of the Konko-Kyo Church of Izuo, Osaka, Japan, and my wife, Mary Braybrooke, representing the World Congress of Faiths.[11]

In February 1975, a spiritual symposium was held at Sarah Lawrence College, New York, on 'Mysticism and Meditation', led by Pir Vilayat Inayat Khan, the Sufi leader, Shimano Eido Roshi, a Zen master, Rabbi Herbert Weiner, a teacher of the Jewish mystical tradition and Rev. Robley E. Whitson, author of the influential book *The Coming Convergence of World Religions*.[12]

Spiritual Summit V, New York

The next major gathering of the Temple of Understanding was the Fifth Spiritual Summit Conference held at the Cathedral Church of St John the Divine, New York, in October 1975, on 'One is the Human Spirit'. The imaginative programme opened with a colourful ceremony at the Cathedral, at which the Dean, the Very Rev. James Parks Morton, the Rev. Toshio Miyake and Dr Jean Houston, Conference Chairperson and President of the Foundation for Mind Research, spoke briefly before Dr Margaret Mead, the distinguished anthropologist, gave the keynote address. She suggested there was 'new hope' for the human race, because it shared a common problem – threats in the atmosphere. 'Whereas people fought each other in the name of trivial boundaries they now, together, face the challenge of pollutants and airborne warfare.' 'At the heart of each religion,' she said, 'we find the same overriding concern for our common humanity.'[13]

A large part of the conference was spent in panel discussions, one on each morning from Monday to Thursday. The first was on 'Unity with Diversity', suggesting that the world faiths were complementary rather than rivals. 'Many flowers make the garden beautiful,' said Munishri

Chitrabhanu, 'and the world will be sustained and beautified by different approaches to life.'[14] On Tuesday, 'Ecology and the Spiritual Environment' was discussed. Two main viewpoints emerged. The first was that man's technological growth is unbalancing the ecology and tending to destroy it. The second was that man and technology are part of a much larger evolutionary process. Dr Edgar Mitchell, the former astronaut, expressed the second approach. 'Technology is neither good nor bad, it just is. It is our problem to adapt to what is, not to revert to what was. We must develop better ways to use our tools.'[15] An interesting aspect of the discussion was the participation of a Sioux and a Hopi medicine man.

On Wednesday the theme was 'Creating the Future Community'. Different degrees of emphasis were placed on the need for unity and diversity. Rabbi Weiner stressed the need for diverse religious traditions, saying, with William James, that the Divine is much too large for any one faith to express it. Pir Vilayat Khan, however, looked to the younger generation as pioneers of a new syncretic community which will encompass all religious traditions. Dr Homer A. Jack, of the World Conference on Religion and Peace, stressed the need to solve urgent, immediate problems before speculating on the future community. Religious groups needed to develop experts for advisory positions in practical matters of state and on political decisions. The fourth morning was devoted to 'Women, Religion and World Community'. This panel discussed the role of women and asserted their equality.

In the afternoons, seminars were held to discuss further the issues raised in the mornings and to help prepare the Joint Statement, which was read at the United Nations. This was a historic occasion, as, although Pope Paul VI had addressed the UN in 1965, this was the first time that representatives of the world religions had gathered at the UN. Even so, the objection of some countries to a religious presence meant that the gathering had to be held in the Dag Hammarskjold Auditorium rather than the General Assembly. The programme began with a meditation by Sri Chinmoy, Director of The Peace Meditation of the United Nations, and was followed by an introduction by Charles Mills, President of the Temple of Understanding and by remarks by Edna McCallion, President of the Religious Non-Governmental Organizations at the UN. Secretary-General Kurt Waldheim gave a brief address, assessing the present and future role of the UN. Dr Ewart Cousins introduced the religious leaders who spoke: Srimata Gayatri Devi; Lord Abbot Kosho Ohtani, Chief Abbot of the Nishi Honganji Temple in Kyoto; Rabbi Robert Gordis, former President of the Synagogue Council of America; Mother Teresa, who had by then established the Missionaries of Charity in India; and Dr Seyyed Hossein Nasr, then Director of the Iranian

Academy of Philosophy, Teheran. The speakers stressed the responsibiltiy of the UN and the need for it to take note of humankind's spiritual aspirations. Lord Abbot Kosho Ohtani said that 'religion must assume an important role' in helping to solve the world's problems.[16] Mother Teresa directed attention to the poor. 'Let us today, when we have gathered to prove to the whole world that we are one, let us be one in this love to the poorest of the poor in the world.'[17]

After the religious leaders had spoken, Dr Jean Houston read the Joint Statement, and Benedictine monk Brother David Steindl-Rast, OSB, Chairman of the Centre for Spiritual Studies, ended the session with a prayer, for which all were asked to stand. 'Let our standing be a mindful gesture – mindful of the ground on which we are standing, the one little plot of land on this earth not belonging to *one* nation, but to all nations united. It is a very small piece of land, indeed it is a symbol of human concord, a symbol of the truth that this poor, mistreated earth belongs to all of us together. As we stand, then like plants standing on a good plot of ground, let us sink our roots deep into our hidden unity. (Allow yourself to feel what it means to stand and to extend your inner roots.) Rooted in the soil of the heart, let us expose ourselves to the wind of the Spirit, the one Spirit who moves all who let themselves be moved. Let us breathe deeply the breath of the One Spirit, the one Spirit who moves all who let themselves be moved. Let us breathe deeply the breath of the One Spirit. Let our standing bear witness that we take a stand on common ground. Let our standing be an expression of reverence for all those who before us have taken a stand for human unity.'[18]

The Joint Statement said that the technological unity of humankind had yet to be matched by social and moral unity and this required the utilization of religions' spiritual resources. Religion itself had often been divisive, but there had been a move towards unity within and between world religions. 'The great religions and spiritual movements of our time stand ready to unite around their common spiritual and moral vision and to contribute to the development of a morality and ethics which is mindful of and actively concerned with basic human rights and freedoms, the natural world and our shared environment, and the vital needs for world peace.'[19] The statement praised the UN for its achievements, but said that immense tasks remained and that there had been insufficient progress on disarmament, economic development and human rights. There was reference to the need for world-wide religious freedom, and the conference recommended that the UN should consider the 'creation of an agency which will bring the much-needed resources and inspirations of the spiritual traditions to the solution of world problems'.[20]

The statement is well written, although general in its terms. Its main significance seems to be in asserting the united concern of religions about the future of mankind and in urging the UN to recognize and make use of the spiritual resources of the world religions. Probably, as so often, the lasting impact of the conference is on and through those who took part.

Unlike most inter-religious conferences, this was not just a matter of words. Each day at 8.30 a.m. and at noon, meditative rituals from the various religions were held. On Monday evening, a new symphony, 'One is the Spirit of Man', especially written for the occasion by Maia Aprahamian, was performed by the Symphony for United Nations. Performances were also given by Hamza El Din, Donald Swann, the Levittown Madrigal Singers, the Newark Boys Choir, the First Musicians, and other groups. The Sufi Order presented five times a Cosmic Mass, which had a cast of three hundred people. Written and narrated by Pir Vilayat Khan, an elaborate pageant depicted the evolutionary stages of the world religions and suggested how they might eventually meet on a transcendental plane of universal understanding. An art exhibition was also arranged to coincide with the conference.

The opportunity to appreciate art and music and also to meditate, enriched the gathering, as it allowed delegates to share experiences together as well as discussing concepts. Indeed, several people have suggested that shared experiences are more likely to develop a sense of oneness than are speeches and debates.

Changes in Organization

During the seventies there were several changes in the leadership of the Temple of Understanding. At the Board meeting in December 1970, Charles J. Mills of Byram, Connecticut, was elected President and Mrs Hollister became Chairman of the Board, which relieved her of day-to-day details of the work. Charles Mills, a graduate of Yale, had been an executive of the FMC Corporation before retiring to devote himself full time to the Temple of Understanding. Dr Ditzen, as Vice-President, continued to be Chairman of the Committee on Plans and Programmes. In 1972 Finley Peter Dunne, who had been Executive Director since 1964, retired and was succeeded by John Gillooly. Gillooly, who had taught European and Russian history at the University of Massachusetts, came to the Temple of Understanding from the Laymen's Movement at Wainwright House in Rye, New York, of which he was Executive Director. In 1975 Mrs Hollister retired as Chairperson. She was invited to remain as Honorary Chairperson, but was succeeded by Finley Peter Dunne as Chairperson. For a time inflation and financial pressures hampered the work of the Temple of Understanding. As a result, the offices were moved from Washington and were for a time located at Wainwright House, Rye, New York.

Insight

In 1976 the first issue appeared of a new journal of world religions called *Insight*, published by Finley Peter Dunne and edited by Professor K. L. Seshagiri Rao, Professor of Religious Studies of the University of Virginia, Charlottesville, supported by a strong advisory editorial board. In 1980 *Insight* merged with *World Faiths* to become *World Faiths Insight*, the joint publication of the World Congress of Faiths and the Temple of Understanding, which Professor Rao and I co-edited until 1991, when Rev. Alan Race, an Anglican clergyman who is author of *Christians and Religious Pluralism*, succeeded me as co-editor. In 1991 the Temple of Understanding decided it was unable to continue as a co-sponsor.

· 12 ·

The Temple of Understanding II

In the early eighties, the Temple of Understanding appointed Edward J. Bednar, former Trappist monk, as President. He had previously been Organizing Secretary of the 1977 Petersham conference for Inter-Monastic Dialogue and was Steering Chairman of the 1980 East-West Monastic Symposium on 'The Monk as Universal Archetype'. He continued his concern to foster dialogue between monks of different religious traditions. He also focussed the Temple's attentions on the theme of 'Reverence for Life'.

'Reverence for Life'

'Reverence for Life' was a concern close to Ed Bednar's heart. He wrote a long paper on the subject early in 1983.[1] In 1981, a Gandhi Commemorative meeting was held on the subject. The following year, in June 1982, to coincide with the United Nations Special Session on Disarmament, the Temple of Understanding organized a conference on 'Reverence for Life'. The intention was to give a focus for spiritual and religious concerns related to the Special Session. Peace activists, such as the Jesuit priest Daniel Berrigan, Dr Homer A. Jack of WCRP and Msgr Bruce Kent of the Campaign for Nuclear Disarmament took part. The event was preceded by the World Peace March.

Later that year, Ed Bednar set out on a journey to India, via Britain, Rome, Jerusalem and Mount Sinai. He spent six weeks in India meeting with representatives of the Sarvodaya (non-violence) movement which carries on the work of Mahatma Gandhi. On his way back to the USA, Ed Bednar stopped in Japan. There he visited Hiroshima and met with peace and interfaith workers in the country.

Declaration on the Oneness of the Human Family

During his travels, Ed Bednar consulted with those with whom he met on two matters: the spiritual dimension of nonviolence and the possibility of holding the next Spiritual Summit Conference at Mount Sinai. The discussion on the spiritual dimension of nonviolence centred on a draft 'Declaration of Principles for a Global Spirituality' (later revised as the 'Declaration on the Oneness of the Human Family') which had been prepared by Dr Robert Muller, who at the time was Secretary of the Social and Economic Council of the United Nations. The hope was that the draft, suitably revised, might be adopted at the projected summit meeting.[2]

Ed Bednar discussed the possibility of holding a meeting in Sinai with Fr Xavier Eid of the Cairo Interfaith Fellowship and with Archbishop Damianos, in whose jurisdiction Sinai lay. It was generally felt that the political situation in the Middle East had deteriorated after the assassination of President Sadat of Egypt and that it might not be a suitable venue for the spiritual summit.

Spiritual Summit VI, New York

These explorations were taken further by S. William Stansmore, a Vice-President of the Temple, who was also at the time Executive Director. In the summer of 1983 Bill Stansmore and Judith Hollister undertook a trip to see major supporters of the Temple of Understanding and to enlist their participation in Spiritual Summit VI, with Mount Sinai still being considered as a possible site. The trip began with a reception in London, followed by a visit to the Secretariat for Non-Christians in Rome. From there they proceeded to visit more supporters in Jerusalem and in Cairo, concluding the trip in India with Mother Teresa and His Holiness, the Dalai Lama. To the surprise and delight of both travellers, the concept of the Sinai gathering was enthusiastically endorsed, with promises to attend from the Vatican and the Dalai Lama. By early 1984, however, the Egyptian government had ruled that the volatility of the situation in the Middle East made such a high profile event too much of a security risk, and that the plan would be 'unfeasible and dangerous'.[3]

It was, therefore, decided to hold the Sixth Spiritual Summit in New York in October 1984. The gathering was held partly at the Cathedral of St John the Divine and concluded at the Church Centre for the United Nations, which is across the street from the UN Secretariat. The programme itself centred on a 'Declaration of Oneness for the Human Family' which had again been drafted by Dr Robert Muller. This preliminary draft was ratified by the spiritual leaders present, who represented 2.5 billion people – over one-half of the Earth's population. It merits being reproduced here.

A convergence of world religions towards a 'Global Spirituality' might suggest the following points in common:

1. The Oneness of the Human Family, irrespective of colour, sex, creed, nation or any other distinctive characteristic.

2. The harmonious place of the individual person in the total order of things, as a unique entity of Divine Origin, with a basic relationship to the Universe and Eternity.

3. The Importance of spiritual exercises, meditation, prayer, contemplation, and the inner search as links between human life and the universe.

4. The Existence of an incipient conscience at the heart of humanity which speaks for what is good and against what is bad for the human family; which advocates and fosters understanding, co-operation and altruism instead of division, struggle and indifference among nations.

5. The value of Dedicated Service to others, with a compassionate response to human suffering, with special attention to the oppressed and the poor, the handicapped and the elderly, the rejected and the lonely.

6. The Duty to give thanks and express gratitude for the abundance of life which has been given to humanity, an abundance not to be selfishly possessed or accumulated, but to be shared and given generously to those who are in need, with a respect for human dignity and a sense of social justice.

7. The need for Ecumenical Agencies and World Religious organizations to foster dialogue and collaborative arrangements, and to bring the resources and inspirations of the religions to bear upon the solution of world problems.

8. A rejection of violence as being contrary to the sanctity and uniqueness of life and a total acceptance of the precept – 'Thou shalt not kill'.

9. An affirmation of the law of Love and Compassion as the great transcending force which alone can break the nemesis of war and establish a Planet of Peace.

10. The Evolutionary task of human life and society to move through the eternal stream of time towards interdependence, communion, and an ever expanding realization of Divinity.[4]

The moving and beautiful opening ceremony was held in the Cathedral. The procession was led by 'Children as Teachers of Peace'. After a Bidding Prayer, Judith Hollister welcomed the congregation and then introduced Dr Robert Muller, by then Assistant Secretary-General of the United

Nations, who read the Declaration. Following the hymn 'City Not Made With Hands', Dr Karan Singh, founder of the Virat Hindi Samaj, gave an address and a second one was given by Dom Helder Camara, Archbishop of Olinda and Recife, Brazil. After a 'Meditation in Movement' by the Omega Liturgical Dance Company, a further address was given by His Holiness the Dalai Lama. The celebration concluded with the Service of Light. The Cathedral was dimmed and the distinguished spiritual leaders each offered a prayer from their tradition and lit a candle. Finally, during the hymn 'Joyful, Joyful, We Adore Thee', the children gave lights to the congregation – a very moving moment for all assembled there.[5]

The participants included Thich Nhat Hanh; Abbot Thomas Keating; Rabbi Wolfe Kelman; Archbishop Iakovos, Primate of the Greek Orthodox Church in America; Rev. Toshio Miyake; and Elie Wiesel, author of *Night*. Besides the help of Dr Robert Muller of the UN, great assistance was given by the Very Rev. James Parks Morton, Dean of the Cathedral of St John the Divine.

Changes in Personnel

Soon, succeeding Abbot Thomas Keating, James Parks Morton was to become President of the Temple of Understanding and its offices were to move to two tiny rooms in the clerestory of the catehdral. At this time, Fr Luis M. Dolan, a Passionist priest of Irish extraction from Argentina, who was working with the Movement for a Better World, also began to take an active part in the affairs of the Temple and was later to become the Director for International Programmes.

In the same year, Dr Kusumita Priscilla Pedersen became Executive Director. Dr Pedersen, who is a follower of Sri Chinmoy, received her doctorate in Buddhist Studies at Columbia University and was Professor of the History of Religions at Brown University and the University of Notre Dame before joining the Temple's staff. She enriched its work with her wide knowledge of the world's religions and the leading practitioners, as well as with her efficiency and organizing skills. At the same time, the Rev. Daniel Anderson, a Lutheran minister, also joined the staff of the Temple of Understanding. Dan Anderson exhibited great patience and a gift for gaining people's trust as he carried out his duties as Director of the emerging North American Interfaith Network.

The Global Forum

Another Spiritual Summit was projected for 1985 or 1986, with Thich Nhat Hanh and Elie Wiesel amongst possible speakers. This did not materialize, although work continued for some time on drawing up a document on 'The State of the World; A Spiritual Perspective'.[6]

In the autumn of 1985, an important meeting was held at Tarrytown in New York State. This brought together a 'core group' of religious and parliamentary leaders. The initiative had been taken by Akio Matsumura, the founder and Executive Director of the Global Committee of Parliamentarians on Population and Development. The meeting was co-sponsored by the Temple of Understanding and the Global Committee. It was co-chaired by Dean James Parks Morton and by the Honorable Sat Paul Mittal, a member of the Indian Parliament. The meeting constituted itself 'The Global Spiritual and Parliamentary Forum on Human Survival' and called for a global conference of the world's spiritual and parliamentary leaders.[7]

Thanks to the energy of Akio Matsumura, the Executive Coordinator, the first such conference was convened, with considerable speed, at Oxford, England, in April 1988. With the detailed organization in the hands of Wilfred Grenville Grey, the British director, the conference attracted distinguished spiritual and parliamentary leaders, including Mother Teresa of Calcutta; the Dalai Lama; Dr Robert Runcie, the Archbishop of Canterbury; Rev. Nikkyo Niwano; the astronomist Carl Sagan; and the ecologist James Lovelock.

A further gathering was held in Moscow in January 1990, thanks in large measure to Dr E. P. Velikhov, Vice-Chairman of the USSR Academy of Sciences, who had taken an active part in the Oxford Conference. Participants included Javier Perez de Cuellar, Secretary-General of the United Nations; Metropolitan Pitirim; Mrs Gro Harlem Brundtland, former Prime Minister of Norway; Lord Jakobovits, Chief Rabbi of the British Commonwealth; Sheikh Ahmad Kuftaro, the Grand Mufti of Syria; Elie Wiesel, the Nobel Peace laureate; and Dr Karan Singh, then Ambassador of India to the United States. The highlight of the conference was a major address by Mikhail Gorbachev given at the Kremlin, in which he stressed the urgency of acting internationally to preserve the environment – an urgency echoed in the Moscow Declaration.[8]

More recently, at the headquarters of the Kurozumi-Kyo sect of Shinto in Okayama, Japan, a 'Shinto International Workshop on Global Survival and Peace' was held on 1 to 2 November 1990, combining prayer and liturgy, scholarly presentations, and open discussion. Plans are in hand for the next meeting to be held in Kyoto, Japan, early in 1993. Regional gatherings are also planned for Indonesia; Atlanta, Georgia; the Pacific Rim; and the Soviet Union.[9]

The Global Forum is not itself an interfaith organization. Rather it exists to bring together spiritual leaders and parliamentarians, along with journalists, scientists, artists and business leaders, to address the problems of human and global survival. It believes, however, the religions have a vital contribution to make on these subjects, and that the spiritual contribution must draw on all the religious traditions of humankind, including the spiritual traditions of indigenous peoples. Indeed, the Global Forum partly fulfils the hopes of the pioneers of the interfaith movement that, as people of different religions came to know and trust each other, so they would learn to work together to solve the great issues facing humankind.

Although the Temple of Understanding and the Global Committee of Parliamentarians on Population and Development were its parents, the Global Forum is a new and independent organization. Indeed it is a robust and vigorous youngster. The Temple, especially through the hard work of Dean James Parks Morton and Dr Kusumita Pedersen, devoted considerable energy to the formation of the Global Forum.

Changes and New Projects at the Temple

Dr Pedersen, in the summer of 1988, left the Temple to continue as Joint Secretary for the Forum with responsibility for the religious dimension of its programme and to devote more time to teaching and writing. At that time, the Rev. Daniel Anderson became Executive Director of the Temple and Fr Luis M. Dolan became Director of International Programmes.[10] In the spring of 1990, Dan Anderson relinquished his post and was succeeded by Dr Peter Laurence, formerly Director of the Interfaith Center at Wainwright House, a lay education centre in suburban New York.

Under Dr Pedersen's leadership, the Temple arranged important educational programmes in the New York area. In the fall of 1986, a series was arranged on 'Teachings for Peace'. The format and content of the Temple of Understanding's newsletter was also improved. Dr Pedersen also took an active part in the two Ammerdown meetings of representatives of international interfaith organizations and the Temple is fully committed to plans to mark 1993 as A Year of Inter-Religious Understanding and Co-operation. In October 1986, the Temple of Understanding was one of the interfaith organizations invited by the Vatican to partake in the World Day of Prayer at Assisi.

The North American Interfaith Network

At the Ammerdown meetings of international interfaith organizations, the need was recognized for regional networks of interfaith organizations. The Temple of Understanding, through the good offices of Rev. Daniel

Anderson, agreed to encourage such a development in North America. Various meetings and discussions were held, including a conference on 'The Challenge of Religious Pluralism' at St Olaf College, Minnesota, in July 1987. At the same time, the first *North America Interfaith Directory* was published by the Temple of Understanding.[11]

In the following year, at the end of October 1988, the new North American Interfaith Network (NAIN) held its first continental assembly, a conference entitled 'A North America Assisi: Learning to Live Together' in Wichita, Kansas. Two hundred and thirty-five people attended, representing twelve major religions of North America. Speakers included Dr Beatrice Medicine, Professor Emeritus at the University of California, who spoke on 'Repression and Revitalization: American Indian Belief Systems'; Bishop Seigen H. Yamaoka, Buddhist Churches of America, on 'The Challenges of Environment for the Religious Community'; Dr Mahmoud Ayoub, Executive Director of the Canadian Institute for Advanced Islamic Research, on 'The Challenges of Peace for the Religious Community'; Dr Seshagiri Rao, Professor of Religion at the University of Virginia, on 'The Challenges of Justice for the Religious Community'; Dr Victor Goldbloom, President of the International Council of Christians and Jews, on 'Inter-Religious Dialogue as a Force for Change', and Dr Diana Eck, Professor of Comparative Religion and Indian Studies at Harvard Divinity School, who spoke on 'Religion at the Crossroads: Religious Diversity, Religious Fundamentalism, and Inter-Religious Dialogue Today', and said that 'Our vision and our loyalties, as well as our airplanes, must indeed circle the planet'.[12]

A second assembly of the North American Interfaith Network was held in Seattle, Washington, in July 1990. The theme was 'Ethics in Action: In the Home, the Workplace and the Environment'. The keynote speaker was Anantanand Rambachan, a Hindu scholar from St Olaf College. The gathering ended with a multifaith programme of music and prayer. Perhaps one of the most important outcomes of this conference was the adoption of a constitution for the North American Interfaith Network and the election of its first Executive Committee, a group chosen to be broadly representative of the religious spectrum of the United States and Canada. Also in that summer of 1990, the Temple of Understanding published the second edition of the *North America Interfaith Directory*, this time in conjunction with the Network.[13]

International Programmes

Under the guidance of the energetic Fr Luis Dolan, the Temple has developed a series of international tours and consultations. In the autumn of 1989 a 'Himalaya High Holy Days Retreat' was arranged by Judith Hollister to coincide with the formal opening of the India Chapter of the Temple of Understanding, chaired by Dr Karan Singh. In July 1990 the Temple arranged an inter-religious consultation in Japan. In early September, a tour of Eastern Europe was arranged by Fr Dolan, including visits to Germany, Poland, Czechoslovakia, Hungary and the Soviet Union. In 1991 a tour of the holy places of the Middle East, with seminars and explorations in Egypt, Israel, Jordan, Syria and Lebanon took place. The Temple is also looking forward to arranging a series of conversations between Christians and Indigenous People in Latin America in 1992, to coincide with the five hundredth anniversary of the 'discovery' of America.

1991 has seen the development of a number of new activities for the Temple. The publication of its newsletter has increased in frequency and a series of 'Roundtables and Retreats' has begun, with monthly presentations at the United Nations in conjunction with the Pacem in Terris Society of the United Nations staff. The programmes, all on contemporary religious themes, have included such topics as 'Perspectives on the Gulf Crisis', 'Religious Diversity in the Soviet Union', 'Does Religion Promulgate Prejudice?' 'The Buddhist Experience', 'Global Responsibility: In Search of a New World Ethic', 'Interfaith Harmony in a Pluralistic World', 'Unity and Diversity of Islam', and 'Peace is Every Step'. Presenters included scholars and religious leaders such as Professor Hans Küng, Dr Karan Singh, Dr Mahmoud Ayoub, and Thich Nhat Hanh. At the same time, the Temple has initiated the production of a series of television programmes on similar themes, for distribution through cable TV systems in major cities throughout the United States and Canada. Leadership for these activities has come from Judith Hollister, Dr Karan Singh, Dean James Parks Morton, and Vice-Presidents Werner Mark Linz, Leonard Marks, Dr Mohammed T. Mehdi, and Rabbi Marshall T. Meyer together with Dr Peter Laurence, Fr Luis M. Dolan and the Temple's distinguished Directors and Advisors, all of whom serve in their individual capacities, and do not represent the official sanction of any religious institutions.

Conclusion: 'We are already One'

In thirty years the Temple of Understanding has grown from small beginnings to involve important religious leaders of all traditions. The initial focus on a building has somewhat faded, but the emphasis on meditation and inter-religious communication has continued. The conferences and programmes have been primarily directed to increasing understanding and relationships between religious persons and communities. Although matters of topical concern have been discussed, no organization has developed to try and see that recommendations are implemented. Rather, in its conferences and its educational work, the Temple of Understanding has helped people to learn more about faiths other than their own and to break down exclusive attitudes to others.

Meanwhile, the Temple has grown quietly but steadily around the world. Under the leadership of Dr Karan Singh, the India Chapter is developing 'Centres' in the major cities of India. In Japan, Rev. Toshio Miyake of Konko-Kyo Church in Osaka and his grandchildren continue the activities of the Temple of Understanding. The work of Fr Luis Dolan has stimulated interest in Eastern Europe, South America and the Middle East. Yet much remains to be done, if the world is to move closer to the vision of religious fellowship and co-operation.

The Temple of Understanding, like the World Congress of Faiths, points to a unity which transcends the differences of the world religions. The Temple expressly repudiates syncretism and takes a positive view of differences – that they contribute to a richer whole. In his preface to *The World Religions Speak*, Finley Peter Dunne writes of the Temple of Understanding that its purpose is not syncretistic. 'There is no intention of trying to combine any religion with any other, no thought of changing the elements of creed and faith, ritual and scripture, ethics and cultural content that give each religion of mankind its distinctive character. Rather, each religion is honoured . . . for its own unique traditions. The differences . . . are to be cherished, both for themselves and the sanctities and beauties they reveal, and for the insight they give us into the true nature of each of them.'[14] Yet this statement needs to be taken with the words of Thomas Merton, spoken at the First Spiritual Summit Conference in Calcutta, which remain a promise and a challenge. 'My dear brothers, we are already one, but we imagine that we are not. What we have to recover is our original unity. What we have to be is what we already are.'[15]

· 13 ·

World Fellowship, World Thanksgiving and World Interfaith Association

World Fellowship of Faiths

There are several other inter-religious organizations which have an international dimension. Here we will concentrate on three bodies: The World Fellowship of Faiths, World Thanksgiving and the World Interfaith Association.

In 1933, an interfaith gathering was again held at Chicago, in conscious imitation of the 1893 World's Parliament of Religions. From this a continuing body was established, which in 1941, set up The World Fellowship Center near Conway, North Hampshire, USA.[1]

The initiators of the First International Assembly of the World Fellowship of Faiths, which was regarded by its organizers as the Second World's Parliament of Religions, were Charles F. Weller and Kedarnath Das Gupta. In 1918, Weller, who had been a social worker since 1896, started the League of Neighbours. This was a body to help alien groups adapt to and interpret themselves to American society, which often showed little interest in the culture of newcomers. Das Gupta found equally little appreciation of Indian aspirations amongst British people, when he came to England. In 1908, to promote greater sympathy, he organized The Union of East and West and also produced some thirty plays about Indian life. In 1920, when Rabindranath Tagore visited the USA, Das Gupta accompanied him and then stayed on. In 1924 he met Weller and they decided to merge the League of Neighbours and the Union of East and West and to create The World Fellowship of Faiths.

The Fellowship of Faiths arranged meetings in several American cities. At these, representatives of different faiths spoke on such subjects as 'Peace and Brotherhood'. From 1928 to 1932 a quarterly journal, *Appreciation*, was published.

In May 1929 a Fellowship of Faiths meeting was held at Chicago. This revived memories of the 1893 World's Parliament of Religions and the idea emerged of holding a Second Parliament in 1933 to coincide with the Second World Fair, which was then being planned.

Soon preparations began in earnest. By June 1932 letters inviting their participation, signed by Rabbi Stephen S. Wise, were on their way to religious leaders around the world. Any attempt 'to develop a new religion or to unite divergent faiths' was disavowed. 'The all-embracing spiritual Oneness of the Good Life Universal', the letter stated, 'must be accompanied by appreciation for all the indivualities, all the differentiations of function, by which true unity is enriched.'[2]

The main meetings, or 'culminating convention', as it was called, took place from 27 August to 17 September 1933. At these and at the preparatory and supplementary meetings, two hundred and forty-two addresses were delivered by one hundred and ninety-nine 'spokesmen of All Faiths, Races and Countries'. The papers, mostly of a high quality, are collected and condensed in the book called *World Fellowship*, which was edited by Charles Weller.

Considerable attention was paid to contemporary problems, such as economic projects to cure poverty; the position of youth and of sexual and racial discrimination; the problems caused by technological developments; and to the dangers of war and world chaos.

The teaching of the world religions on many matters was described. There was also discussion of other efforts to build up inter-religious and international co-operation. There was a message from Professor Wadia of the International Fellowship of India and from the organizers of the Indian All Faiths League.

Dr Herman Neander, Rector of Esthuna, Sweden, spoke of Rudolf Otto's Inter-Religious League. Otto denied any desire to create an 'esperanto religion'. 'Yet despite the great variety that exists amongst religions, one thing binds them together: the religious character and impulse as such and a common antagonism to materialism and irreligion . . . A silent sympathy attracts the religious to the religious.'[3] Otto hoped that religions might together support efforts for international justice and world-brotherhood and provide the League of Nations with a necessary spiritual foundation.[4] Dr Neander also referred to the plans for a World Conference for International Peace through religion.

Sir Francis Younghusband, who was soon to found the World Congress of Faiths, referred to by Charles Weller as 'The Second International Congress of the World Fellowship of Faiths', spoke on 'Fellowship with the

Universe'. A message was sent by His Holiness Jagadguru Shri Shankaracharya about India's first All Faiths Conference, held in June 1933, in preparation for the Chicago gathering, which he had hoped to attend. The conference voted to set up an All Faiths League.

The organizers were satisfied with the gathering, which had a strong sense of unity. None of the speakers 'assumed that their faith was the one and only way of salvation'.[5] The whole event, Weller believed, would 'help to mark a new world era in human progress', 'contributing towards a fuller realization of worldwide human unity.[6]

The World Fellowship has continued to work for human unity and understanding from its World Fellowship Center, which was founded by Charles Weller in 1941. For the last twenty years the director has been Rev. Dr Christoph Schmauch, a minister of the United Church of Christ, who had previously represented the Christian Peace Conference at the UN. Christoph Schmauch has continued to play an active part in the Christian Peace Conference and a feature of the World Fellowship has been a concern for dialogue with humanists and Marxists. The World Fellowship has wide links throughout the world and in 1989, Christoph Schmauch visited India twice and also attended the WCRP Assembly in Melbourne. The World Fellowship has been one of the first organizations to express support for the Year of Inter-religious Understanding and Co-operation.

To avoid confusion, the World Fellowship needs to be distinguished from another body, The World Fellowship of Religions, which is sometimes called the World Fellowship of Faiths, which was founded in the 1950s by Acharya Sushil Kumarji Maharaj, an eminent Jain leader. In 1957 he convened a World Conference of all religions in New Delhi, which was inaugurated by the President of India. Subsequent interfaith gatherings have been held and the movement supports various welfare programmes.[7]

World Thanksgiving

Early in the sixties some leading citizens in Dallas, Texas, USA, wanted to express the religious feelings of the citizens in a way which was inclusive. The concept of thanksgiving had played an important part in American life and in Dallas itself, Thanksgiving Day had been celebrated publicly at least as early as 1861.[8]

It was agreed to create a garden in the centre of the city and then to build a Chapel of Thanksgiving which would be universal in character and open to everyone. The distinctive and beautiful chapel, designed by Philip Johnson, was opened in 1976, which was the two hundredth anniversary of the country. The following year, the Hall of Thanksgiving was opened by Robert Müller, then Assistant Secretary General of the UN.

Increasingly, World Thanksgiving, led by its energetic and far-sighted founder, Peter Stewart, has developed its educational work and its world outreach. Each year a Thanksgiving Declaration is prepared and signed by twelve spiritual leaders. On one occasion this was presented to the Secretary General of the United Nations and on another to President Bush, to mark two hundred years of Presidential Thanksgivings.

Seminars have been held to see how thanksgiving relates to various aspects of life. The first Harvard seminar explored the concept of thanksgiving in Hinduism, Buddhism and Islam. The second Harvard seminar related to the way in which Christians, Jews and Muslims give thanks. Subsequently, a Convocation of World Thanksgiving was held, led by Cardinal Koening. Distinguished speakers, including the Dalai Lama, the Archbishop of Canterbury, Dr Runcie, and John Templeton, who has endowed the Templeton Prize, have spoken at World Thanksgiving Center. Meetings about Thanksgiving have been held in various places, including the Jerusalem Chamber at Westminster Abbey, during the Vancouver Assembly of the World Council of Churches, and recently, in Liechtenstein. It is hoped to arrange a gathering in Northern Ireland. A book on *Thanksgiving in Islam* by Muhammad Abdul-Rauf has been published.[9]

Thanksgiving has been found to be an unthreatening way for people of different faiths to come together, as they do not have to discuss competing truth claims. World Thanksgiving has therefore made an important contribution in bringing people of different faiths together in a relaxed atmosphere where friendship and trust can grow. World Thanksgiving has also shared in the process of bringing together interfaith organizations and was represented at the World Day of Prayer for Peace at Assisi.

The World Interfaith Association

The World Interfaith Association reflects the energy and devotion of Dr Jacques Fisher. He was born in Breslau, Germany, which is now the Polish city of Wroclaw. The Fisher family, which was Jewish, included many writers, thinkers and statesmen. During the middle of the 1930s, the Fishers settled in Warsaw, where they were later to experience the horrors of life in the Ghetto.

When Dr Fisher's parents were discovered sheltering orphans, they, with the orphans, were sent to the concentration camp at Treblinka, from which they never returned. Jacques Fisher himself was hidden by a Catholic friend of the family. He escaped to Austria, but was later captured by the Nazis and sent to an internment camp. After his liberation by the US army in May 1945, he helped to form a group in Austria, known as 'The Refugee Liaison Committee' to help survivors of the war. He was also working with the UN in Austria in its care for orphans and refugees.

During the sixties, he was mainly concerned with commercial activities in Africa. It was in 1963 that he first met Sir Zafrullah Khan, who was at the time President of the UN General Assembly. Together, they conceived the idea of a world wide interfaith movement. Sir Zafrullah was also to give his support to the World Congress of Faiths and the Temple of Understanding.

The World Interfaith Association has stressed the importance of exploring the common ethical heritage of all religions. As Dr Fisher has said, 'Only through deeper understanding between all religions can the aspiration of humanity towards happiness and harmony be fully realized and the destructive forces of materialism be finally overcome'.[10]

The World Interfaith Association helped to arrange during Pope John XXIII's visit to New York in 1965 for him to address the International Convocation of Peace on Earth. In 1987 the Association sponsored a 'Round Table for Peace' at Geneva. A number of religious leaders, including the Dalai Lama, signed a resolution urging the vital need for world peace.

Dr Fisher has been generous in his support for various interfaith initiatives and has attended a number of important conferences, including the 1989 conference in Costa Rica on 'Seeking the True Meaning of Peace' and the conference on 'War Never Again', held in Warsaw in 1989 at the invitation of Cardinal Josef Glemp, the Archbishop of Warsaw and Primate of Poland.

Dr Fisher is also the founder of The World Association for Orphans and Abandoned Children and a leading campaigner against war toys. He is also hoping to establish a World Interfaith Centre in Jerusalem, where 'people who are true to their own faith' can pool their religious experiences. These many activities are all aspects of what has been called Dr Fisher's 'life-long devotion to the cause of world peace and mutual tolerance'.[11]

· PART III ·

Peace through Religion

'How can religion be made to function for peace?'

· 14 ·

1914–1964

By a sad irony, it was on the very day that the First World War began that one of the earliest interfaith conferences for peace held its first meeting. This tragic coincidence highlights the continuing question that such efforts have had to face. 'Can religions, even if they act together, exert any effective influence on political decisions and events?'

Here the interest is with those interfaith bodies, and in particular the World Conference on Religion and Peace (WCRP), for which the search for world peace has been the dominant concern. The World Congress of Faiths, the International Association for Religious Freedom and the Temple of Understanding have both hoped that their work would contribute to peace and world order, but as a long-term result of a revival of spiritual values. WCRP has, by contrast, tried to enable world religions to have effective political influence. Certainly it has helped to create a new climate of friendship between members of different religions. It has educated some religious leaders in an awareness of contemporary problems. Through it, representatives of world religions have called on humanity to live at peace. They have helped to shape public opinion and so to influence political leaders.

WCRP is the most influential of the interfaith bodies working for peace and has support in all continents. Attention will centre on its work. In part it is the outcome of earlier efforts, especially in the USA and Japan, dating back to early in this century. It will, therefore, be helpful first to consider these developments. They show how those primarily involved in peace-work have become aware of the inter-religious dimension of their endeavours. Their initial motivation is therefore different from those who were prompted to search for unity amidst the diversity of humankind's religious beliefs and practices. These earlier efforts also highlight some of the problems involved in this work.

The Nineteenth Century

The beginnings of interfaith action for peace date to 1914. All religions proclaim the virtues of peace, although most have been perverted to sanction war.[1] The first Christians were pacifists and, within the churches, there have always been peace-makers. After the long Napoleonic Wars, there was a renewed interest in the search for lasting peace. The initiative rested with certain far-sighted individuals. The motivation seems to have been as much ethical and moral as specifically religious. The groups were mainly pacifist. Peace societies were developed simultaneously in England, the USA, where the American Peace Society was formed in 1828, and on the Continent of Europe, especially in France and Switzerland.

At first the peace societies in different countries were rather unrelated. In 1843 the first International Peace Congress was held. Further meetings were held at regular intervals and they focussed attention on a programme of international arbitration as a replacement of war. Charles Bonney, the inspirer of the World's Parliament of Religions, was one of the supporters of these ideas. Gradually, these suggestions percolated the public consciousness.

By the end of the nineteenth century, A.C.F. Beales estimated that there were four hundred and twenty-five peace bodies in the world.[2] Slowly, some churches had become more interested. Suggestions too about a system of international justice were beginning to interest some national leaders. In the first years of this century the US government negotiated a pattern of arbitration with thirteen other nations, but these efforts, known as the Hay treaties, were wrecked by the Senate. Two Conferences were also held at the Hague in 1899 and 1907. They encouraged the growth of international arbitration, but it was not until after the First World War that the Permanent Court of Justice was established.

Charles Macfarland in his *Pioneers for Peace Through Religion*, summarizes the developments in the nineteenth century in this way. 'From 1815 to 1867, the Peace Movement was primarily ethical and essentially religious, but not ecclesiastical. From 1867 to 1890, there was an increasing emphasis on the political aspect, mainly in the form of proposals for arbitration. From 1890 to 1914, peace propaganda became effective in inducing *exploration* by governments. Thus by 1914, while much had been accomplished, the arbitration idea was generalized and had not taken obligatory form. The Hague Tribunal had no clear code of international law. While the concept of a Society of Nations appeared on the horizon there was little or no suggestion of any restrictions or limitation, nor even any definition, of national sovereignty.'[3]

The Church Peace Union

In February 1914 Andrew Carnegie, an industrial magnate, invited some Protestant, Roman Catholic and Jewish representatives to his house to discuss 'how religion can be made to function for peace'. His guests were eminent people and included Dr John Mott, who was to be a leader of the Ecumenical Movement, Dr Mead, a Unitarian from Boston who was Director of the World Peace Foundation, Rev. Charles S. Macfarland, a Congregationalist who was general secretary of the Federal Council of the Church of Christ in America, Rev. Jenkin Lloyd Jones, who was at the time pastor of All Souls Church of Chicago, who had been active at the World's Parliament of Religions and who described himself as an uncompromising pacifist and Hon. Marcus M. Marks, a leading member of the New York Jewish community. Cardinal Gibbons of Baltimore and Rabbi Dr Emil G. Hirsch of Chicago, although not present, had expressed their support for Andrew Carnegie's initiative.

Carnegie, as a Scottish youth, was influenced against the church because of the violence of theological controversy. In later manhood, he was influenced by the Swedenborgians. They fostered his idealism on world peace and his sense of a religious unity which lay beneath theological arguments.[4]

At the meeting at his house in February 1914, Carnegie asked his guests to become trustees of money which he wished to give for the abolition of war. From this came into being the Church Peace Union, in which twelve religious organizations – including Roman Catholic, Protestant and Jewish groups – co-operated. At the time such co-operation was still very unusual. The day after the gathering, Edwin Mead, one of the participants said to Charles Macfarland, who was to become a leader of the Peace Union, 'May not the time come when all religions will unite for peace?'[5]

In August of that year members of the Church Peace Union shared with members of the World Alliance for International Friendship in a conference at Constance in Germany. Sadly, they met there in August 1914, on the very day that war was declared. Despite the dangers, they proceeded with the meeting. A message was read from the Archbishop of Canterbury. Much time was spent in prayer. On the advice of the Mayor of Constance, the meeting was abandoned on the second evening, but not before a continuation committee had been set up, which quickly convened in London. Because of the outbreak of war, some of the delegates had a difficult and dangerous time getting home.

World Conference for Peace through Religion

Although the Church Peace Union continued to keep in touch with other peace organizations, a decade was to pass before the hope of holding an interfaith conference for peace was again suggested. On 11 December 1924, Dr Henry Atkinson, who was General Secretary, presented to the Church Peace Union 'a plan to hold a World Religions Congress on behalf of International Friendship and Goodwill'. The outline suggested forming an international committee of a thousand members, drawn from all religions. They would be invited to serve as individuals, rather than as representatives of a religion. This principle, because of the lack of hierarchical or representative structures within most religions, has been found necessary at almost all interfaith gatherings. The conference, Atkinson suggested, should be autonomous and the committee, when set up, should decide its venue. He tentatively suggested 1930 as a date for the conference. The Church Peace Union accepted the proposal and agreed to shoulder reponsibility for setting up and calling the Congress.[6]

The earliest announcement of the plan is interesting as it shows what its originators had in mind. The representatives, it said, 'will not meet to discuss or compare religions, nor to form a league of faiths, least of all to find a least common denominator of their beliefs. They will assemble in order, if possible, to harness to the cause of international goodwill and peace the spiritual force of all their religious faiths'. The results that were hoped for were that:

1. It might create a clearer knowledge of the record, ideals and attitude of each religion in its relation to world peace.
2. Each religion would be challenged and stimulated to set itself in the best light and to emphasize its noblest ideals and principles.
3. Leaders would be drawn together in a better mutual understanding.
4. A realization of common objectives would help promote unity of spirit and action.
5. There might emerge the possibility of a co-operation, through a loose form of organization, whereby all the religions of the world might exert a united pressure at critical times.[7]

Another document voiced the hope that agreement might be expressed on

1. Human brotherhood as essential to all religions.
2. The fact that world peace could only be established by the recognition of universal brotherhood.
3. The possibility of world religions co-operating by each working in their own sphere for the attainment of these ideals.[8]

Atkinson was asked to seek support for the proposal, especially amongst the religions of the East. Advice was sought from many quarters, including Sir Eric Drummond, who was Secretary General of the League of Nations and from Franklin D. Roosevelt, a future President of the United States. Sponsors in America included Jews, Protestants and Roman Catholics and some people who were not identified with any religious body. There was considerable support, although there was also opposition from some who thought the idea chimerical or utopian and from some Christians who feared that Christian claims would be compromised.

By 1928 Atkinson had got together a preliminary committee which included religious leaders from India, China, Japan, Ceylon, Britain, Sweden, Germany, France, Holland, and the USA. Amongst the religions represented were Christianity, Judaism, Hinduism, Confucianism, Islam, Shintoism, Buddhism and the Baha'i religion as well as the Theosophical Movement.

One hundred and ninety delegates – one hundred and twenty five of them Christian – attended a Preliminary Committee meeting at Geneva in September 1928. Dean Shailer Mathews, an advocate of the Social Gospel, was elected chairman. At the meeting it was decided to call a conference in '1930 if possible'. At the committee meeting various speakers, including Dr Joseph Hertz, Chief Rabbi of the British Empire, the missionary C. F Andrews, who was a friend of Gandhi and Professor Hauer of Germany who was to become leader of the German 'Faith Movement', outlined the fundamentals of their religions. There were some devotional times at which a book of worship was used which had been prepared by Professor Robert Hume, known for his study of the Upanishads. The book of worship contained selections from the sacred scriptures of the world.

The Preliminary Committee adopted a statement of purpose. It said that the conference's sole intention 'will be to rouse and to direct the religious impulses of humanity against war in a constructive worldwide effort to achieve peace . . . The Universal Conference designs neither to set up a formal league of religions, nor to compare the relative values of faith, nor to espouse any political, ecclesiastical, or theological or social system'. The specific objects would be to state the highest teaching of each religion on peace and the cause of war, to record the efforts of religious bodies to further peace, to seek out ways in which people of all religions can work together for peace, and to look for opportunities for concerted action.[9]

The Preliminary Committee elected a central committee of seventy people, which next met at Frankfurt in August 1929. Before that meeting, Atkinson canvassed wide support.

Atkinson visited India, China, Japan, and several other countries. He met Mahatma Gandhi and Rabindranath Tagore. He even managed to set up committees in India, Burma, Ceylon and Japan and discovered at least a dozen groups who were trying to secure similar co-operation. In Japan, especially, the Japan Religious Association had also envisaged a World Conference. On hearing of the American plan, they postponed their own scheme and decided to co-operate with the Church Peace Union. They did, however, in 1928 hold a National Religious Conference, attended by about fifteen hundred people.[10]

In the interval, an administrative committee, appointed by the Central Committee in Geneva, met in Paris in December 1928. At this it was agreed that the Church Peace Union should remain the administrative agency, with Shailer Mathews as chairman and Atkinson as secretary. The Paris meeting also set up a small committee which reported to the Frankfurt meeting of the Central Committee on the preparations required for the conference. Because of the conference's importance, it suggested that the topic 'What can religions contribute to the establishment of Universal Peace' be divided into three issues to be explored separately by three commissions. The three questions to be addressed were:

1. What are the influences in the world that make for war?
2. What are the spiritual resources of mankind with which these influences can be met?
3. How can these resources be set in motion and directed to bear upon the causes of war?

A fourth commission should look at the practical question of how these resources could be activated. The group also recommended that the number of addresses should be strictly limited and that outstanding religious leaders should be invited to preach, where possible, in an appropriate church or synagogue.[11]

The Central Committee, at its Frankfurt meeting in 1929, decided to change the name to World Conference for International Peace through Religion. The proposed date of the conference was deferred to 1931.

At the next Central Committee Meeting at Berne in August 1930, the date was again postponed – this time to 1932. Washington was chosen as the venue. It was now felt that preparations pointed to a 'world-wide movement rather than to the holding of a single meeting'. Other assemblies were envisaged in Geneva and Tokyo. Visitors to the Berne Committee meeting included Rabindranath Tagore and Professor Salvadore de Madariaga of the League of Nations. At the next Central Committee meeting, held at Geneva in August 1931, plans were again both enlarged and deferred.

The Commission reports show a strong desire to submit to the will of God and not to use religion as a 'means'. Considerable attention was given to the relation of religion and education, and also to the attitude of religions to peace and justice and the question of the practical contribution which they can make. It was now thought that effective interfaith committees for peace were needed in local areas. In effect, the work for which the conference was originally envisaged was now seen as a necessary preliminary to holding such a conference. Answers to questions about the contribution of religions to peace and the establishment of local committees were now desired before an international conference should be held. Inevitably, as the scope and the objectives had become so enlarged, the conference was deferred.

Japan

Meanwhile in Japan, a National Religious Conference for International Peace was held in May 1931, with three hundred and forty-five delegates. Addresses were given by the Prime Minister of Japan and by religious leaders. On the third day, at a general meeting, twelve resolutions were adopted unanimously. Part of the main resolution, as it comes from one of the earliest conferences, is worth quoting:

> If all religionists in the world co-operate and do their utmost, then our ideal of a warless world will not only exist in our religious faith but also it will become a matter of practical international affairs. Therefore, we appeal to public opinion at home and abroad, proclaiming our belief and decision:
>
> 1. The Conference declares that we religionists should assume responsibility for the frequent occurrences of war.
> 2. The Conference declares that all religions can and ought to co-operate to bring about international peace, admitting the unique characteristics of each religion.
> 3. It is our conviction that the moral law should govern international relations as well as personal relations . . .
> 7. The Conference hopes for the total removal of all racial and religious discrimination.
> 8. The Conference declares that religionists should take the leadership of the League of Nations and the Treaty for Renunciation of War.

The Conference also urged the establishment of an institute for studying the means and ways of promoting international peace through the co-operation of all religions. It suggested the creation of a permanent religious peace movement to make a world league of religions, and pledged Japan's leadership in such a movement. These high hopes were to be bitterly disappointed by events leading up to and during the second World War. Yet, a few of those involved in the 1931 conference were again to become active in post-war interfaith work for peace, and Japan has indeed become one of the leaders in the World Conference on Religion and Peace, of which the first conference was held in Japan at Kyoto.[12]

Further Delays

It seems that the next meeting of the Central Committee of the World Conference for International Peace through Religion was not held until September 1937, again at Geneva. In the meantime, the international situation had deteriorated and the 'economic debacle on the part of the nations' had made the original plans for the conference impossible. Shailer Mathews had again visited India and the Near East. The agenda centred on the question, 'How can religion function in the field of international affairs?' It was agreed that the conference should be held at an early date, if possible in 1939. Meanwhile regional conferences might begin at once and an approach should be made to the World Alliance for International Friendship to include the findings of the committee in its programme for 1938. In a message, which proved to be the committee's final message, it was affirmed that only religion could create the spirit of goodwill necessary to effect the changes required to create lasting peace. Before a conference was held, the world was plunged into war.

Even so, Charles Macfarland claimed a reserve of strength was gathered by the movement. 'First, new connections and associations have been made between men of goodwill among the religions of East and West, including Britain and India. Secondly, the Executive (or Central) Committee has gathered a fund of experience and information, the want of which, in earlier years, retarded its efforts. There is now a new basis of understanding. Thirdly, the organization of forces will be ready when the moment comes.'[13]

With hindsight, it seems that the efforts were too ambitious. For a conference on the scale and of the scope envisaged, the preliminary preparations were perhaps ideally necessary, but circumstances are never ideal, and if one waits for perfection, one waits for ever. Even so, the smaller committee meetings and preparatory commissions created many fruitful and on-going contacts and produced some useful material – as much perhaps as would have come from a single large isolated conference. Indeed, the failure in fact to convene such a conference may reflect hidden doubts about its value. The question is whether it is best to start from the top with an international conference and hope that from this local initiatives will follow, or whether to be fruitful, local groups are needed first. It seems that the Central Committee increasingly came to recognize the prior need of local groups. The committee also wrestled with the question, which remains the central problem of interfaith efforts for peace: how in practice can religions effectively promote international peace and justice? In the harsh world of power politics, moral exhortation and public opinion are often ignored. Certainly they were not strong enough to stem the fateful tide of violence which was rising in the thirties. Economic depression also worked against the committee. The Christian theological mood had also become less sympathetic to contact with other faiths.

War

The Second World War did not completely extinguish the hope of inter-religious co-operation for peace. In 1943 a statement entitled *Pattern for Peace* was signed in the USA by various religious bodies, including the National Catholic Welfare Conference, the Synagogue Council of America, the Federal Council of the Churches of Christ in America and some Orthodox Christian groups. The statement asserted that Moral Law must govern World Order and that the rights of individuals, of the oppressed, and of minorities should be respected. It called for an International Institution to maintain peace with justice and for inter-national economic co-operation.[14]

In Britain when the Atlantic Charter was proclaimed, Sir Francis Younghusband, the founder of the World Congress of Faiths, arranged a series of meetings on an inter-religious foundation for the Atlantic Charter.[15]

At the San Francisco Conference, which laid the foundations for the United Nations, non-governmental organizations concerned for peace were invited. After the war, the Church Peace Union concentrated on building up support for the United Nations – the USA not having been a member of the League of Nations. The Church Peace Union also went beyond the World Council of Churches in creating links with Roman Catholics and Jews. A committee report, from the late forties, showed that the desire for wider contacts had survived. 'Our leadership must not be exclusively Catholic, or Protestant or Jewish, but must be inspired by a sincere effort to achieve interfaith solidarity in action for world peace.'[16] Yet it was not until the nineteen sixties that significant developments occurred.

It is true that many religious people, in the period after the Second World War, were deeply concerned for peace and there was much discussion about the morality of nuclear weapons. This concern, however, expressed itself primarily through denominational gatherings and state-ments. For example, The World Council of Churches, established in 1948, issued a number of statements through its Commission of the Churches on

International Affairs. The National Council of Churches of Christ in the USA explored in depth some international issues and Pope John XXIII's encyclical, *Pacem in Terris*, gave prominence to Catholic concern, whilst some American Jewish bodies issued statements on contemporary issues. Yet there was no attempt at combined inter-religious activity for peace.

The clientele of the peace movements was restricted to particular groups. The Church Peace Mission worked mainly among Protestants, whilst the Catholic Association for International Peace was, as its name implies, for Catholics. By the mid-sixties, however, the Fellowship of Reconciliation included Catholics and, in the USA, because of the Vietnam War, it was increasingly in contact with Buddhists. The Jewish Dimensions for Peace was a new initiative. The Council of Religion and International Affairs, which was the new name for the Church Peace Union, maintained an interfaith interest and published some material and held a few small conferences. The churches in the fifties and early sixties, however, were basically unconcerned with interfaith dialogue and co-operation.

· 15 ·

Towards the World Conference
on Religion and Peace

The National Inter-Religious Conference on Peace

The first large interfaith meeting for peace to be held in the USA, after the Second World War, did not take place until 1966. The 'National Inter-Religious Conference on Peace', which was held in Washington DC, from 15–17 March, was attended by almost five hundred clergy and lay people.

The first steps were taken by three clergymen from the Boston area: Dr Dana McLean Greeley, who was then President of the Unitarian Universalist Association, Bishop John Wesley Lord, then the Methodist Bishop of Boston and Bishop John J. Wright, who at the time was the Roman Catholic Bishop of Worcester, Massachusetts. They were joined by Rabbi Maurice N. Eisendrath, who was President of the Union of American Hebrew Congregations of New York. The first small committee meeting was held in 1963. Amongst the early associates were Rabbi Balfour Brickner, Msgr Edward G. Murray, who was secretary of the US Inter-Religious Committee on Peace, Bishop Daniel Corrigan, who was the Episcopal Bishop of New York and Dr Homer A. Jack.

Dr Homer Jack who was to become a central character in this story was born in Rochester, New York in 1916. He earned three degrees from Cornell University and also graduated from the Meadville Theological School (Unitarian) at the University of Chicago. Dr Homer Jack, a Unitarian Universalist minister, had worked professionally in race relations. In 1966 he was the Director of the Department of Social Responsibility of the Unitarian Universalist Association of the United States and Canada and a founder member and an Executive Director of SANE, a secular disarmament organization. He was also a member of the secretariat of the National Inter-Religious Conference on Peace. The author of thirteen books, in 1984 he received the Niwano Peace Prize and in 1985, the Adlai Stevenson Award in Chicago. He has throughout his tireless work for peace been actively supported by his wife, Ingeborg.

In January 1965 an exploratory conference was held at the Church Centre for the United Nations. Soon afterwards the organizational form of the conference was conceived. In addition to Rabbi Eisendrath, Dr Greeley, Bishop Lord and Bishop Wright, Bishop John Hines of the Episcopal Chuch and Archbishop Iakovos of the Greek Orthodox Church, agreed to become conference co-chairmen. An executive committee was formed and a secretariat, consisting mainly of denominational executives with special responsibilites in the field of international relations, was set up.

The conference was completely unofficial, sponsored only by the six co-chairmen and other prominent leaders of church and synagogue. A suggestion that religious organizations might participate officially was found to create difficulties and was not pressed. A number of religious groups did, however, contribute to the costs. Prior to the conference, some of the co-chairmen met with U Thant, the Secretary General of the UN. He and Lyndon Johnson, the President of the USA, sent messages of goodwill to the conference.

The conference was primarily a working conference, with three concurrent workshops on 'Living with the Changing Communist World', 'China and Conflicts in Asia' and 'Intervention, Morality and Limits'. Members of the workshops received background papers in advance and a prepared position paper – which in the third group was substantially changed. To be included in the final report, each paragraph or idea in the paper had to be agreed by at least two-thirds of the workshop. Another subcommittee prepared a Conference declaration, which had to be agreed by a three quarters majority. It is interesting to note these ground rules, as one observes the evolution of decision-making mechanisms.

The purpose of the conference, as defined by the co-chairmen, was fourfold:

1. To bring together clergymen and laymen from all peace-oriented viewpoints to discuss the relation of religion to peace.
2. To analyze in depth the basic religious statements on war and peace and on the moral principles in world order, to find parallel moral principles and to seek approximate guidelines.
3. To discuss current problems from the viewpoint of these principles and proximate norms.
4. To analyze existing religious programmes in Washington, at the

UN, on the local level, and in the world community, and to recommend further co-operation so that organized religion can play its role in governmental decisions affecting war and peace.[1]

To what extent were these purposes achieved? Dr Homer Jack mentions amongst the achievements, 'the rich, uninhibited, mature dialogue on some prime questions of our time, communism, China and intervention', 'Substantive recommendations for effecting peace in Vietnam', and 'the experience of working together showed that previous rigidities have been relaxed'. The reports, he claims, justifiably, 'compare favourably with other such statements of policy from governmental and non-governmental groups'. An indirect achievement, he adds, 'was that the publicity about an *inter-religious* conference on peace raised hopes, not only among members of various denominations and faiths, but also among the general public. Many were inspired that church and synagogue could unite, however unofficially, to think through some of the deeply ethical problems of our times, ones that cannot be left solely to governments.'[2] Dr Jack also referred to the problems that the conference uncovered. Some church people were very new to dealing with war/peace issues and there were deep divisions among participants. Others felt that church and synagogue had nothing special to say, although there were signs that some churches were appointing experts with specialized knowledge in these fields. A third problem was that some churchmen, especially evangelicals, refused to attend inter-religious gatherings. It is also true that although called interfaith, the conference participants were predominantly Jewish or Christian.[3]

Besides the discussion of specific issues related to the Communist world and intervention in Vietnam, there was some consideration of the nature of religion's involvement in political matters. A valuable contribution was made by Dr John C. Bennett, a minister in the United Church of Christ, who was President of the Union Theological Seminary. Answering the charge that high matters of state belong 'to the experts or to policy-makers, who live with the changing details of the problems and may have access to classified information' and that religious leaders are outsiders who lack the competence to speak, he argued that there were at least six areas in which 'persons who combine religious perspectives and moral sensitivity with a careful attempt to understand the relevant facts, though not specialist or insiders in the government, have a duty or right to speak'.[4] First, they should call attention to the immediate human consequences of any policy, even if they must also consider the possible human consequences of any change of policy. Secondly, the determination of the goals of policy was a matter of moral choice, and he suggested some such goals. Another area of moral concern was the means used to achieve any or all of these ends. Fourthly, Bennett suggested that religious groups could help the American people see the world as it appeared to peoples in other continents. Another area was in bringing to the fore and questioning the presuppositions of policy, expressed or unexpressed. Finally, churches and synagogues, he suggested, should criticize the false uses of religion and morality, in assumptions about 'a holy war' or 'honour' or 'obligation'.[5]

Other keynote speakers concentrated on specific issues or were content with generalities: but at a luncheon session three leading religious journalists were invited to speak on 'The Limitations and Possibilities of Organized Religion Acting for Peace'. Arthur Moore, editor of the *Methodist World Outlook*, noted that the vast majority of statements by religious groups 'have no effect whatsoever except to make the drafters feel good'.[6] They are not so much scorned as completely ignored and are usually a waste of time. Either such statements are so general – 'We are against war and in favour of peace' – or if they try to be specific they reveal deep divisions amongst religious people. If such differences are merely papered over, the statement loses any weight. There was also the question of authority. In whose name were statements made? Moore ended by saying, 'We must begin to realize that it is not our role to give the world answers that we already possess, but to join with the world in searching for the answers – in trying to find the connection between the great ethical insights that we proclaim and the events, ominous and confusing, taking place in the world today.'[7]

It is significant that although the fact that the conference was interreligious attracted public attention, those attending were less concerned to congratulate themselves on meeting than to concentrate on specific issues. To some extent, the 1966 conference had still to assert the right and duty of religious leaders to have this interest. Now, nearly twenty five years later, it is common to hear expressions of opinion on contemporary and controversial issues by religious leaders. International public opinion has become increasingly significant, partly because of the continuous growth in media coverage of world news. Yet the vital question of what impact religious people can in practice have on world affairs has persisted and underlies the attempts of The World Conference on Religion and Peace[8] and other bodies to become increasingly relevant.

Towards Kyoto

The declaration issued by the 1966 National Inter-Religious Conference on Peace suggested the need for a 'world inter-religious conference on peace in 1967, encompassing participation of all the world's religious traditions'.[9] 1967 proved to be far too soon, but by October 1970, such a conference was in session.

The US Inter-Religious Committee on Peace, which had been considerably strengthened by the 1966 conference, soon afterwards asked Rev. Herschel Halbert of the Department of Christian Social Relations of the Episcopal Church and Dr Homer Jack to visit some world religious leaders to explore the possibility of a world conference. After a major world tour, they reported back to the committee in April 1967. Since 1945, they said, there had been no large scale effort to bring together religious leaders of the major world religions to discuss substantively the problems of world peace. The need to convene such a gathering was widely felt, but the task of organizing it was formidable. It involved, at least, the following problems:

1. Bringing the leaders of the world religions to the same stage of readiness to talk substantively about the issues of world peace.
2. Finding a site which would be politically and religiously neutral.
3. Securing balanced initial sponsorship so that the conference would not be dominated either by United States religious leaders or Judeo-Christian leaders.
4. Obtaining funds to pay the international travel costs of many, if not most, of the delegates.[10]

It was also suggested that a preparatory symposium would be necessary to plan the large world conference. This might be held in New Delhi, with perhaps the Gandhi Peace Foundation as co-sponsor or in Tokyo, with an *ad hoc* inter-religious committee as co-sponsor.

After discussion, it was agreed to hold the seminar in India, in conjunction with the Gandhi Peace Foundation of which Sri G. Ramachandran, a Member of the Indian Parliament, was then chairman. It was also decided to send a representative delegation, prior to the conference, to make an official call on the World Council of Churches in Geneva, on the Vatican in Rome and on the Ecumenical Patriarchates in Istanbul and Jerusalem. After the symposium the American team visited Saigon and then shared in a Japanese-American Inter-religious Consultation on peace in Kyoto. The American team, gathered by Rev. Herschel Halbert, included Dr Ralph D. Abernathy, a close associate of Martin Luther King, Jr, as well as Rabbi Eisendrath, Dr Greeley and Bishop Lord.

The New Delhi Symposium, 1968

The New Delhi Symposium began with a Gandhian religious service, with material from several religious traditions. Dr Zakir Husain, a Muslim who was then President of India – and also a Vice-President of the World Congress of Faiths – welcomed the delegates. Keynote addresses were given by Bishop John Wesley Lord and Sri Jayaprakash Narayan, the veteran Sarvodaya worker, who was scathing in his comments on religions in India. 'They do not seem to be even concerned with the questions of peace.'[11]

An important part of the symposium was the discussion on the sanctions for peace within the respective religious traditions. The papers were of an unusually high standard. Swami Ranganathananda, of the Ramakrishna Mission, who was also to be a participant in the Temple of Understanding's Second Spiritual Summit Conference in Geneva in 1970, claimed that 'the concept of man upheld in Hinduism is the most vital source of its sanctions for peace. The discovery, by the sages of the Upanishads, of the true nature of man as the Atman, the immortal divine self, and its unity with Brahman, the infinite self of all beings, constitutes the greatest single source of the universality and humanism of Hinduism and its perennial sanction for peace'.[12] Professor K. G. Saiyandain, a member of the Asian Institute of Educational Planning and Administration in New Delhi, explained the limited circumstances in which Islam permitted war and the stringent conditions laid down to control it. Rabbi Eisendrath spoke of the passion for peace in Judaism and was guarded in his comments on Israel.

Dr Gopal Singh, then a member of Parliament and who was also a Vice-President of the World Congress of Faiths, author of several books on Sikhism, spoke of the Sikh reverence for truth from any quarter. He quoted the words of the third Guru Amar Das, 'The world is on fire. Save it, O God, save it in Thy mercy through whichever door it cometh to Thee'.[13] John Burt, Bishop coadjutor of Ohio, suggested four ways in which Christians could work for peace with members of other religions. They should together denounce national idolatry, suggest non-violent ways to overcome poverty, racism and oppression, find ways of developing and using the world's resources for human good and stress the unity of all people under God. The Ven. Baddeema Wimalawansa Theo, Principal of the Sri Lanka Vidyalaya in Colombo, quoted the tenfold virtues which the Buddha said should be adhered to by every ruler and indicated their contemporary application. Dr Bool Chand, who was director of the Ahimsa Shadh-Peeth in New Delhi, spoke of the teaching of *ahimsa* (non-violence) in Jainism. There were also talks about Zoroastrianism by Dastoor N. D. Minochehr-Homji from Bombay and about the Hindu Vira

Shaivite teaching by Jagadguru Shri Gangadhar Rajayogeendra Mahaswamiji Moorusaviramath.

Another session, appropriately as it was the Gandhi Centenary, was devoted to the 'Relevance of Gandhi as a Religious Force for Peace'. Before the session, participants had visited Rajghat, the national shrine where Gandhi's body had been cremated. Attention was also given to what organized religious groups were doing for peace. There was a moving address by the Civil Rights leader, Ralph David Abernathy. Angelo Fernandes, Archbishop of New Delhi, who was to take a leading role in WCRP, spoke of the work of the Second Vatican Council, whilst Rev. Riri Nakayama, of the Hozenji Buddhist Temple in Tokyo, told of peace work in Japan. Jambel D. Gomboev, who was chairman of the Religious Board of Buddhists in the USSR, spoke about the position of Buddhists in his country.

Part of the symposium was spent in three simultaneous panels on Social and Economic Development, Freedom and Human Rights and Peace-Making and Peace-Keeping. Only the third of these moved beyond generalities, with, as one result, producing a note of dissent from Jambel D. Gomboev of the USSR. The symposium Message is also very general, but it was significant that it was agreed by members of so many religions. Dr Greeley, in his assessment, says there was real dialogue without syncretism or the hiding of differences. The lack of Shintoists, of Muslims from outside India, of Africans and Latin Americans was a weakness.[14]

Two sessions were devoted to the question of a world conference. Dr Homer Jack, after recalling pre-war attempts, outlined above, suggested the major purposes of convening a world conference on religion and peace. 'The first purpose would be to acquaint the leaders of the world religions with the sanctions and traditions each major religion has within it for world peace and for more just international relations . . . We still know too little about each other's religions . . . A second purpose would be to ascertain if, indeed, there are principles or middle axioms on international relations and peace which we do have in common . . . and which would take priority over our differing national entanglements. Another purpose would be to discuss several specific international problems from the viewpoint of certain provisional, common religious principles in the effort toward common action. A fourth purpose would be to show the world's people that world religions are indeed alive to the problems of peace in this world, as well as to the eternal problems of the spirit. The final purpose of a world conference would be to develop a corps of co-workers across religious and national lines, who might be called upon, indeed mobilized, in any international emergency. They could take action for peace, such as issuing joint statements or participating in joint deputations in specific crises, doing so irrespective of their particular religion or nationality, but from the perspective of their religions.'[15]

Dr Jack also mentioned likely difficulties. Even so, it was agreed to form an Interim Advisory Committee, which asked Archbishop Fernandes to take the chair. The idea was welcomed when the American delegation met with religious peace workers in Japan. The Committee, which in 1969 was replaced by the Preparatory Committee, agreed to work for a world conference in late 1969 or early 1970. The Japanese agreed to hold preparatory conferences to ensure full Japanese participation.

Planning for Kyoto, 1970

At the Interim Committee's second meeting in Istanbul in February 1969, Archbishop Fernandes was named President and Dr Dana McLean Greeley, who had been active from the beginning and Rev. Nikkyo Niwano, were elected chairmen. Other co-chairmen were to be Dr R. R. Diwakar, of the Gandhi Peace Foundation, Rabbi Eisendrath, Professor Mahmud Husain, Bishop Lord and Bishop Wright, who later became a Cardinal. Rev. Toshio Miyake of Japan, was elected treasurer. Dr Homer Jack was named secretary-general, with Rev. Shuten Oishi of Japan and Sri G. Ramachandran of India as joint secretaries. The Japanese invitation to hold the conference in Kyoto was accepted and a budget of $300,000 was set.

Following the Istanbul meeting, an international office was opened in Boston. Further contacts were made with religious leaders. For a time there was a hope that Pope Paul VI might visit the conference, but fears of Japanese student demonstrations discouraged this. Several Vatican secretariats, however, continued to be interested and supportive. Initial contacts at the World Council of Churches, when the American mission visited Geneva, were disappointing. The WCC attitude to interfaith dialogue was, however, about to change, with the appointment of Dr Stanley Samartha, from Bangalore, to head its new Sub-Unit on Dialogue with People of Other Faiths and Ideologies. Dr Eugene Carson Blake, the General Secretary, agreed to speak at the conference and three staff members of WCC attended. The Archbishop of Canterbury showed no interest.[16]

The Preparatory Committee met in Kyoto in December 1969. To try to ensure balanced and representative attendance, a quota system for delegates, according to continents and religions was agreed. This has been a continuing feature of WCRP conferences. Dr Jack was asked to undertake a round-the-world trip to recruit delegates. To ensure that a message emerged from the conference, an Interim Message Committee was appointed. After some debate, it was decided that each plenary session would open with a prayer service. Because the conference hall was a 'public' building, it was agreed that these should not be full acts of worship, but the offering of public prayers. Each major religious tradition represented at the conference would be responsible for one of these prayer services. To avoid any suggestion of syncretism, the prayers were to be strictly of the tradition offering them.[17] The Preparatory Committee also worked out ways by which the conference should be self-governing and plans were made to ensure full press coverage.

The Japanese office was opened in May 1970 in Fumon Hall in western Tokyo, in space donated by Rissho Kosei Kai. In June, the international office moved there and only moved to Kyoto on the eve of the conference.

The original Exploratory Mission in 1967 had identified four problems: where to meet, how to ensure that all delegates were equipped to participate, how to avoid a preponderance of Christian and/or Western delegates and where to find travel costs for delegates. The choice of venue was easiest. Japan was politically acceptable to all states and the Japanese government agreed in advance to give visas to all overseas delegates validated by the Secretary-General, even if the delegate's country of origin was not recognized by the Japanese government. To help delegates reach a similar level of understanding of the issues to be discussed, the Preparatory Committee agreed that a pre-conference study packet was to be prepared well in advance and be sent to each registrant. US religious leaders clearly played an important role in preparing for the conference, but to avoid domination by them, Indian and Japanese committees were also involved in the work. The willingness to subsidize travel costs for delegates from Asia, Africa and Latin America, helped to ensure a reasonable balance at the conference and reduced 'cultural imperialism'. Finance was largely dependent on the generosity of the Japanese and American committees. Of the estimated $300,000 budget, the Japanese and Americans each offered to raise a third. It was hoped that religious leaders in other countries would raise the remaining third, but this did not happen. As a result, the conference was almost entirely financed by Americans and Japanese: but not, despite rumours, by the CIA or Japanese government. 'This world conference is being paid for solely by private funds, overwhelmingly from religious groups. No government or political party has contributed funds.'[18]

The criteria had been met sufficiently to make it possible to go ahead with the conference. Some fifty years after the idea was mooted at the Church Peace Union, an inter-religions conference on peace was in session.

· 16 ·

The WCRP Assemblies

Kyoto, 1970

The first Assembly of the World Conference on Religion and Peace began in Kyoto on Friday 16 October 1970. Earlier in the week, several Japanese academic institutions together arranged a Consultation on Inter-religious Dialogue, with reference to peace. The opening session of the Assembly, which some 2,000 visitors watched from the galleries, began with Buddhist prayers and messages of greeting. After an election of officers, Archbishop Fernandes gave his presidential address. Later in the morning, Sir Zafrulla Khan spoke on 'The Fundamentals of Peace'. In the afternoon, Dr Homer Jack spoke on the background and purposes of the conference. After certain business matters, participants met in simultaneous groups, according to their religion.

On the Saturday morning addresses were given by Dr Hideki Yukawa, a Nobel Laureate in physics, on 'The Creation of a World Without Arms' and by Professor Zwi Werblowsky, who was Professor of comparative religion at the Hebrew University, Jerusalem. The participants then went to one of three simultaneous commissions (or workshops) on either disarmament, development, or human rights. In the afternoon, Dr Eugene Carson Blake, of the World Council of Churches, spoke on 'Development' – the theme of one of the commissions. Later, there was a panel on peace action, in which Dr Blake, Dr Ralph D. Abernathy, President of the Southern Christian Leadership Conference, and the Venerable Thich Thien Minh, Vice-President of the Executive Council of the Unified Buddhist Church of South Vietnam, participated.

Sunday was spent in the respective commissions. In the evening some participants met according to nationality. On Monday delegates went on a day tour to Nishi Honganji Temple, the Tenrikyo headquarters, Todaiji Temple and to Heian Jinga Shrine. On the Tuesday the three commissions met for the last time. Later, there were five panels on more practical aspects of peace-work. In the afternoon, Archbishop Helder Camara of Brazil spoke on 'Religions and the Need for Structural Changes in Today's World'. The three commission reports and the conference message were given a first reading, but not debated.

On the sixth and final day, 21 October, the commission reports were debated and approved, although only after heated discussion on the Middle East. The conference message was approved and also the report of the Follow-Up Committee, with its plans for a continuing body. The Buddhist peace-worker, Venerable Thich Nhat Hahn gave a closing summary and critique, which he called 'Saved by Man'.

Underlying the discussion of specific issues, the question of the practical impact of religion on world affairs kept bubbling to the surface. Dr Blake, having said that traditional religious attitudes sometimes stood in the way of development, suggested the positive contribution that religious communities could make. They could add their views to the 'current debate on the meaning and goals of development – and to the search of different societies for new cultural foundations and a new ethos'.[1] They should educate their followers to be aware of humankind's interdependence and the need for justice. Professor Werblowsky, critical of religions' record in the field of peace, said that the mere citing of 'peace-texts' was of little value. Inner peace, too, was not enough. 'The salvation of the world through the transformation of all hearts is an eschatological concept and not a social programme'.[2] He looked at the possible conflict between justice and peace and pointed to the variety of social attitudes within even one religious tradition. Delegates at the conference should be clear that they were using the term religion in a selective and prescriptive sense. Religionists, he warned, 'have to guard against two subtle dangers: the danger of getting intoxicated with their own verbiage, and the danger of overestimating the significance of what they are doing'.[3] There was also the danger that the nearer religionists came to the centres of power, 'the more they get caught in the inevitable ambiguities of compromise and of the political game . . . and generally of walking – like Agag – very delicately'.[4]

'The Kyoto Conference', he went on, 'will be more than a wasteful exercise if instead of producing high-sounding declarations of principles, or beautiful phrases about peace, brotherhood, freedom and human rights, or making the participants "feel good", it will succeed, in its group discussions and commissions, in addressing itself to the task of isolating problem areas, assessing their dynamics as well as the extent to which the dynamics of religion can impinge on them and interact with them, and sketching out concrete modes of action both inside the religious world and in the contact of the latter with other sectors of society . . . Ultimately, it is not to the world but to themselves that religionists have to send a message . . . The challenge for religionists is not what to say, but how to be.'[5] This was a useful reminder of the two constituencies that religious peace workers have to address: their own religious communities and the secular world. Dr Abernathy stressed the need for religious people to speak out in the name of the poor and oppressed – and the suggestion that religious bodies should be the 'voice of the voiceless' has become quite common. Archbishop Camara hoped that 'if the religions of the world get together to support Action for Justice and Peace, something that seems absurd may become possible, what seems utopian may become a reality'.[6]

In the Kyoto Declaration, delegates expressed their deep conviction that the religions of the world have 'a real and important service to render to the cause of peace'. They listed the convictions that they had in common, such as belief in the unity of the human family and the equality, dignity, and sacredness of each individual and the profound hope that good would finally prevail. Confessing that religious people had often betrayed their ideals, they referred to the grave problems of the world that had been discussed. Speaking as individuals, but in the name of 'the powerless whose voice is seldom heard', they insisted on the fact that 'men and all their works are now united in one destiny'. Promising to educate public opinion to be aware of mankind's unity and of the futility of war, they expressed their backing for the United Nations.[7]

The Commissions were more specific. The report on disarmament outlines the steps needed to reduce the threat of war. The internationalism and commitment to non-violence are obvious. The Human Rights commission pointed to the sufferings of various oppressed and minority groups, whilst the report on development is a sensitive treatment of the issue. In effect, however, they all see the major role of religions in influencing public opinion, by spreading information about the real situation in the world and by deepening a sense of human unity. The Youth Commitee said young people 'are beginning to get sceptical of conferences which merely pass pious resolutions without formulating programmes of action. Therefore, to prevent this conference becoming another high failure, we recommend that the continuation committees immediately draw up programmes of action which will be implemented immediately'.[8] It was, indeed, in the work of the Continuation Body that the conference was to have a lasting influence. The achievements of the conference itself were considerable and it gave to the Continuation Body its mandate.

Kyoto's Achievements and Disappointments

As the long history of efforts to convene such a conference shows, the fact that it took place at all was a great achievement – only possible through the immense hard work and dedication of a few people, notably Dr Homer Jack. The reports show good temper, widespread agreement, a forward-looking attitude to religion, and real concern for the issues of the day. The religious leaders who attended were of a high quality and there was a good balance. There were over two hundred delegates and all major world religions were represented. Although the ninety-six Christians were the largest group, they were not in a majority. There were one hundred and twenty members of other faiths. The one hundred and thirty-nine Asian and African delegates easily outnumbered the seventy-seven Westerners. With visitors, journalists and others, more than one thousand people were involved in the conference. Another achievement, mentioned, by Dr Homer Jack, was the mature facing of the Vietnam War. He mentions also two by-products. 'One was that religionists in several countries, notably Japan and India, developed a co-operative relationship among themselves.'[9] The other was a glossary of words and phrases on international relations for Japanese speaking delegates and on Japanese religions for Westerners.

Dr Jack mentions some disappointments. The fears that too few Hindus and Muslims would attend came true. Those who came were often from an academic background, rather than influential in the life of a faith community. This was partly because of a lack of funds to subsidize travel and partly because not enough work had been done to identify delegates. The death, on the eve of the conference, of President Nasser of the United Arab Republic may have prevented Muslims coming from Egypt. It may be that the Hindu and Muslim worlds failed to appreciate the significance of the conference. The same may be said of the lack of Western European Protestants. Twenty-one West Europeans attended, of whom only five were Protestant. The Church of England was not represented. There were too few women and too few young people. No one came from China, even though deliberately, no one had been invited from Taiwan or South Korea. The fact that finance came almost entirely from the American and Japanese committees, with small gifts from IARF and the Inter-Religious Organization in Singapore – showed a narrow basis of interest and support. The lack of worldwide publicity was disappointing. There was good media coverage in Japan, but little elsewhere. Another disappointment was that some delegates 'appeared to be of nation states first and only second, adherents of a religious faith'.[10]

The Venerable Thich Nhat Hanh, in his concluding critique, judged the conference a success. Fears that it would be dominated by Christians and Westerners had proved unfounded. Nor had it been too political and too little religious. Various peace groups had made useful contacts. There had been tensions, but none likely to break up the conference. 'Religious discrimination and ideological conflicts were not considerable, were not deeply felt.'[11] He found the commission reports more specific and advanced than he had expected. There were, however, weaknesses, especially that, 'the schedule is too tight'.[12] This, he said, did not allow sufficient time to get to know each other in depth. The balance between length of time and cost is always difficult and too few big conferences allow for small enough groups, although meal times allow for personal conversations. Thich Nhat Hanh wondered also whether 'the Grand Hotel was too chic for peace workers'.[13]

Thich Nhat Hanh's remarks highlight the tension between the need to produce documents at such a conference and the desire to develop individual friendships. The latter are often what one remembers afterwards, although the documents are important for further lobbying on the issues discussed. They can be presented to the United Nations, to governments and to religious bodies and a response called for. Their production can, however, dominate discussion. I felt at the second conference at Louvain – the first WCRP Assembly that I attended – that the voting on verbal amendments, in a Commission of over one hundred people, hindered real discussion of the issue in hand. At Melbourne, far more was left to the commission's drafting group which noted suggestions made. This is perhaps a measure of the rapport and trust that has developed.

Louvain, 1974

The pattern set by Kyoto has been maintained, with modifications, at subsequent assemblies. An International Preparatory Committee met at Louvain, or Leuven, Belgium, in March 1974. Again an international secretariat was formed. The budget was set at $185,000, half of which was to be used to subsidize travel for delegates from Asia, Africa and Latin America. The money came almost entirely from Japan, America and Western Europe – the latter mostly from Catholic sources. The choice of Louvain helped to increase European participation, but only from thirty-five to forty-two, although the overall number of delegates was smaller – one hundred and seventy-three as compared to two hundred and nineteen at Kyoto. The number of fraternal delegates increased considerably from nine to thirty-one. Asians still made up the largest group with eighty-one delegates, many from Japan. Seventy-three delegates were Christians and there were about twenty each of Hindus, Buddhists and Muslims.

There were fewer speeches – only from Cardinal Suenens of Belgium, the Ven Thich Nhat Hanh and Archbishop Fernandes, as chairman. Cardinal Suenens, on the opening day, 28 August 1974, indicated that the conference was not directly for dialogue, but for looking together at the fundamental needs of humanity. In his opening address, he stressed both the unity of the world and its inequalities. Religions were an inestimably fruitful force, he said, for humanizing mankind. Archbishop Fernandes also spoke of the many problems facing mankind and of the disappointments of the early seventies. 'The first development decade was a flop; UNCTAD III (The United Nations Conference on Trade and Development) as good as a failure. The year 1971 brought in the international monetary crisis . . . There has been war and skirmishes.'[14] The conference theme 'Religion and the Quality of Life' was urgent and appropriate, because the current malaise was 'a moral and spiritual one affecting the whole of man and all mankind'.[15] 'It will have to be a deeper understanding of religion that can meet today's challenges: one's prayerful regard for God not turning our eyes away from worldly tasks but sharpening our vision of what must be done. The quality of man's life in the last quarter of the century depends among other things on whether the spirit of religion, as concretized in prayer and contemplation, can establish an active link with life as it is and with the caravan of history'.[16] Archbishop Fernandes then looked at some areas of special concern.

Thich Nhat Hanh, in part reiterating his critique at Kyoto, said, 'It is *not* for producing more papers that we have come to Louvain. Documents, even the most perfect ones, are not sufficient to make peace. It is our way of life, arising from the spirit of love and understanding and co-operation, that will make peace.'[17] We have come to encounter each other, as people, people who have truly lived our religious life' – with the opportunity at the conference to live the religious life of others.[18]

Participants spent most of their time in four simultaneous commissions, on disarmament, development, human rights and on environmental issues, and in two working parties, one on population and the other on religious freedom, and also in six panel discussion groups. Despite Thich Nhat Hanh's words, a lot of time was spent in producing documents. There was time to meet others over meals and on the day tour which began at the Breendonk concentration camp, near Antwerp, and which then visited the First World War graves and memorial at Ypres, and concluded with a civic reception at Bruges. Prayer services were again held, although many found the presence of photographers disruptive. The conference concluded with a moving convocation in St Peter's Church, Louvain. Before this, participants walked for a mile through the ancient city to draw attention to the needs of the flood-stricken people of Bangladesh. The convocation included various prayers, a message from a Youth Conference at Taize, the reading of the Louvain Declaration and closing prayers led by Father Paul Verghese, now better known as Metropolitan Paul Mar Gregorios, which began:

> Lord of the Universe!
>
> Lord of all mercy and grace!
> Fountain of all good!
> Ground of all being!
> We invoke Thee by many names,
> Allah, Parmeshwar, Satchidanand,
> Ahura Mazda, Adonai Elohenu,
> God our Father. Father of us all,
> Thou art good, Thou art all good,
> Thou alone art all good.
> Unto Thee we bow our heads,
> In thy presence we bend our proud necks.
> OM SHANTIH, SHANTIH, SHANTIH,
> SALAM, SHALOM SHLOMO.[19]

The Declaration began by recalling that 'of all the things learned at Kyoto, none has marked us more deeply than the discovery that the integrity of the commitment of each to his own religious tradition permits, indeed nurtures, loving respect for the prayer and faithfulness of others'. Hoping that the 'long era of prideful, and even prejudicial, isolation of the religions of humanity is gone forever, we are resolved henceforth to serve humanity together each in the way most in keeping with the convictions of his spiritual family and local circumstances'.[20] Calling on governments to stop the proliferation and increase in nuclear weapons, the Declaration confessed that 'we have not known how to mobilize religious people so that they might contribute effectively to the prevention of even limited local or civil wars'.[21] Different views on the use of violence were recognized, but respect for conscientious objectors was called for. 'Liberation Plus Development Equals Peace' is the heading of a section of the Declaration. 'We have come to see human liberation, economic development and world peace as a dynamic triangular process.'[22] There is concern for basic human rights and a call for religious bodies to avoid entangling political alliances.

The environmental crisis was also discussed and it is interesting how early inter-religious conferences were in giving attention to this. Delegates pleaded 'with our religious communities to evoke among their peoples a fresh sense of awe before the mystery of existence and a recovery of the values of humble self-restraint in the conduct of personal and social life. We appeal to the religious communities of the world to inculcate the attitude of planetary citizenship, the sense of our human solidarity in the just sharing of the food, the energy, and all the material necessities of existence which our generous habitat provides.'[23]

The Declaration is a sensitive document. Whilst concentrating on central and urgent issues, it is self-critical and avoids the tone of a superior lecture to the world, which such statements sometimes adopt. The reports of the commissions are also carefully thought out.

Princeton, 1979

The third Assembly was held at Princeton, New Jersey, from 29 August to 7 September 1979 – rather longer than previous assemblies. Forty-seven countries and ten major religions and a broad spectrum of 'fraternal delegates' were represented by the three-hundred and fifty-four participants. Princeton was unquestionably the most representative gathering of WCRP to that date and provided an important platform for religions to address the political and economic needs of the world. For the first time, there were delegations from the USSR and the People's Republic of China.

There was a 'New York Day', with a procession to a multi-religious service at St Patrick's Cathedral, at which Cardinal Cooke spoke, and a gathering at the United Nations headquarters, at which Secretary-General Kurt Waldheim made a brief address. There was also a 'Washington Day' which included a reception for delegates by President and Mrs Carter. Speakers at the conference included Mr A. K. Brohi, a former cabinet minister of Pakistan, on 'The Contribution of Islam to the problems of World Peace', Swami Chidananda, of the International Divine Life Society at Rishikesh, on 'Hinduism and Its relevance to WCRP', Rev. Jesse Jackson, a civil rights leader who was later to seek the Democratic nomination for the Presidency, on 'Our Religious Mission', Senator George McGovern, who had once stood for President, Andrew Young, the US Ambassador to the UN, Zwi Werblowsky, Congressman Robert F. Drinan and by Archbishop Fernandes, Dr Greeley and Dr Homer Jack.

Archbishop Fernandes, as President of WCRP, spoke of the need for WCRP to sharpen its focus. From the outset, it had been an exercise in a 'supportive, common enterprise of world-building at economic, social, cultural and political levels but inspired by beliefs and ultimate attitudes to life'.[24] 'Religious dialogue', he said, 'does not necessarily mean that two persons speak about religious experiences, but rather that they speak as religiously committed persons with their ultimate commitments and religious outlook on subjects of common interest.' He quoted from one of the speakers at Kyoto who had said they were engaged 'in contributing to a very definite concept of religion and to a new concept of fellowship. The new – and prescriptive – concept of religion implies that whatever else religion may be, it loses its authenticity and credibility if it ignores its social responsibility'.[25] WCRP, Archbishop Fernandes said, was 'an exercise in applied religion . . . trying to create a unity of conscience or, if you prefer, a universal conscience around the basic convictions shared by all living faiths'.[26] Religion had an integrating role, in which the 'inner work' was as necessary as the outer.[27] Religions must question the emphasis on growth and wealth creation.[28]

Dr Greeley asked bluntly whether delegates genuinely accepted the principle of inter-religious co-operation. 'Can even we honestly put the causes of religion, peace and humanity on a par at least with our own church or faith?'[29] He bewailed the 'selfish religious institutionalism, what I call even religious idolatry and chauvinism, that I see so prevalent in so many quarters in the contemporary scene. If we think national idolatry is bad is not religious idolatry worse?'[30] He said WCRP was 'challenged to overcome the ethical indifference and the sense of helplessness alike that among religious people stand in the way of the realization of a better world here and now'.[31]

Dr Homer Jack, for the first time giving a substantive address at an Assembly, spoke with characteristic forthrightness on 'The New Abolitionism'. He suggested a seven point programme for a great new crusade to say 'no' to nuclear war. It should make clear the absolute moral rejection of nuclear arms and suggest practical steps by which the world community might rid itself of its massive stockpiles.[32]

The Rev. Jesse Jackson had recently returned from South Africa and voiced the sufferings of the blacks. 'When dogs bite children in Soweto, deep down in South Africa, we must bleed all over the world.'[33] He called for action by the American government to bring pressure on South Africa.

The published *Findings* summarize the work of its three commissions and three seminars. The Commissions were on 'Religion and International Economic Justice', 'Religion and International Security' and 'Religion and Human Dignity, Responsibility and Rights'. The seminars were on 'Religion, Education and Peace Commitment', 'Strengthening the Spiritual Dimensions' and on 'Multi-Religious Dialogue and Action in Conflict Situations'.

The contents of the *Findings* demonstrate two significant developments within the WCRP: its continuing politicization and its initial exploration of religion *per se*, or 'our common spiritual foundations in the formulation and formation of world community'.[34]

The Princeton Declaration encapsulates especially the political and economic conclusions of WCRP III. A strong stand was taken against arms proliferation, especially of nuclear weapons. 'A global, moral, and religious campaign which will say NO to ANY KIND OF WAR BETWEEN NATIONS OR PEOPLES is our call to governments, religious groups, and all men and women of conscience and faith.'[35] Equally strong statements were made in favour of human rights and against religious intolerance. The importance of religious education for peace was stressed. Sexual and racial discrimination and apartheid were condemned. There was a call for a new, just and equitable economic order. Concern was voiced for the rights of conscientious objectors to military service. Conservation of natural resources was stressed and there was a call for 'a style of human life in harmony with all of nature'.[36]

A theme of approval of and correspondence to certain ethical concerns of and resolutions pending before the UN is clear in the Declaration. This showed the degree to which WCRP, as a Non-governmental organization (NGO), was influential at the UN. The New York offices of WCRP are opposite to the UN building.

Dr Homer Jack soon afterwards assessed the strengths and weakness of the Princeton Assembly. It was more representative and, even if Western Christians still seemed to dominate, there were larger Japanese and Indian delegations. More of the delegates were members of local WCRP committees, so the conference was less 'a collection of individuals'. The Assembly seemed ready for co-operative service and action projects. The ten member Chinese delegation played a creative role – it was the first time that any of the delegation had left China since 1950. Participants dealt better with 'persisting problems of religious nomenclature or semantics . . . With sensitivity to Buddhists and some others, participants tended to use the terms, truth and the transcendent, in Assembly statements more than the word, God'.[37] Participants were also ready to criticize their own religious institutions. In a background paper, Dr Stanley Samartha had said that 'too often religions are part of the problem', whilst one seminar admitted that 'comparing our faith with practice, we confess our failure as religionists to be clear channels through which this vital force can flow' and continued, 'too often religiosity has led to a religious power closed to the problems of the world'.[38]

The disappointments that Dr Homer Jack mentions were, first, that the findings 'may not be as sharp and striking as those of the two previous conferences'. Despite good preparatory papers, 'the resultant output appears competent, but hardly notable'.[39] Then, the Assembly failed to study and make judgments on that 'which it should have been able to do best: those conflict situations in the world which, at least in part, are based on religion'.[40] It was hard, he says, to recruit participants from Northern Ireland or the Middle East. The conference failed to attract adequate funds from religious groups or from foundations and had to be run 'on the cheap'. The media coverage was disappointing and few reporters came to Princeton. The arrival of the Chinese delegation gave excellent advance publicity but it was not followed up. It had been hoped to run a parallel conference for visitors, but this did not prove possible. Another disappointment at all the first three world conferences was 'the inability of some participants, although still a minority, to put international justice above national practices . . . The goal in the future as in the past, is for participants from religious organizations to attempt to put universal values above parochial national ones, however difficult it may be for all.'[41]

Princeton differed from the previous assemblies in certain ways. There were more Muslims. More attention was devoted to the spiritual aspects of religion. Mr Brohi and Swami Chidananda both gave a lot of information about the teaching of their respective religion. The Swami stressed the important role that WCRP could play in projecting an accurate image of a religion.[42] One seminar was specifically on spirituality. More attention had been given to thinking about the purposes and pattern of religious services. There was a little more free time for participants and the Assembly itself was longer, although the ten day duration may have discouraged some people from coming. Fewer prominent religious leaders attended, but some world leaders, such as Jimmy Carter and Kurt Waldheim spoke.

Nairobi, 1984

The fourth Assembly was the first to be held in Africa. The venue was Nairobi, Kenya and the dates 23 to 31 August 1984. By now, Dr John Taylor had become Secretary General. Dr Taylor was born in Birmingham, England, in 1937. He studied at Cambridge and McGill Universities, specializing in Islamic studies. After working at the Selly Oak Colleges, Birmingham as a Reader in Islamic Studies, he became a staff member and then Director of the Sub-Unit on Dialogue at the World Council of Churches. He, therefore, brought to WCRP wide experience in international interfaith dialogue.

Nearly six hundred people took part on the theme 'Religions for Human Dignity and World Peace'. More Africans took part. People came from some sixty countries. Unfortunately, however, the Kenyan authorities would not offer visas for citizens from the Soviet Union and East Germany, although some people came from other East European countries. There were many young people and a large number of women. 'The range of participating organizations was impressive and it was particularly encouraging that many authoritative religious bodies chose to send fraternal delegates or observers. This marked the way, WCRP/International is moving beyond a level of participation among enthusiastic individuals to a level of participation by people who are responsible representatives of their communities', wrote John Taylor.[43]

Delegates had a chance to see something of Kenya and the context of the Assembly was significant. There seems to have been more emphasis on the spiritual character of the Assembly, with the recognition that WCRP is essentially an inter-religious organization. Considerable attention was given to the material used in worship and meditation.

Many difficult subjects, such as the Middle East, were raised in a spirit of understanding. Some national delegates showed a defensiveness, but perhaps issues had not been discussed sufficiently by national chapters prior to the assembly.

There were addresses from The Hon. P. V. J. O. Nyakiamo, who was Minister of State in the office of the President of Kenya, from Archbishop Fernandes, who quoted words of Dr Zakir Hussain, a former President of India. 'For religions to play their historic role in the supreme challenge of the century, the move towards one world community, they will have to look beyond dogmas, rituals and practices which obstruct the flow of life from different religious circles towards a new sense of harmony and collaboration.'[44] Desmond Tutu, at that time Bishop of Johannesburg, challenged the system of apartheid, which values a person by their skin colour, with the teaching of Judaism and Christianity that all are made in *imago dei* (in the image of God). He saw also in other religions grounds for giving high value to each individual human being. 'All major religions have a high doctrine of man and woman . . . The adherents of all major religions are under obligation to promote the well-being of all human beings.'[45] Religions were therefore constrained to be concerned about the quality of life and to be accused therefore of meddling in politics.

The Memorial Lecture for Maria Alberta Lucker, a great worker for WCRP from Germany, was given by Dr Erika Wolf, a former member of Parliament in the Federal Republic of Germany. Maria Lucker, she said, reiterated three tenets of WCRP. 'Firstly, the call for more spirituality . . . (second) concentration on deepening intercultural co-operation and (thirdly) the involvement of more young people.'[46] There were talks too by Dr Andre Chouraqui, a Jewish scholar who had translated the Bible into French, and by Dr Inamullah Khan, Secretary-General of the World Muslim League, on 'Islam Means Peace'.

The Youth Conference, held before the main conference, suggested various ways of increasing the 'sense of being together in a common work'.[47] The Women, who also met prior to the main Assembly, were motivated by three concerns, 'a sense of urgency with respect to peace, an awareness that religious people are impelled to turn principles into action, and a sense that women have a special role to play in raising and speaking to the world's problems'.[48]

Dr John Taylor, who was appointed Secretary-General of WCRP IV in October 1983 and Secretary-General of the World Conference on Religion and Peace in February 1984, asked three questions in his report. First, 'Is Religion a Force for Peace?'. He warned that 'the very credibility of religion in today's world is at stake in the failure of religious people to be effective peacemakers'.[49] His second question was 'Is WCRP an Instrument for Peace-Making?'. He stressed the importance of inter-religious understanding in a world where so often members of one religion fail to understand another's beliefs and react with bitterness or violence. The inter-religious character of WCRP in no way lessened a person's loyalty to his or her own faith. He mentioned the need to work with other organizations. WCRP had also recognized that the search for peace must go hand in hand with the search for justice. Thirdly, he gave an affirmative answer to his question 'Can this Assembly be a Sign of Hope?'

The three commissions were on 'People of Faith Working Together for Peace', 'Human Dignity, Social Justice and Development of the Whole Person', 'World Peace and Disarmament'.

The Declaration affirmed that participants met 'as men and women rooted in our own religious traditions' – answering the persistent criticisms that inter-religious activity involves disloyalty to one's own faith community. 'We have shared in worship and meditation', the Declaration continued. 'We have discovered once again that our differences of culture and religion, far from being a threat to one another, are a treasure.'[50] Delegates were critical of the strife between religions and of the failure of religious people to take a lead in speaking out on moral and ethical issues. The presence of many young people and women was welcomed. The context of Africa was noted and delegates were especially aware of the human rights abuses in South Africa. The need to be more specific was acknowledged. 'We are convinced that a major new priority of WCRP must be to address ourselves to areas of chronic regional tension and conflict in Southern Africa, the Middle East, South and Southeast Asia, Central America and Europe.'[51] The urgency of disarmament, development and human rights were again stressed. There was also emphasis on the vital need for Peace Education.

Looking forward from the Assembly, Dr John Taylor spoke of the need to co-operate more closely with religious organizations, with inter-religious organizations, with peace movements and with political bodies.[52] He stressed the urgency of continuing to address the issue of nuclear weapons. He called also for the building-up of regional and national WCRP networks and for the increasing of finance. Another development many looked for was a practical way of working together for peace and justice.

Melbourne, 1989

The fifth Assembly was marked by the generous hospitality of the Australian hosts. An abiding memory will be the charm and wisdom of David Penman, Archbishop of Melbourne, who was chairman of the host committee, who, tragically, was to die a few months after the conference. He made clear that Australia is becoming a multi-cultural and multi-religious society and that the Assembly was important in helping Australians themselves to recognize this. 'Australia's population of 16 millions has 140 different ethnic peoples, representing over 75 languages (apart from 200 plus extant Aboriginal dialects) and practises an incredible variety of religious traditions.'[53] He stressed too that Australians were increasingly appreciating the Aboriginal heritage. At the conference, Aboriginals arranged a cultural evening. Most of the religious communities in Melbourne shared in offering hospitality and I particularly remember the friendliness of a visit to a Mosque. As usual, there was a day outing, which gave delegates a chance to appreciate something of Australia's wild life.

Each morning began with prayers, led by members of one tradition. Sadly many delegates arrived late, disturbing the atmosphere and the discipline of prayer and meditation was not perhaps as central as might be expected at an inter-religious conference. The opening ceremony, however, included moving prayers – some offered by Rev. Etai Yamada, Chief Abbot of the Tendai-sect, who had brought a very ancient lamp from his temple. Immediately following the conference, the Third World Day of Prayer for Peace was held at Mornington. It was preceded by a dawn vigil on the beach which more than compensated for the lack of atmosphere at other times of prayer. Despite the intense heat, which made it hard for some people to concentrate, the Day of Prayer was an inspiring conclusion to the week.

The Assembly was preceded by lively and successful conferences for women and for young people. At the opening session, Bob Hawke, Prime Minister of Australia spoke about the multi-cultural nature of Australian society. He spoke too about his government's support for efforts to ban nuclear weapons. He affirmed also his country's strong opposition to apartheid in South Africa and he gave a special welcome to Archbishop Trevor Huddleston, a lifelong opponent of apartheid, who was later to address the conference. Archbishop Paul Reeves, the Governor General of New Zealand, was another speaker. There was an encouraging video message from ex-President Jimmy Carter. Charles V. Willie, Professor of Education and Urban Studies at Harvard, gave the Dana McLean Greeley Lecture. 'Religious leaders', he said, 'have a good understanding of the principle of difference and the principle of complementarity', but they had difficulty in getting this across to political leaders, who 'continue to believe that peace is a function of power, that weakness invited violence, that individuals, groups, and nations should fight for love and justice and kill, if necessary, to protect freedom'. 'There is no way to characterize these beliefs', Professor Willie said, 'except to call them silly.'[54] He went on to speak about the importance of peace education.

The overall theme was 'Building Peace Through Trust – the Role of Religion'. Dr John Taylor highlighted the need for trust to be built among nations and within nations. He spoke of the need for a sense of trusteeship for our economies and our environment. He spoke too of a sense of trust – and therefore hope – in ultimate values. There were four commissions, each divided into two sections. They were on disarmament and on regional conflicts; human rights in the family and in the global community; economic and social development and ecological balance and human environment and, fourthly, on non-violence for self-renewal and for building peace and on education for peace.

The Assembly was characterized by a sense of hope. The intermediate Nuclear Forces Treaty had been signed and a cease-fire agreed between Iran and Iraq. There was also the hope that humankind will enter the next century 'with a better understanding of our common humanity and common destiny'.[55] The Declaration spoke also of an 'increased awareness of the importance of moral values in human life'.[56] Further, the Assembly rejoiced that the United Nations was 'being revitalized' and that 'educational systems involving the media and other forms of communication are being developed in order to educate people for peace and justice'.[57] Delegates also noted with gratitude that 'a willingness on the part of many religions is emerging whereby they contribute their finest and deepest inspirations and co-operate with each other and with all who share common concerns in order to achieve lasting peace, a humane social and physical environment, a world not suffering from poverty, oppression, avoidable sickness and death, including the ravages of AIDS, endemic wars, discrimination and the other powers that plague our peoples'.[58]

The sense of hope did not blind the delegates to the real problems that still exist, such as the nuclear threat, the use of chemical weapons, the widespread use of torture and the dangers to the environment.

Religious people, the declaration affirms, can help preserve the improvements and address the problems by keeping 'alive the conviction that the achievement of human happiness and fulfilment is dependent upon higher spiritual powers, powers which enable us to believe that peace is possible'.[59] The Assembly agreed four ways in which it could help build peace through trust:

1. We build trust through disarmament and through the strengthening of institutions for conflict resolution. This kind of trust implies risk and vulnerability because it depends on acceptance of mutual dependence rather than a reliance on mutual terror . . .
2. We build trust through the protection and preservation of human rights for all people . . .
3. We build trust by the creation of economic systems that provide for and assure the well-being of all and that conserve and respect the ecological balances of nature.
4. We build trust by educating ourselves and our children for peace, and through the use of non-violent methods of change and conflict resolution . . . Non-violence is love and love is the most powerful force against injustice and violence.[60]

The Assembly declaration ends with these words, which express the sense of hope and inspiration: '"Lead us from fear to trust". Lead us from common terror to common security as we surrender our reliance on armaments, accept and love our enemies. Lead us from casualness to responsibility as we recognize in the suffering of others our oneness in the human family. Lead us from greed and selfishness to compassionate service as we acknowledge that the inheritance of the earth and all creation is not only to us, but to others and all succeeding generations. Lead us from ignorance to knowledge, from violence to non-violence as we learn of one another, as we overcome our suspicions, as we grow in patience and the ability to love and as we ourselves experience true inward peace.'[61]

In the time since the conference there has been dramatic progress in the search for peace between the great powers and some reduction of nuclear weapons. Eastern Europe has been transformed and dialogue between the South African government and black leaders has begun. Yet the resurgence of extremism and fundamentalism in many religions has come as an unpleasant surprise. 'The unexpected shock of the late eighties', Dr Robert Runcie, the Archbishop of Canterbury, said in the summer of 1989, 'is to discover that all over the world – in most religions and cultures – there are those who believe they should *not* tolerate others, should avoid completely those whose beliefs they consider in error.'[62] Religion itself remains as much a threat to peace as a power for peace.

· 17 ·

WCRP's Achievements

Assemblies are high profile occasions. It is, however, the on-going work of an organization which helps to achieve its objectives.

At the Kyoto Conference, it was agreed to form a continuing inter-religious body to be called the World Conference of Religion for Peace. This was to engage in at least four programmes:

1. To initiate inter-religious seminars and conferences at all levels in order to create a climate for the peaceful resolution of disputes among and within nations without violence.
2. To encourage the establishment of national and regional inter-religious committees for peace.
3. To develop an inter-religious presence at the United Nations and other international conferences, whereby the influence of religion can be directly exerted to resolve conflicts.
4. To encourage the further development of the science of inter-religious dialogue for peace.[1]

Over the years WCRP has been faithful to this charge.

Building Up Local Chapters

The first two items belong together, as the development of WCRP national chapters and regional structures has been accompanied by the holding of conferences and seminars. The Asian Conference on Religion and Peace was established in 1976. In 1982, for example, WCRP/Africa was established during a WCRP Consultation held in Nairobi during August of that year. The following August an All-Africa Assembly on Peace and Religion was held in Nairobi and was also attended by members of the International Preparatory Committee for the Fourth Assembly of WCRP, which was held in Nairobi in the following August. Nearly one hundred religious leaders from Africa attended the All-Africa Assembly on 'Religion for Peace in Emerging Africa'. Subjects discussed included 'Threats to Peace in Africa' and 'Religion, Ideology, and Peace'.[2]

Gradually the WCRP network has spread around the world. There are now national chapters in over twenty countries. One of the most recent to have a fulltime worker is in Australia. To give a few examples, in Pakistan, there are regular monthly meetings and extra meetings on special occasions. The group hosted the WCRP International Executive Committee in 1985. In that year, the Year of Youth, an Essay Competition was arranged and the following year, the Year of Peace was observed. The chapter has co-operated with the government to help combat the spread of narcotics. The Sri Lanka National Council for Religion and Peace was formed in 1978, at a meeting at which Dr R. R. Diwakar spoke. Dr A. T. Ariyaratne, the Sarvodaya leader, plays an active part. WCRP in Sri Lanka has tried to help alleviate the ethnic problem and it has been a centre for peace education. WCRP/UK, under the leadership for many years of Canon Gordon Wilson and Hannah Stanton, has had a programme of regular meetings and organized the imaginative Youth Peace Bus from London to Moscow and back. In West Germany about six hundred people receive regular information about WCRP and there are well established groups in Stuttgart and Munich.[3]

The number of groups is impressive. They are to be found in many parts of the world and in countries where different religions are dominant. All serve as a focus for inter-religious understanding and co-operation in their countries and are linked to regional bodies, as well as to WCRP International. The difficulties of building up a truly international inter-religious organization with strong local roots is enormous and the considerable measure of success – always with limited finance – is a tribute to the work of Dr Homer Jack and Dr John Taylor.

Regional Conferences and Delegations

Regional conferences are also important. Again only a selection can be mentioned. The first Asian Conference on Religion and Peace was held in Singapore in 1976, after a preliminary meeting in 1975. It meets regularly and has had several successful conferences, including an Asian Inter-religious Youth Forum. In Europe, a European Committee of WCRP was formed in 1975 with Dr Maria Lücker as general secretary. It has held several conferences. At Melbourne, delegates were presented with a Latin American report that pointed to the grave problem of foreign debt, to the genocidal policy towards aboriginal people and the violation of human rights by dictatorships.

Besides the conferences arranged nationally and regionally, WCRP International has organized inter-religious delegations to various countries. In May 1982 a ten person group visited Beijing to discuss with the leadership of China disarmament issues, including the Second UN Special Session on disarmament. The Mission was received by Mr Ji Pengfei, a member of the State Council of the People's Republic of China and was hosted by Mr Zhao Puchu, President of the Buddhist Association of China.[4] In 1985 a WCRP/International Team visited South Africa, although not all of the intended party were allowed to enter the Republic. The team visited people of all races, many of whom were victims of police brutality. They also took part in a service of thanksgiving at which Rev. Dr Allan Boesak preached just after he had been released from twenty-five days of solitary confinement. Delegates, however, were unable to attend The Bishop Tutu peace lecture, because it had been banned by the authorities.[5]

Work at the UN

The United Nations, in fulfilment of the third task of WCRP, has been the focus of much activity. In 1970, WCRP received accreditation at the UN through the Office of Public Information (OPI). An application was also made for consultative status with the Economic and Social Council (ECOSOC). In 1973 consultative status in Category II was granted, which allows WCRP to observe meetings of ECOSOC and its commissions and other bodies, to circulate statements, alone or with other Non-Governmental organizations (NGOs), and, on occasion, to make oral interventions.[6] Part of the work has been to make contact with the UN community. In 1971 Archbishop Fernandes and other officers met U Thant, then Secretary General, and there have been regular contacts. Dr Homer Jack was a well known figure at the UN headquarters in New York and often took the lead in getting NGOs to act together, especially in efforts which led eventually to 'The Declaration on the Elimination of All Forms of Intolerance and of Discrimination Based on Religion or Belief'.[7] It is said that WCRP represents a wider constituency than most NGOs and it has been very active at the UN. In 1980, for example, WCRP made an oral intervention in the debate about human rights in Kampuchea during the thirty-sixth session of the UN Commission on Human Rights.

At the end of 1990 WCRP was represented at the UN summit meeting of heads of states and governments on 'The World's Children'. Earlier, WCRP with UNICEF had arranged a conference on 'The World's Religions for the World's Children', in which about one hundred and fifty people participated, drawn from all religions and about forty countries.

The conference drew up the 'Declaration of Princeton', which was presented at the summit meeting.[8]

In the July 1976 Newsletter Dr Homer Jack wrote, 'People often wonder, what does the Secretary-General do between world conferences? WCRP opened our international office opposite UN Headquarters just to inject religious insights into the ongoing agenda of the UN. In the past few weeks, your Secretary-General has done the following: We hosted a small working lunch of diplomats to work out next steps in the strategy to adopt a UN Declaration Against Religious Intolerance. We worked with the Quaker Office at the UN on a weekend conference of diplomats preparing for a crucial session of the Ad Hoc Committee on the Role of the UN in Disarmament. We prepared a report for this Committee which has been widely circulated in the UN community and also a report on a Special Session of the UN General Assembly devoted to disarmament. We are chairman of a committee preparing a major paper on strengthening the role of the UN in the field of human rights. With all these efforts of restructuring the UN, there is fear that the role of non-governmental organizations (NGOs) might be lessened or lost, and so your Secretary-General was one of three representatives who intervened with the Chairman of the UN's Ad Hoc Committee on Restructuring to make sure that their conference room paper continues the role of NGOs.'[9] Evidence of WCRP's activity at the UN is the large number of briefing papers that it produced on current issues.

Representation at International Bodies

Besides its activity at the UN in New York and at Geneva, WCRP has been represented at many international conferences. In the December 1986 Newsletter, Dr John Taylor gives some picture of his activities. In July, he attended The International Council of Christians and Jews Colloquium in Salamanca, Spain, to which for the first time some Muslims were invited. In September, he was in New York representing the Geneva-based Special NGO Committee on Disarmament at the Advisory Board on Disarmament Studies. Then in San Francisco, Dr Taylor attended the consultation of the Japanese and American chapters of WCRP being held there. Then followed three days of visits to people in Canada who were interested in the work of WCRP. On the way back to Geneva, Dr Taylor stopped in London and then in Frankfurt for discussions with IARF. In October, he attended the Islamic-Christian Friendship Society's meeting at Marl in West Germany and the World Peace Conference in Copenhagen. Towards the end of October, Dr Taylor was in Assisi for the World Day of Prayer for Peace and then in Rome. Early in November, he was in London as an observer at a preparatory meeting for the Global Forum of Spiritual and Parliamentary Leaders for Human Survival and then attended the WCF Annual Conference, at which the main speaker was Dr Cantwell Smith, who has been a pioneer in the study of world religions. Dr Taylor also attended a meeting of WCRP/UK. By mid-November, he was in Sri Lanka, to meet with leaders of WCRP and Sarvodaya there and then travelled to India, to Madras, Madurai and Calcutta and on to Bangladesh for meetings with WCRP there and back to India to New Delhi, Chandigarh, Goa and Bombay, helping to get WCRP/India established. It is an amazing record for five months (or four months, if August is omitted) and it is only a sample of the international travel undertaken by WCRP's staff and the international contacts of the organization and its participation in the activities of many related bodies.[10]

Dialogue for Peace

The fourth task of 'encouraging inter-religious dialogue for peace' is harder to assess. Peace-education and its importance is a recurring subject both at international gatherings and at national meetings. At the Melbourne Assembly attention was given to work of 'Conflict Resolution'. WCRP has given constant support to educational efforts and has promoted youth activities. Slowly peace studies are becoming part of the curriculum in some schools and a few universities have departments devoted to this subject.

WCRP managed to attract religious leaders from both the Soviet Union and China, at a time when there was much hostility between these two countries – even though the WCC was unable to do this. To do so, WCRP had to make certain political decisions. For example, delegates were not invited from Taiwan, nor was the Dalai Lama invited.

WCRP also managed to reflect a more or less non-aligned position during the cold war period. This is the more remarkable, given that the US support for WCRP was strong.

Practical Projects

Two areas which WCRP has had difficulty developing are practical projects and making an impact on regional conflicts.

The First Asian Conference on Religion and Peace, held at Singapore in November 1976, launched the Boat People Project, with Ven Thich Nhat Hanh as the director. Sadly, the project was 'a very flawed effort'.[11] At the Nairobi Assembly, $400,000 was pledged for the victims of drought and refugees in Africa. Dr John Taylor writes of this, 'This amount is very small compared with the amounts which are being given by many other religious organizations . . . but the basic principles proposed from WCRP that religious communities should respond co-operatively and should avoid any sense of competition or self-aggrandizement in their aid operations remain truer than ever. It is also a matter of principle that WCRP should not be seen to be empire-building in terms of trying to centralize or organize activity in its own name. Accordingly, the generous gifts of individual members of WCRP and of the organizations which they represent are being channelled through existing projects where an inter-religious spirit and practice are evident.'[12] Whilst rightly, members of WCRP want to show their practical concern to relieve suffering, it would be impossible for WCRP, with its small staff, to become a relief agency.

Situations of Conflict

The failure to which Dr Homer Jack refers in his assessment of the Princeton Assembly[13] to address conflict situations, which are based, at least partly, on religion, continues. For Dr John Taylor, 1987 began 'with a particularly troubling visit to Jerusalem, the occupied territories and Egypt. I felt the need', he writes, 'to consult members of our International Council who live in the area to see whether WCRP can help to promote some reconciling action for peace and justice in a situation where frustration and fear on all sides of the conflict combine to create new sufferings and bitterness . . . So far as WCRP is concerned in our limited response to the Middle East situation, I believe that we should continue to work with all NGOs at the UN in their concerns for peace-making; it would be particularly helpful if we could have help from both Jewish and Muslim colleagues in this respect in New York and Geneva. Within the area we must try to keep alive the hopes for a meeting of young people who come from both sides of the conflict between Israelis and Palestinians. On a wider regional level we should hope for a small regional meeting for potential participants from the area to the Melbourne Assembly who might meet earlier within their own region.'[14] The difficulty is that felt by other bodies, such as the International Council of Christians and Jews, on how to be of help, especially from outside. Tragically, in areas of conflict those religious people who speak for moderation and peace are often not listened to, whilst others play on religious differences to exacerbate the divisions and bitterness.

The recurring problem is how effective religious people can be in the struggle for peace. The prayers and protests of many religious people failed to avert the Gulf War. Certainly, from outside, strength and encouragement can be given to those who struggle against an unjust regime, as for example in South Africa. It is much harder where religious people are on both sides of the conflict. Perhaps only the growth of strong local interfaith groups can be of real help, although it is almost impossible for these to grow where there is already conflict. It may be encouraging that in countries like Britain and the USA, where interfaith activity is quite broadly based, interfaith organizations seem to have survived the 'Salman Rushdie affair.'

More generally, political leaders seldom acknowledge those who influence them. At the Global Forum on Human Survival in 1990, however, President Gorbachev admitted that it was popular concern that had forced politicians to act on ecological issues and that popular concern was stimulated by a few visionary individuals.[15] Religious people are influential in shaping public opinion and the wave of prayer and concern for peace has played its part in creating the new climate in international affairs.

Part of the achievement of WCRP has been in encouraging religious people and especially the leaders to make informed comment on social and political issues. For some religions, this is quite a new development, although the contrast sometimes made between Semitic and Indian religions is often overstated.[16] At the same time, WCRP has challenged religious people to speak together. It has, therefore, served as a critique of traditional religions: challenging them to see that their spiritual concerns need to be expressed in practical comment and action and challenging their isolationism and frequent intolerance.

At the Global Forum on Human Survival, many spiritual leaders felt that they were marginalized. 'We are merely the icing on the cake', said one Hindu swami. The decorative robes were photogenic, but after one opening meditation, the Dutch politician who was chairing the session said, 'Now, the real work begins'. Some religious representatives felt the politicians only saw them as useful educators of their communities, making known what politicians and others had decided. Few political leaders seemed to see that the global crisis is essentially spiritual. Yet leaders in all religions speak of the need for a new sense of values and a recognition of our interdependence not only with each other but with the planet. Robert Muller has said that the next century will be spiritual or it will not be. Religious leaders recognize that the root of the contemporary crisis is spiritual. WCRP has helped to give many of them the confidence and expertise to proclaim this clearly and to challenge the priorities of politicians and nations.

· 18 ·

Other Peace Groups

The distinctive feature of the World Conference on Religion and Peace is that it is an inter-religious organization committed to work for peace and justice. There are other religious peace groups and other bodies which bring together people of different faiths to work for particular causes.

The Gandhian Movement

People of many faiths shared in the Gandhian movement which sought the independence and regeneration of India. In his teaching of *ahimsa*, non-violence, Mahatma Gandhi was influenced by Jainism and Buddhism, and by the example of Christ's death, as well as by his Hinduism. He was open, he said, to truth from whatever source and at his ashram prayer services regularly included readings from the scriptures of the world. His influence has been pervasive, far beyond those groups which specifically trace their origins back to Gandhi.

In Delhi, the Gandhi Peace Foundation, as we have seen,[1] hosted the Symposium, which helped prepare for the first meeting of WCRP. Vinoba Bhave, with his Bhoodan (Land-gift) movement and Jayaprakash Narayan, by his political stance, continued the work of Gandhi in India. Peace Brigades International, the Civil Rights Movement in America, the Chipko Movement to protect the forests of Uttarakhand, the Sarvodaya Movement in Sri Lanka and many other groups own the influence of Mahatma Gandhi.[2] Shri Jagadguru has suggested that all the great religions are pervaded with truth, nonviolence, compassion and unity. These need to be translated into action. When that happens, the world will have Peace. 'There is no religion without peace, no peace without religion.' Peace must be just to endure.[3]

Gandhi was deeply influenced by Jainism's emphasis on *ahimsa* (non-violence). Inspired by His Holiness Acharaya Tulsi, the Jain Peace

Movement, Anuvrat Movement, has arranged two international conferences on 'Peace and Nonviolent Action'. The first was at Ladnun in December 1988 and was attended by over one hundred and fifty delegates from several countries. The conference agreed the Ladnun Declaration. The second conference was held at Rajsamand-Udaipur in February 1991.

The International Fellowship of Reconciliation

The International Fellowship of Reconciliation (IFOR), which had Christian origins, is now open to people of all faiths. As we have seen, the Peace Conference at Constance in August 1914 had to be abandoned, because of the outbreak of war.[4] Two of the participants, Henry Hodgkin, a British Quaker and Friedrich Siegmund-Schultze, pacifist chaplain to the German Kaiser, travelled on the same train as far as Cologne. There, as they shook hands in farewell, they promised that they were 'one in Christ and can never be at war'.

From this vow, the Fellowship of Reconciliation (FOR) was born. Four months later, at a meeting at Trinity College, Cambridge, the organization was formed and Hodgkin was elected the first chairman. In 1915 Hodgkin visited the USA and at a meeting on 11 November – the very date, three years later, on which the Armistice was to be signed – the American FOR was founded, with Gilbert A. Beaver, as the first chairperson. Other leaders included the Episcopalian Bishop Paul Jones, who had been deprived of his office as Bishop of Utah because of his pacifism, and the Unitarian, John Haynes Holmes. It took longer to establish the German branch, 'Versohnungsbund'. Schultze was arrested twenty-seven times during World War I.

In its work for peace, FOR has given particular attention to the rights of conscientious objectors and was effective during World War I in getting President Wilson to stop the inhumane treatment of some conscientious objectors in the USA.

In 1919 The International Fellowship of Reconciliation was formed. Its first secretary was Pierre Ceresole, the Swiss pacifist, who pioneered the idea of work camps, in which volunteers came together to undertake work of reconstruction. In 1932 IFOR led a Youth Crusade across Europe in support of the Geneva World Disarmament Conference. As clouds of war spread, IFOR established Embassies of Reconciliation and initiated peace efforts not only in Europe, but also in Japan and China.

The involvement with Asia increased after the Second World War, partly thanks to the efforts of the Australian FOR and Peace Churches there. In 1954 the American FOR launched a six-year Food For China Programme. The Vietnam War, thanks to the untiring efforts of the USA

FOR Executive Secretary Alfred Hassler, led to close co-operation with Buddhist peace movements. In 1968, at the height of Vietnam's suffering, FOR sponsored a world tour by the Buddhist monk Ven Thich Nhat Hanh, whose poems and writings have become widely known. In 1970 the Dai Dong project was founded which involved thousands of scientists around the world grappling with the problems of war, the environment and poverty. IFOR's work has grown also in the Philipines, Latin America and the Middle East, partly thanks to the decades of seminars on active non-violence led by Jean and Hildegard Goss-Mayr, recipients of the 1990 Niwano Peace Award.[5]

When the American FOR was formed, it took over the British 'basis', which was couched in orthodox Christian terminology. Various attempts to rewrite this led, in 1930, to the adoption of a new statement. This says that love 'seen pre-eminently in Jesus must serve as the true guide of personal conduct', but the statement was written to make it easier for those who were not orthodox Christians to join. In fact, immediately after the adoption of the statement, the National Council instructed its staff to find one or more Jewish members of the Council.

In the 1950s the National Council received recurring proposals that the Statement should be redrawn, but no action was taken until 1963, when staff were instructed to initiate wide-ranging consultation on this question. By 1965 a new Statement was ready and was adopted at the Council meeting. The third paragraph of the Statement reads:

> The Fellowship seeks the company of those of whatever faith who wish to confront human differences with nonviolent, compassionate and reconciling love. The fellowship began as a movement of protest against war, with its roots in the ethic of love as found pre-eminently in Jesus Christ. Many of its members today are motivated by a commitment to God as revealed in Jesus Christ, and to a life of obedience to Christ as Lord. The participation of others is nourished in the historic faith and community of Judaism, with its prophetic emphases on universalism, justice and love. Still others affirm their faith in man and in the unity and interdependence of the human race, and their intent that life shall be made truly human.
>
> Any requirement of credal uniformity thus is alien to the spirit of the Fellowship; . . . It is a special role of the Fellowship to extend the boundaries of community in radical directions, as it seeks the resolution of cultural conflicts by the united efforts of men of many faiths.[6]

The lead in broadening the basis of membership taken by the American FOR has been followed by IFOR, which is now open to members of all religions. One of the IFOR's newest branches, in Bangladesh, includes Muslims, Hindus and Christians.

Religious Peace Groups

There are many religiously motivated peace groups.[7] Some are for members of one religion, such as The Jewish Peace Fellowship or the Jain or Buddhist Peace Fellowships. Others are for members of a particular denomination within a religion, such as the Anglican Pacifist Fellowship or Pax Christi. There are also religious groups which campaign specifically against nuclear weapons, such as the Christian Campaign Against Nuclear Defence (CCND) or JONAH, Jews Organized for a Nuclear Halt. Increasingly these peace groups are working together. In December 1988, for example, the Asian Buddhist Conference for Peace and the Christian Peace Conference held a joint meeting at Khabarovsk, USSR.[8]

Prayer for Peace

Many of these groups also support The Week of Prayer for World Peace. This was the initiative of a small group of people in Britain, in 1974, led by George Appleton, who had been Archbishop in Jerusalem and Edward Carpenter, who was Dean of Westminster. The work was for many years undertaken by Canon Gordon Wilson and his wife Jean from their vicarage in Crewe. It was modelled on the widely observed Week of Prayer for Christian Unity. A week in October, which included United Nations Day, was set aside and a simple leaflet prepared, with prayers and thoughts drawn from the religious traditions of the world. This is now widely distributed, partly thanks to the support of Rissho Kosei Kai. Sometimes there are public services of prayer in connection with the week.[9]

'The Prayer for Peace' has also become widely known. The prayer, written by Satish Kumar, who had been a Jain monk was first used by Mother Teresa of Calcutta at a meeting at St James's Church, Piccadilly, London, on 7 July 1981. It was officially 'launched' at an interfaith service held at Westminster Abbey on Hiroshima Day, 6 August 1981. The prayer which has been translated into many languages,[10] is:

Lead me from Death to Life,
from Falsehood to Truth,

Lead me from Despair to Hope,
from Fear to Trust,

Lead me from Hate to Love,
from War to Peace

Let Peace fill our Heart,
our World, our Universe.

The opening of Buddhist Peace Pagoda in London, one of several around the world, was also marked by prayers from people of different traditions.

The importance of prayer for peace was given great emphasis at the World Day of Prayer for Peace, when Pope John Paul II invited leaders of all great religions to join him at Assisi on 27 October 1986 for a day of prayer for peace. This is discussed below.[11]

There are a variety of other prayer initiatives. One of the most imaginative was 'One Million Minutes of Peace', inspired by Brahma Kumaris. People around the world were invited to donate some minutes of each day to prayer for peace.[12] Other examples are prayers, arranged by The Freedom, Justice and Peace Society of New Jersey, in connection with Human Rights Day on 10 December,[13] or those held in connection with the environment on Earth Sabbath in June.[14]

Co-operative Religious Action

Increasingly people of many religions are coming together in peace related concerns. In 1973 the World Council of Peace convened in Moscow the World Congress of Peace Forces. More than three hundred religious representatives met at the monastery of Zagorsk. From this the suggestion was made to hold an international conference for followers of different religions to discuss contemporary aspects of peace. This was eventually held in 1977 and was called 'The World Conference of Religious Workers for Lasting Peace, Disarmament and Just Relations Among Nations'. It was attended by nearly six hundred and fifty people, drawn from many religions. Observers came from the Vatican, the World Council of Churches, and the World Muslim League. Only eight people attended from the USA, where questions were asked whether the conference was independent of the Soviet government.[15] A second conference was held in May 1982 and attracted wider support, including the evangelist, Billy Graham. Metropolitan Filaret of Minsk, chairman of the preparatory committee, stressed that the distinctiveness of religions was recognized, but 'for all their differences, all religions recognize the ideas of love, fraternity and peace as the highest principles of human inter-relations . . . All religions have a common responsibility to contribute effectively to the common effort for the safeguarding of life against a nuclear catastrophe'.[16]

In the spirit of the Assisi World Day of Prayer for Peace, the Community of St Egidio arranged in the following year an interfaith meeting for peace. Such meetings have now become annual events under the auspices of *Incontri Internazionali Uomini e Religioni* (International Meetings of People and Religions), which was set up in 1988. Meetings have been held in Rome in 1987 and 1988, in Warsaw in 1989, in 1990 in Bari, Italy and in 1991 in Malta.

In June 1989 a major conference on 'Seeking the True Meaning of Peace' was held in San Jose, Costa Rica. The conference was co-hosted by the University for Peace of the United Nations and the Government of Costa Rica. Attention was given to drawing up a Declaration of Human Responsibilities for Peace and Sustainable Development, to be presented to the UN. The Dalai Lama and the President of Costa Rica, Dr Oscar Arias Sanchez, both Nobel Laureates, played an active part. The conference stressed the need for a new paradigm of thought incorporating our spirituality and human values.[17]

Nearly two years later the United Nations University of Peace in Costa Rica sponsored another interfaith consultation, this time on 'World Religions and Global Threats'.

Participants from outside Central and Latin America were clearly moved by hearing from indigenous religious leaders about the sufferings of their people during the Spanish Conquest five hundred years ago and about the continuing exploitation and discrimination which they experience.

It was hoped that the 1992 observation of the Evangelization of the Continent would be marked by repentance and by positive efforts at inter-religious reconciliation as Christians recognized past mistakes and sought a new relationship with the indigenous people.

Coming soon after the shock of the Gulf War, the religious leaders were deeply aware that religion has often been a cause of conflict and that the causes of fanaticism and fundamentalism need urgently to be studied and addressed. They also felt that war should no longer be an instrument of politics.

The conference ended with participants sharing in a mass, which commemorated the assassination eleven years before of Archbishop Romero. In an unprecedented gesture of hospitality in that country, a rabbi, a Hindu swami and a representative of the indigenous people were invited to speak during the mass.

Inter-religious co-operation is increasingly taking place on many issues. In 1984, a United Nations Interfaith Colloquium against Apartheid was held in London, chaired by Bishop Trevor Huddleston.[18] Amnesty International has published pamphlets on 'Religions and the Death

Penalty' and 'Arguments for Human Rights'.[19] There has been interfaith concern about the plight of religious believers in Eastern Europe.

It is, however, the environment which now, with peace, is a major focus for inter-religious activity. In 1986 the World Wildlife Fund, to mark its twenty fifth anniversary held an interfaith ceremony in Assisi. The celebration was introduced by Prince Philip, the Duke of Edinburgh. Dr Karan Singh, President of the Virat Hindu Samaj and a leader of the Temple of Understanding, Rabbi Arthur Hertzberg, Vice-President of the World Jewish Congress and other leaders took part.[20]

The Global Forum on Human Survival, which has already been discussed, also focusses on environmental issues.[21] The dialogue of politicians and religious leaders is still very new. At the Moscow Global Forum, scientists, artists and representatives of the media also participated. Slowly there is a recognition that the major challenges of today require a sharing of the insights of people with many skills and backgrounds. Increasingly, religious thinkers are part of that process. No longer do they pontificate from afar, but, recognizing their own fallibility and limited knowledge, they now are part of the discussion – and to that discussion people of all religions have a contribution to make.

Many of those, however, who are most deeply concerned about the environment think of themselves as belonging to 'the New Age'. The New Age movement is hard to describe and not organized. 'It refers' writes Clifford Longley, religious correspondent of *The Times*, 'to a ground swell, an uncentralized movement of many diverse constituents, which seeks to reunite the spiritual and the natural order which hard science and soft secularism have put asunder.'[22] Members of it draw upon the inspiration of all religions and the accusation is sometimes made that the movement is syncretistic, treating 'all religions as equivalently true, even as needing to be synthesized into a new whole'.[23] References to the Earth Mother particularly alarm some Christians who regard this as a new paganism. A characteristic of interfaith movements has been to respect the integrity of particular religions. They will now have to consider how far they can work together for goals which they share with those who are more impatient with religious boundaries.

The way that people of many religions are now co-operating in a variety of causes is itself evidence that the work of interfaith organizations to overcome hostility and suspicion between believers has achieved some success. Many, however, still question such co-operation. Further, as Clifford Longley says, there is a danger when 'religions are recruited to some other cause than their own, (when they are) not treated as ends in themselves but as spiritual support for some other vision'.[24] This is why it

remains important that believers from the world religions share their
vision and seek to articulate what they hold in common and make clear its
application to the pressing problems of peace, justice, the needs of the
hungry and the preservation of the planet.

PART IV

Bilateral Conversations

'Tell me your hundred beautiful names for God and I will tell you mine.'

· 19 ·

Bilateral Conversations

In a family, there are times when the whole family wishes to be together. At other times two members of the family want to talk by themselves. In the same way, there are occasions when multifaith dialogue is appropriate and other times when discussion between members of two religions is more helpful – just as there is a need for intrareligious and ecumenical efforts within each world religious community.

Conversation between members of different religions is not new. There was religious and philosophical dispute in ancient India and in the Roman Empire. During the European Middle Ages, there were Christian-Jewish disputations. In the late eighth century CE, Abbasi Khalifah al-Mahdi and the Chaldean patriarch Timothy I met and conversed. Later, in 1219, an audience was granted to St Francis of Assisi by Ayyubi Sultan al-Malik al-Kamil at Damietta.

Such meetings were individual and exceptional. Of course, where different religious communities occupied the same geographical space, there was the necessary conversation of daily life. The Islamic world, with its *dhimmi* system, particularly regulated the position of members of other religions and Christendom when it tolerated the presence of Jews, did so under strict supervision.

It is only quite recently that members of one religion have sought to study another faith and become acquainted with its practioners not for the purpose of refuting their beliefs and trying to persuade them to change their religion but in order to understand.

Christian-Jewish dialogue has the longest history, which is why it will receive the most attention. Pioneering attempts to overcome centuries of prejudice and misunderstanding began to be made in the period between the two World Wars. The horrors of the Nazi attempt to exterminate the Jews gave new urgency to this task. During and after the Second World War, national councils of Christians and Jews began to be formed, which have now come together in the International Council of Christians and Jews. From the sixties, this 'unofficial' work has been paralleled by official conversations between representatives of the Jewish world, on the one hand, and representatives of Christian churches. The World Council of Churches and the Vatican have, on the Christian side, taken the lead in this.

The churches also have taken the initiative in encouraging Christian-Muslim dialogue and, subsequently, Christian conversations with members of other religions. The bilateral conversations, which they have initiated, are dealt with in this section of the book. They have also arranged multifaith consultations which are discussed later in the account of the work of the Vatican Secretariat for Non-Christians and of World Council of Churches' Sub-Unit for Dialogue with People of Living Faiths.[1] Slowly other world religious bodies, such as the World Muslim Congress are sharing responsibility for these meetings.

A number of other churches, universities, national interfaith bodies and voluntary groups have also initiated bilateral dialogue. Whilst an attempt will be made to give an impression of these developments, it is impossible to give a complete picture. The emphasis in this book is on the development of continuing international organizations which exist to encourage interreligious understanding and co-operation. Yet such international developments gain their vitality from the widespread growth of local and national dialogue, the promotion of which achieves the purposes of international interfaith organizations.

It is noticeable that it's often Christians who have taken the initiative in starting conversations. As a result, Christians are usually one of the partners to bilateral conversations, although meetings of Jews and Muslims are just beginning. It maybe that the universalism inherent in Christianity, which inspired missionary outreach, also inspires the search for understanding and co-operation. This does not mean, as members of other religions sometimes suspect, that Christians who engage in dialogue are using it as a covert way to gain conversions. Lines of demarcation between Indian and Far Eastern religions have not been so rigid.

Naturally each bilateral conversation has its own character, determined by the religions which are party to the conversation. Further it may only be particular traditions in conversation. It is important not to forget the varieties within each religion. It is a common experience early in bilateral conversations, for members of each religion taking part to want to withdraw and sort out what they think their religion teaches. The character of the conversations is also determined by their locality. It makes a difference whether dialogue with Muslims takes place in an Islamic or European country. Similarly, Israel provides a special context for Jewish-Christian meeting.

The character of conversations is also determined by the purpose of dialogue, although this is often not sufficiently clarified. Dr Tarek Mitri of the Middle East Council of Churches, in a survey of Christian-Muslim relations writes, 'One intellectual, involved for many years in dialogue initiatives undertaken by the WCC, pointed out that the first years were rich, as far as theological exchange is concerned, but subsequently there was more emphasis on possible practical co-operation. In his opinion, this might have been a cover for the unwillingness to do rigorous work in theology. Another Muslim intellectual, equally involved and rather appreciative of Christian-Muslim encounters, recognizes the pertinence of theological dialogue but fears it may have been a diversion from the more serious problems, political or religio-political.'[2]

In considering the widespread growth of bilateral religious conversations, it is therefore necessary to try to keep in mind, whether the discussions are between official representatives of religious bodies or are the freer conversations of individuals; to be aware of the tradition in their own religion to which a person belongs; to remember the local context; and to be sensitive to the purpose of the dialogue.

· 20 ·

The International Council
of Christians and Jews

It was in the period between the two World Wars that the relationship of
Jews and Christians began to come to the fore. Some Christians recognized
the need to combat anti-semitism and to relieve the sufferings of the Jews.
In 1934, for example, the General Assembly of the Church of Scotland
recognizing the 'age-long sufferings of the Jewish people' and aware of 'the
present outbreaks of anti-Semitic fanaticism' declared their heart-felt
sympathy for the Jewish people and that their ill-treatment was 'abhor-
rent'.[1] Too few Christians followed this lead. It was only after the Second
World War, as the horrible attrocities of the Holocaust sank into the
consciousness of Christians, that Christian-Jewish relations began to
attract more attention.

The nineteenth-century illusion of tolerance and emancipation for Jews
in Europe was destroyed by renewed persecutions in Russia and by the
Dreyfus affair in France. The assassination of Tsar Alexander II in 1881
was followed by a new pogrom which shattered any hope of gradual
emancipation. Many Jews fled to Western Europe or America, but a few
went to settle in the land of Palestine, whilst others stayed on as persecuted
minorities. Then in 1894, the notorious Dreyfus affair showed the limits to
liberalism in France. Dreyfus, a Jewish officer, was found guilty of treason
on evidence eventually shown to be perjured. This event seems to have
inspired Theodor Herzl to write his pamphlet *Der Judenstaat* and to start
the political Zionist movement.

1924–1940

The beginnings of organized efforts at Jewish-Christian co-operation date
back to 1924. It was the year of a Presidential election in the USA. The

Democratic Party candidate, Governor Alfred E. Smith, often known as Al Smith, was a Roman Catholic. He became the victim of a scurrilous campaign largely led by the Ku Klux Klan. With their slogan, 'America for the Americans' and their clear anti-semitism, they were a threat to all minorities. To combat their influence, the Federal Council of Churches of Christ in America and B'nai B'rith set up a Committee on Good Will between Jews and Christians. Four years later, when Al Smith again sought nomination, the attacks on him were renewed. Now Roman Catholics joined with Protestants and Jews to launch the National Conference of Christians and Jews (NCCJ).

This was based on a belief in a 'spiritual interpretation of the universe'. The purpose was to 'promote justice, unity, understanding and co-operation among Protestants, Catholics and Jews and to analyse, moderate and finally eliminate intergroup prejudices which disfigure and distort religious, business, social and political relations, with a view to the establishment of a social order in which the religious ideals of brotherhood and justice shall become the standards of human relationships'.[2]

The work of the NCCJ was in the broadest sense educational, including research and speaking tours by teams consisting of a Protestant, a Roman Catholic and a Jew. From 1934 'Brotherhood Weeks' began to be held annually. In the late eighties such a week was still held in Manchester, England, although in many places, thanks to feminist influence the name has been changed. Everett R. Clinchy, a Presbyterian minister, who was the first Executive President, was an imaginative and dynamic leader. He propounded what he called a 'scientific formula' for improving human relations:

First, reduce the social distance, the isolation between the various religious and racial groups so that democratic communication may be kept alive. Secondly, discover the economic and sociological forces which make for prejudice and deal with the several factors individually. Hold the guiding star in the sky of men's aspirations, political democracy above totalitarianism, industrial democracy above economic injustice, freedom of the human spirit above tyranny, peace above war, essential justice for all groups above privilege for any one.[3]

NCCJ explicitly rejected charges of indifferentism. A statement adopted in 1949 said, NCCJ 'strives for brotherhood in those ways which are acceptable to Protestants, to Catholics, and to Jews – not on the basis of removing religious differences'. The Conference 'acknowledges the freedom of the Catholic or the Jew or the Protestant to hold that his faith is the one true faith. It does not affirm such a holding by any one of the three, for it could obviously do so only at the expense of the other two – but neither does it disaffirm. It is not indifferentist, therefore, it is simply as it must be, non-preferential'.

The statement declared that NCCJ did not sponsor joint worship, exchange of pulpits, or common observance of Christian and Jewish holy days, nor did it disapprove of such practices on the part of those who in good conscience participated in them. 'It was not an "interfaith" organization, but rather a "civic agency" seeking "to promote affirmative co-operative action among Protestants, Catholics and Jews in areas of common civic concern".'[4]

In Britain the story also goes back to 1924. This was the year of the Religions of Empire Conference.[5] This was also the year in which the Social Service Committee of the Liberal Jewish Synagogue felt that 'in spite of serious differences of belief, Jews and Christians were at one in their desire to bring nearer the Kingdom of God on earth'.[6] The Committee, with some other organizations, convened a gathering for 'Jews and Christians to confer together on the basis of their common ideals and with mutual respect for differences of belief'.[7] The Conference on 'Religion as an Educational Force', was held in November 1924. It aroused so much interest that the *ad hoc* committee was given a more permanent status and eventually in 1927, a Society of Jews and Christians was established.

The aims were:

1. To increase religious understanding, and to promote good-will and co-operation between Jews and Christians, with mutual respect for differences of faith and practice.
2. To combat religious intolerance.[8]

The society, later known as the London Society for Jews and Christians arranged various lectures. A selection of these were published, in 1934, under the title *In Spirit and in Truth*.[9] Because the activities of the society were viewed critically by those suspicious of indifferentism, there is a defensive note in some of the papers. Hewlett Johnson, who was then Dean of Canterbury, in his introduction, asserted that there is common ground and that Jews and Christians need each other. But he then makes clear that his Christian commitment was not compromised. 'Christianity is the central point in the wide circle of light which shines forth from a heavenly Father . . . I long to commend to others what I see.'[10]

Tragic events on the Continent were soon to demand more than scholarly discussion. Hitler came to power in 1933 and began to implement antisemitic policies, whilst the situation in Palestine was becoming increasingly difficult. Refugees from Germany started to make their way to Britain and on their arrival some Christians, led by Dr George Bell, the Bishop of Chichester, tried to help them. Meanwhile Jewish organizations were finding it increasingly difficult to cope with the flood of refugees.

In 1938 Anglican, Free Church and Roman Catholic churches agreed to support a Christian Council for Refugees. The Rev. W. W. Simpson, who was to devote his life to improving Christian-Jewish relations, was appointed secretary. Bill Simpson was at that time a Methodist minister in North London in an area which included much of the Orthodox Jewish community of Stamford Hill. He had, however, already become interested in Judaism at school and university. The authorities of the Methodist Church had also encouraged him to devote two years to the study of contemporary Jewish problems. He had been for that period a part time student at Jews College, a rabbinic seminary in London. He had also studied traditional Christian approaches to Jews.[11] He was, therefore, well prepared for his work for the Council for Refugees.

The Council of Christians and Jews

Besides help to refugees, it was also becoming apparent to some Christian leaders that efforts should be made to promote better relations between Jews and Christians. Mrs Kathleen Freeman, a prominent Anglican lay-leader, and one time president of the National Council of Women, discussed this with Rabbi Mattuck of the Liberal Synagogue. She also talked to Bishop George Bell and to the Rev. Dr James Parkes, an Anglican priest and scholar who for several years had devoted his time to studying the part played by Christian teaching in fomenting antisemitism.

Together with Rev. Henry Carter, a leading Methodist, they approached William Temple, the Archbishop of Canterbury. He agreed to call together a meeting of leading Christians and Jews. As a result, in March 1942, a Council of Christians and Jews was set up 'to check and combat all forms of religious and racial intolerance; to promote mutual understanding and goodwill between Christians and Jews in all sections of the community; to promote fellowship between Christian and Jewish youth organizations in educational and cultural activities; and to foster co-operation between Christians and Jews in social and community service'.[12]

It is significant that the aims make no reference to antisemitism. This was deliberate, because Archbishop Temple persuaded those responsible for setting up the Council that antisemitism was only one of many expressions of racial and religious intolerance which was symptomatic of deeper disorders. It may be also that to have focussed on antisemitism would not have enlisted as much support, because at that stage the full implications of Hitler's policies were not recognized.

The Council devoted itself to educational work helping members appreciate the teachings, beliefs and practices of the other religion. No attempt was made to mask the distinctiveness of either faith community. Together Jews and Christians agreed to combat all forms of discrimination and to promote the ethical values which they held in common.

Besides the Archbishop of Canterbury, the Moderator of the General Assembly of the Church of Scotland, the Moderator of the Free Church Federal Council, the Chief Rabbi, Dr H. J. Hertz, and the Archbishop of Westminster, Cardinal Hinsley (after some deliberation) backed the Council and agreed to become Joint Presidents. Quite recently in 1988, the leader of the Greek Orthodox Community, the Archbishop of Thyateira and Great Britain, has become a Joint President. Suggestions that the Reform or Liberal Jewish Communities should have a Joint President have always been resisted on the grounds that the Chief Rabbi, who is the leader of the Orthodox Jewish community, claims to speak on public matters and in relationship to the churches for the whole Jewish community. The Queen is the Patron. The body was therefore assured of official approval and backing, although it has remained a voluntary organization, answerable for some years to a Council and now to the Executive, which is elected by the members. The Council has had to raise its own funds, which have come mostly from the generosity of individual Jews and Jewish trusts. No Christian denomination, as such, has given substantial financial backing, although individual Christians and some churches have been generous. It may be that in the future the Christian and Jewish communities will need to take official responsibility for the funding of CCJ.

When the Council was established, W. W. Simpson, who had been active in the initial work to set up the Council, was the obvious choice to be secretary – a post which he held until 1974.

Abortive Efforts to Form an International Council

Soon after the establishment of the British Council of Christians and Jews (CCJ), a small group of Jews and Christians from Britain and America dined together at the invitation of Sir Robert Waley-Cohen, who was one of the outstanding leaders of the Anglo-Jewish community and Treasurer of CCJ. The American guests were Fr Edward Cardinal, a Catholic priest, Rabbi Morris Lazaron and Rev. Everett Clinchy. They had come to study the effect of the 'Blitz' on the morale of the British people. Naturally enough, conversation turned to the work of CCJ and NCCJ. In subsequent correspondence it was agreed to hold an International Conference of Christians and Jews as soon as possible after the end of the war. Oxford was the chosen venue and the conference met there at Lady Margaret Hall in August 1946.

Representatives of other existing organizations for understanding between Jews and Christians were invited. For example, Alan Paton, who two years later was to write his famous book, *Cry the Beloved Country*, represented the South African Society of Jews and Christians, which had been formed in the thirties, but which soon after the Oxford Conference was to wither in a climate hostile to its purposes.[13] Individuals from other European countries, where there was no organization, were also invited. In all, there were well over one hundred participants from fifteen countries.[14] Special permission was obtained to include two Christian pastors from Germany, Dean Grüber from Berlin and Hermann Maas from Heidelberg. A Jewish participant, several years later, described their presence as 'profoundly impressive – one might say traumatic'.[15]

On the eve of the conference, a crowded public meeting was held in London. Speakers included The Archbishop of Canterbury, the theologian, Professor Reinhold Niebuhr, the politician, R. A. Butler and Rabbi Dr Leo Baeck. The latter's appeal for tolerance and understanding, so soon after his release from the Theresienstadt concentration camp, made an unforgettable impression.

The theme of the Conference was 'Freedom, Justice and Responsibility'. Considerable preparatory work was done and much of the time was spent in six commissions.[16] A youth commission was also formed. The commissions' reports were published. The second commission agreed a declaration on 'Fundamental Postulates of Judaism and Christianity in Relation to Social Order', which Dr W. R. Matthews, the Dean of St Paul's Cathedral, said was of 'considerable interest for all who are concerned about the future of civilized man'.[17] A resolution was sent to the Paris Peace Conference.

Two other decisions were made at Oxford. It was agreed to hold an emergency conference as soon as possible on the problem of antisemitism in Europe. This took place at Seelisberg in 1947. It was also agreed that a 'Continuation Committee be set up to make plans for the establishment of an International Council of Christians and Jews',[18] but this was not to be fulfilled for nearly thirty years.

Seelisberg, 1947

Seelisberg is a village in Switzerland overlooking the meadow in which in 1291 three neighbouring cantons joined together in a 'perpetual federa-

tion' and laid the foundations of what was to become the Swiss
Confederation. The conference was mainly a gathering of experts. The
outstanding personality was Professor Jules Isaac, whose seminal study
Jesus et Israel was just about to be published.[19] The organizing secretary
was Dr Pierre Visseur from Geneva, who was the secretary of the Conseil
International de Chretiens et Juifs.

In an Address to the Churches, the conference set out what were soon to
be known as 'The Ten Points of Seelisberg'. They are worth quoting in full,
as many Catholic and Protestant statements on a new Christian approach
to Judaism can be traced back to the ten points:

1. Remember that One God speaks to us all through the Old and
New Testament.

2. Remember that Jesus was born of a Jewish mother of the seed of
David and the people of Israel, and that His everlasting love and
forgiveness embraces His own people and the whole world.

3. Remember that the first disciples, the apostles and the first
martyrs were Jews.

4. Remember that the fundamental commandment of Christianity,
to love God and one's neighbour, proclaimed already in the Old
Testament and confirmed by Jesus, is binding upon both Christians and
Jews in all human relationships, without any exception.

5. Avoid distorting or misrepresenting biblical or post-biblical
Judaism with the object of extolling Christianity.

6. Avoid using the word 'Jews' in the exclusive sense of the enemies of
Jesus, and the words the 'enemies of Jesus' to designate the whole
Jewish people.

7. Avoid presenting the Passion in such a way as to bring the odium
of the killing of Jesus upon all Jews or upon Jews alone. It was only a
section of the Jews in Jerusalem who demanded the death of Jesus, and
the Christian message has always been that it was the sins of mankind
which were exemplified by those Jews and the sins in which all men
share that brought Christ to the Cross.

8. Avoid referring to the scriptural curses, or the cry of a raging
mob: 'His blood be upon us and our children', without remembering
that this cry should not count against the infinitely more weighty
words of our Lord, 'Father, forgive them, for they know not what
they do'.

9. Avoid promoting the superstitious notion that the Jewish people
are reprobate, accursed, reserved for a destiny of suffering.

10. Avoid speaking of the Jews as if the first members of the church
had not been Jews.[20]

The Seelisberg Conference also urged that the Oxford suggestion of an International Council of Christians and Jews 'should be implemented without delay'.[21] At a conference at Fribourg in 1948, on the theme of Intergroup Education, a constitution for an international council was adopted. But when it came to the ratification of this by national councils, problems arose. The British, French, German and Swiss organizations all agreed, but not the American. Everett Clinchy had put much energy and enthusiasm into the preparations for an international council. Yet on his return to the USA from Fribourg, he was advised by UNESCO and some European educators that in some countries, where there were 'Christian Democratic parties', the word 'Christian' had unacceptable political connotations. A broader platform would be necessary effectively to combat antisemitism and other forms of group prejudice. On Clinchy's advice, NCCJ decided not to ratify the Fribourg constitution. Everett Clinchy himself now threw his energies into a new organization, known as 'World Brotherhood'. For a time this made considerable progress in a few countries, but then, because of lack of finance, quietly disappeared from the international scene.[22]

An International Consultative Committee

The American failure to ratify the proposed Fribourg constitution brought to an end plans for an international council. W. W. Simpson did what he could to maintain international contacts. Eventually in 1962 the time was ripe to form an International Consultative Committee of organizations concerned with Christian-Jewish co-operation. Progress towards this was impeded by the dominant theological climate amongst Protestants which was unsympathetic to interfaith understanding and by Catholic charges that Christian-Jewish organizations were 'indifferentist'.

Shortly before the Second World War, in 1937, the International Missionary Council had met at Tambaram, South India. In preparation for the gathering, the Dutch missionary theologian Hendrik Kraemer wrote his *The Christian Message in a non-Christian World*.[23] In this he argued strongly for the discontinuity between the Gospel and world religions. It was only after the war that his influence and that of the great Swiss theologian Karl Barth, to whom Kraemer was indebted, began to spread in the English-speaking world. The mood now was unsympathetic to other world religions and the emphasis fell on the uniqueness of Christ. Mission and the call to conversion were stressed. At the Amsterdam meeting of the World Council of Churches (1948) the failure of the churches to oppose antisemitism was deplored as it was a barrier to sharing the Gospel with Jews. The impetus for a new Christian understanding of Jews came, therefore, from a dawning awareness of the anti-Jewish nature of much Christian teaching and of the responsibility of Christians for many of the sufferings of the Jews. The impetus did not come, at this stage, from dialogue with world religions. Indeed, with the exception of some individuals such as W. W. Simpson or Edward Carpenter of Westminster Abbey, it was not until the eighties that the Christian-Jewish dialogue movement and the interfaith movements began mutually to influence each other.

In 1950 the Vatican issued a directive to the Catholic hierarchy warning them against involvement with the International Council of Christians and Jews. This came as a nasty shock. The grounds for this warning was the supposition that the movement was an 'indifferentist' organization, which tended to ignore or minimize the differences of religious faith and practice. In most countries the directive was ignored as by the time of its issue, no International Council of Christians and Jews existed. In Britain, however, Cardinal Griffin, the Archbishop of Westminster, asked the Vatican for a ruling on whether the directive applied to his participation in CCJ. Four years later, he was informed that it did and that he and all Catholics, clerical and lay, must withdraw from the Council. No satisfactory explanation of the reason for the directive or for this ruling was ever given. Some contacts with Catholics on a private friendly basis were maintained, but it was not until 1964 that the ruling was rescinded. In that year, the new Archbishop of Westminster, John Heenan addressed the Annual Meeting of CCJ and gave 'some public explanation of what has happened during the last few years'.[24]

By then, an International Consultative Committee of Organizations working for Christian-Jewish co-operation had been established. During the fifties informal contact had been maintained between European organizations for Christian-Jewish co-operation. These included the French Amitie Judeo-Chretienne, the German Co-ordinating Council (DKR), the Austrian Aktion gegen den Antisemitismus, the Amicizia Ebraico-Cristiana in Florence, a Swiss group and CCJ. Thanks largely to the work of Bill Simpson, a series of private and informal meetings took place, out of which grew an Informal Liaison Committee of Secretaries of Organizations of Christians and Jews. In December 1960, at a meeting in London, it was agreed to review the role of the Liaison Committee and its secretariat. By this time in Israel, with its religious 'mix' of Jews from many countries and of many traditions, Christians of almost all denominations, Muslims as well as smaller religions such as the Druze, an Israel Committee for Interfaith Understanding had been formed. Christian-Jewish organizations had also been established in Argentina and Uruguay.

A constitution for an International Consultative Committee of Organizations working for Christian-Jewish Co-operation was prepared and the body was formally established at a meeting at Frankfurt in January 1962. Its main objective was to provide for 'consultation between member organizations on matters of common concern in the field of Christian-Jewish relations'.[25] It could recommend action, but had no authority over member groups. Membership included those groups active in the Liaison Committee, although the French Amitie Judeo-Chretienne did not agree to participate until 1964. The Dutch Het Leerhuis became a member and was followed by other national bodies. To everyone's delight, at long last in 1974, Dr David Hyatt, who had just been elected President and Chief Executive Officer of the American NCCJ, brought NCCJ into membership. In 1974 at a meeting in Basle, at NCCJ's suggestion, the name of the organization was changed to The International Council of Christians and Jews. This was at once welcomed by Msgr Dr A. C. Ramselaar, a Catholic leader from the Netherlands and past Catholic doubts were quickly forgotten. Bill Simpson who had been General Secretary of the Consultative Committee became the unpaid secretary of the new Council. As he had by this time retired as General Secretary of CCJ, he was able to bring his great energy and experience to this task, ably supported by Ruth Weyl, his part-time secretarial assistant.

In 1966 the International Consultative Committee held a major international conference in Cambridge. This also marked the twentieth anniversary of the first international conference which had been held at Oxford in 1946. Although the conference was only half the size of the Oxford meeting, several eminent scholars and leaders attended. These included Fr Edward Flannery, Dr Samuel Sandmel and Alice and Roy Eckardt and Rabbi Marc Tannenbaum from the USA and Dr James Parkes, Ven. C. Witton-Davies, the Archdeacon of Oxford who for many years was chairman of CCJ and Rabbi Dr I. Levy, who for many years has been Honorary Secretary of CCJ, from Britain.

The conference issued a critique of The Vatican II Declaration *Nostra Aetate* and the WCC New Delhi statement on Christian relations with the Jews. It also produced a definition of dialogue, which is still of value. 'The dialogue is essentially a dialogue between persons, an attitude to life and not a mere technique. It is a relationship which has been found in experience to be capable of deepening the spiritual life of all participants alike, for each is given in dialogue full opportunity to express his own position in all freedom. It has proved an enrichment of their faith in God to committed Jews and Christians, and has dispelled many misunderstandings of each about the faith and practice of the other. We believe that it is not only consistent with our several loyalties to church and synagogue, but that it also increases interreligious harmony as we face together the problems and needs of our changing world.'[26] A further conference was held in 1968 in Toronto.

The International Council of Christians and Jews

In 1975 the International Council of Christians and Jews (ICCJ), as it was now officially known, met in Hamburg. 1975 marked the thirtieth anniversary of the liberation of the concentration camps and Hamburg was close to the site of Bergen Belsen, one of the camps. In 1976 ICCJ met in Jerusalem and focussed on the significance of Israel in Jewish-Christian dialogue. An extensive programme of visits in different parts of the country was arranged by the Israel Interfaith Committee, which had joined ICCJ in 1966. At this conference Rabbi Dr N. Peter Levinson, from Germany, was elected President in succession to Mme Claire Huchet-Bishop from France.

A conference or 'colloquium', as it was usually called, now became an annual event. In 1977 it was held in Southampton, England, to celebrate Parkes' eightieth birthday and to commemorate the centenary of the birth of Jules Isaac – two scholars who had made an ineradicable contribution to building a new relationship between Jews and Christians. The conference was also the occasion of the official opening at the University of the Parkes Library which holds the remarkable collection of books and pamphlets on Christian-Jewish relations that James Parkes had gathered together.

The next year ICCJ met in Vienna and the Austrian hosts made members aware of the lurking danger of a recrudesence of Nazism. In Vienna various organizational changes were made. Dr David Hyatt of NCCJ was elected president. Dr Franz von Hammerstein, who had just finished his term of service at WCC, was appointed part time General Secretary. A search now began for new offices. The West German Government generously made available the house in Heppenheim in which Martin Buber had lived from 1916 to 1938. After much discussion, it was felt that the association with the spirit of the great philosopher and teacher, Martin Buber, whose book *I and Thou* stressed the importance of personal relationships and of dialogue was of great symbolic importance for ICCJ. Martin Buber House, as it is now known, was not, however, convenient for Dr Franz von Hammerstein, whose other duties in Berlin had become increasingly demanding.

In his place, in 1979 it was agreed to appoint Dr Jacobus (Coss) Schoneveld, a Pastor of the Netherlands Reformed Church who had studied for several years in Israel. In 1980 he moved to Heppenheim and took up his post as General Secretary. Very quickly, the new General Secretary helped ICCJ to relate to other international bodies, such as WCC and the Vatican secretariat. He also helped ICCJ to focus on educational priorities, especially the purging of Christian text books of anti-Jewish bias and on a new approach to the teaching of history. Following a consultation of thirty scholars and specialists, in May 1985 a *Guidelines on the Teaching of History and Particularly on the Place of Jewish History in the Teaching of General History*, which challenged widespread 'distortions, omissions and stereotypes' was produced.[27]

In 1979 Sir Sigmund Sternberg, who was Joint Treasurer of CCJ in Britain, was elected Chairman of the Executive of ICCJ. He has brought great energy and enthusiasm, as well as wide contacts to ICCJ and helped to give the work a higher profile. In 1985 this was recognized when the Pope made him a Knight of the Order of St Gregory – only the second Jew to receive so high an honour.

Meanwhile, conferences had been held in Madrid in 1978, at the invitation of the Centro de Estudios Judeo-Cristianos there, in New York in 1979 on 'The Battle for Human Rights in the Aftermath of the Holocaust' and in Sigtuna, Sweden, in 1980, where the impact of the Holocaust, this time on theology, was again considered. In 1981 ICCJ met in Heppenheim, with 'Images of the Other' as the theme.

In 1982 Israel's invasion of Lebanon provoked a crisis in Christian-Jewish relations. Indeed the policies of the Israeli government and the actions of its army have caused considerable strains in Christian-Jewish dialogue. Those Christians involved in the dialogue are often accused by other Christians, especially by Arab Christian leaders in the Middle East, of pro-Israeli bias and of ignoring violations of human rights. Because of these divisions, it was perhaps fortuitous that the 1982 colloquium was held in the divided city of Berlin. At this meeting, Donald Coggan, a former Archbishop of Canterbury and for a time Chairman of CCJ, became ICCJ's Honorary President. Following the meeting, a magazine called *From The Martin Buber House*, was introduced to strengthen contact between member organizations. More recently in 1987 an ICCJ newsletter has been started, which is more popular in its outreach.

The 1983 colloquium was held in Amersfoort, in the Netherlands, on 'The Search for Peace'. For the first time East Europeans attended, including the young historian and Arabist Dr Stefan Schreiner. Together with Dr Alexander Scheiber, Director of the Rabbinic Seminary in Budapest, he was elected to the Executive at the next annual meeting in 1984. During the following decade, ICCJ has given growing attention to building up contacts in Eastern Europe. In November 1985 a consultation on 'Jewish-Christian Dialogue and its Contribution to Peace' was held in Budapest and there have been subsequent gatherings, for example at Buckow in East Germany in 1987.

In 1984 at Vallombrosa, near Florence, the colloquium, which was the first that I attended, reviewed the state of Christian-Jewish dialogue, with the theme '1984 and Beyond – Purpose and Strategy in Jewish-Christian Relations'. Those who had pioneered the dialogue were becoming increasingly aware of the need to pass the task to a new generation, who had not themselves personally lived through the period of the Holocaust and the rebirth of Israel. Before the Colloquium, the ICCJ Executive were received in private audience by Pope John Paul II. He stressed his deep interest in the dialogue and spoke of dialogue as 'a modest, but in the end very effective way to peace'.[28]

The following year, at the invitation of the recently formed Irish Council of Christians and Jews, the colloquium was held in Dublin. The Chief Rabbi of Ireland, Dr David Rosen, in an opening address, suggested the need to move beyond tolerance and to recognize a 'diversity of paths to God'.[29] The notes on 'How to present Jews and Judaism in the preaching and teaching of the Roman Catholic Church', recently issued by the Vatican, aroused some hostile comment. At the gathering, a deepening of personal relationships was encouraged by the introduction of Interaction Group Activities. Attempts were also made to come together in the 'acknowledged presence of God' by the introduction of times of spiritual sharing. Conferences had always provided opportunity for Jews, Catholics and Protestants to have their own separate times of prayer and worship, although Reform and Liberal Jews were sometimes uneasy about being expected to join the Orthodox and Anglicans were not sure whether they were Protestant or Catholic! There was, however, no joint or interfaith prayer. Some people would have liked this, but for others it would have caused insuperable difficulties. Even so, the desire at a religious conference to spend sometime together before God was widely felt. It was clear that this could not be instead of the regular prayers of any faith community, but had to be of an informal experimental nature. In my view, this innovation helped to deepen the spiritual depth of the gathering.[30]

In 1985 the annual ICCJ-Sternberg award was presented for the first time to The Rabbinic Seminary in Budapest, in memory of Rabbi Professor Alexander Scheiber, one of the first East Europeans to attend an ICCJ Colloquium. In subsequent years, it has been presented to Fr Marcel Dubois, for his pioneering theological work in Israel, to Dr Gertrud Luckner, who was active in the German resistance and who has made a significant contribution to Catholic-Jewish relations in German-speaking countries, and in 1988 to the Sisters of Sion, an international Catholic order devoted to encouraging Christian appreciation of Judaism. In 1989 the recipient was Professor Paul van Buren, who is writing a four volume Christian theological study which gives full weight to the continuing reality of the Jewish people and to the new understanding of Christian-Jewish relations.

At the 1986 Salamanca Colloquium, for the first time Muslims were invited to participate. The theme, appropriate to its Spanish setting, was 'Cultural and Religious Encounter Between Jews, Christians and Muslims – Lessons from the Past'. Pointing to the bitter divisions in so many places, Professor Hasan Askari from Britain spoke of the failure of all religions, whilst Professor Hava Lazarus-Yafeh from the Hebrew University in Jerusalem spoke of the difficulty but importance of combining loyalty to one's own faith with reverence for different traditions.[31] A particularly memorable feature of the gathering was the joint study of texts from the Bible and the Holy Qur'an in which Christians, Jews and Muslims took part together.

Although it was generally agreed that the primary task of ICCJ was to concentrate on the Christian-Jewish agenda, with its many unresolved issues, it was also recognized that trilateral dialogue was important and needed to be persued. In 1988, therefore ICCJ, in co-operation with the West German Konrad Adenauer Foundation's International Institute held a Symposium near Bonn. There were forty-three participants, including people from Lebanon, Morocco and Nigeria. It is hoped to continue this initiative, which, amongst other benefits, makes clear that the coming together of Christians and Jews is not over against Muslims or other religious traditions. This is especially important whilst the public image in the West of Islam is so negative.

The active part played by women in the Salamanca Colloquium has led to a developing programme for women. The Montreal Colloquium in 1988 was preceded by a Women's conference on the Role of Women in Religion, at which Pauline Webb, a British Methodist made a memorable speech.[32] The following year at Lille, the colloquium was again preceded by a Women's seminar. Renewed attention has also been given recently to increasing the involvement of young people. A number of youth conferences have been held since the sixties. The one in Berne, Switzerland, in 1987, arranged by a young Swiss pastor, Christoph Knoch, was particularly enthusiastic and gave its members the confidence to make a big contribution to the subsequent Fribourg Colloquium. Young Leadership Conferences were also held before the Montreal and Lille colloquia. In 1990 the Young Leadership conference was held in Israel on the topic 'Interfaith in the Land of Faiths: The Roots of Justice, Peace and Love in Judaism, Christianity and Islam'.

The 1987 Fribourg Colloquium on 'Overcoming Prejudice', looked back forty years to the Seelisberg Conference, famous for its Ten Points.[33] Two of the participants in the Seelisberg Conference, Chief Rabbi Alexandre Safran, who was in 1947 Chief Rabbi of Romania and who subsequently became Chief Rabbi of Geneva, and W. W. Simpson, for whom sadly it was to be his last ICCJ Colloquium, gave vivid talks recalling the beginnings and describing the progress during forty years. Dr Clemens Thoma of Lucerne drew attention to the need for Christians to find theological space for Judaism, a point which is being increasingly recognized.[34] The American educationalist, Mrs Judith Banki warned Jews not to think that Christianity was at heart anti-Jewish. Christians today, she said, should not be blamed for the sins of their forbears. 'The past cannot be forgotten, it has to be faced and overcome. Jews need Christians to work with them, to eradicate the inherited prejudices which still permeate our cultural heritage.'[35] At the Colloquium, there was heated talk about recent difficulties in Catholic-Jewish relations, such as the beatification of Edith Stein, who was a convert to Judaism from Christianity, about the creation of a Carmelite convent at Auschwitz, which was the scene of the terrible slaughter of so many Jews, and about Pope John Paul II's reception of the President of Austria, Kurt Waldheim, who was suspected of involvement with certain Nazi war crimes.

The 1988 Colloquium was held in Montreal, Canada. Fifteen years before Canada, which in the 1930s had an unsympathetic attitude to refugees, had promulgated a law declaring itself to be a multicultural society. The government was vigorously opposed to prejudice and discrimination, so Canada was a good venue for a colloquium. Holding it there was also an important effort to strengthen the ties between European and North American co-workers. Unfortunately it came at a time when, because of financial difficulties, the Canadian CCJ was having to cut back on its work.

The subject was 'The One Way and the Many Ways – Dilemmas of Pluralism'. Rabbi Howard Joseph of Montreal spoke of a theology of humility. A recognition of the finite nature of any human understanding of the divine should lead to an acknowledgement that a faith system which is true for some need not be true for all. Fr Bernard Dupuy, former secretary of the Catholic Bishops Conference in France suggested that the Creator in accepting the infinite variety of all beings was less disturbed by differences between Judaism and Christianity than their adherents seemed to be. Dr Subhi Abu-Gosh, Director of Muslim Courts in Israel, whose presence again showed the importance ICCJ now attaches to trilateral discussion, gave a Muslim view of religious pluralism. Dr Pauline Webb, former head of Religious Broadcasting on the BBC World Service, said dialogue was an affair of the heart.[36]

In 1989 the Colloquium was held in Lille, France and recalled the two hundredth anniversary of the French Revolution, with its declaration on human rights. As Professor Pierre Pierrard, President of the host organization Amitie Judeo Chretienne, pointed out the declaration gave rights to Jews as individuals, but ignored their peoplehood. The French revolution also set a precedent for the use of terror as an instrument of state. Dr Arthur Hertzberg of New Hampshire, USA, said he thought the Christian reality was quite different from Jewish reality and he expressed doubts as to whether a pluralist world was according to the will of God,[37] although it seemed to be the reality. Thus, the issue discussed at Montreal and at previous conferences surfaced once again – the relationship of the two religions to each other. Real acceptance of the other must surely imply recognizing that, as Rabbi David Rosen said at Dublin, there is more than one path to God.[38] More than three hundred people participated in the Lille gathering from some twenty-five countries, including Australia, Bulgaria, Nigeria, Uganda and Uruguay.

A Decade of Growth

This in itself is evidence of how ICCJ has grown in the last decade and of how it has extended its membership and range of contacts.[39] The number of national councils has grown and many of them have become more dynamic and influential. Links are being established with the newly formed CCJs in Victoria and New South Wales, Australia and with groups in Latin America. A few Christian scholars in Africa are becoming interested in the dialogue. Jews and Christians from Eastern Europe have become involved and women and young people have taken an increasingly active part. Relationships with the Vatican and WCC have been strengthened. Contact has been opened up with Muslims and with international interfaith organizations. It is sad, in the midst of so much progress, that the Israel Interfaith Committee is in difficulties. It is sad also that the 1990 Colloquium, planned for Jerusalem, had to be postponed because of the difficult political situation in Israel and the West Bank. The Young Leadership Conference there did go ahead. In place of the Colloquium, a consultation was held in Prague in August 1990, at which the Czechoslovak CCJ was received into membership of ICCJ. The 1991 Colloquium was held at Southampton. The venue was chosen partly because the British Council of Christians and Jews was preparing to celebrate its fiftieth anniversary and partly because the library of James Parkes, an Anglican pioneer of a new Christian appreciation of Judaism, is housed there. The theme was 'When Religion is Used as a Weapon. The Use and Misuse of Religion in Defence of National and Fundamental Values'. The colloquium, aware of developments in Eastern Europe, and of the effects of the Gulf War, examined the question of how national identity can be affirmed without chauvinistic excesses. It also looked at problems created by 'fundamentalism'.

Looking ahead to the nineties, Sir Sigmund Sternberg, Chairman of the ICCJ Executive, mentions four tasks on which ICCJ should concentrate in the years ahead. The first is to make more widely known what has already been achieved. There is still considerable ignorance amonst church and synagogue members of the new emerging relationship between Jews and Christians. Secondly, in both communities the revival of extremism and fundamentalism and the missionary efforts of some Protestant groups pose a threat to dialogue. Thirdly, Christians need to reflect on the theological implications of their new understanding of Judaism and it is to be hoped that Orthodox Jews will become willing to engage in discussion of theological matters. Fourthly, Sir Sigmund calls upon Jews and Christians to do more together in the way of common action for justice and peace, in partnership with all people of faith and good will.[40]

· 21 ·

Official Conversations

Although ICCJ has high level support, it and its member organizations are voluntary, unofficial bodies. The last twenty years have also seen growing official dialogue between Jewish representatives and representatives of the churches. These have produced reports of the meetings and, on the Christian side, have encouraged the churchs to prepare statements expressing their new thinking on the relationship of the churches to Jews and Judaism.

The Jewish Participants

Through the centuries, because of Christian hostility, Jews have been defensive and were often forced to withdraw into introverted ghettos. References to Christianity were usually hostile, although, as in Mediaeval Spain, there were periods of cultural exchange. In the nineteenth century, when in central and Western Europe Jews were allowed out of the ghetto, exchange on equal terms became possible. But emancipation brought its own temptations to assimilate. At the same time Christians renewed their efforts to convert Jews, so no real dialogue was possible. The late nineteenth century, as we have seen, pointed to the limits of tolerance.[1] It has been said of the period up to the Second World War that Jews and Christians 'engaged not in dialogue but in double monologue. Christians wanted to prove the superiority of their faith; Jews were primarily concerned with bettering their lot in society. Christians wanted converts; Jews, civil rights. Jews were forced to talk religion where they meant social betterment'.[2] There were, however, some seminal figures. Although the philosopher Hermann Cohen, who was Professor at Marburg from 1876–1912, wrote extensive critiques of Christianity, he had a sense of the deep relationship between Judaism and Christianity, especially in its Protestant manifestations. Franz Rosenzweig (1886–1929), an Existentialist thinker, proposed the doctrine of the Two Covenants. Martin Buber, best known for his book, *I and Thou*, accepted the reality of Christianity as a path to God and asked Christians to say the same of Judaism. Other scholars, such as Claude Montefiore, a Liberal Jew, or Joseph Klausner, a Jewish nationalist, began to study Jesus and Paul.[3]

The Holocaust shattered these initiatives and Jewish energy was absorbed in reconstructing world Judaism. For many Jews the horrors of the Holocaust confirmed their worst suspicions of Christianity. The Orthodox thinker Eliezer Berkovits warned against friendly approaches by Christians. It is in fact amazing that so many Jews have been willing to enter into friendly dialogue. In part the motivation has been to help Christians become aware of the deep-rooted anti-Judaism of traditional church teaching. Jules Isaac, the French scholar, was amongst the first to expose the Christian teaching of contempt. Others hope to gain Christian sympathy for Israel. Orthodox Jews, on the whole, reject 'theological' dialogue, which grapples with questions of ultimate truth. The leading American rabbi, Joseph Dov Soloveichik, argued that faith communities can only communicate on 'secular grounds' or 'human categories'. The life of faith is so intimate that it cannot be communicated to those outside the community. He opposed 'any attempt to debate our private individual faith commitment'. He did, however, endorse dialogue on humanitarian and cultural concerns and admitted that these discussions 'will, of course, be within the framework of our religious outlooks and terminology'.[4]

The Orthodox Rabbinical Council of America, in its guidelines on dialogue, welcomed discussion of universal religious problems, but rejected debate of 'our private individual commitment' or consideration of 'truth'. They felt that dialogue on 'religious-spiritual aspects of our civilization', for example on war and peace, secularism, civil rights or moral values, was important, but rejected inter-religious dialogue concerning the 'doctrinal, dogmatic or ritual aspects of our faith . . . There cannot be mutual understanding concerning these topics, for Jews and Christians will employ different categories and move within incommensurate frames of reference and evaluation'.[5] Individual Orthodox rabbis have been ready for a wider dialogue, as have many Liberal and Reform Jews in Britain and Reform and Conservative Jews in USA. Even so, it is important to recognize that Jews and Christians often approach dialogue with different expectations. Otherwise, this imbalance can cause frustration. For Jews, an understanding of Christianity is not necessary to their understanding of their own faith. Once when Franz Rosenzweig was asked what Jews thought of Jesus, he replied 'They don't'. Christians, however, cannot understand their own faith without coming to terms with Judaism.

'What impels the Jew to dialogue with Christianity', writes Henry

Siegman, a former Vice-President of the Synagogue Council of America and Executive Director of the American Jewish Congress in New York, 'are not *theological* but *historical* considerations. For the Jew, the problematic of Christian-Jewish relations is determined by a history of Christian attitudes and actions towards the Jew which diminished his humanity and inflicted on him suffering and martyrdom . . . His concern is for his present and future survival'. This, he adds, does not mean that the Jew 'fails to appreciate the potential the dialogue holds for mutual religious support and for the contribution that can be made jointly with Christians, and with men of other faiths, in resisting the forces of our society that threaten to empty life of transcendent meaning and to rob the individual of his *tzelem Elokim* (divine image).[6]

Siegman, in this important paper, goes on to say that for Jews Christians must grapple with their guilt and he criticizes *Nostra Aetate* for its failure to yield 'a sincere examination of the Christian conscience'.[7] He stresses the importance of Israel and the difficulties created by Christian missions. He admits that Jews have failed to consider the implications of their own traditions for a meaningful pluralism. 'We have been forthright in calling Christianity to account, but we have been somewhat less than daring in initiating a process of self-examination.'[8]

Siegman's article explains why so often Jews and Christians approach the dialogue with different agendas. 'All too often, we are so intent on our own agendas that we pass each other like ships in the night.'[9] His article also explains why there has been no Jewish statement on Christianity, comparable to the statements on Judaism issued by the Vatican or the WCC. Jewish interest tends to be historical or practical. In Israel, it is scholars rather than rabbis who have been active in dialogue.[10] The hope has been that Christians will recognize how anti-Jewish their teaching has been and will be able to correct this. Very importantly, Jews have hoped that Christians will desist from missionary pressure on them and will join them in combatting the antisemitism that still lurks in many places. They have hoped too that Christians will be sympathetic to the rebirth of Israel and her struggle to survive. In recent years, however, this latter hope has often been in vain.

The Roman Catholic Church

In 1986 Pope John Paul II visited the Great Roman Synagogue and spoke there. It has been said that this journey to the Rome Synagogue was the longest journey made by this much-travelled Pope. In it he crossed over nearly two thousand years of history. It also, as he said, brought to a close the period initiated by the Pontificate of Pope John XXIII and by the

Second Vatican Council. 'The general acceptance of a legitimate plurality on the social, civil and religious levels has been arrived at with great difficulty.'[11]

At the synagogue, the Pope repeated the words of Vatican II that the church 'deplores the hatred, persecutions and displays of anti-Semitism directed against the Jews at any time and by anyone'. He also said, 'I would like once more to express a word of abhorrence for the genocide decreed against the Jewish people during the last War, which led to the holocaust of millions of innocent victims'.[12]

The International Catholic-Jewish Liaison Committee

Yet as the Pope said, his visit, in some sense marked the end of the period since Vatican II. The year before also marked fifteen years of regular meeting between Catholic and Jewish representatives – between what became known as the Commission for Religious Relations with the Jews, on the one hand, and The International Jewish Committee on Inter-religious Consultations (IJCIC), on the other. In between the consultations contact was maintained and smaller planning meetings held.

In 1966 Pope Paul VI approved the setting up of an office, within the Secretariat for Promoting Christian Unity, for Catholic Jewish relations.

In 1974 Pope Paul VI established a Commission for Religious Relations with Jews. It is officially described as 'attached to but independent of the Secretariat for Christian Unity'.[13] This link, rather than with the Secretariat for Non-Christians, reflected a recognition of the close bond between the church and the Jewish people and the traditional view that the first schism in the church was the break with Judaism. Meanwhile, the Jewish IJCIC had come into being.[14]

In 1969 an informal meeting with some Jewish scholars was held near Rome. Early in the next year, Pope Paul VI set up a liaison committee which with IJCIC formed a Catholic-Jewish liaison committee. At the planning meeting in December 1970, a memorandum was drawn up distinguishing two main areas of concern. One was questions concerning the mutual relationship of Jews and Christians and the other was on questions of common concern.[15]

While the Vatican would prefer an exclusively religious dialogue, the Jews have raised political issues, often ones related to Israel. This is seen particularly in the agendas of the initial meeting. The International Catholic-Jewish Liaison Committee first met in Paris 1971 to consider human rights and religious freedom and to consider the relationship between religious community, people and the land in Jewish and Catholic traditions. In 1972, at Marseille, the latter subject was again the topic for discussion. At Antwerp in 1973, it was 'People, Nation and Land'. In 1975, at a meeting in Rome, when the Jewish delegates were received by Pope Paul VI, the Vatican document, *Guidelines*, was discussed and also the concept of human rights in the two traditions. In 1976 the meeting was in Jerusalem. This was particularly significant as the Vatican still did not (and does not) recognize the existence of the state of Israel. At the meeting, there was a joint assessment of major developments in Christian-Jewish relations. In 1977, in Venice, the topic was 'The mission and witness of the Church'. At the 1977 meeting, Professor Tommaso Federici gave an important paper on mission. He distinguished sharply between 'proselytism', which was viewed as coercive, and witness, which proclaims the Church's belief in the action of God in history and especially in Christ. Organized attempts to convert Jews are repudiated.[16]

In 1978 in Toledo and Madrid, the subject was education: 'The image of Judaism in Christian education and the image of Christianity in Jewish education.' In 1979 at Regensburg, education was again considered, this time for dialogue in a pluralistic society. There was also discussion of religious freedom. In 1981, in London, the subject was 'The Challenge of secularism to our religious commitments'. In Milan in 1982, the topic was the sanctity and meaning of human life in the present situation of violence. Then at Amsterdam in 1984, 'Youth and Faith' was discussed. The 1985 Rome meeting marked the twentieth anniversary of *Nostra Aetate* and included an analysis of the Vatican *Notes*. The eight-hundred and fiftieth anniversary of Maimonides birth was commemorated. The programme for the future was discussed.

At the end of its twelfth meeting in Rome in 1985, the International Liaison Committee committed itself to a programme of action for the immediate future. The six main points are:

1. To disseminate and explain the achievements of the past two decades to our two communities.
2. To undertake an effort to overcome the residues of indifference, resistance and suspicion that may still prevail in some sections of our communities.
3. To work together in combatting tendencies towards religious extremism and fanaticism.
4. To promote conceptual clarifications and theological reflection in both communities and to create appropriate forums acceptable to both sides, in which this reflection can be deepened.
5. To foster co-operation and common action for justice and peace.
6. To undertake a joint study of the historical events and theological implications of the extermination of the Jews of Europe during

World War II (frequently called the 'Holocaust' or, in Hebrew, *Shoah*).[17]

At its meeting in 1990 the International Catholic-Jewish Liaison Committee, alarmed by the resurgence of antisemitism in parts of Europe, stressed the need to uproot sources of religious antisemitism. It was suggested that Catholic statements on the subject should be translated into the vernacular languages and distributed as widely as possible.[18]

Vatican Statements

The decree *Nostra Aetate*, promulgated in October 1965 by the Second Vatican Council, was a decisive turning point in Catholic-Jewish relations. Although there was bitter controversy surrounding earlier drafts of the resolution, *Nostra Aetate* turned its back on centuries of hostility.

It begins by recalling the spiritual bond that links the people of the New Covenant to Abraham's stock and by affirming God's continuing covenant with the Jewish people. The document commends dialogue. Most important the charge of deicide is repudiated. The decree also condemns all persecution and particularly displays of antisemitism.[19]

Gerhard Riegner, who for many years was Secretary General of the World Jewish Congress and active in the dialogue throughout, looking back after twenty years, summed up the eight major principles that *Nostra Aetate* established like this:

1. The Declaration stresses the spiritual bond between the Church and the Jewish people.
2. It acknowledges that it received the 'Old Testament through the people with whom God concluded the Ancient Covenant'.
3. It acknowledges the judaic roots of Christianity, starting with the Jewish origin of Jesus himself, of the Virgin Mary and of all the Apostles.
4. It declares that God does not repent of the gifts He makes and the calls He issues and that Jews remain 'most dear to God'.
5. It states that what happened in the Passion of Christ cannot be charged against all Jews without distinction then living, nor against the Jews of today.
6. It declares that the Jews are not rejected or accursed by God.
7. It proclaims the Church's repudiation of hatred, persecution, displays of antisemitism at any time and by anyone.
8. It fosters and recommends mutual understanding and respect through biblical and theological studies and fraternal dialogues.[20]

The last principle, in Riegner's view, was the most important with its stress on mutual understanding and *respect*. 'It definitely closes the era of friction and enmity. But it leaves also behind it the eighteenth-century concept of religious tolerance. In proclaiming mutual respect as the guiding principle in interreligious relations for the future it constitutes a real milestone in Christian-Jewish relations and opens a new vision for the future.'[21] It is interesting that this is the same point on which, as we have seen, Pope John Paul II concentrated in his address at the synagogue.

Various national and provincial synods have sought to extend and apply the teaching of *Nostra Aetate*. Of particular importance are two documents emanating from the Vatican on the tenth and twentieth anniversaries of *Nostra Aetate*. In 1974 Pope Paul VI set up a Commission for Religious Relations with the Jews. In the following year, it produced *Guidelines and Suggestions for Implementing the Conciliar Declaration Nostra Aetate*. In 1985, to mark the twentieth anniversary of *Nostra Aetate*, the Commission for Religious Relations with the Jews published *Notes on the Correct Way to present Jews and Judaism in preaching and catechesis in the Roman Catholic Church*.

Although these documents show progress on many matters, there are still causes of friction. The Jewish world does not understand why the Vatican has not recognized the state of Israel. This is a problem peculiar to the Roman Catholic Church, for only it, being also the Vatican State, has diplomatic relations. Some Jews feel, wrongly I believe, that this means that Catholics have not really changed their old beliefs that the Jews were rejected by God. It is rather that the Vatican does not recognize a state whose boundaries are not internationally agreed and perhaps because the Vatican wants to retain influence in the Muslim world, so as to protect Christians there. Clifford Longley, the Religious Correspondent of *The Times*, himself a Catholic, has argued, however, that the Vatican would have had more influence if it had had diplomatic relations with Israel.[22]

The beatification of Edith Stein, the siting of a convent at Auschwitz, the Pope's willingness to receive Yasser Arafat, leader of the PLO and also Kurt Waldheim, President of Austria, who has been accused of collaboration with the Nazis, have also caused misunderstandings.

Yet despite the difficulties, as Geoffrey Wigoder of the Hebrew University says, 'the changes that have occurred within a mere two decades have been impressive.[23]

The World Council of Churches

The World Council of Churches (WCC) brings together over three

hundred Protestant, Anglican, Orthodox (since 1961) and Pentecostal
churches. It has no legislative power over member churches, but strong
moral authority. There is a Sub-Unit for Dialogue with People of Living
Faiths, which subsumes the Consultation on the Church and the
Jewish People (CCJP). This itself is a successor to the International
Missionary Council's Committee on the Christian Approach to the Jews
(IMCCAJ), which was formed in 1931. CCJP is elected by the working
group of the Sub-Unit and is composed of Christians who are concerned
for the Jewish people and for the theological integrity of the church.
Whereas IMCCAJ was almost exclusively oriented towards mission,
CCJP is predominantly concerned for dialogue. In addition to its theological concern with the Jewish people, WCC, mainly through its department on International Affairs, has made various comments on the
situation in the Middle East.

Dialogue Meetings

In 1962 informal discussion began between some Jewish leaders and
members of the WCC about the possibility of a joint consultation. This
was eventually arranged at the Ecumenical Institute at Bossey in
August 1965, and was jointly organized by the WCC and the Synagogue Council of America. Discussion centred on common social concerns, rather than theological problems. The general theme was 'the
Situation of Man in the World Today'. The report emphasized that 'the
Jewish people have often preserved truths of the revelation of God
through the Old Testament to which Christians have often been blind.
In particular Judaism has an abiding message for the Church in its
stress on the revelations through the Law and the Prophets that God is
Lord over every realm of life, material as well as spiritual.'[24]

Despite intentions expressed at the consultation, there was no quick
follow-up. It was not until June 1968 that Jewish representatives again
met with members of the WCC. At the meeting, which was held in
Geneva, there was a review of developments in Christian-Jewish relations since 1961. Areas of common concern were defined, such as
economic and social justice, international peace and security and
human rights. It was agreed that meetings should take place regularly
and a small group was set up to plan future consultations.

The next consultation was at Geneva in May 1969. The main issues
considered were Jerusalem in Jewish and Christian traditions and religious education and prejudice. A report was given on a meeting of some
Christians and Muslims. In the following year, the emphasis was on

current issues. It was agreed to put the consultations on a more permanent basis and a small steering committee, with five Jews and five
Christians, was set up. In October of the same year (1970), a consultation was held at Lugano on 'The Quest for World Community: Jewish
and Christian Perspectives'.

In April 1972 a smaller group met to prepare for the next consultation, held at Geneva in December 1972. The topic 'Quest for World
Community' was pursued and the papers published. Current issues,
such as racism in Southern Africa, human rights in the Soviet Union
and the Middle East conflict were also raised. A pattern of smaller and
larger meetings in alternative years was established. In 1975, in
London, the theme was 'The Concept of Power in Jewish and Christian
traditions'. In 1976 a smaller meeting was held in Jerusalem, always a
significant venue. Time was given to reviewing the progress of the past
decade. There was a report on the WCC Nairobi Assembly and relief
that WCC had not followed the UN in equating Zionism with racism.
Jewish members hoped that the WCC might follow the Vatican in
issuing guidelines.

In 1977 the theme of the meeting in Zurich, was 'Nature, Science and
Technology'. In 1980 the subject was 'Religion and the Crisis of Mod-
ernity', at a meeting held in Toronto. In 1984, at Cambridge, USA, the
subject was 'Religious Pluralism: Its Meaning and Limits'. Unfortunately, the meeting planned for May 1987 in Geneva on 'Tikkum Olam
or the Meaning of Creation' was cancelled at the last moment because
of illness.

Other more specific meetings have taken place. Members of the
WCC Central Committee have met with Jewish representatives in the
places where the committee has met – for example in Buenos Aires in
1986. In the same year the first dialogue meeting between Jews and
African Christians, sponsored by WCC and IJCIC, took place in
Nairobi. There have also been meetings between IJCIC and member
churches of the WCC, such as the Anglican Communion, the Lutherans
and the Orthodox churches.

WCC Statements

At its first Assembly, at Amsterdam, in 1948, the WCC showed its
awareness of Jewish suffering. 'We cannot forget that we met in a land
from which one hundred and ten thousand Jews were taken to be
murdered. Nor can we forget that we meet only five years after the
extermination of six million Jews.' Yet there was no hint of Christians
being at least partly responsible for these sufferings. It was also made

clear that the evangelistic task included the Jewish people. The church's failures in love and the 'image of the Jews as the sole enemies of Christ', which the church had often fostered were a hindrance to evangelism (not a cause of antisemitism!). Antisemitism is condemned clearly as a 'sin against God and Man'. The existence of Israel was noted, but the WCC did not express a judgment on the 'complex conflict of rights'.[25]

At the 1961 New Delhi Assembly, the WCC repeated its condemnation of antisemitism and made clear that blame for the crucifixion should not fall upon the Jewish people of today. 'In Christian teaching the historic events which led to the Crucifixion should not be so presented as to fasten upon the Jewish people of today responsibilities which belong to our corporate humanity and not to one race or community.'[26]

At both the Uppsala (1968) and Nairobi (1975) Assemblies, statements were adopted about the Middle East situation, but there has been no discussion about the theological significance of Judaism and the Jewish people at a WCC Assembly since 1961.

Even so, important work on the Christian understanding of Judaism has continued in the WCC and its member churches. By 1982, after a long process of discussion, *Ecumenical Considerations on Jewish-Christian Dialogue* were commended for study by the Central Executive. Recently, the various statements by the WCC and by member churches have been published in *The Theology of the Churches and the Jewish People*. A study of these documents shows wide agreement that:

1. The covenant of God with the Jewish people remains valid.
2. Antisemitism and all forms of the teaching of contempt for Judaism, especially teaching about deicide, are to be repudiated.
3. The living tradition of Judaism is a gift of God.
4. Coercive proselytism directed toward Jews is incompatible with Christian faith.
5. Jews and Christians bear a common responsibility as witnesses to God's righteousness and peace in the world.

The document recognizes that there is not yet a common mind in the churches on the question of mission nor on the relation of Covenant and Land, especially in relationship to the state of Israel.[27]

The failure of the churches to repudiate missionary activity has disappointed Jews and is a hindrance to dialogue. There was some disappointment that at the Canberra Assembly of the WCC in 1991 there was no statement denouncing antisemitism. Jews also feel that the World Council of Churches, which had often issued statements hostile to Israel on the political situation, is not deeply committed to Israel's right to exist.

Israel, therefore, remains a stumbling block in Jewish dialogue with both the Vatican and the WCC. This gives special significance to the dialogue in Israel.[28]

· 22 ·

Israel

If Christian-Jewish dialogue everywhere is affected by the existence of Israel, the situation in Israel should be seen in its own terms. Interfaith activities there are related to and coloured by the political tensions and uncertainties. They are also linked to efforts to foster inter-communal understanding.

Because its population is religiously very mixed, Israel seems an obvious centre for interfaith dialogue: but developments have been restricted by features peculiar to the situation in the country. 'At the beginning of 1975', wrote Dr Ezra Spicehandler, of the Hebrew Union College, 'there were over 360,000 Jews in Jerusalem – drawn from over sixty communities from Harbin to San Francisco, from Bokhara to Melbourne; 60,000 Muslims of various persuasions; and 20,000 Christians representing dozens of Christian confessions, Roman and Greek Catholic, Protestants of almost every denomination, Armenians, Ethiopians, Copts, Greek and Russian Orthodox.'[1] Yet, writing at the same time, Dr Jacobus Schoneveld, who was then Theological Adviser in Jerusalem to the Netherlands Reformed Church and who is now General Secretary of ICCJ, said, 'It must be admitted that the Holy Land is an underdeveloped area in matters of interfaith and ecumenical relations'.[2] Fifteen years later, the position is still the same. The variety of people in Jerusalem has perhaps increased, with the immigration of more groups of Jews, although the local Arab Christian population is said to have declined. If anything, partly because of the intafada, the possibilities of dialogue have become more difficult, although if they are even more urgent.

There are many factors that inhibit dialogue. Relations between religious groups were formalized and defined by the *millet* system, which derives from the time of Arab conquest of Palestine. Whilst the Muslims reserved a privileged position for themselves, they allowed a degree of independence to the religious minorities under their rule. This was not limited to matters of liturgy, but included personal and family rights. The British, during the Mandate between the Wars, continued the system. The State of Israel, from its inception, established a Ministry of Religions to aid, protect and safeguard the rights of various communities. Each community appoints its own ministers, rabbis or imams, administers its own property and exercises jurisdiction over its members in matters of marriage, divorce and maintenance. The system, whilst preserving a limited autonomy for the communities, also isolates them from each other. Fr Marcel Dubois, a Catholic priest who has lived in Israel since its creation, described the relations of the heads of communities, Bishops, Rabbis, Imams and Ministers of Government, as consisting of 'exchanges of courtesy, relations of strict justice, defence or recognition of rights according to the *status quo*, whose norms Israel has accepted; all this is in short mutual respect and respect for what Claude Levi-Strauss would have called the synchronistic system with all that makes up tradition and immobility'.[3]

Orthodox Jewish rabbis are often not willing to enter into dialogue with others. Many Jews came from Oriental countries, where they escaped Christian 'oppression' and have only a peripheral interest in Christianity. Other Jews, especially from Eastern Europe, who knew Christian persecution, are glad at last to work out their own destiny free from Christian pressures. Their primary concern is to give political and social expression in Israel to the biblical imperative. These other concerns leave little time or energy for dialogue, and, in any case, only a minority of the population is religiously observant. Amongst the observant, fundamentalism is a growing phenomenon, shown for example in the campaign against the opening of a branch of Utah's Mormon Brigham Young University.[4]

The Jews who are involved in dialogue are scholars. Professor Shamaryahu Talmon, of the Hebrew University, has said their 'theological involvement is of a nature which more often than not does not express itself in pastoral activities. Their motivation to participate in the dialogue arises out of a historical cultural consciousness, no less, and sometimes more than out of their religious persuasion'.[5] Mostly they are of Western European or American background. Their interest springs partly from a desire to ensure that Christians are aware of the roots and dangers of antisemitism and to help gain friends for Israel, and partly from an historical concern with the origins of Christianity in relation to Judaism. Hardly any see any relevance of Christianity to their own faith commitment, although a few have a real appreciation of the person of Jesus. Some Jews are also involved in dialogue more as social-community workers concerned to build bridges of understanding between different groups.

Scarcely any Muslims have wished to involve themselves in interfaith dialogue – and certainly not at any official or public level. Arab-Israel hostility does not allow the necessary atmosphere of trust. Indeed, East Jerusalem Arabs are reluctant even to meet socially with Jews.[6] There is little scholarly Muslim leadership. Jerusalem has never been a centre of Islamic scholarship. After the 1948 flight of many Arabs from Israel, 'Israel was left with a considerable Arab population, but an Arab population without intellectuals, because among those who had left were all the intellectuals'.[7] A new generation of Israeli Arab intellectuals, mostly born in Israel and educated in Israeli schools and universities, has now grown up, but because of their educational background, they are not deeply versed in the Muslim intellectual tradition. A few have been willing to enter into dialogue on social and educational rather than religious issues. No such possibility has existed amongst Arabs in the occupied territories – and recently the situation in these territories has deteriorated.

Arab Christians, who are a majority of the indigenous Christian population, are also reluctant to share in dialogue. As a minority amongst a minority, they do not wish to draw attention to what separates them from their Muslim Arab brothers. Events in Lebanon have made them feel their marginality in the Middle East and a number of Christians have emigrated to the West. Those who have stayed have no history of dialogue and mostly lack the theological sophistication of those who would be their partners in dialogue. The Orthodox and Eastern Churches are not only disinterested in interfaith co-operation, they take little part in Christian ecumenical activities. The Uniate Churches – those in communion with Rome – are largely untouched by new Vatican teaching. Arab Christians feel no responsibility for the Holocaust and do not recognize that traditional teachings and liturgies have contributed to antisemitism. Indeed, they often feel that they, as Palestinians, are the innocent victims of Western guilt about the Holocaust. Further, the language of dialogue is usually English, in which Arab Christians may feel at a disadvantage. Fr Elias Chacour, speaking as an Arab Oriental Christian, observed that English was only his fourth foreign language and that his mentality, logic, style and approach to reality was different from those who took the lead in dialogue.[8]

Even amongst Western Christians, only a limited number take part in dialogue. Those who adopt a missionary stance towards Judaism do not wish to and would not be welcome. Dr Schoneveld said of the Ecumenical Theological Research Fraternity in Israel that 'it has kept aloof from all who were filled with a missionary zeal towards the Jewish people'.[9] Some Evangelical Christians, especially those associated with the 'International Christian Embassy' may give strong support to Israel. Yet, whether or not they are actively missionary, their hope is that the conversion of the Jews will be the prelude to the second coming of Christ.

Only a limited circle of people are engaged in interfaith dialogue. The Baha'is and the tiny handful at home in Eastern religions do not make any noticeable contribution. What Ezra Spicehandler said some time ago is still largely true. 'Those active in the interfaith movement are mainly Western European and American Christians and Western European and American Jews. The Christians are almost all clergy, while the Jews are laymen or non-orthodox clergy.'[10] There are a few exceptions and sometimes those from Israel who attend international conferences are able to participate in dialogue whilst abroad. Naturally for those deeply involved in Israeli life, peace is the uppermost priority although more theological dialogue may be the interest of the many scholars from overseas who spend time in Jerusalem.

Interfaith Activities

Despite all the difficulties and limitations, as Geoffrey Wigoder says, 'Israel is the scene of fruitful activity and dialogue'.[11] The first tentative efforts were made during the period of the Mandate. These were led by Martin Buber and another distinguished thinker Hugo Bergmann.

In 1957 the Israel Interfaith Committee, now known as the Israel Interfaith Association, was established with representatives of religious bodies in the country: Jews, Christians (Catholic, Orthodox and Protestant), Muslims and Druze. The inaugural meeting was attended by about one hundred people. Professor Mazar, the President of the Hebrew University, took the chair. A statement of purpose said, 'Since the establishment of Medinat Israel, the question of the relations between adherents of Judaism and the adherents of other religions has attained an unprecedented degree of moral and social significance', mentioning the holy places and the moral obligations thereby imposed on the Israeli government and people, the statement goes on, 'the relation between the majority in Israel and members of other religions in this sensitive area, constitute a probestone of the human and spiritual content of Israel's sovereignty and are likely to have an influence on ties between Israel and the nations of the world – as well as between Jews and non-Jews in other countries . . . The aim of this Council is to cultivate fellowship and tolerance between religious groups by means of broad educational endeavours which face up to existing difficulties and which seek to pave the road to mutual confidence. The council will seek to create contacts with similar organizations abroad.'[12]

The movement did not at first make much headway, except for occasional publications and reception and lectures. There was no on-going programme. Early in the seventies the committee was reactivated, largely through the initiative of Professor Werblowsky, a distinguished scholar of world religions. Mr Joseph Emanuel has for many years been the energetic full time secretary. Finance has always been a problem and recently the Committee has seemed in danger of collapse, because of prevailing suspicion about all meetings of Jews and Arabs. This gives added point to the words of the founders, quoted above, that the relation between religious communities will 'constitute a probestone of the human and spiritual content of Israel's sovereignty'.

There are two main areas of the Committee's work: amongst inhabitants of Israel and with visitors to the country. In Israel, the committee has helped to arrange meetings between members of the various communities. Those in Jerusalem have often been on theological matters, those in Galilee more often on cultural topics. There have been local groups in several cities. The committee has also done great work in making visitors aware of the contemporary religious situation in Israel. Often it has arranged speakers for parties of visitors, or for Christians staying in Israel to join a Jewish family for Passover or for the Sabbath. It has worked with other organizations to arrange some important seminars and colloquia. In November 1970, for example, an international colloquium was held on 'Religion, Peoplehood, Nation and Land'. In May 1972 a congress was held in Jerusalem on 'Black Africa and the Bible'.

Very recently, an Inter-religious Co-ordinating Council in Israel has been formed and held its first Annual Meeting in Jerusalem in January 1991. This is an umbrella organization on which many dialogue groups in Israel are represented.

There are a variety of other activities. In 1965 the Rainbow Group, of Jewish and Christian academicians, was established privately. Professor Zwi Werblowsky, the first chairman, described it as 'a private closed club of self-confessed, unrepentant intellectuals who meet for theological, intellectual labour'.[13] Canon Peter Schneider, an Anglican clergyman of Jewish birth, who was working in Israel, was the first secretary. At the monthly meetings, a paper is read and lively discussion follows. Some years ago, Dr Schoneveld, who was then secretary said, the group 'has come beyond the academic level and has evolved as a circle of friends, in which genuine confidence has been reached, so that most discussions no longer divide on merely Jewish and Christian lines but rather on the particular religious and social issues involved. This, however, has not been achieved because political and other sensitive issues were shunned. Rather the opposite is true'.[14]

Dialogue is also carried on at the Ecumenical Theological Research Fraternity in Israel and at numerous institutions such as the Ecumenical Centre for Theological Research at Tantur, at the Swedish Theological

Institute, at St Isaiah House, at the Martin Buber Centre for Adult Education and elsewhere.

At Nes Ammim, near Haifa, a Christian village was formed to identify with Israel. Its aim has been 'to serve Israel with investment, economic initiative and technical know-how. The desired outcome of this project, in human and moral terms, should be the experience of Israelis that there exists a genuinely Christian attitude of goodwill, service and profound respect for Jewry and Judaism; and a more concrete experience by Christians of the realities, values and problems of Jewish life and creative efforts in Israel'.[15] When it started in 1963 there were ten adults and two children. The village has grown steadily. It had at first to make clear that there was no missionary intention. Now with an attractive guest house, the village plays an important role in interpreting Israel to Western Christian visitors.

Another fascinating community is the hermitage Lavre Netofa, not far from Nazareth, founded by Fr Albuna Ya'akov Willebrand. The aim is to bring about an appreciation of Judaism, Christianity and Islam amongst Arabs and Israelis and to revive Eastern style monasticism.

For other groups the focus is less theological or dialogical, but more on community understanding and peace building. Neve Shalom is a community in which Arabs and Jews learn to live together 'in mutual respect and understanding'.[16] It also runs a School of Peace to which come young people from both communities. The recently formed Clergy for Peace also focusses 'on the present, on current events, not some far off theological discussion'.[17] It is a partnership between local clergy – mainly Christian and Jewish, but with a few Muslims and Druze. In 1989 the organization helped to arrange for Rabbi Levi Kelman to speak at a Melkite (Greek Catholic) church service near Acre.

The Issues

Jewish-Christian dialogue in Israel is conditioned by two events. The tragedy of the Holocaust and the rebirth of the Jewish nation.[18] 'The first impetus', wrote Professor Shemaryahu Talmon of the Hebrew University, 'to initiate interfaith meetings between Jews and Christians was given in the early post-second world war years by the experience of the Holocaust. The perpetration of the most horrible crimes in all history propelled Jews and Christians into an endeavour to analyze the psychological, social and theological factors which had made possible the indescribeable events of the war years. Jews had to discover for themselves to what degree a meaningful, renewed coexistence with Christianity was yet possible. Their endeavour was complemented by the heart-searching of conscientious

Christians in the Western world, who on their part scanned their own past as individuals and analyzed basic tenets of Christianity in the attempt to diagnose the theological-historical roots of antisemitism, aiming at conceiving ways and means of interpretation and self-education, which would safeguard Christians and Jews – indeed safeguard humanity – from the very possibility of another such hellish debacle.'[19] 'The founding of the State of Israel', he continued, 'introduced a new dimension into the dialogue situation. For many Jews and Christians the major issue of dialogue soon became the Israeli Jew and Jewry in the State of Israel. This shift could best be discerned in the direction which the dialogue took in post-war Germany. Wittingly or unwittingly, the Christian-Jewish encounter became pinpointed on the encounter of the new, or supposedly new, Germany with the sovereign State of Israel'.[20]

It was not until two decades after the war that Christian churches began to make official statements on Christian-Jewish relations. They were in part prepared for by the work of individual Christians, often living in Israel, who were very conscious of the burden of Christian guilt. If some of the pioneers may have over-compensated for this, they also had to justify their attempts to build a new Christian theology of Judaism to their fellow Christians.

Jewish confidence in Christian repentance was almost destroyed by the Six Day War. The silence of Christians during the war and their seeming unconcern over Israel's fate disillusioned Jewish partners in dialogue. The experience, however, convinced those Christians involved in the dialogue, that the question of the Land was central to Jewish-Christian dialogue. As Dr Hartman, a Jewish scholar put it, 'Christianity could have come to terms with the existence of the Jewish people in Tel Aviv – Tel Aviv could be disposed of as a manifestation of Zionist, secular, political nationalism. But when the Jews came back to Jerusalem, Judaism was back as a living force'.[21]

The silence of Christians outside Israel at the time of the Yom Kippur War was another disillusionment to Jewish partners in dialogue, eased a little by support from some Christians within Israel. Most Western Christians in Israel tried to adopt a mediating position in the hope that they could assist the process of reconciliation.

The Lebanon War and the prolonged *intafada* in the occupied territories and the Gulf War have made the situation more difficult. Jews often feel that Christians have been unsympathetic to their position. Certainly some who have worked with the Palestinians or who feel that the church should be on the side of the poor and oppressed have been very critical of Israeli actions. Comparing the action of the Israelis towards the Arabs to that of the Nazis to the Jews has caused deep pain and resentment. Because the indigenous churches' membership is mostly Arab, many Western churches have expressed solidarity with them, although some evangelical churches have taken Israel's side. Others, who through the dialogue have come to recognize the centrality of Israel in Jewish self-understanding, seek to be even-handed. Yet for Jews who see the Return in covenantal terms, this, says Geoffrey Wigoder is unsatisfactory. For them, 'there are ritual and ethical responsibilities as well as the duty to be, in the words of the Bible, "a beacon to the gentiles"'. The call should be to Jews to fulfil the social justice demanded of them as part of the covenant.[22]

It is inevitable that the political tensions in Israel and the West Bank should cloud the dialogue. Yet Israel has a continuing importance for other aspects of Jewish-Christian dialogue. It is there above all that Christians can be helped to rediscover the bonds that unite them with Jews and Judaism.

· 23 ·

Christians and Jews:
Conclusions

The suggestion has been made that Christian-Jewish dialogue has reached a 'plateau' or 'theoretical limit'. Rev. Allan Brockway, who was responsible for Christian-Jewish dialogue at the WCC in the eighties, said in 1988, 'Two years ago I suggested to you that the relation between the Church and the Jewish people was at a turning point, that "dialogue" as a formal process had reached a plateau on which we could sustain the present relationship but from which we could not move on to the necessary next stages . . . I proposed then that we – Christians and the Church – needed to "regroup" in order to discover what we had learned from the dialogue years.'[1] Dr A. Hertzberg, referring specifically to Jewish-Catholic dialogue, has suggested that the dialogue has reached its theoretical limit and that no further change is possible. The churches, he says, have by now defined their positions in the new circumstances while the Jews have also made their stands clear.[2]

Quite recently a number of books reviewing the progress made in the dialogue have appeared.[3] This suggests that this is a time for stock-taking. Some Christian leaders of the dialogue feel that a new understanding of Judaism has been affirmed but that the theological implications for the churches' self-understanding have yet to be recognized. Allan Brockway has written, 'Those churches which incorporate the continuing reality of the covenant between the Jewish people and God into their official theology establish a premise with far-reaching implications, both for their relations with the Jewish people and for Christian theology itself. By and large, however, the development and implementation of those implications remain in the future.'[4]

Geoffrey Wigoder writes that from a Jewish perspective, the Christian view of the Jews is still beset by major problems. The literal story of the crucifixion continues to foster negative attitudes towards Jews and Judaism. 'Christianity retains an innate triumphalism' and still in some quarters perpetuates a missionary approach. Real understanding of Jewish concern for the Land is often lacking and criticisms of Israel are widely resented.'[5]

Wigoder recognizes that 'the new-found triumphalism of certain Jewish right-wing Orthodox and nationalist circles is detrimental to any form of moderation, including interfaith understanding'.[6] Rabbi Dr Jonathan Sacks, the Chief Rabbi of Britain, has also spoken of 'deep religious revivals, built on intense hostility to the assumptions of the modern world' – assumptions which include the virtue of tolerance. 'The kind of theology that speaks of tolerance and openness and dialogue with the modern world is seen by many believers in search of meaning, truth and identity, as a compromise that lacks content and authenticity. And the result is that the most passionate believers today, in all our several faiths, are more concerned with their own destiny than with our collective destiny.'[6] Jonathan Sacks goes on to restate 'the Interfaith Imperative'.

It is in part the very development of the dialogue which has provoked the backlash. No one who enters into deep dialogue with members of another faith is unaffected by the experience. Christians who have been much involved are calling for theological rethinking. This, to opponents, confirms their criticism that dialogue leads to a weakening of the faith. The reply would be that faith is purified and strengthened by dialogue.

It is to be hoped that both the unofficial bodies for dialogue and the framework for official contact are strong enough to resist outspoken criticism and opposition. Real trust and friendship has been painstakingly built up since the Second World War. There may still be disagreements and tensions between those involved, but they have more in common than they have with extremists in their own faith communities.

· 24 ·

Christians and Muslims

The relationship of Christians and Muslims has at times, especially during the Crusades, been as bitter as that of Christians and Jews. In this century, scholars have helped members of both religions to a truer understanding of each other. In the last decade, there has been the beginning of official discussions between Muslims on the one hand and representatives of the Vatican or the World Council of Churches on the other.

Meetings arranged by the World Council of Churches

Cartigny, 1969

The first Christian-Muslim meeting initiated by the World Council of Churches, was held at Cartigny, near Geneva, in March 1969, following a prior planning meeting held during the previous year. Twenty-two Muslims and Christians met together for four days. The aide-memoire, prepared at the end, stressed the need for Christians and Muslims to meet, discussed what the two religions have in common, looked at the questions which the modern world poses for both religions, and considered the nature and tasks of dialogue.

Four reasons were given for the necessity of dialogue between Muslims and Christians. The first was the specific historical roots which the two religions have in common. Secondly, an attitude of self-criticism is inherent in each religion. Thirdly 'the increased mobility and mixing of populations which has made meetings of Christians and Muslims much more common, and has increased the responsibility of the two religions to find ways of living together in the same society'.[1] The fourth reason mentioned was 'the common responsibility of both religions with regard to the political problems in the Near East'.[2]

At this first meeting certain tasks were identified. One was the way in which both religions were presented in textbooks and religious instruction. Every caricature should not only be avoided 'but also struggled against'. Another was dealing with the problems arising from the growing mixing of Muslim and Christian populations. Thirdly, the question of mission and proselytism was raised. Fourthly, it was asked whether common prayer between Christians and Muslims was possible. The fifth question was 'What responsibility do Islam and Christianity have in regard to the human and social problems of our time (nature and function of the modern state, emancipation of women, relationships between rich and poor nations, etc).'[3]

Broumana, 1972

Although Christians and Muslims both took part in the multi-lateral dialogue at Ajaltoun in 1970,[4] the next bi-lateral meeting was not until July, 1972 at Broumana. Forty-six people attended, almost equally from the two religions. They came from twenty countries. The memorandum mentioned the reasons for meeting and considered the hopes for dialogue. It stressed three guiding principles for dialogue: 'frank witness . . ., mutual respect . . . and religious freedom'.[5] The responsibility of Christians and Muslims to achieve interracial, intercultural and international community and to be concerned for society was agreed. It was felt that the concept of revelation in both religions should be studied more carefully.

The question of sharing in each other's devotions, which is not often mentioned in reports, was also discussed. 'Where Muslims and Christians meet together we are not only listening to each other, but we are listening to God. On occasion, therefore, Christian and Muslim individuals or groups may also express their mutual understanding and trust in opening themselves to each other's devotional idiom, notably of *dua*, of supplication and meditation. Though conscious of our real and imagined differences in such actual or vicarious spiritual partnership, and though anxious to avoid misleading others, some of us felt that it was feasible to attempt this kind of interpenetration of mutual recognition and responsiveness to God.'[6]

Legon and Hong Kong

In 1974 another multi-lateral meeting was arranged. This was held in Colombo in April 1974 and ten Muslims took part.[7] In the same year, the first of two regional Christian-Muslim gatherings were held. This was at Legon, Ghana, in July 1974. The other was held at Hong Kong in January of the next year. The reports are particularly interesting, as they are more detailed and specific than previous world meetings.

The Legon meeting was the first Christian-Muslim meeting on an African regional basis and was marked by a desire for mutual awareness and caring. 'Christians should be willing', the report says, 'to share with their Muslim neighbours those facilities and opportunities for religious, educational, social and economic advancement which Christians happen to possess. A similar spirit may be expected from the Muslim side.'[8]

Examples of concrete, local collaboration are given. Joint prayers for the welfare of a whole community, goodwill messages on each other's feast days and the exchange of information about important events in each community are suggested. In schools, religious instruction should be provided for all religious groups represented. 'Christian and Muslim schools should be open to the principle of providing teachers and educational materials for the respective religious communities.'[9]

The discussion of family life and mixed marriages is very sensitive and insists that the primary duty of both religions is to help the individuals concerned. 'It is a matter of widespread concern that religions should not attempt to impose conditions on people whose emotional involvement, of which marriage is the natural climax, makes them ready and prepared to cross religious barriers, particularly when such conditions pertain to children as yet unborn. Religious leaders should never try to exploit the emotional vulnerability of such people for their own narrow confessional interests, but must instead help these people to fulfil their potential and discover for themselves what is true for them. Where religious counsel is requested from one or the other religious tradition, such help must be given, with the welfare and harmony of the people concerned as the over-riding consideration. It is unhealthy both for a normal family life and for the spirit of dialogue that religious competition should be extended into the field of family life and responsibility.'[10] Any suggestion that medical care should be conditional on religious confession is also condemned.

At the Hong Kong meeting, those present affirmed that their faiths enjoined a loving relationship with each other. They believed both religions had a responsibility to work together for political and social harmony and should defend each other's interests They deplored 'the deliberate and unnecessary multiplication of competitive charitable organizations and social agencies'.[11] By contrast, they commended the Inter-Religious Co-operation for Community Organization in Indonesia, which tried to meet direct human need in the country's big cities. Like their fellows at Legon, they argued that 'schools providing religious instruction for children from different religious communities should arrange to have such instruction given by qualified persons belonging to the respective communities'.[12] They rejected the view that because an educational institution had a religious foundation, it should only teach that religion.

Mission and Da'wah

Following the Nairobi Assembly of the World Council of Churches in 1975,[13] a consultation was held at Chambesy in Switzerland, in June 1976, to study the Christian concept of mission and the Muslim understanding of *da'wah*.[14] It was recognized that mission and *da'wah* are essential religious duties in the respective religions, but the importance of religious freedom was also affirmed. 'The conference was grieved to hear that some Christians in some Muslim countries have felt themselves limited in the exercise of their religious freedom and have been denied the right to church buildings. The Muslim participants regard such violation as contrary to Islamic law as well as to the principle of religious freedom.'[15] The Christian participants expressed their regret for Western imperialism and recognized that much missionary work had ulterior motives.

Cartigny, 1976

In the autumn of 1976, a meeting was arranged at Cartigny, near Geneva, to plan together the next steps in Christian-Muslim dialogue. It was especially important as it laid a foundation for the institutional consultation that continues to develop.[16] At the meeting it was agreed that preparation and sympathy for dialogue needed to be encouraged at all possible levels within both communities. The report says that whereas dialogue is usually thought of as conversation, it is often part of people's daily experience. Three areas of encounter, education, family life and prayer, were discussed in detail. Clarification on certain socio-political issues was required in the future. These included 'Faith and Politics in Islamic and Christian Thought' and 'Social Justice and Development'. Specific situations such as the Lebanon, faith and politics for Arab Christians and the place of Muslims in Europe needed attention. On theological matters, revelation; inter-religious attitudes; faith, science and technology; the future of humanity and Christian mission and Islamic *da'wah* are mentioned as deserving further study.

Beirut, 1977

In November 1977 a consultation was held in Beirut, Lebanon, on 'Faith, Science and Technology and the Future of Humanity'. Participants were well aware of the stark situation in Lebanon and of the gap between the heights of true faith and attrocities of the recent warfare. Three themes were pursued at the meeting. One was a historical and conceptual analysis. For this a paper was presented by Dr Wilfred Cantwell Smith on 'A Historian looks at faith, science and technology'. The second theme was 'Ecological and Socio-political concerns'. The third

area was 'Theological Concerns'. This included a discussion of humanity's
relation to nature and of the role of Jesus Christ as seen by Christians and
Muslims. On the latter subject, 'Christians present were moved at Muslim
insistence that the question be taken seriously, and the suggestion that so
long as doctrinal formulations were not stressed Christ could become an
important symbol for Muslims too (as indeed he is in the Qur'an), as
humanity wrestles with the deepest problems of science, technology and its
own future. The symbol of the cross, its meaning for Muslims and for
Christians, the role of suffering and of willingness to suffer, of potential
defeat and ultimate victory for persons as they plunge into the present
crisis received considerable attention. Also the question was addressed of
the connotations of the cross for not only person but city, for society and
social justice.'[17]

Chambesy, 1979

In March 1979 a planning meeting was held at Chambesy, Switzerland.
The variety of situations in different parts of the world, which mean that
Christian-Muslim relations are themselves varied, was recognized. Continuing suspicions of dialogue were also recognized and the group insisted
'that dialogue must never be used as a tool for proselytism. Organized
missionary activities generate tensions between Christians and Muslims
which are causing increasing concern. In order to build trust and
confidence for the sake of future relations between us these activities
should be restrained'.[18] The need for dialogue at official, popular and
academic levels was affirmed. In a cautious note on prayer together, the
group said, 'We desire to avoid all confusion and syncretism which may
come from attempts to worship together. We may however expect to
invoke God's blessing on all we undertake together and to listen together to
our respective scriptures.'[19] The group also insisted that 'all planning
should continue to be undertaken jointly by both partners'.[20] This may
sound fairly obvious, but too often one group has tried to push its agenda.
The meeting sketched out a programme of action for the next few years,
giving particular encouragement to regional consultations.

Meeting of Youth

In 1980 the first official Muslim-Christian youth dialogue was held at
Bossey in Switzerland. The role of religion in promoting change was
discussed and the ambiguities of cultural dominance. Participants also
sketched their visions of the future. The fear of dialogue being misused for
conversionist activity was talked about and missionary activities were
criticized.

Sri Lanka, 1982

In 1982, a conference was held in Sri Lanka on 'Christians and Muslims Living and Working Together: Ethics and Practices of Humanitarian and Development Programmes'. Significantly, this meeting, held at the invitation of the Sri Lankan Minister for Muslim Affairs, was jointly organized by WCC and the World Muslim Congress, which has its headquarters in Karachi. As a result, it was recommended that the two bodies should establish a joint planning committee to intensify the dialogue. It was hoped that representatives of other international Islamic organizations and of the Roman Catholic Church would also become involved. The plight of refugees and the problems of minorities were discussed. The Christian participants stayed on after the meeting to evaluate it. They stressed the urgency of Christian-Muslim dialogue.

Regional Consultations

In recent years, as suggested at Chambesy in 1979, a number of regional consultations have been held. The first in Porto Novo, Benin in March 1986, was on 'Religion and Responsibility'. The role of the Islamic state was discussed. At Bali, Indonesia, in December 1986, the subject was 'Advancing Together into the Next Century'. Again religion and the state and religion and family life were main topics. At Kolymbari, Greece in September 1987, and at New Windsor, USA in March 1988, questions of religious pluralism, increasingly characteristic of much of the Western world, were discussed. 'Religion and Life' was the subject of the meeting at Usa River, Tanzania in June 1989. These regional meetings, in Stuart Brown's words 'were designed to consider issues of local importance, to reinforce local interfaith communication and to contribute to the development of an international network of veterans of dialogue'.[21] What has been learned in these regional consultations will be of value to the WCC as it sets about elaborating a set of 'ecumenical considerations' for Christian-Muslim dialogue.

Progress and Problems

In his assessment of Christian-Muslim dialogue at the Review Meeting of the WCC Sub-Unit at Casablanca, Morocco, in June 1989, Dr Tarek Mitri observes that many Muslims still suspect that dialogue is a new mode of mission and evangelization. 'The credibility problem is far from being solved.'[22] Of those Muslims who are ready for dialogue, few are interested in theological discussion. There is greater interest in practical issues and in 'discerning together spiritual meanings in the sufferings and struggles of daily life'.[23] Initially, Dr Tarek Mitri writes, the dialogue was

with 'liberal-modernist' Muslim intellectuals. This has been followed by
attempts to build lasting and acceptable relations with Pan-Islamic
bodies, on the assumption that they are 'more representative'. Dr Mitri
warns, however, of the temptations which may not have been avoided.
'One is to aspire towards contributing, from outside, to an Islamic reform
(or perhaps reformation). Another is to consider institutional Islam as the
legitimate representative of the majority, the real Islam, as it were. The
issue of who represents Islam, of who can speak on its behalf authorita-
tively, is controversial amongst Muslims around the world. Christians
cannot always follow their own criteria or preferences, as they look for
partners.'[24] He mentions the need to dialogue with mystical Muslims and
militant Muslims, recognizing that the partners in dialogue and the
agendas are inextricably linked. He stresses the need to involve the 'silent
Muslims' – the great majority who as yet are not interested in dialogue. He
also points to three unfinished tasks: 'Proselytism, the misuse of Church
diakonia and other forms of organized missionary activity; religious
freedom and other rights of religious minorities, as well as human rights;
religion and state, models of society and problems of modernization and
secularization.'[25] A further issue, identified by Dr Michael Mildenberger
from Germany, is the position of Muslim minorities in Christian countries
and Christian minorities living in the Islamic world.[26]

The Vatican

Visits

During this same period there have been the beginnings of official
contact between the Vatican and the Muslim world. The Secretariat for
Non-Christians, now renamed The Pontifical Council for Inter-religious
Dialogue, was set up in 1964.[27] The second President, Cardinal Pignedoli
from Italy developed a policy of travelling widely to visit religious leaders
and of welcoming delegations to Rome. In 1974, for example, he travelled
to Saudi Arabia to meet King Faysal and other leaders. Later in the year
he visited the Supreme Council for Islamic Affairs in Cairo. Such visits
have become characteristic of the work of the secretariat. Soon after Msgr
Arinze, who was quickly made a Cardinal, became head of the department, he attended the Fourth Assembly of the World Conference on
Religion and Peace. Following that he journeyed to Indonesia. Later, he
attended an Islamo-Christian consultation at Windsor Castle, chaired by
the Crown Prince of Jordan. In 1985 he went to Cordoba for the
celebration of the twelfth centenary of the mosque/cathedral, attended a
regional Episcopal Conference in West Africa and journeyed with Pope

John Paul II during his visit to Morocco.[28] In subsequent years he has continued to travel widely.

Numerous guests have been welcomed at Rome. In 1977, for example, a delegation came from Indonesia in November, led by the Minister for Religious Affairs, Dr Mukti Ali and, in the following month, from Iran, led by Professor Sayyed Hossein Nasr. The following year, the Mufti of North Yemen and his suite were guests in Rome.

Meetings Sponsored by the Secretariat

Unlike the WCC Sub-Unit on Dialogue the Vatican secretariat, whilst participating in many meetings, has arranged few itself. One very important event was the Islamic-Christian Dialogue held in Tripoli in February 1976, although it proved to be a controversial occasion and did not go as planned. It arose from a visit to Cardinal Pignedoli by Dr Shehati, Secretary for Foreign Affairs of the Libyan Socialist Union. In prior discussion the purely religious nature of the gathering was stressed. It had been intended that the delegations should each consist of twelve members and that a few observers should be invited. The Catholic delegation was taken aback to find some five hundred guests were present. Throughout, the Catholics were given generous hospitality, but the Muslim delegation 'carried out its "dialogue" by systematically attacking the Catholic delegation'.[29] It was in preparing the final declaration that difficulties occurred. The declaration included two paragraphs, numbered 20 and 21, which attacked Zionism as 'an aggressive racialist movement', affirmed 'the national rights of the Palestinian people and their right to return to their lands' and 'the Arab character of the city of Jerusalem' and demanded 'the liberation of all prisoners in occupied Palestine and of all occupied territories'.[30] The Cardinal, on hearing the declaration, made known the Catholic disagreement with these paragraphs, which the Vatican repudiated.

The other sections of the Declaration are unexceptional and show quite a measure of agreement and understanding. In reflecting on the meeting, the report in the *Bulletin* says that despite the final episode, the gathering showed the necessity and urgency of dialogue, in the sense of mutual listening and acceptance, with Muslims. It also showed the difficulties. 'There is a discrepancy of history, of culture, of social evolution, of religious mentality, which only now we fully realize.'[31] The most concrete result of the days in Tripoli and the most valid methodology for dialogue seem, for the moment, to be meeting and personal welcome: to feel and call each other brothers in the name of the same God.'[32] The conference also showed, despite the assurances asked for by the Catholics that it would be purely religious, how easily dialogue can be perverted for political purposes.

In May 1985 the Secretariat helped to organize a colloquium on 'Holiness in Islam and Christianity' at the Pontifical Institute of Arabic and Islamic Studies in Rome. Twelve Muslim and twelve Christian scholars participated.[33] The links built up by Fr Thomas Michel in Turkey lead to a colloquium being held at the Gregorian University in 1988. This was attended by twelve professors from different theological faculties in Turkey and twelve scholars from Catholic institutions in Rome. In the same year, the secretariat hosted a Christian-Muslim encounter at Assisi on 'Co-existence in the midst of Differences'. A small group of Christians and Muslims from the countries of North Africa attended. 'Three factors contributed to its success', writes Fr Michael L. Fitzgerald of the Secretariat, 'the prior preparation in the different countries, the Franciscan spirit in Assisi and the concluding audience with Pope John Paul II.'[34]

Educating the Church for Dialogue

The staff of the secretariat is supported by expert consultants for each religion. In 1979, for the first time, a Plenary Assembly of the secretariat was held, bringing together the members, consultors and experts. At the meeting, an examination was made of progress in Christian-Muslim dialogue. Subsequent plenary meetings have been held at Grottaferrata, near Rome in 1984 and 1987. In 1989, a two day meeting was held just for the consultors on Islam.

An important part of the Commission for Religious Relations with Islam, set up in 1975 which is part of the Secretariat, has been to educate members of the Roman Catholic Church on dialogue with Islam. In 1981 a revised version of *Guidelines for Dialogue between Christians and Muslims*, which was first issued in 1969, was published.[35] In the same year a selection from the Pope John Paul II's speeches, which touched on Christian-Muslim relations was produced.[36] At the Synod of Bishops, held in Rome in October 1983 Msgr Jadot reported on the Secretariat's work, with special reference to Islam. In Rome too, interdicasterial meetings are held two or three times a year to allow members of other departments of the Roman Curia to be brought up to date on different aspects of Christian-Muslim relations. It fell to the secretariat too to make arrangements for the Muslim guests to the Assisi World Day of Prayer.

Other Activities

Whilst the Vatican and the WCC have taken many initiatives in the field of Christian-Muslim relations, numerous other bodies have been active. The Centre for the Study of Islam and Christian-Muslim Relations at Selly

Oak Colleges, Birmingham, provides study courses and undertakes research. The Islamic Foundation in Leicester takes part in dialogue with Christians and people of other faiths. Professor Hasan Askari, who was for some years at the Centre in Birmingham, has set up his own Inter-religious Foundation in London. The report of the Vatican Secretariat lists many other organizations which have arranged consultations.[37]

The growing number of Muslims in Europe has stimulated Christians there to a greater concern for good community relations and for interfaith understanding. The World of Islam Festival in London created some interest and prompted some reflection on Christian attitudes to Islam.[38] In February 1978 the Conference of European Churches arranged a consultation in Salzburg, for representatives of churches in East and West Europe and for representatives of specialized organizations to consult with Muslim lecturers and specialists.

Jews, Christians and Muslims

Muslims and Christians, like Jews, look back to Abraham, as the father of the faithful. Because of their common semitic origin, some have felt there should be a special relationship between these religions, and this desire is expressed, for example, in the Standing Conference of Jews, Christians and Muslims in Europe.

It was early in the sixties that some young Jews and some young Germans began to develop a curiosity about each other. Rabbi Lionel Blue and Rabbi Dow Marmur made contact with Pastor Schoneich and Pastor Maechler, and arranged the first interchange between an English synagogue and a German church.

The unsettled situation in the Middle East made both Jewish and Christian participants aware of a third religion, Islam. Already, too, there was a considerable Muslim community in Europe, about which there was widespread ignorance. Helped by Bishop Scharf, Pastor Maechler organized a meeting in Berlin between a number of Jewish, Christian and Muslim religious leaders and students. The meeting took place at the end of the war of 1967, not far from the Villa in Wannsee, where the 'Final Solution' was planned.

One meeting led to another, so that trust and confidence began to grow. By 1971 it was felt that the time had come to form a loose organization, known as the Standing Conference of Jews, Christians and Muslims in Europe. The Standing Conference has four main aims; to help educate ministers of religion; to provide better information about the three religions; to encourage religious minorities in their search for identity in the European setting; and to improve public relations between religious minorities, the Standing Conference, and society.[39]

In 1972 the first European Conference was held in London, in February – somewhat interrupted by the power cuts caused by the miners' go-slow. The subject was 'The Faith of our Fathers – the Fate of our Children'. The main addresses were given by Rev. Michael Hollings, Dr M. Navearn, and Rabbi Dr Louis Jacobs.

The second European Conference was held near Haarlem in Holland in March, 1973, attended by some fifty people. The conference explored the role of religion in a secularized time. A few accepted a positive, critical function of secularization, but the majority warned against its dangers. The third conference was held at Berlin in November 1974 on 'Violence and its Roots'.

Branches of JCM have now been established in Germany, Great Britain and Holland. These have arranged a number of smaller gatherings, interchange of theological students and lectures. The annual meeting at Bendorf-am-Rhein, Germany, for students from the three religions have been especially important.

When the Standing Conference was set up, it was felt that the existing structure of interfaith co-operation mirrored the past, not the present, reality. There were a number of Christian-Jewish councils and friendship organizations to combat antisemitism. It was difficult to enlarge these to include Muslims. On the other hand, interfaith organizations which included all religions were too general for the dialogue desired between the 'Abrahamic' religions. Now the possibility is growing of Jewish-Muslim bilateral conversations.

Conclusions

There is plenty for Christians and Muslims to discuss and to do together. In his report in 1979, Mgr Rossano declared, 'Dialogue with Muslims will certainly be one of the principal tasks of the Church in the future'.[40] In his Preface to *Christians Meeting Muslims*, published in 1977, Dr Mülder, who was moderator of the Sub-Unit for Dialogue, rightly said that 'when compared to a history of many, many centuries of tensions, these ten years show a remarkable development, a new spirit of co-operation, a real effort towards mutual understanding'. He warns, however, 'that ten years is a short period and that the sapling of dialogue is still very tender and continually in danger of being uprooted'.[41] The danger comes from those on both sides who, theologically, reject the approach of dialogue and from explosive political and social situations which would wreck the new-found friendship and trust. 'Much goodwill', as Dr Mülder says, 'on both sides is needed to overcome tensions.'[42]

Recent events in the Islamic world, with the rise of very rigorist Islamic regimes in Iran and elsewhere have increased the difficulties of dialogue. The prolonged repercussions of the publication of Salman Rushdie's *The Satanic Verses*, which most Muslims regarded as an insulting and blasphemous attack on their religion, have given political importance to the relation of Islamic states to Western nations – showing the different suppositions of the democratic states which have been influenced by Christianity.

The regained self-confidence of the Muslim world suggests that dialogue with Islam will be of increasing importance. Yet this very self-confidence may make some Muslims feel that dialogue is a form of compromise. The Qur'an teaches respect for the 'people of the Book' (Jews and Christians) – and some Muslims have extended this to Hindus and Buddhists: but there is a clear belief that the message of the Prophet is the final word of God. Mr A. K. Borhi, Minister for Religious Affairs of Pakistan, for example, has said that Islam is not 'just one religion among others', it is 'in some sense the totality of the religious experience of all mankind'.[43] Christians have often made similar claims for their religion. Some people, therefore, have suggested that the next major struggle for supremacy in the world will be between the Islamic nations and the Western powers, which in such a competition would increasingly find unity by stressing their Christian heritage. The alternative is dialogue by which members of both faiths seek the understanding and peace to which the founders of their religions bore witness.

· 25 ·

Dialogue with Hindus

The mutual influence on each other of Hinduism and Christianity has grown steadily during the last one hundred and ninety years. Although there was a Christian presence in India from at least the second century CE, mutual interaction dates from the missionary era and especially from the beginning of the nineteenth century. Leading figures of the Hindu Renaissance, such as Ram Mohun Roy, Keshub Chander Sen, Rabindranath Tagore or Dr Radhakrishnan, were influenced by Christianity. Equally, Europeans, such as the philosopher Schopenhauer or Annie Besant, who became a leader of the Theosophical Movement, were affected by Hinduism.

There have been various interfaith movements in India, but paradoxically the hospitality of Hinduism has sapped their growth. Leaders of the Hindu Renaissance have affirmed the equality of religions. Swami Vivekananda, as we have seen, declared at the World's Parliament of Religions that 'to the Hindu, the whole world of religions is only a travelling, a coming up of different men and women through various conditions and circumstances to the same goal'.[1] Dr Radhakrishnan, as mentioned earlier, looked for the emergence of a universal religion, of which the various historical religions are the branches.[2]

The view that all religions are really the same and the acceptance of different spiritual paths as equally valid has made for tolerance. It has, however, perhaps made Hindus too tolerant of differences and not especially interested in reconciling or overcoming them. Thus the dynamic necessary to interfaith work has been lacking. At the same time, to members of semitic religions, the Hindu approach seems to evade questions of truth. For them, it has been unhelpful to be told that all religions really say the same thing, when they are convinced that they do not. Christians have often, therefore, recoiled from the embrace of Hinduism for fear that their integrity and their claims for the uniqueness of

Christ might be compromised. Whilst there has been a growing concern that Christianity in India should not appear alien, but be expressed in an Indian idiom, there has been a constant fear lest the particularity of the Christian Gospel be endangered. Thus the Hindu assertion that all religions really say the same has led to an easy acquiescence in difference, so robbing interfaith movements of their drive, whilst frightening away from close contact Christians who have feared that they might be put in a false position. Together with this, the relation of religions has been complicated by political issues. The desire of many Muslims, during the struggle for independence, for a Muslim state, led often to hostility towards Hindus. Before independence, Christians were often identified with the alien ruling power, and since independence have been concerned to show that they were active Indian citizens. The Sikhs, whose homeland was split by partition, had to spend many years struggling for a Punjabi state.

In any case, the views of most nineteenth-century Christian missionaries were hostile to Hinduism. Only gradually did Christians become interested in sympathetic study of Hinduism and then in dialogue.

An exception to such nineteenth-century hostility was William Miller, who was Principal of Madras Christian College at the turn of the century. He believed that Hinduism had a place in God's plan. 'Future generations', he wrote, 'will see clearly . . . that Hinduism and the Hindus are embraced within the limits of God's plan. The time will come when it will be deemed simply foolish to deny that Hindu thought, as truly as Greek philosophy, or Roman law, is a factor in the building of the historic fabric of which the foundation was laid when Abraham was called and of which the cornerstone is Christ.'[3] He spoke of Christ fulfilling the aspirations of Hinduism, but also of Christianity needing to be fulfilled by the contributions of other religions. As Dr Kaj Baago notes, Miller's view and that of Bernard Lucas of the London Missionary Society, need to be distinguished from the idea of fulfilment usually associated with J. N. Farquhar and his influential book, *The Crown of Hinduism*. 'Whereas Farquhar always maintained that the fulfilment of Hinduism in Christianity would happen through a *replacement* of Hinduism by Christianity, Miller and Lucas expected the fulfilment to take place through a *development* of all higher religions, Christianity included, into a World Religion with Christ as centre.'[4]

Miller expressed his support for the World's Parliament of Religions, but, apart from attempts within the Brahmo-Samaj, (a founding member of IARF) and by Keshub Chander Sen, in his Church of the New Dispensation, to include material from all religions, the first interfaith

developments were associated with Mahatma Gandhi and his independence movement.

Mahatma Gandhi

Gandhi was guided by five underlying principles in his discussion of the
relation between religions. First, *Satya* (Truth) and *Ahimsa* (Non-Violence) served as the key to unlock the mysteries of all religions. Second,
the Bhagavadgita was the clue to the scriptures of the world. Third, the
principle of equi-mindedness enabled him to look for agreement, rather
than differences, between religions. Fourth, the experience of the seeker
served as the final norm of judgment about truth and the validity of a
religious doctrine. Finally, a religion had to be studied through the
writings of a known votary of that religion. He believed that all principal
faiths constitute a revelation of Truth, but, as they are expounded by
fallible men, they are all affected by imperfections. Beneath the
differences of the actual religions, he proclaimed a religion of humanity
that underlay them all. He never tired of pointing out to adherents of
different religions that they all believed in one God. Addressing Hindus
and Muslims, he said, 'We believe in one and the same God, the
difference of nomenclature in Hinduism and Islam notwithstanding.'[5]
He thought of the underlying religion or *dharma* as a 'belief in the ordered
moral movement of the universe' and in personal terms as the search for
truth.[6]

He appealed to the adherents of different religions to recognize their
underlying unity. 'The need of the moment', he wrote in *All Religions are
True*, 'is not one religion, but mutual respect and tolerance of the devotees
of different religions. We want to reach not the dead level, but unity in
diversity. Any attempt to root out tradition, effects of heredity, climate
and other surroundings, is not only bound to fail but is sacrilege. The
soul of religion is one, but it is encased in a multitude of forms . . . God is
one, whatever the name given him.'[7] In the spirit of *swadeshi* (acceptance
of our immediate situation) he recognized the particularity of each
religion to which an adherent should remain loyal, but he pleaded for
harmony and mutual understanding.

Gandhi, on the basis of his own experience, made various suggestions
for relating one religion to another. The first step to effect understanding
was a serious and reverent study of other scriptures, with an impartial
mind, from the standpoint of their adherents. Equally important was the
willingness to live together with people of other faiths. This was not so
much geographical or spatial proximity, as a social relatedness, which
rejected the predominant caste and communal mentality.

'I hold', he wrote, 'that believers who have to see the same God in others that they see in themselves must be able to live amongst all with sufficient detachment. And the ability to live thus can be cultivated not by fighting shy of unsought opportunities for such contacts, but by hailing them in a spirit of service.'[8] As a further step, he suggested active participation by all religious communities in constructive programmes of nation-building. Understanding between religions resulted from their adherents actively sharing in such constructive ventures as the improvement of village sanitation, education of villagers, or the removal of untouchability. 'The edifice of unity', he said, 'can rest on constructive work alone.'[9] This is an important insight, as too often interfaith meetings have been all words and no action.

In an atmosphere of mutual tolerance, he thought each religion should be ready to adopt and adapt good things in other religions. Equally, each religion should work for the good of others. 'Our inmost prayer should be that a Hindu should be a better Hindu, a Muslim a better Muslim and a Christian a better Christian.'[10] He opposed the efforts of missionaries to win converts, although when pressed by C. F. Andrews, he admitted that on occasion an individual, for his spiritual growth, might wish to change religions.

Gandhi was particularly concerned to reconcile Hindus and Muslims and opposed the partition of India on independence. He attracted members of various faiths to his movement and at his Ashrams, devotions included readings from the scriptures of the world. He was not particularly concerned with theological differences, but wished to see members of all religions working together for the development of the nation.

A number of Christians joined the Gandhian movement and formed part of the Gandhian inner circle. Amongst the missionaries were C. F. Andrews, Verrier Elwin and Ralph Richard Keithahn, whilst Indian Christians included Rajkumari Amrit Kaur, S. K.George, Aryanayagam, Bharatan Kumarappa and J. C. Kumarappa, who wrote *The Practice of Precepts of Jesus*.

S. K. George

We may concentrate on S. K. George, as he was most active in promoting inter-religious fellowship. In 1932 when he declared his support for Gandhi, he was compelled to resign his post at Bishop's College, Calcutta. He had an unsettled life, scratching a living from occasional teaching jobs and from his writings. He and his wife espoused a variety of good causes, including the Inter-Religious Student Fellowship and The Fellowship of the Friends of Truth.

The Inter-Religious Student Fellowship was an offshoot of the International Fellowship. The International Fellowship, of which A. A. Paul was
founder secretary, came into being during the period of the national
struggle for independence, with a view to creating mutual understanding
between people of different races and religions in India. It became a forum
for inter-religious discussions and international encounters. From this was
born the Inter-Religious Student Fellowship, with the organization of
which S. K. George helped in the thirties and forties. The aims and basis
of the Inter-Religious Student Fellowship declared that the religious
attitude was of permanent value to mankind and always deserved reverent
recognition. The fellowship desired to encourage mutual respect, appreciation and sympathy of religions for each other, and to this end said 'it is
absolutely necessary that no member of the fellowship should claim for his
religion any exclusive and final possession of truth'.[11] Further, 'we do not
desire to persuade any within the fellowship to our own religious belief and
practice.'[12]

This was to renounce the missionary thrust of the Church, and George
believed that Christianity should not seek to replace Hinduism, but find its
place within it, as 'a structure of Hinduism'.[13] Hinduism, he held, had 'a
place for Jesus among the many leaders and teachers it reverences as
revealers of God to man, nay as incarnations of God in his aspect as the
Lover and Redeemer of men. Its conception of a favourite God, Ishta
Devata, would sanction even an exclusive worship of him to those who find
in such adoration the way to God-realization. But it would definitely place
him in its own setting among the diverse modes and ways in which the
Unfathomable and the Eternal manifests itself to mortal minds. Who can
say that this is not the setting in which he will find his permanent place in
the religious heritage of the race, at any rate in India.'[14] It is not surprising
that with such views, which for most Christians would have meant an
abandonment of their convictions, George did not attract many Christians
to the Inter-Religious fellowship, and with independence achieved both
the International Fellowship and the Inter-Religious Student Fellowship
went out of active existence.

The Fellowship of the Friends of Truth

The Fellowship of the Friends of Truth is also no longer active in India,
having been largely replaced by the Bhoodan-Gramdan Movement. The
British branch, formed in 1956, however, continues to hold conferences
and meetings and to publish a newsletter.[15]

The Fellowship grew out of the experience of members of the Society of
Friends working and worshipping together with Gandhi and some of his

followers. Horace Alexander, an English Quaker, was walking through some fields in East Bengal with Gandhi one day in January 1947. 'It seems to me', Alexander said, 'that what the world, especially India, needs above all today is some religious fellowship which can be joined by adherents of all the chief religions. I am not now thinking of a Syncretistic movement . . . I am thinking of a union of hearts, a fellowship in which men of each faith . . . all find themselves at one, because they are seeking together to practice the truth of God in the world. And I have wondered whether the Society of Friends, the "Quakers" so called, could help to provide such a meeting ground.' After some thought, Gandhi agreed that the Quakers would be the best society: 'but only on one condition. Are they prepared to recognize that it is as natural for a Hindu to grow into a Friend as it is for a Christian to grow into one?' Horace Alexander replied: 'Some would agree to that condition and some would not. I, for one, am one of those who would readily accept that position, not only for Hindus but for Muslims and others'.[16] The Friends, as a society, felt unable to commit themselves to the idea. Still today the views of Quaker Universalists, who question the centrality of Jesus in the Quaker tradition, are disputed. A number of individual Quakers, however, did support the suggestion.

At a meeting held at the Friends Rural Centre, Rasulia, in 1949 the Fellowship was formed.[17] S. K. George took a leading part, being at times secretary and editor of the *Quarterly*. Meetings were held in different parts of the country and quite a membership was built up. With the death of George in 1962, the quarterly ceased publication. For a time, a newsletter was published by G. Ramachandran, a well-known member of Parliament, who had founded Gandhigran, which was a rural, social and educational development in South India, which was also the headquarters of the Fellowship of the Friends of Truth.

The specific interfaith movements, inspired by Gandhi, may have disappeared in India, but his approach to the relationship of religions is still influential amongst those who seek to perpetuate his ideas. The Bhoodan-Gramdan movement attracts workers from different faiths. As we have seen, the Gandhi Peace Foundation acted as host for one of the preparatory meetings that led to the Kyoto World Conference on Religion and Peace.[18] Perhaps the special contribution of Gandhi was linking interfaith fellowship and practical action together, and many of those who came to share his ideas on the relation of religions were attracted by his work of nation-building.[19]

Chenchiah

An Indian Christian, who also hoped that religions could work together in building the new India, was Chenchiah. He was a lawyer and rose to be Chief Justice of Pudokottai High Court. He was an ardent nationalist and was concerned that Christianity should adapt to the needs and aspirations of India. He contributed to the book *Rethinking Christianity*, and was for a time editor of *The Pilgrim*, which was concerned with the relation of Christianity to other religions. He devoted most of the March 1950 issue of *The Pilgrim* to advocating 'the desirability of co-operation of religions in the new national set-up of India'.[20] Where religions had met in a spirit of brotherhood, they had first discovered what they had in common, but then became aware of their differences. The need now for renewal required a pooling of resources. His aim, therefore, was 'to stress the importance of the study of comparative religion – for the formation of a universal faith – and to point out what common practical efforts religions have tried to draw together and co-operate'.[21] His mention of some practical attempts at co-operation are especially interesting. He described the common celebration of festivals in Madras: he pleaded for a place for common prayers in every town: he asked Christians to take the lead in suggesting common prayers at times of grave national crisis, and he mentioned the small groups which he had started, consisting of Christians and Hindus who joined together in prayer for the sick. He spoke, too, of the beginnings made in the field of common worship. Criticized by Dr Kraemer, Chenchiah made clear that he rejected the 'facile maxim' that all religions lead to the same goal. Inter-religious co-operation was the story of how 'life-forces of three different religions brought together are coalescing and producing – a new type of life'.[22]

'Discontinuity'

Chenchiah's was a voice in the wilderness. Although in the wake of the 'fulfilment' theory, Christian missionary scholars had studied Hinduism sympathetically, by the forties the mood had changed, under the influence of Hendrik Kraemer, who argued in his *The Christian Message in a Non-Christian World* that the church's primary task was 'the announcement of the Message of God which is not adaptable to any religion or philosophy'.[23] The general view of Christian thinkers in India in the forties, as represented for example by Dr Marcus Ward's *Our Theological Task*, was that whilst it was right to interpret the Gospel in Indian terms, there was an unchangeable fundamental core of the Christian faith that could not be altered. At the same time, the partition of India, accompanied by bloody communal fighting, had embittered the relations of Hindus and Muslims. Attention, too, was directed to the problems facing newly independent India, and Christians were concerned to discover their identity in the new situation.

CISRS

It was thanks to Paul Devanandan, through the newly-formed Christian Institute for the Study of Religion and Society (CISRS) at Bangalore, of which he became director in 1956, that Christian attention was again directed to Hinduism. He was aware of the resurgence of the ancient religions of Asia and of the cultural influence of Hinduism in the newly independent India. He wanted Christians to play a full part in nation-building. Through the institute he arranged occasions for dialogue between Christian and Hindu thinkers, and also stimulated Christian thinking about the relationship of the church to contemporary Hinduism.

One of the first seminars, for example, held at Nagpur in 1958, took as its theme 'The Christian Approach to Renascent Hinduism'. Many of the papers and discussions at these seminars are recorded in *Religion and Society*, the bulletin of the Institute. The debates of the sixties are a preview of the discussions in the World Council of Churches in the seventies. It can be seen that gradually there is less fear of compromising the finality of Christ and of the risk involved in dialogue. Increasingly, dialogue is thought to have its own inherent value and is not regarded as a new form of evangelization. It is recognized that as part of his commitment the Christian has certain beliefs about Jesus and that he brings these to the dialogue, but the purpose of dialogue is a common search for truth. There is some tension between those who stress common humanity as the basis for dialogue and those who put emphasis on sharing religious experience. Besides the growing openness to dialogue, the seminars have led to a deepening understanding by Christians and Hindus of each other's beliefs. The discussions have been mainly at an intellectual and doctrinal level and have generated a considerable literature.[24]

'Christian Revelation and World Religions'

At the same time, some Roman Catholic theologians were coming to speak of the world religions as the ordinary means of salvation. In November 1964 a conference on 'Christian revelation and non-Christian religions' was held, under the auspices of the thirty-eighth International Eucharistic Congress (Bombay), in St Pius College, Goregaon. The preceding week, the Second Vatican Council had approved the decree on 'The Attitude of the Church Towards Non-Christian religions'. An inaccurate report of the conference circulated in some newspapers and provoked some controversy. Even so, the suggestion that salvation was available to non-Christians – even if, as speakers argued this was based on Catholic teaching – was still at the time surprising to many members of the Church. Some of the speakers further suggested that this salvation was mediated through the world religions. The four papers by Hans Küng, Piet Fransen, Joseph Masson and Raymond Panikkar were influential in making known the new thinking in the church, which has become widely accepted since Vatican II.[25]

Abhishiktananda and Bede Griffiths

Whilst learning about Hinduism and theological consideration of the limits to salvation preoccupied some Christians, others attempted to enter into the spirituality of Hinduism. The group which centred around Swami Abhishiktananda, who as a Catholic monk had adopted the way of life of a sannyasin, included for a time the Swiss Ambassador Jacques Albert Cuttat and the Anglican priest, Fr Murray Rogers. The Upanishads were read in a meditative way 'to enter as authentically as possible into the experience which has moulded the religious soul of India'.[26] This search for a spiritual, meeting point has become increasingly influential, as the works of Swami Abhishiktananda have become known outside India. Bede Griffith's ashram in South India has also been a place of pilgrimage and renewal for many from the West. The ashram and Bede Griffith's writings have stimulated many to seek a spiritual meeting point of religions.[27] A number of ashrams, both Christian and Hindu, are also centres of inter-religious dialogue.

Recent Developments

The last twenty five years have seen a growing interest by Christian thinkers in India, both Protestant and Roman Catholic, in Hinduism. They study it deeply and have penetrating discussions with Hindu scholars. It is uncertain whether this interest is shared by ordinary church members, but in the churches there is a concern that the Christian faith should be expressed in an Indian idiom. The approach of the theologians is clearly from a Christian standpoint. They recognize that they can learn from this dialogue; but it is dialogue between separate communities, not an interfaith movement.

Albert Nambiaparambil

At a more ordinary level, the Catholic Bishops Conference of India since 1973, under the supervision of Father Albert Nambiaparambil, has initiated various experiments. One approach is through 'Get Togethers on Dialogue', with individuals coming together for two or three days to 'study the nature, scope, demands, difficulties, risks, and concrete possibilities of interreligious dialogue in that particular region'.[28]

Another experiment is through 'Live-Togethers', where participants of different religions come together for prayer, meditation and shared reflections. They discuss such topics of common concern as 'what my religion means to me, my attitude towards other religions, prayer and religious experiences in my life, my religion and my suffering neighbours', and they consider how to foster mutual unity and communal harmony. The Dialogue Commission is in touch with several ashrams, dialogue centres and dialogue groups in different parts of India. Recently it has arranged a number of multi-religious retreat-prayer sessions, and has promoted multi-religious evening panels in all major cities on 'Values in a Fast Changing World'.

Fr Albert Nambiaparambil, whose energy and enthusiasm are boundless, is active in several international bodies including IARF, WCRP and WCF. He, has also taken the initiative in forming The World Fellowship of Inter-Religious Councils (WFIRC). This was set up following a World Conference on Religions held at Cochin in November 1981 on the subject 'Religion and Man'. WFIRC has held a number of meetings and convened a major conference in October 1991, as part of the preparations for the celebration of One Hundred Years of the Interfaith Movement to be held in Bangalore in 1993.

All four of the international interfaith organizations which are cosponsoring the Bangalore celebrations have links in India. The Brahmo Samaj has for many years been a member of IARF and there are other member groups. WCRP has a well established chapter in India and the Temple of Understanding has recently formed an Indian group. In the South of India, there is a branch of the World Congress of Faiths.

Many other groups have arranged inter-religious conferences and only a few can be mentioned as examples. In 1974 the World Fellowship of Religions held an international interfaith conference in New Delhi.[29] Brahma Kumaris, with its headquarters at Mount Abu in Rajasthan, has sponsored the 'One Million Minutes of Prayer for Peace' and 'The Global Co-operation for a Better World' movements, which have brought together people of many religions. ANUVIBHA, the Anuvrat Global Organization, sponsored by His Holiness Acharya Tulsi, a Jain, has held inter-religious conferences on peace. The 1988 Conference produced the Ladnun Declaration. The League of Devotees Worldwide, based in Bombay, inspired by Swami Bhaktipada, promotes a programme of Interfaith Dialogue Towards Harmonious Coexistence under the name 'Religion in the Year 2000'. They arranged a big conference in May 1990. The India Heritage Foundation, inspired by Swami Chidanand Saraswati, which promotes accurate knowledge of Hinduism, also sponsors interfaith programmes. In January 1986 the Philosophy Department of Madras Christian College sponsored a Seminar on 'Interfaith Dialogue for National Integration and Human Solidarity'. This was supported by the University grants Commission and may be a sign that religious studies, in addition to the study of philosophy, may soon be encouraged in Indian universities.

Conclusion

Despite some recent increase in communal violence and religious extremism, the Indian religious climate is favourable to interfaith co-operation. It is beneficial to those elsewhere if Indians play a full part in world bodies and if Christians there contribute their insight to the world church. Despite the numerous initiatives, no comprehensive structure or network for dialogue has yet been established. An even more important task, as Gandhi saw, is to translate the friendship and openness that exists between many religious leaders into the promotion of communal harmony and the uplift of the people.

· 26 ·

Meetings with Buddhists, Sikhs and Traditional Believers

Dialogue is spreading. In different places across the world, some Christians are likely to be engaged in conversations with members of other religious groupings in the area. Much that is happening is not recorded, or, if it is, only in local newsletters. The WCC Sub-Unit has tried to stimulate some of this dialogue and to be in touch with what is happening. It is not possible here to give more than one or two examples but such will be sufficient to illustrate the complex network of inter-religious relations which are emerging and on which the higher profile international conferences depend for their vitality. It is again noticeable that nearly always Christians are one party to the conversations.

Conversations with Buddhists

In recent years growing attention has been paid to Christian-Buddhist dialogue. The WCC Sub-Unit for Dialogue has sponsored some Christian-Buddhist conversations. One was held in Geneva in March 1972, when Christians, Buddhists and Cao Daists met to discuss 'Christian and Buddhist Contributions for the Renewal of Society in Vietnam'. The conflict in Vietnam had brought together Christians concerned for peace and some Buddhist monks. The Vietnamese monk Ven Thich Nhat Hahn, for example, became well known to peace and interfaith groups in the West.

The second Christian-Buddhist consultation was on 'The Religious Dimensions in Humanity's Relation to Nature'. This was held in Colombo, Sri Lanka in February 1978. In December 1984 another consultation was held in Hong Kong on 'Conflict and Reconciliation – Resources within our Religious Traditions'.

The Vatican Secretariat has had growing contacts with the Buddhist world. Japanese Buddhists were among the first guests of other faiths to be welcomed to Rome by Cardinal Marella, who was the first President of the Secretariat.[1] Members of the Secretariat have visited many Buddhist communities.

Much Christian-Buddhist dialogue has been local in character. In Sri Lanka, in the fifties and sixties, the nation was establishing its identity. The church was keen to escape its colonial past and to be seen to have an active role in the new society. The dialogue of those years in which Dr Lynn de Silva played a pioneering role, helped to change Christian and Buddhist perceptions of each other. Dr Rienzie Perera has described the activities: 'Coming together from time to time to exchange ideas and read papers on given topics; responding to books and articles written by Buddhists or Christians; attempting to educate Christians about people of other faiths; dealing with ethnic conflicts and building communal harmony.'[2] The method was what he calls 'conference methodology'.

Today, Dr Rienzie Perera writes, Sri Lanka is gripped by a socio-economic and political revolution. Buddhism is closely linked with this revolution and deeply involved in the political life of Sri Lanka. This has made many Christians suspicious of Buddhists. At the same time there has been a revival of crusading Christian evangelism. The climate is therefore inimical to dialogue. Philosophical or theological discussion, for example, about the 'soul', seem to many irrelevant when issues of violence affect daily life. Dialogue, he suggests, may therefore arise out of engagement with the struggle in Buddhist society rather than by arranging conferences.

The emerging Buddhist-Christian dialogue in North America has a theological and academic character. A group led by Professor Masae Abe and Professor John Cobb has now met five times. Leading theologians have participated. The twenty-eight participants come from North America, East and South Asia and from Europe. As a continuing group, members have learned to trust each other and have grown in mutual understanding. Dr John Berthrong, Dean of the School of Theology at Boston University, describes the changes. 'The Christians have learned that Buddhism has a long and noble history of social ethics. And the Buddhists have realized that the Christian notion of God is not some kind of simple-minded anthropomorphism. Old images have been replaced with the realization that Buddhism and Christianity are evolving, living communities of faith.'[3]

In North America itself, Buddhism is said to be the fastest growing religion, although it is still small in absolute numbers. Buddhists are divided between American converts and immigrant communities, New Buddhists groups are emerging all the time. Dialogue is very varied, but an umbrella organization called the Society for Buddhist-Christian Studies tries to give coherence to this development.[4]

Christians have also taken the initiative to encourage dialogue with Buddhists in Thailand. There is also now a National Council for Inter-Religious Dialogue in Thailand on which all the officially recognized religions are represented. There are similar councils in other countries of South East Asia. In Hong Kong, a Confucian-Christian dialogue was held in June 1988, with the support of the WCC.

There has also been quite a lot of unofficial dialogue, both at an academic level and in attempts to explore the spirituality of the two religions. The Zen Buddhist monk, Rev. Eshin Nishimura for example, has spent time at a Quaker centre in the USA and at various monasteries in Europe. He is active in the Zen and Christian colloquy.[5] Amongst Christians, the Catholic priests Dom Aelred Graham and Fr William Johnston and the Quaker Douglas Steere have tried to enter deeply into the Zen tradition.[6]

Dialogue with Sikhs

Dialogue with Sikhs has mainly taken place in the Punjab and in Western Europe and North America, although some Sikhs have been active in Inter-religious Councils in South East Asia. The first Sikh-Christian Conference was held at Baring Union Christian College, Batala in the Punjab in October 1963. This led to the establishment of the Christian Institute of Sikh Studies at Batala, but there was no follow up to the conference.[7] In 1969 the newly opened Department of Religious Studies at Pattiala University held a large inter-religious conference to mark the five hundredth anniversary of the birth of Guru Nanak.[8] In 1987 a Sikh-Christian Dialogue meeting was arranged by the National Council of Churches in Delhi. This concentrated on trying to understand the complex situation in the Punjab, which has made dialogue so difficult.

In Britain the initiative was taken by members of the United Reformed Church, who arranged the first of a series of Sikh-Christian consultations in 1984. The first meeting concentrated on the difficulties which Sikhs faced in observing their religion in an alien Western context. The 1985 consultation considered spirituality and its practical implications. Further consultations have been held.[9] Similar consultations have been held in Canada and the USA.

Dialogue with Traditional Religions

The WCC Sub-Unit has arranged three meetings concentrating on relations between Christians and members of African traditional religions. The first meeting was held in Ibadan, Nigeria in 1973 on Primal World Views. The second on 'Humanity's relation with Nature' was held at Yaounde, Cameroon in 1978. The most recent meeting was at Mindolo Ecumenical Foundation in Zambia in 1986.

A Consultation with traditional Cultures was held in Honolulu in 1982. In 1987 a dialogue meeting of Christians and followers of Native Spiritual Ways was held at Sorrento, in British Colombia, Canada. Earlier, at the Vancouver Assembly of the World Council of Churches, Native Canadians played a significant part. Attempts have also been made to begin dialogue with Aboriginals in Australia.

There is some feeling that dialogue with traditional religions has been neglected. Partly perhaps this is because there are no written texts readily available for study. It may reflect the condecension of the West. The environmental crisis, however, is making more people aware that we neglect at our peril traditional spiritual teachings, which emphasize our oneness with nature.

It is noticeable that African participation in the international interfaith organizations is limited. There is a need too to broaden Latin American participation. People from some areas of the world and some smaller religious groups, such as Jains and Zoroastrians, are still too little involved in the interfaith movement, which is impoverished by their absence.

PART V

Religions Engage in Dialogue

'To walk together towards Truth
and to work together in projects of common concern'

· 27 ·

Religions Engage in Dialogue

As relationships between members of world religions grow, some religious bodies are seeking official contact with members of other religions. Christian observers have been invited to some international Islamic conferences. The World Muslim Congress, through its Secretary general, Dr Inamullah Khan, plays an active part in interfaith organizations. The Japanese Buddhist movement, Rissho Kosei Kai, led by Rev. Nikkyo Niwano, does the same. In 1969 Patiala University in the Punjab invited scholars of all faiths to an International Seminar on Guru Nanak. The Jewish world has established IJCIC for inter-religious dialogue. Many religious bodies now invite speakers of other religions.

The Christian church has attempted to put its approach to others on to an organized basis. In 1964 the Vatican established its Secretariat for Non-Christians, which in 1989 was renamed the Pontifical Council for Inter-Religious Dialogue. In 1971 the World Council of Churches (WCC) set up a Sub-Unit on Dialogue Between People of Living Faiths and Ideologies. Some national councils of churches, such as the British Council of Churches, with Rev. Kenneth Cracknell and now Rev. Dr Clinton Bennett as secretary, have departments for inter-religious relations. A number of denominations also have small committees for interfaith matters, with may be a part time officer. The United Church of Canada's appointment of the Rev. Dr John Berthrong was perhaps the first such full time appointment. Considering the size and importance of the task, the churches have been reluctant to make available the necessary resources and personnel.

Clearly the work in this field of representative religious bodies is quite different in intention and structure from that of interfaith organizations. As Fr Fitzgerald, who is secretary of the Pontifical Council for Inter-Religious Dialogue has written, 'The Council cannot be considered an "interfaith organization". It is rather an office of the central organ of the

Roman Catholic Church for promoting interreligious dialogue'.[1] At times, the work appears to be that of religious diplomacy, but at other times valuable and far-reaching inter-religious dialogue has been encouraged.

Representative religious bodies have to spend as much time interpreting religious dialogue to their own members as engaging in it. In each religion there are those who view dialogue with suspicion, either because they suspect that it is a cover for missionary activity or because they feel it weakens the missionary imperative.

Here, as in other aspects of the interfaith movement, it is Christians who were the first to take an initiative. It is, therefore, on the work of the Vatican Secretariat and the WCC Sub-Unit that we shall concentrate. There is not room to describe the work of national councils of churches nor of particular denominations. An exception will be the work of the Unification Church, which has seen the encouragement of interfaith dialogue as a central part of its vocation, to which it has devoted considerable resources. The initiatives of other world religious bodies will be mentioned briefly.

· 28 ·

The Pontifical Council for Inter-Religious Dialogue

The Declaration on the Relationship of the Church to Non-Christian Religions

The Second Vatican Council's Declaration on the Relationship of the Church to Non-Christian Religions marks the beginning of a fresh approach of the Catholic Church to members of other faiths. Not that the Council's thinking was entirely new, but the sensitive approach suggested by some Catholic theologians was given official approval.

The preparation of the Declaration had a chequered history.[1] It began with Pope John XXIII indicating to Cardinal Bea that he wished the Council to make a statement on the Jews. Originally this was to be included in the Decree on Ecumenism, as chapter four, with chapter five on religious freedom. At the second session of the Council, the first three chapters on the schema of this decree were voted, but the other two were held over for lack of time. Between the second and third sessions, some Cardinals made clear that they thought Jewish-Christian relations were outside the topic of ecumenism, whilst others indicated their fears that any statement about Jews would offend Arab countries, where Christians were a tiny minority.

Before the third session, a draft text was leaked to some newspapers. When the Council Fathers returned to Rome, they were not presented with this text, but with a new one. In the new draft, the rejection of the charge of deicide had disappeared and more attention to Muslims had been added. The Declaration was very fully discussed by the council and, after some amendments, approved by a large majority. Even if, in the light of the original draft, there was some disappointment with the Declaration, it is a significant document.

The Declaration stresses what human beings have in common. 'For all peoples comprise a single community.'[2] It is recognized that from ancient times, 'there has existed among diverse peoples a certain perception of that hidden power which hovers over the course of things'.[3] Reference is made to the contemplation of the divine mystery in Hinduism, to Buddhism's acknowledgment of the 'radical insufficiency of this shifting world',[4] and to some of the teachings of other religions. 'The Catholic Church', the Declaration continues, 'rejects nothing which is true and holy in these religions. She looks with sincere respect upon those ways of conduct and life, whose rules and teachings, which, though differing in many particulars from what she holds and sets forth, nevertheless often reflect a ray of that Truth which enlightens all men. Indeed she proclaims and must ever proclaim Christ "the way, the truth and the life" (John 14.6), in whom men find the fullness of religious life, and in whom God has reconciled all things to Himself (cf II Corinthians 5. 18–19). The Church, therefore, has this exhortation for her sons; prudently and lovingly, through dialogue and collaboration with the followers of other religions, and in witness of Christian faith and life, acknowledge, preserve and promote the spiritual and moral goods found among these men, as well as the values in their society and culture.'[5] Then follow separate sections on the Muslims and the Jews. Finally, all forms of discrimination are condemned.

Although the Declaration recognizes a search for God in other religions and mentions dialogue and collaboration, no attempt is made to define it. It is set within the context of the search for human unity and the assumption that such unity is ultimately to be found in Christ, to whom the Church is called to witness. Whilst the approach to members of other religions is to be by way of friendship and co-operation, the Declaraion does not imply any alteration of the Church's self-understanding, and indeed, should be read in the light of the Dogmatic Constitution on the Church (*Lumen Gentium*). The underlying missionary intention of the Church is clear, too, in the work designated for the Vatican Secretariat for Non-Christians.

Dialogue and Mission

Following the Second Vatican Council, Pope Paul VI established the Secretariat for Non-Christians. In a discourse to the Sacred College, the Pope explained its purpose:

Moreover we have decided to create a separate Secretariat for Non-Christians, so that there shall be a means of coming to some kind of dialogue, both considerate and faithful, with all those *who still believe in*

God and adore him. With the help of this initial step and of yet others, we intend to make a clear demonstration of the *Catholic dimension of the Church* which, at this time, and in this conciliar atmosphere, not only embraces in the bonds of understanding, friendship and fraternal consideration, those who are inside the Church, but once more looks outside to find some basis for dialogue and contact with all souls of goodwill.[6]

It was made clear from the beginning that the creation of the Secretariat did not mean that Mission had been replaced by Dialogue. 'The preaching of the Gospel', wrote Fr Humbertclaude, the first secretary, 'remains still the most important way of achieving the task assigned by God to his Church, that of making the nations aware of the Good News of Salvation.'[7] The word 'mission', however, had been abused and misunderstood and respect for the liberty of the soul had at times been infringed. Various new difficulties faced missionary work, including the fact that Christianity was almost always the religion 'attributed to the old colonists and so to the old oppressors'.[8] Equally the Church had become 'far more clearly aware of the universal brotherhood of man in God and of the new universal redemption by Jesus – diversity of religion or the absence of any belief can no longer be opposed to this brotherhood of man. If other religions are no longer moving towards her, the Church must take the first steps to bring herself to them. It must strain itself to the utmost to gain as wide a contact as circumstances allow'.[9] The Secretariat's particular task, Fr Humbertclaude continued, 'is to prepare the ground, in order to make it capable of receiving the seed, and then to leave it to germinate quietly and peacefully'.[10] The Secretariat was more concerned with whole groups than with individuals.

Dialogue was possible because there was a certain common ground among men – 'examples of religious feelings, of patience, of assiduity in work'.[11] Moreover people had complementary qualities. Fr Humbertclaude distinguished between pre-dialogue, which aimed 'to create conditions which are necessary for strict dialogue – mutual understanding, the beginnings of a conversation, the establishment of contact'.[12] 'As to dialogue considered in its strict theological sense, which itself presupposes a certain amount of confidence and sympathy, as well as the admission that the truth which another possesses is worth discussing, this will be limited to start with to disentangling the genuine main principles of others from all errors of interpretation, all the prejudices, and from all the elements, historical and otherwise, with which they have been falsely coloured. This supposes that the partners in dialogue are capable and, as far as possible, representative.'[13]

'With a doctrinal basis firmly established, we come to a mutual agreement as to what are common or converging elements, and what are the opposing elements. If the opposing elements are considered afresh, it will be seen that some of them, even if they do not seem to be converging already, could perhaps converge after a more detailed study. In this way the area of basic agreements will continue to grow. In this situation, however, absolute truth, or what at least appears to be absolute truth, can never be sacrificed. In the case of those elements which are irreducible, since truth can only be one, recourse must be had once again to research to try to discover what exactly is true. When this is done, what is true must be adopted, and what is false rejected, using as a basis the light which has been mutually agreed upon from the beginning.'[14]

This article is valuable as it makes clear the Secretariat's understanding of dialogue, which is seen as complementary to the Church's overall mission of proclaiming the gospel. The view that other religions have 'saving significance' is expressly rejected and the salvation of non-Christians is seen as a secret dialogue between God and the individual soul.[15] Dialogue, rather like the Church's educational work in a previous generation, is a *preparatio evangelica (preparation for the gospel)* to remove hostility and misunderstanding and to make communication possible.

It is interesting to compare Fr Humbertclaude's article with a lecture given in 1989 by Cardinal Francis Arinze, the present President of the Council. He describes inter-religious dialogue as 'one of the elements in the carrying out the mission of evangelization which Christ gave to his Church'.[16] He makes clear that dialogue does not aim at changing the other's religious allegiance, but at mutual conversion to deeper obedience to God. Interreligious dialogue is not an effort to unite all religions in one, which 'would be the error of syncretism'.[17] Inter-religious dialogue, he says, 'is a meeting of heart and mind between followers of various religions . . . It is walking together in projects of common concern'.[18] He gives various reasons why dialogue is important. One is the fact that Christians are only a minority of the world's population and that for many reasons there is more meeting of people of different religions in the modern world. The reasons are also theological. 'The entire human family has only one origin' and every person has something of the divine image.[19] Further, 'all human beings are included in the great and unique design of God in Jesus Christ, even when they are not aware of it'.[20] Dialogue is witness to Christ and is 'part of the total mission of the Church'.[21] Christ should be proclaimed. Yet, he insists that dialogue is appreciative of other religions. In it, 'the Church discovers the working of God in the other religions, elements of truth and grace, seeds of the Word, seeds of contemplation, elements which are true and good'.[22]

In both the article by Fr Humbertclaude and the lecture by Cardinal Arinze, there is an acknowledgment of the open nature of dialogue. There can be no hidden conversionist agenda. There is also appreciation of the working of God in other religions. Yet they are seen in the context of the Christian understanding of God's plan of salvation. Whilst dialogue is fully respectful of the other, it does not require any change in the Church's understanding of her mission.

A History of the Secretariat

The Secretariat for Non-Christians was set up in 1964.[23] Cardinal Paolo Marella was appointed President, Fr Pierre Humbertclaude secretary and Msgr Rossano as under secretary, although he became secretary from 1973 to 1983. The first task was to choose consultors. Their first regular meeting was held in January 1965. It was also necessary to clarify further the Church's evaluation of other religions and its understanding of dialogue in relation to mission. Initially, therefore, the work of the Secretariat was internal – considering the Church's attitude to other faiths. Various *Guidelines* were published. Although some non-Christian visitors were received at Rome by Cardinal Marella, it was Cardinal Pignedoli, who was President from 1973–1980, who encouraged visitors and also himself visited religious leaders around the world. He hoped to 'create an atmosphere of understanding and, if possible, friendship'.[24] During his Presidency some meetings with members of other religions were arranged. His sudden death in 1980 was a blow to the secretariat. He had summed up his work as 'a service of friendship . . . founded on spiritual and eternal values'.[25]

He was succeeded by Mgsr Jean Jadot, a Belgian. Now, rather than itself arranging meetings, the secretariat encouraged its staff to attend conferences organized by other bodies. In 1984 Mgsr Jadot resigned and was followed by Mgsr Francis Arinze, from Nigeria, who was soon appointed a Cardinal. Cardinal Arinze has travelled extensively and attended many meetings. The year before his appointment, Fr Marcello Zago had become secretary. He was a specialist in Theravada Buddhism. In 1986 Fr Zago was elected Superior General of his congregation and resigned as secretary. He was succeeded by Fr Michael Fitzgerald, an Englishman, who has a degree in Arabic. In March 1989, as part of the reform of the Roman Curia, through the Constitution *Pastor Bonus*, the secretariat was renamed the Pontifical Council for Inter-Religious Dialogue. 'Although not modifying in any way the work of this office', writes Fr Fitzgerald, 'the change is significant. It can be taken to imply that this department, together with those for promoting Christian Unity and for

Dialogue with non-Believers, "have come to stay and should not be regarded as temporary or experimental offices". The new title moreover is positive, rather than apparently discriminatory, and in fact corresponds much better to the role of the department'.[26]

The Secretariat's work

There are two main aspects of the Secretariat's work. The first is the attempt to build up relationships with other religious groups. The second is to study and assess honestly other traditions, so as to see where there is agreement and disagreement.

A considerable number of religious leaders, including the Dalai Lama, a group of Shinto priests, and a delegation from the Supreme Council for Islamic Affairs of Cairo, have been invited to Rome and received by the Pope or members of the Secretariat. In receiving the Ambassador of Iran, the Pope made reference to Zoroaster, and when he himself visited the Far East in 1971, he specifically addressed the non-Christians of Australia and of the Philippines. Cardinal Pignedoli and Cardinal Arinze have invited numerous religious leaders to Rome.

The other main aspect of the Secretariat's work is reflected in its publications, such as the *Guides for Relations with non-Christian Religions: Meeting with African Religions, Guidelines for a Dialogue Between Islam and Christianity, Meeting with Buddhism, Meeting with Hinduism,* and the popular booklet, *Religions in the World.* These aim to give a clear statement of the religion concerned and to show where they agree and disagree with Catholic truth. A similar approach is seen in *Religions: Fundamental Themes for a Dialogistic Understanding,* edited by R. Caspar PB. Useful as they are, they may seem to predetermine the Catholic position in approaching those of other faiths. In fairness, however, it must be said that increasingly in the *Bulletin,* members of other faiths are asked to contribute, and in 1972 non-Christian professors were invited to address the regular meeting of consultants.

In 1984 after much work and several drafts, *A Directory for Dialogue* was approved by the Pope and published in the official *Acta Apostolicae Sedis.* The document describes dialogue as a process 'in which Christians meet the followers of other religious traditions in order to walk together towards truth and to work together in projects of common concern'.[27] Dialogue, it is said, is one element of the Church's mission.

A further aspect of the Secretariat's work, which is clear from copies of the *Bulletin,* is its effort to maintain contact with dialogue meetings taking place in various parts of the world. There are several reports of meetings arranged by the Commission for Dialogue of the Catholic Bishops

Conference of India and of the situation in African and Asian countries. The Catholic Church too has been represented at gatherings of the Temple of Understanding and the World Conference on Religion and Peace. It also has a close working relationship with the WCC Sub-Unit.

The World Day of Prayer for Peace

Although the World Day of Prayer for Peace was the initiative of Pope John Paul II, making the detailed arrangements with representatives of other religions fell to the Secretariat. In the context of the International Year for Peace, the Pope invited other religious leaders to come on pilgrimage to Assisi, the city of St Francis, to pray and fast for peace in the world. Representatives of all religions took part. After an initial welcome by the Pope at the Church of S. Maria del Angeli, each religious community prayed on its own. Then all came together in the courtyard of the Basilica of St Francis to offer prayers of their tradition in the presence of all. At the end, olive branches were distributed and all exchanged handshakes or embraces of peace and friendship. It was explained that whilst people were together to pray, they did not pray together. There was no common prayer.[28]

The Pope made clear that his participation was as a follower of Jesus. His own deep faith made him reverent to the faiths of others. There was no intention of seeking a religious consensus. 'Our meeting', he said, 'attests only that in the great battle for peace, humanity, in its very diversity, must draw from its deepest and most vivifying sources.'[29] Defending his initiative in the face of some criticism, the Pope stressed the unity of the human family, which for Christians is based on both God's act of creation and of redemption. The Church, he said, has 'the task of being, not merely the symbol of this unity, but its "effective sign", actually working to bring about reconciliation among people and with God.'[30]

The day was a very special event. All who were there felt the guidance of the Spirit. Many in other parts of the world participated by their own prayers. It was in late 1986 that President Reagan first met Mr Gorbachev in Iceland and the thaw in the Cold War began. The day has become a landmark and the example and spirit of Assisi have inspired many recent efforts at interfaith co-operation and prayer for peace.

· 29 ·

The World Council
of Churches

'Dialogue within the WCC constituency has made great strides in relatively few years', writes Marlin van Elderen, who is on the WCC staff.[1] Since the establishment of a Sub-Unit on Dialogue Between Men of Living Faiths and Ideologies (now called the Sub-Unit on Dialogue with People of Living Faiths) in 1971, the World Council of Churches has become increasingly interested in interfaith dialogue.

This is not an entirely new interest. Christian Study Centres, especially in India and other parts of Asia, have for some time arranged dialogues with members of other faiths.[2] The Ecumenical Institute at Bossey has held meetings involving people of different faiths and ideologies. As early as 1956, a study project, *The Word of God and the Living Faiths of Men* was approved by the World Council of Churches Central Committee meeting at Galyateto, Hungary. Various consultations were held in connection with this study, notably one at Kandy, Ceylon, in 1967, which brought together for the first time Protestant, Orthodox and Roman Catholic theologians to consider the relationship between Christians and men of other faiths. There was some discussion of the subject at the New Delhi (1961) and Uppsala (1968) assemblies.

The subject, however, was given special attention at the meetings of the Executive and Central Committees of the World Council of Churches at Canterbury in August, 1969. Various factors made it clear that this was a subject requiring greater attention.

1. The World Council of Churches was receiving with increasing frequency invitations to take part in inter-religious gatherings. In 1969 it was invited to the Temple of Understanding Conference at Geneva and the World Conference on Religion and Peace at Kyoto.

2. In many countries, there was a demand that Christian communities should co-operate rather than compete with other religious groups.
3. Migration was creating a multi-religious situation in countries where this had not previously existed. Some young people were turning away from Christianity to these new religions.
4. The need had already been recognized to give serious attention to the underlying attitudes of faith that help or hinder programmes of development in pluralistic situations.
5. In several parts of the world there was hostility or conflict between different religious communities.

'These situations', wrote Dr S. J. Samartha, 'demand that, where necessary, the World Council should cooperate with other World Religious Organizations to enlist the resources of all faiths to tame political passions, reduce tensions, and to bring about conditions that help to restore peace and harmony.'[3]

The Central Committee discussed this matter and passed the following resolutions:

Believing that Christian Mission and Faithfulness to the Gospel imply a respect for men of all faiths and ideologies, the Central Committee
(a) Welcomes the increased emphasis on dialogue with men of other faiths and secular ideologies.
(b) Encourages the Department (on Studies in Mission and Evangelism) to study further the relation between dialogue and mission, as well as the relation between our common humanity with other men and our new humanity in Christ.
(c) Approves the plan for an Ecumenical Consultation on Dialogue with Men of Other Faiths in March 1970 in Beirut.[4]

The Sub-Unit

At the WCC Central Committee meeting at Addis Ababa in January 1971, it was decided to set up the Sub-Unit on Dialogue Between Men of Living Faiths and Ideologies. Dr Stanley Samartha, an able and experienced theologian from India, was the first secretary. He was succeeded by Dr John Taylor, a Methodist from England, who is now Secretary General of WCRP. The present secretary is Dr Wesley Ariarajah, a Methodist from Sri Lanka. The Sub-Unit has had a small staff of specialists in a particular religion. The first moderator was

Professor Hans Margull. He was succeeded by Dr Mulder from the Netherlands and he, in turn, was followed by Professor Diana Eck from USA.

Three aspects of the World Council of Churches' involvement can be distinguished. Bilateral consultations, some of which have already been considered, multilateral consultations and the continuing debate about the Christian theology of dialogue.

Multilateral Consultations

Multilateral consultations were held at Ajaltoun, near Beirut in March, 1970, and at Colombo, Sri Lanka, in April 1974. At Ajaltoun, forty people from seventeen countries took part. Members of four major faiths, Hindu, Buddhist, Christian and Muslim, were brought together, for the first time under the auspices of the World Council of Churches. 'The key note of the consultation was the understanding that a full and loyal commitment to one's own faith did not stand in the way of dialogue. On the contrary, it was our faith which was the very basis of and driving force to intensification of dialogue and a search for common action between members of various faiths.'[5]

The Colombo meeting was attended by fifty people from five religions and from twenty-two countries. In comparison with the Ajaltoun gathering, Jews were invited to this conference. It had been jointly planned by a group consisting of members of all the faiths concerned. Christians, although the largest group, were in a minority. The theme was *Towards World Community*, and the group made a sober analysis of the problems and possible contribution of religions. The meeting called for further exploration of dialogue and of the means of co-operation for social justice.

In recent years, the emphasis has been on bilateral consultations. The next multifaith meeting was not held until 1983. This was a gathering in Mauritius in preparation for the Vancouver assembly of WCC. A similar preparatory meeting was held in Hong Kong in 1990, before the Canberra assembly. In November 1987, a multilateral dialogue meeting for South Asia was held in New Delhi and later that year there was a consultation on Spirituality in Interfaith Dialogue in Kyoto, Japan.

The Theological Debate

Not all Christians have been happy about the World Council of Churches' involvement in dialogue. Considerable attention, therefore, has been given to the Christian theology of dialogue. This was the theme of a consultation at Zurich in 1970. The reflections of that meeting and the experience of the Ajaltoun consultation were considered at the 1971 Central Committee, which set up the Sub-Unit and which also accepted an *Interim Policy Statement and Guidelines*.

This, first of all, recognized dialogue with people of living faiths and ideologies as one of the major current concerns of the ecumenical movement. Commenting, Dr Samartha says, 'Given the great difference in the cultural backgrounds and theological traditions of the members of the Central Committee, it is remarkable that such a statement was accepted at all'.[6] Secondly, the statement acknowledged that dialogue must take place in freedom and involved living relationships, not just talking. Dialogue offered to Christians the promise of discovering new dimensions of understanding their faith. It required respect for the integrity of partners in dialogue, but the Christian started from his standpoint of faith in Jesus Christ. Thirdly, some guidelines to the churches were suggested.

Reactions to the statement were received from churches in several countries. Analysing these, Dr Samartha suggested that certain significant issues emerged:

(a) The approach to or the meeting point of dialogue, particularly as it touches the question of Truth.

(b) The theological basis of dialogue with discussion swirling around 'Christo-centric' and 'Theo-centric' standpoints, leading inevitably to questions of the work of the Holy Spirit in the world.

(c) The place of 'mission' and 'witness' in dialogue; pushing the discussion beyond the alternatives of seeing dialogue either as a 'betrayal of mission' or 'a new tool for mission' in the post-colonial era.

(d) The motivation, purpose and possibilities of dialogue with people of certain ideologies, e.g. Marxists, Maoists, secular humanists, etc., recognizing the need to take this discussion beyond the intellectual confines of Europe and also noting that 'religion' and 'ideological' questions are closely related.

(e) The possible contributions dialogue can make towards the quest for spiritual resources for living in community, supporting personal and social life in an age of science and technology.

(f) The place of worship and prayer in the living context of dialogue between people of living faiths as they struggle to seek the meaning of the transcendent in the contemporary world dominated by things and machinery and impersonal forces that seem to be relentlessly marching along devouring their own creations.[7]

The Nairobi Assembly

The different attitudes to dialogue within the churches came to the fore at the World Council of Churches 1975 Assembly at Nairobi. In the debate of Section III on 'Seeking Community', 'Asian Christians spoke almost as one and gave witness to their experience of life in a pluralistic society, of their existence as a minority among great masses of Hindus, Buddhists and Muslims. They told of various levels and densities of community and dialogue, within daily contacts of living together, in working together for nation-building, in sharing moral and human concerns and ideals, in shared prayer to God and meditation on the holy scriptures and the holy men of various traditions. They told of how such experience of community, at the religious and theological level in particular, had given them new insights into the Bible, had deepened and strengthened their Christian faith, enhanced their world view and freed them from many fears they had inherited from missionaries, and from narrow clannish conceptions of God and his Christ.'[8] They were supported by Africans and a few Europeans, but were strongly opposed by 'Evangelicals from Scandinavia, Western Germany and England' who argued that Christ 'is present only in the Word and Sacraments'.[9]

Because of the opposition to dialogue, the section's report was amended by the assembly in a conservative direction. This upset many Asian and African theologians, who 'were surprised and shocked at the summary way in which some of their deepest Christian experiences were dismissed and discarded on very flimsy theological grounds. They asked themselves: "Is every Christian experience and every theological initiative, which is not North Atlantic, invalid, inadmissable and unworthy of a hearing?"'[10]

At the subsequent meeting of the Central Committee in Geneva in 1976, the continuing work of the Unit was agreed to, although it had to be restricted by the financial cuts which were affecting the whole World Council of Churches' organization.

Chiang Mai

Two years after the Nairobi Assembly, a Consultation was held at Chiang Mai, in Thailand, in April 1977. This progressed beyond the sharp division apparent at Nairobi.

The theme at Chiang Mai was 'Dialogue in Community'. This was intended to point to the living context in which dialogue occurs. There is dialogue within a community, which involves growth in mutual care and understanding. There is also dialogue between communities for the sake of a wider community of peace and justice. This can happen at a local, national or international level. By relating dialogue within the community to dialogue between communities, the statement links the search for Christian unity to the wider search for human unity. It also sets dialogue in the context of Christian service. 'We see dialogue', the statement says, 'as a fundamental part of our Christian service within community.'[11] It is therefore in no way a secret weapon of 'aggressive Christian militancy' but 'a means of living out our faith in Christ in service of community with our neighbours'.[12] Seen also as sharing in the *missio Dei*, the statement affirms that the relationship of dialogue gives opportunity for authentic witness.

The Consultation was aware of the tension in the relation of the Christian community to the community of humankind. The term 'world-community' was avoided, partly because people in Asia, Africa and Latin America are suspicious that it really implies the imposition of a 'secular Western Christendom' and partly because people in the West thought it suggested 'a creeping syncretism that might lead to one religion for the world'.[13] Instead 'the vision of a world-wide "community of communities" commended itself to us as a means of seeking community in a pluralistic world. The vision is not one of homogenous unity or totalitarian uniformity, but it is for Christians related to the kingly rule of God over all human communities'.[14]

It was recognized that engaging in dialogue in community raised penetrating questions about the place of peoples of other faiths and ideologies in the activity of God in history; but these were not answered, only preliminary considerations being outlined. There was also discussion of the various ways in which the word 'syncretism' is used.

The Consultation was clearly an important event. Dr Samartha has described it as 'a step forward because it overcame some of the difficulties and tensions manifested in the Nairobi debate of Section III'.[15] Monsignor Rossano, leader of the Vatican observers, commented 'that from now on we will speak of "Before Chiang Mai" and "After Chiang Mai"'.[16] Part of the importance, besides soothing some of the disagreements of Nairobi, lies in the consultation linking dialogue so closely with the search for community. This relates it to the search for peace, justice and human unity. It, however, avoids any suggestion of a link at a religious level. One Indian theologian, A. P. Nirmal felt the discussion were timid. 'We ask for an "adequate" theological basis for dialogue rather than re-examining our theological traditions and formulations in the light of specific dialogical experiences. We are preoccupied with our concern to safeguard the uniqueness of Jesus Christ or the finality of Jesus Christ or our total commitment to Jesus Christ before entering into a dialogical situation, rather than examining the adequacy of the doctrine of the uniqueness of Jesus or the nature of our commitment to him in the light of actual dialogue experience.'[17]

Vancouver

At the Sixth Assembly of the WCC, held in Vancouver in 1983, a new openness to people of other faiths was evident. Twenty years before, when the assembly was held in New Delhi, people of other faiths were not even allowed to attend as accredited press representatives. At Nairobi, a few guests of other faiths were present. At Vancouver, they were invited to address a plenary session. Besides the official programme, there was an extensive range of dialogue meetings for visitors and for the general public.

The theological dispute was, however, by no means at an end. The report *Witnessing in a Divided World* included the sentence: 'While affirming the uniqueness of the birth, life, death and resurrection of Jesus to which we bear witness, we recognize God's creative work in the religious experience of people of other faiths.' In the debate, a number of objections were made to this and the sentence was referred back to the drafting committee. At the subsequent meeting of the Central Committee, the words 'religious experience' were deleted and were replaced by the 'seeking for religious truth'.[18] 'What is recognized here as belonging to God's creative work' commented Dr Emilio Castro, 'is not the achievements of other religions, but the searching for truth within those religions.'[19] A searching is recognized, but no finding is affirmed. There is no acknowledgment of God's presence with people of other religions.

At the WCC World Conference on Mission and Evangelism in San Antonio, Texas, in 1989, one section report took this step. 'Our ministry of witness among other people of other faiths presupposes our presence with them, sensitivity to their deepest faith commitments and experiences, willingness to be their servants for Christ's sake, affirmation of what God has done and is doing among them and love for them.'[20] The WCC evangelism secretary, Dr Raymond Fung saw this as a departure from the Vancouver position, whilst Dr Wesley Ariarajah saw this section of the report as the strongest affirmation of dialogue ever made at a missionary meeting.[21]

Questions about God's presence with people of other faiths were at the heart of the four-year study programme on *My Neighbour's Faith and Mine*, which the Sub-Unit initiated. In January 1990 a consultation was held at Baar, near Zurich in Switzerland, to consider the results of this study. The statement affirms that 'People have at all times and in all places responded to the presence and activity of God among them . . . We acknowledge that among all the nations and peoples there has always been the saving presence of God . . . We affirm that God has been present in their seeking and finding.'[22] The statement goes on to say that 'the saving presence of God's activity in all creation and human history comes to its focal point in the event of Christ'.[23]

The statement says that inter-religious dialogue needs to transform 'the way in which we do theology'.[24] This fits with one of the achievements of the Sub-Unit in expanding the scope and meaning of dialogue. It is no longer confined to the Sub-Unit, but has begun to be seen as a way of working which is influencing other commissions. In 1988 the Sub-Unit jointly sponsored a conference on Women in Interfaith Dialogue with the Sub-Unit on Women in Church and Society.

At the Canberra Assembly, guests of other faiths were again present and played a more prominent role. There was no debate on the theological significance of other faiths, but there was an important debate on gospel and culture, partly because of the presence of some of the Aboriginal people of Australia at the assembly. The Gulf War, which overshadowed the Assembly focussed attention on Christian–Muslim relations. There were some complaints that denunciation of antisemitism was muffled.[25]

Conclusion

Obstacles to dialogue remain. Many people of other faiths are still suspicious that 'dialogue is simply a stalking horse for mission'.[26] On the other hand, conservative Christians regard dialogue as a betrayal of mission. Discussion around this issue is bound to continue, for, as Marlin van Elderen writes, 'No one has yet come up with a satisfactory formulation of the relation between witness and dialogue'.[27]

Insofar as the World Council of Churches speaks for Protestant, Anglican, Orthodox and other churches, it suggests that the Christian church is still ambivalent in its attitude to other world religions. The same ambivalence may be seen in denominational statements.[28] Indeed the variety of opinions expressed at the World's Parliament of Religions in Chicago, in 1893, is still prevalent in the churches today. Those who have shared deeply in dialogue witness to the enrichment that they have received. Most members of WCC would accept dialogue, on the basis of our common humanity, on issues of peace, justice and the environment. The points on which there are still disagreement are whether members of other religions can have saving experience of God's love and whether other religions have a place in God's purposes and are channels of divine love.

Evangelical churches which are not members of the World Council of Churches are clear in their opposition to dialogue. Indeed WCC's support for dialogue is one of their grounds of criticism of the WCC. Unlike the WCC, they seem reluctant to listen to the experience of Christians in Asia and Africa and to the testimony of those who have engaged deeply in dialogue. In its growing openness to dialogue, the WCC has shown itself to be a global body, able to free itself from the cultural arrogance of the Western world.

· 30 ·

Other Religions' Initiatives

Other religions do not have as centralized structures as the Christian churches, but increasingly they have begun to engage in inter-religious dialogue at an official level. The question of who represents a religion has always caused some difficulty, as within every religion, there are different groups and movements. Normally participants in inter-religious gatherings do so as individuals, but efforts are usually made to invite people who carry authority within their religious community.

Judaism

The growth of official international contacts necessitated the creation of a special Jewish structure for this purpose. No such body existed when the first Jewish-WCC meeting took place in 1965. It was felt that the Jewish representation was rather limited. In 1969, therefore, the World Jewish Congress and the Synagogue Council of America agreed to co-operate and act jointly in the field of Jewish-Christian relations vis-à-vis representative bodies of the Christian churches. They formally established the International Jewish Committee on Inter-Religious Consultations (IJCIC) and invited other bodies to join. The American Jewish Committee accepted the invitation in March 1970, while the B'nai B'rith Anti-Defamation League and, shortly afterwards, the Jewish Council in Israel for Inter-Religious Relations formally became members of the International Committee in 1973. It is this body, IJCIC, widely representative of world Judaism, which relates to the Vatican, the WCC, and to world confessional bodies.

Islam

Various Muslim groups have engaged in dialogue, including the Islamic Conference of Jeddah, the World Muslim League and the World Muslim

Congress, as well as famous centres of learning such as the University at Al-Azhar. At the Cartigny meeting of members of WCC and some Muslims in 1976, it was agreed that future consultations should be jointly planned. An example of this was the 1982 Sri Lanka Consultation, which was initiated and organized co-operatively by the World Muslim Congress and the WCC. Since 1986, representatives of the interfaith offices of the WCC and the Vatican have met regularly with their counterparts from the world Islamic organizations.

The World Muslim Congress also makes a valuable contribution to the international interfaith organizations. Its Secretary-General, Dr Inamullah Khan, has been a regular participant in many international interreligious conferences. The World Muslim League has an officer in Geneva to work on inter-religious affairs.

Buddhism

Buddhists are playing an increasingly active role in interfaith work, partly because of growing social awareness. The World Buddhist Fellowship is often represented at international inter-religious gatherings.

In Japan, Buddhists, especially from newer movements, have been active in support of interfaith dialogue. Dr Shinichiro Imaoka, who lived to be over one hundred and who was a great pioneer of inter-religious co-operation started his work in the twenties. He soon became president of the Japan Free Religious Fellowship. He took a leading part in arranging the first National Religious Conference for International Peace Through Religion, which was held in Japan in May 1931. Thirty-seven years later, in 1968, with Rev. Riri Nakayama, Chief Priest of the Buddhist Temple Hozenji in Tokyo, he headed the *ad hoc* Japanese committee which met with the US Inter-Religious Committee on Peace.

Rev. Nikkyo Niwano, founder and President of Rissho Kosei Kai, who is a winner of the Templeton Award for Progress in Religion, has given generous backing to both WCRP and IARF and to other groups. His efforts he says are based on the conviction 'that the essential meaning of every religion is essentially the same'.[1] Nipponzan Myokoji have built peace pagodas and organized marches for peace in several cities across the world.

Some Shinto groups, such as the Tubaki Grand Shrine and the Konkokyo Church of Izuo, led by Rev. Miyake are active in support of both IARF and WCRP. Other new Japanese religious movements have been active in inter-religious work, such as Ittoen and Oomoto.

His Holiness the Dalai Lama's support for many interfaith activities has been very significant. He is a Patron of the WCF and has spoken for it on several occasions and for the Temple of Understanding. His ready willingness to participate in The World Day of Prayer for Peace at Assisi in 1986, encouraged other leaders to take part. He spoke at the Oxford Conference of the Global Forum on Human Survival. He has travelled to all continents in pursuit of peace and inter-religious harmony.

In Korea, the Won Buddhists have been supporters of WCRP from its early years. Their founder, Sot'aesan, who was born in 1891, had a vision of the essential unity of religions. In commemoration of the centenary of his birth, the Won Buddhists arranged an academic and an interfaith conference. The latter was concerned to see how inter-religious organizations could promote peace and the reunification of Korea.

The work for peace, good community relations and social uplift has led some Buddhists to increasing co-operation with people of other faiths. Ven Bhikkhu Buddhadasa and his Garden of Liberation in Siam has inspired Thai and foreign monks to carry the Buddhist message of social concern to many parts of the world. The efforts of Suchart Kosolkitiwong, a self-appointed World Peace Envoy, who tried to establish an International Federation of Religions, were less successful. In Sri Lanka, Dr Ariyaratne has worked steadfastly for peace and communal harmony. Dr Buddhadasa Kirthisinghe, the representative of the Maha Bodhi Society in New York, was unceasing in his efforts for interfaith understanding. Best known of Buddhist workers for peace is the Vietnamese monk, Ven Thich Nhat Hanh, whose poems and writings are widely appreciated.

In 1989 forty-five Buddhists from Asia, Europe and America met to see how they should respond to global problems and the search for social justice. They decided to form the International Network of Engaged Buddhists (INEB), which has these objectives:

1. To promote understanding between Buddhist countries and various Buddhist sects.
2. To facilitate and engage in solving problems in various countries.
3. To help bring the perspective of engaged Buddhism to bear in working on these problems.
4. To act as a clearing house of information on existing engaged Buddhist (and relevant non-Buddhist) groups and activities, and aid in the co-ordination of efforts wherever possible.[2]

In pursuing these goals, Engaged Buddhists recognize the need to work closely with those of other faiths who share similar concerns.

Hinduism

Hinduism is the least structured of religions and there does not seem to be any co-ordinating group for inter-religious dialogue. Many groups, such as the Divine Life Yoga Society, the Sai Baba movement, the International Society for Krishna Consciousness, the Ramakrishna Movement, the India Heritage Foundation, as well as groups mentioned above[3] and many other bodies have sponsored interfaith gatherings. Indeed it is an assumption of many Hindus that all religions are, at heart, the same or lead to the same goal.

The Sikh World too, especially through the Guru Nanak Foundation, takes part in inter-religious gatherings. Pattiala University arranged an inter-religious symposium in 1969 to mark the five hundredth anniversary of the birth of Guru Nanak. Political unrest in the Punjab has prevented further initiatives. Individual Sikhs play an active part in many inter-religious organizations. One example is Mr Mehervan Singh, who for twenty years was the honorary secretary of the Inter-Religious Organization of Singapore.

A Vocation to Encourage Unity

For several religious groups, the search for religious unity is central to their vocation. Others may regard some of these groups as syncretistic, but they have all played their part in building a new relationship of understanding between people of different faiths. New Age movements, too, will also tend to stress spiritual unity. Here we shall briefly mention the Theosophists, the Unitarians and the Baha'is. In the next chapter we shall discuss in some details the efforts in this field of the Unification Church.

Theosophists

Theosophists can claim to have been amongst the first to suggest a unity of religions. Carl Jackson says that its philosophy has been of 'catalytic significance in religious thought in the nineteenth and twentieth centuries'.[4] Although the teaching has its roots in the ancient world, it is usually identified with the doctrines promoted by Mme Helena Petrovna Blavatsky (1831–91). She was a Russian-born mystic who founded the Theosophical Society in 1875.

The Theosophical Society affirms the following objectives:

1. To form a nucleus of the universal brotherhood of humanity, without distinction of race, creed, sex, caste or colour.
2. To encourage the study of comparative religion, philosophy and science.
3. To investigate unexplained laws of nature and the powers latent in man.

The society insists that it is not offering a new system of thought, but merely underscoring certain universal concepts of God, nature and man that have been known to wise men in all ages and that may be found in the teachings of all the great religions. Emphasis is placed on mystical experience. A distinction is made between inner, or esoteric, and outer, or exoteric, teaching. It is said that all the historic world religions contain inner teaching which is essentially the same, despite external differences. This teaching is monistic in character, suggesting an all-encompassing underlying unity. Theosophy has also shown a preoccupation with the occult.

The Theosophical Society should not be described as an interfaith movement. Its emphasis on an underlying unity of religions does not give the recognition to the separate identity of religions, which is a characteristic of interfaith organizations. Critics consider theosophy syncretistic and accuse it of trying to reconcile religions to its predetermined philosophy.

Be that as it may, Theosophy has been a means of introducing many Westerners to the wisdom of the East. Some theosophists, notably Henry Steel Olcott and Annie Besant, played a part in the spiritual renaissance of Buddhism and Hinduism at the end of the last century and the beginning of this century. Besides the Theosophical Society, the teachings of theosophy have influenced Westerners through a variety of other organizations, such as Rosicrucianism, The Liberal Catholic Church, World Goodwill and the Lucis Trust.

Unitarians

Unitarians have had a significant influence in several inter-religious organizations. The International Association for Religious Freedom, as we have seen, was a Unitarian initiative and Unitarians continue to play an important part in it. Some of the leaders of the World Congress of Faiths, such as Lord Sorensen or Rev. Arthur Peacock, were Unitarians. Dr Homer A. Jack, the first Secretary General of WCRP, is a Unitarian and so was Dr Dana McLean Greeley, who had a leadership role in both WCRP and IARF. The Brahmo Samaj too, which has played an part in IARF, was founded in Calcutta in the early nineteenth century by Ram Mohun Roy, who was himself influenced by Unitarian missionaries.

Bahá'ís

Bahá'ís proclaim the oneness of humanity and the underlying unity of religions. The Declaration of the Báb in 1844 made this clear. It includes the words, 'Become as true brethren in the one and indivisible religion of God, free from distinction, for verily God desireth that your hearts should become mirrors unto your brethren in the Faith, so that ye find yourselves reflected in them, and they in you'.[5] Bahá'u'lláh taught that world unity is the last stage in the evolution of humanity towards maturity. 'God has chosen to reveal himself through his messengers, among them Abraham, Moses, Zoroaster, Buddha, Jesus, Mohammed and the Báb. They are one and all the exponents on earth of Him who is the central Orb of the Universe'.[6] 'There can be no doubt whatever', he said, 'that the peoples of the world, of whatever race or religion, derive their inspiration from one heavenly source, and are the subjects of one God'.[7] He told his followers 'Consort with the followers of all religions in a spirit of friendliness and fellowship'.[8] Abdu'l-Bahá said, 'The gift of God to this enlightened age is the knowledge of the oneness of mankind and of the fundamental oneness of religion'.[9]

With such beliefs, Bahá'ís have been active in support of inter-religious work. During Bahá'u'lláh's lifetime, the Bahá'í Faith, despite much opposition, had spread to fifteen countries. Already the task of bringing together people of different religions was being pursued in Iran, Iraq, India, Russia and Egypt.

At the 1893 World's Parliament of Religions, Rev. Henry H. Jessop, in his paper, referred to Bahá'u'lláh. He spoke of the interview granted by Bahá'u'lláh to Professor E. G. Browne, a Cambridge scholar. This was the first public reference to the Bahá'í Faith at a large gathering in America. It created considerable interest in the Bahá'í Faith, which began slowly to spread in the West. By the end of 1898, three groups of Western pilgrims had visited Bahá'u'lláh's son and successor, 'Abdu'l–Bahá. Soon afterwards, an American woman, Sarah Farmer, became a Bahá'í and put her centre in Green Acre, Maine at the disposal of her new faith. The centre still functions as a Bahá'í school and meeting place for people of all faiths.

In 1911 'Abdu'l-Bahá gave his first public address, from the pulpit of City Temple, London. His message reaffirmed belief in the oneness of religion. 'The gift of God to this enlightened age is the knowledge of the oneness of mankind and of the fundamental oneness of religion. War shall cease between nations, and by the Will of God, the Most great Peace shall come; the world will be seen as a new world, and all men will live as brothers.'[10] His address was fully reported in the *Christian Commonwealth*. Wherever he spoke during his European tour, 'Abdul-Bahá repeated this message.

At the Religions of Empire Conference in 1924,[11] two papers were presented on the Bahá'í Faith. Lady Blomfield, a British Bahá'í, gave a reception for all the conference participants.

When twelve years later, the World Congress of Faiths met in London, Canon George Townshend presented a paper at the request of Shogi Effendi, the Guardian of the Bahá'í Faith. It was called 'Bahá'u'lláh's

Ground Plan of World Fellowship'. The chairman for the session, Viscount Samuel, said, 'If one were compelled to choose which of the many religious communities of the world was closest to the aim and purpose of this Congress, I think one would be obliged to say that it was the comparatively little known Bahá'í community. Other faiths and creeds have to consider, at a congress like this, in what way they can contribute to the idea of a World Fellowship. But the Bahá'í Faith exists almost for the sole purpose of contributing to the fellowship and unity of mankind . . . I suggest that this Bahá'í Community is really more in agreement with the main idea which has led to the summoning of the Congress that any particular one of the great religious communities of the world.'[12]

Following Canon Townshend's presentation, a number of Bahá'ís made contributions. Amongst them was Richard St Barbe Baker, the founder of Men of the Trees, who was later to become a Vice-President of WCF. Another famous Bahá'í, who later became a Vice-President of the World Congress of Faiths, was the potter, Bernard Leach. The Bahá'í community has worked closely with WCF, especially in recent years. There has been at least one Bahá'í on the executive and Bahá'ís have played an active part in the formation of local interfaith groups in Britain. They have also been supportive of the Interfaith Network (UK), the UNA's Religious Advisory Committee and of the Religious Education Council.

From the beginning, individual Bahá'ís have participated in WCRP. In August 1990 a formal international relationship was formed between the Bahá'í International Community and WCRP. In 1987, the Bahá'í Faith became the sixth world religion to join the World Wide Fund for Nature's Network on Conservation and Religion. Bahá'ís also play a full part in The Week of Prayer for World Peace.

A particular Bahá'í initiative is World Religion Day. 'Abdu'l-Bahá suggested that a day be dedicated each year to demonstrate the oneness of religion. Bahá'ís in the West observe this on the third Sunday in January and usually arrange interreligious gatherings. Some have been held in churches and Cathedrals.

Bahá'ís remain true to the teaching of Bahá'u'lláh, the Founder of the Faith, that 'the fundamental purpose animating the Faith of God and His religion is to safeguard the interests and promote the unity of the human race, and to foster the spirit of love and fellowship amongst men'.[13]

· 31 ·

The Unification Church

The Unificationist Church, as its name suggests, teaches and works for the unification of human life. This includes the reconciliation of religion and science and of religions with each other. In his *Divine Principle*, the Rev. Sun Myung Moon wrote, 'The history of the development of cultural spheres shows us a trend toward forming a worldwide cultural sphere, centering on one religion, through the unification of numerous religions. This is proof that human history is leading toward the restoration of one unified world.'[1]

The Unificationist Church has therefore devoted very considerable resources to encouraging the coming together of religions. Speaking at the Fourth International Conference on God, Rev. Moon told participants that 'as representatives of the world's religions, you are called to bring your churches, mosques, synagogues, ashrams, and temples into a co-operative unity for the sake of world peace and human freedom, centred on God. Many people ask what religions can do in this secular age. I answer: the world's religions must provide a stable, universal foundation of values upon which governments can build true peace and harmony, science and technology can be fully utilized for the happiness of humankind, and the world's cultures can be purified, shared, celebrated.'[2]

The Unificationist Church has promoted a variety of conferences on the Unity of the Sciences, on theological matters and to promote peace. It is not possible here to give a full picture of the many activities sponsored by the Rev. Moon and his church. Here we shall concentrate on those specifically intended to encourage interfaith dialogue, particularly the Global Congress of the World's Religions and the Council for the World's Religions.

The Global Congress of the World's Religions

One initiative of the Unification Church was the formation of the Global

Congress of the World's Religions. The sixth annual International Conference on the Unity of the Sciences, which is sponsored by the International Cultural Foundation and founded by the Rev. Moon, was held in San Francisco in 1977. Some participants stayed on afterwards to discuss a proposal prepared by the faculty of the Unification Theological Seminary of Barrytown, New York.

This began by saying that the world family has entered an international era and that the future of the religious faiths is necessarily an interdependent one. 'We are moving towards active participation in one anothers' lives and faiths. Towards this inevitable goal, we propose the formation of a Global Congress of World Religions.'[3] There then followed certain affirmations. First, each religion has its own profound truths and absolute value. Secondly, one purpose of religion is to make a better world, but no religion can do this in isolation and by itself. 'Practical co-operation of the world's faiths in solving specific human problems is required as a means both of releasing new energies against these problems and of acting out spiritual values common to the religions themselves.'[4] The world religions can provide leadership for the new age and bring the human family together in healthy wholeness. 'If the world's religions do not offer the required leadership, the inevitably resulting void is liable to be filled by militarists or reductionist or materialists.'[5] Religions should provide an alternative to the threats of totalitarian communism and reactionary fascism.

The statement proposed a 'global forum in which the religions can take the public initiative which humanity may rightfully expect of them – we support the work of unification of the world's religions. "Unification" is a non-sectarian word which means for us neither union nor uniformity, neither creedal alignment nor imposed or implicit agreement on theological issues. We hold, rather, that there is already a sufficient basis in common, human, spiritual insights which would allow for a problem-solving orientation according to which we could work together even though we disagree doctrinally. We acknowledge that the religious situation is and shall continue to be a pluralistic one: we, too, are comfortable with the mutual tolerance and independence which pluralism implies. At the same time, we are convinced that communication, co-operation and confederation of the world's religions is desirable as an expression of the essential unity of human hearts and necessary as a means of solving basic problems.'[6]

It has been worth quoting this initial document quite fully, as subsequent discussion refined the idea, but did not seriously modify it. The San Francisco gathering encouraged the suggestion. The initiative was left with the Unification Theological Seminary at Barrytown and especially with Dr Warren Lewis, a free churchman from Texas, who at the time was professionally employed to teach at the Seminary. Lewis carried the project forward on two fronts. First, conferences on contemporary African religion were held at Barrytown and Bristol. Secondly, three annual conferences 'Towards a Global Congress of the World's Religions' were held at Boston in 1978, at Los Angeles in 1979 and at Miami in 1980. At both Lewis chaired further discussions of the original idea. At Boston, Dr K. L. Seshagiri Rao, Editor of *Insight*, the journal of the Temple of Understanding, and I, as editor of *World Faiths*, both spoke in an individual capacity. At Los Angeles, Finley Peter Dunne, then a board member of the Temple of Understanding, and the late Dr Isma'il R. al-Faruqi, then Professor of Islamics at Temple University in Philadelphia, Pennsylvania, were the speakers. At the end of the Conference, Ninian Smart, Professor of Comparative Religions at Lancaster and at Santa Barbara, announced the formation of an international, interfaith Committee for the Global Congress. This Committee, functioning as an independent body comprising individuals dedicated to the founding of the Global Congress and known for their inter-religious concerns, were to have the responsibilities of refining the idea, setting the agenda, and calling the Global Congress of the World's Religions into its first session.

At the Conference 'Towards a Global Congress of the World's Religions', held in Miami, USA, from 30 November to 1 December 1980, the Global Congress was inaugurated. I was given the honour of reading the Preamble:

> The flowing together of human energies in the life of our time inspires us religious people to unify our hearts, clarify our understanding, implement our compassion, and co-ordinate our action in the shared responsibility for well-being of the human family and the earth itself on which we live.

> This task belongs to all of us as the history of our race increasingly becomes a common story, but it is particularly expected of those whose minds have been opened to spiritual enlightenment and whose hearts are made tender for the fragile and the suffering.

> We, therefore, today, November 30th, 1980, sensing our religious responsibility, in the name of all we hold sacred constitute ourselves a global congress of the world's relgions.

> We undersign our names – both those who call on God and those who do not – and invite others of like persuasion to join with us and sign their

names, betokening our intention to gather the world's religions into an on-going congress where these high purposes shall be acknowledged, strengthened, and made effective.[7]

It was made clear that the Global Congress was not a new religion nor a syncretism of existing religions. Its purpose is to encourage communication between members of the great religions, both by arranging conferences and by publications.

Soon after the Miami Conference, Dr Warren Lewis' employment at the Unification Theological Seminary was terminated. The leadership of the Global Congress passed to Dr Henry O. Thompson, a Presbyterian who teaches at the Unification Theological Seminary, who is a prolific writer. The Trustees have met annually. The Congress has sponsored a series of inter-religious conferences, several of which have given rise to publications. There is also an interesting occasional newsletter. The Congress is sponsored by the Unification Theological Seminary and depends largely on the active support and generosity of its Principal, Dr David S. C. Kim.

The Council for the World's Religions

The Global Congress has been rather overshadowed by The Council for the World's Religions, which is another initiative sponsored by the Unification Church.

In the late seventies, besides the preparatory conferences for the Global Congress, other theological conferences were initiated by Rev. Moon, with the advice of Professor Herbert Richardson. In 1980, a more formal structure was given to this development by the establishment of the New Ecumenical Research Association, New ERA, under the directorship of John T. Maniatis. The establishment of New Era was marked by a lunch at Rev. Moon's home. From this developed the idea for a conference on 'God: the Contemporary Discussion'. The first 'God Conference', in December 1981, involved participants from over thirty nations and from almost all religions. At the same time, Rev. Moon initiated the 'Youth Seminar on World Religions', a global pilgrimage to religious homelands for a selected group of young people, drawn from the world's religions. To support the inter-religious projects which had developed from New ERA Conferences, the International Religious Foundation (IRF) was incorporated in 1983, with Rev. Chung Hwan Kwak as president.

In the same year, under the auspices of IRF, Rev. Moon initiated the development of the Assembly of the World's Religions. This was under the leadership of Rev. Kwak, Richard Payne, who had several years experience of inter-religious publishing, and Dr M. Darrol Bryant, Professor of Religion at Renison College at the University of Waterloo, Canada. The first assembly was held in 1985 and the second in 1990. There are plans to hold a third in 1993 to mark the centenary of the 1893 Chicago World's Parliament of Religions. Soon afterwards, in 1984, an international panel of advisors from different religions met at Ossining in New York State to discuss setting up a continuing body, which was to become known as The Council for the World's Religions. This also is under the auspices of IRF.

The Assembly of the World's Religions

McAfee, 1985

The first Assembly of the World's Religions, held at the Americana Great Gorge Conference Center, McAfee, New Jersey, in November 1985, was a large and imaginative gathering. Over six hundred people from eighty-five nations took part. Each had written a short paper prior to the conference. Unusually in such a large gathering, there was enough time for small discussion groups. Much attention was given to the meditation and worship as well as to the artistic, imaginative and emotional content. The Plenary Speakers were Rev. Sun Myung Moon, as Founder of the International Religious Foundation, Swami Dayananda Saraswati, Director of Arsh Vidya Peetam, Ven. Samdhong L. Tenzin Rinpoche, Principal of the Central Institute of Higher Tibetan Studies, Dr Ursula King, then at the University of Leads, Dr S. S. Janaki, of the Kuppuswami Sastri Research Institute, Professor Midori Shirato of Rissho University, His Holiness Acharya Sushil Kumar Maharaj, Founder of the World Fellowship of Religions, Ms Meenakshi Gopinath, of Lady Shri Ram College at Delhi University, Dr Joseph Paige of Shaw Divinity School, Metropolitan Paulos Mar Gregorios of the Syrian Orthodox Church of the East, Rabbi Dovid Din, Director of Shaarei Orah Center for Judaic and Mystical Studies, Dr Wande Abimbola, Vice-Chancellor of the University of Ife and Dr A. K. Brohi of the National Hijra Council of Pakistan. There were a number of religious and Cultural performances, including an evening of classical Indian dance and a concert by the New York City Symphony. The Fourth Day of the Assembly was held in New York and included a tour of the city and a gathering at the Metropolitan Baptist Church.

The Assembly was 'an extraordinary event, one that lifted us beyond our ordinary experience and gave us a glimpse of what is possible when we come together out of the deepest dimensions of our respective traditions and lives. It was, as one of the participants remarked "a word of hope in our troubled world"'.[8]

San Francisco, 1990

The second Assembly was held in San Francisco, California, in August 1990. The theme was 'Transmitting Our Heritage to Youth and Society'. The pattern was similar to the first assembly. The programme included a welcoming ceremony, prayer and meditation, dialogue groups, for which participants had written papers, plenary sessions, artistic performances, workshops and a pilgrimage and tour. The morning prayer and meditation sessions were according to a particular tradition, but open to all to attend. The evening meditations were interfaith in character. Speakers at plenary sessions included Metropolitan Dr Paulos Mar Gregorios of the Orthodox Syrian Church of the East, Sheikh Dr Ahmad Kuftaro, Grand Mufti of Syria and Rev. Sun Myung Moon. The plenary panels also attracted very distinguished speakers.[9]

The Council for the World's Religions: Activities

The Council for the World's Religions is a continuing body that has sponsored various activities.

Its aims are:

1. To proclaim the basic oneness of the human family.
2. To promote reverence for the rich diversity of the spiritual heritage of humankind.
3. To call people of all faiths to a sense of their spiritual unity, while respecting what is distinctive in each faith.
4. To foster mutual understanding and co-operation between and within religious traditions of the world.
5. To serve those who seek religious harmony, and to assist co-operation between interfaith organizations.
6. To further the application of common religious insights to the basic problems of humanity.
7. To champion human rights, including the right to freedom of religious belief and practice.
8. To give practical expression to the spiritual aspirations of believers by supporting programmes that alleviate suffering and promote human well-being.
9. To work towards the eventual establishment of a permanent forum for the world's religions in which they may deliberate and strive for common objectives.[10]

A particular work of CWR has been the holding of both inter-religious and intra-religious conferences. At the former participants are drawn from all major religions. For example, at Harrison Hot Springs in British Columbia, in 1987, some sixty people of different religions met to discuss 'Ritual, Symbol and Participation in the Quest for Interfaith Co-operation'. The intra-religious conferences are designed to facilitate communication within one religious tradition. It is a common experience at inter-religious conferences to discover that members of one religion do not speak with a single voice. In every religion, there are differences and sometimes, sadly, bitter divisions. The intra-religious conferences are making a valuable contribution to overcoming these internal divisions.[11]

At both types of conference, the pattern is similar. Much of the time is spent in group discussion. Participants are expected to produce a short paper, well ahead of the conference. This is circulated before the conference to other members of the discussion group. To each paper, one member of the group makes a brief response. This means that the time together can be devoted to discussion in depth, instead, as so often happens, to listening to over-long papers. There are some plenary sessions, as well as times of prayer and worship and some opportunities for relaxation and leisure. In my experience, the conferences arranged by CWR have been some of the most satisfactory and worthwhile. This is largely due to the scholarly and imaginative leadership of Dr Francis Clark, formerly Professor of Theology at the Gregorian University, Rome and a Reader in Religious Studies at the Open University in Britain, who is a Consultant to CWR and to Dr Darrol Bryant. The conferences benefit too from the resources generously made available by IRF and from the staff work of members of the Unification Church.

Another project of CWR has been the Religious Youth Service Programme (RYS). This has brought young people of different religions together on a project of social work for a community. During the time together, there are opportunities to learn about the participants' religions and to learn about the needs of the community in which the visitors are involved.

From these initiatives of CWR, have emerged the impressive journal *Dialogue and Alliance*, which often includes papers given at one of the CWR conferences, and books on interfaith dialogue. A particularly useful publication is the *Interfaith Directory*, edited by Francis Clark. The spur to the preparation of the book was the 1985 Ammerdown conference for interfaith organizations. The Directory is one more way in which members of very different groups may feel together part of a worldwide interfaith movement.[12]

Recently an Inter-Religious Federation for World Peace (IRFWP) has been formed. It appeals, says its Secretary General, Dr Francis Clark, 'to the universal ideals of spiritual and temporal peace which were proclaimed by all the great religious founders, teachers and sages, and which are the common inheritance of humankind'.[13]

The Problems of the Sponsorship

There can be no doubt about the high quality of the work undertaken by the bodies sponsored by IRF. There has, however, been much suspicion of it and some opposition to it. The Rev. Sun Myung Moon and the Unification Church have been the subjects of much hostile publicity. Partly this relates to the source and use of the Rev. Moon's money, partly to his political sympathies, which are regarded as 'right-wing', partly to the proliferation of organizations using different names, and mainly to methods by which his followers are recruited and trained.[14] Methods of fund-raising and over-enthusiastic recruitment have been criticized by the leadership of the Unification Church itself. Some of the external criticisms may have been evoked by jealousy of the movement's growth, and many are still suspicious of the Unificationist activity.

A full study of the Unification Church is impossible here and would require a discussion of 'new religions' in general. The fact that some of the Rev. Moon's teachings differ from traditional Christian views or that some of his followers seem to regard him as the new Messiah is not relevant here. Dialogue allows the other to define his or her beliefs.

The suspicion seems to be that the interfaith programme of the Unification Church is being used to promote that church and to help it gain respectability. Clearly any body may hope for some credit for worthwhile projects, but if there is an ulterior motive for dialogue that may jeopardize the dialogue itself. In a personal statement, Dr Francis Clark and Dr Huston Smith, both Consultants of CWR, point out that many academic, scientific and humanitarian projects are dependent on sponsorship. To accept that sponsorship 'does not mean that we personally, or the CWR collectively, are in any way committed to endorsing the specific religious beliefs and practices of the Unification Church. As we maintain our own very different religious beliefs and practices, so we respect their right to maintain theirs. Nevertheless, when we find that any religious group or any individual believers hold the same ideals of interreligious amity and collaboration that we ourselves hold, then we gladly make common cause with them in working for those common ideals, without presuming to make censorious criticisms of their specific beliefs and practices'.[15]

A large number of religious leaders and scholars have now taken part in conferences sponsored by the Unification Church. Others refuse because of their suspicions, some of which have been outlined above, or because of the criticisms of their colleagues. Clearly it is for each individual to make his or her own decision and this should not affect a person's membership of other bodies.

The relationship of CWR to the interfaith organizations is more complex. CWR appears to claim to be an interfaith organization, but other interfaith organizations see as part of their self-definition, that their governing body should be inter-religious and that their funding should be drawn from several religious communities. It seems to me better to see CWR as the inter-religious programme of the Unification Church. Its status is then similar to the Sub-Unit on Dialogue of the World Council of Churches or the Vatican's Pontifical Council for Inter-religious Dialogue. Both these bodies arrange a series of multi-religious consultations, which people of different faiths attend. There is no suggestion that the integrity of a Jew or a Muslim who attends a consultation arranged by the WCC is compromised. Equally, the Vatican or the Unification Church may, partly because of greater resources, be able to do more for inter-religious understanding than one of the interfaith organizations. That, however, does not make either an interfaith organization. To blur the distinction, which should not imply an evaluation of the usefulness of the work of particular bodies, is likely to cause misunderstanding.

Sadly such misunderstanding does exist. Those in the interfaith organizations know the prejudice that still exists in many religious communities to the whole concept of inter-religious co-operation and dialogue. To be seen to be closely allied to a body of which there are also suspicions might aggravate the difficulties. In the interfaith organizations there are of course some who share the widespread suspicion of Rev. Moon and the Unification Church. It will take time for these suspicions to be dissappated. The way forward to help remove suspicions seems to be for as much personal contact as possible between those who are members of the international interfaith organizations and those who are working with CWR. A recognition of the different status of CWR and the interfaith organizations will also help. Each has work to do and the need to overcome religious intolerance requires all the resources available.

· PART VI ·

Learning about Other People's Beliefs

'A world culture could be built up and a world renaissance made possible if educational institutions throughout the world were inspired by a common study of the spirit of man as reflected in his approach to God.'

· 32 ·

Studying and Teaching World Religions

Providing Accurate Information

Inter-religious dialogue presupposes growing knowledge of other people's religious beliefs and practices. Ignorance is a potent cause of misunderstanding and prejudice. An important task of interfaith organizations has been to provide unbiassed information about the great religions. In the Council of Christians and Jews, for example, the value of education has been seen in removing ignorance and the causes of prejudice, thereby helping 'to check and combat all forms of religious and racial intolerance'.[1] The Inter-Religions Organization of Singapore has also hoped that providing accurate information about the religions practised there has helped 'to create a climate in which religious disturbances are less likely'.[2]

One early example of trying to provide accurate information was The Religions of the Empire Conference held in London in 1924. The conference was arranged to coincide with the British Empire exhibition. Sir Denison Ross, an expert on Oriental languages and joint author of *The Heart of Asia*, in agreeing to become chairman of the organizing committee, insisted 'that the Congress should not take a controversial form'.[3] To ensure this, all speakers from the platform were accorded an equal status. They were not allowed to introduce matters which were either religiously or politically controversial. In any case, their papers had to be submitted in advance to the Committee. No discussion was allowed. The intention of the conference was strictly informative, not comparative.[4] This also was the reason why no papers were given on Christianity or Judaism. This was a deliberate decision of the organizers as 'they considered that their function was chiefly to familiarize those attending the lectures with the religions of the Empire relatively little known in Britain'.[5]

The other condition Sir Denison Ross laid down was 'that the spokesman of each religion should be one who professed such religion'.[6] The papers were given by scholarly adherents of the particular religion and the choice of speakers was well made. Here is an interesting point of principle which is still discussed. Can someone who is not a member of a faith speak adequately of it, or must an outsider inevitably miss the 'feel' of a religion? At the WCF Conference in November 1988, when Professor Hans Küng was the main speaker, several of the respondents objected to him basing his knowledge of other religions on descriptions of those religions made by Christian scholars.[7] This is an issue that has also come to the fore in the teaching of world religions in British Schools. It is often said that the aim is not just to provide information about a religion, but to help pupils understand the world-view of adherents of a particular religious tradition. Certainly it is easier for a member of a religion to convey what it feels like to belong to it: but the number of adherents of Indian religions in Britain who have been readily able to communicate their faith and are at home with current educational methods has been limited. Sympathetic teachers, making use of the wide range of audio-visual aids which are now available, have shown that they can convey to their pupils considerable insight into faiths other than their own.

The International Association for the History of Religions

With the desire for greater knowledge of the world religions, there has been, in this century, a rapid expansion of academic study of the subject, although there has been some debate about the proper name for this discipline. Besides the growth of university departments and of courses at colleges of education, the development has also led to the establishment of organizations to promote the study of world religions.

When *Le Premier Congres International d'Historie des Religions* was convened in Paris in 1901, in connection with *L'Exposition Universelle*, it was devoted exclusively to the scientific study of religions. The circular advertising the conference said that 'the proposed Congress is of an exclusively historical nature'.[8] In the event, the papers justified this claim.

The Paris Congress was to be the first of a series. At each congress an international continuation committee was appointed, with responsibility for arranging the next congress. These were held at Basel (1904), Oxford (1908), Leiden (1912), Paris (1923), Lund (1929) and Brussels (1935). No permanent organization, however, was established until after the Second World War. Soon after the war, Professor Gerardus van der Leeuw helped to found a Dutch Society for the History of Religions. From this body a request went to the surviving members of the continuation committee, appointed at Brussels in 1935, for permission to organize a congress in Amsterdam in 1950. Preparations were also made to form a permanent body consisting of national societies. The desire for a permanent body was partly so that the work could be related to UNESCO.[9]

At the Amsterdam Congress, an international organization was set up with a permanent secretariat. At first the organization was called The International Association for the Study of the History of Religions (IASHR): but the name was later shortened to The International Association for the History of Religions (IAHR). Now a further change to 'The International Association for the Study of Religions' is being considered. The British Association has already made this change, which reflects the diversification of this subject. The first statute states the purpose of IAHR is to be 'a world-wide organization which has as its object the promotion of the academic study of the history of religions through the international collaboration of all scholars whose research has a bearing on the subject'.[10] The intention of Van der Leeuw and the other founders was that the history of religions should not be isolated from other related studies, such as the psychology and sociology of religion[11]: but their overriding concern was for the academic or 'scientific' study of religions.

The post-war period has seen much discussion of methodology in the study of religions. This is well described by Professor Eric Sharpe in his *Comparative Religion*.[12] In this context, the important question is whether the academic study of religions is an end in itself or should serve the cause of interfaith and international understanding. This came to a head after the ninth International Congress which was held in 1958 in Tokyo. This was the first time a Congress had been held outside Europe. Despite initial fears, the registration of scholars from outside Japan was satisfactory. One hundred and thirty came from twenty-six foreign countries, including a large number from the USA and about thirty scholars from Afro-Asian countries.[13] Even so, with the presence of many Japanese scholars, the Congress became aware that the Oriental approach to the study of religions was different to the dominant academic tradition in Europe. 'The West', writes Professor Sharpe, 'had generally tended to look upon religion for scholarly purposes as something static, a collection of data, or alternatively as an organism to be dissected. Typically the West had long been accustomed to spending most of its labours on the ancient religious traditions. Perhaps by the 1950s the approach was no longer purely genetic: but well-established conventions die hard. The East, on the other hand, could as a rule conceive of no purpose for the study of religion other than to deepen one's apprehension and understanding of reality: certainly it could never look upon religion merely as a passive object stretched out on the scholar's operating table. Religion is there to be lived, and if study does not help the student to live better or more fully, then there can be little or no point in it.'[14]

The 'Eastern' view had some 'Western' sympathizers, such as Professor Friedrich Heiler of Marburg University, who delivered an address at the opening session.[15] The issue was also raised by the fact that the Congress was immediately followed by a symposium, arranged as part of a UNESCO East-West project, on 'Religion and Thought in Orient and Occident: A Century of Cultural Exchange'.

Heiler, a pupil and friend of Rudolf Otto, had in 1956 revived Otto's Religious League of Mankind, which was affiliated to the World Congress of Faiths.[16] He began his opening address with the quotation 'Have we not all one Father? Has not one God created us?' He welcomed Arnold Toynbee's book, *An Historian's Approach to Religion*, and its criticism of the exclusive attitude of so many Christians. The modern science of religion, Heiler argued, refuted the narrow Christian view which denied every other revelation and claimed there was no link between the Gospel and world religions. Quoting Schleiermacher's words, 'The deeper you progress in religion, the more the whole religious world appears as an indivisible whole', Heiler outlined 'seven principle areas of unity which the high religions of the earth manifest'.[17] The reality of the transcendent, he said, is immanent in human hearts, is man's highest good, and is ultimate love. The way to God is a way of sacrifice. Equally all religions teach love for one's neighbour as well as saying that love is a superior way to God. 'Thus there is an ultimate and most profound unity of all high religions.'[18] 'One of the most important tasks of the science of religion', he continued, 'is to bring to light this unity of all religions. It thereby pursues only one purpose, that of pure knowledge of the truth. But unintentionally there sprouts forth from the root of scientific inquiry into truth not only a tree with wondrous blossoms but also with glorious fruit – its inquiry into truth bears important consequences for the practical relationship of one religion to another.'[19] 'A new era', he concluded, 'will dawn upon mankind when the religions will rise to true tolerance and co-operation on behalf of mankind. To assist in preparing the way for this era is one of the finest hopes of the scientific study of religion.'[20]

Such questions had normally been avoided by scholars as 'unscientific'. Their unease was increased by the fact that the next Congress was to be held in Marburg, which was Heiler's own university. In an article in the *Hibbert Journal*, Professor Zwi Werblowsky of Jerusalem voiced his dissent, although he did not mention Heiler by name. He argued that whilst individuals who studied religion might advocate mutual understanding and co-operation, they could not do so as students of religion. 'Students of religion cannot by definition preach mutual understanding – if they speak of mutual understanding, then they do so as protagonists of a certain ideology (i.e., of tolerance, charity, liberalism, etc.) but not as students of religion – there is, as I can see it, neither room nor justification for an "Applied Comparative Religion".'[21]

Matters came to a head in Marburg. The Secretary, Professor C. J. Bleeker, presented a paper to the General Assembly of the IAHR on 'The Future Task of the History of Religion'. He mentioned the new dimension, introduced by the presence of Oriental scholars at the Tokyo Congress. He then dealt with criticisms of the UNESCO symposium on 'Religion and Thought in East and West, a Century of Cultural Exchange'. The intention was that the problems should be discussed in a historical context, although some participants may have transgressed the borders of purely scientific research. He admitted that the theme could not be discussed in complete disinterestedness, because it touched directly on the burning issues of the day. Claiming that Oriental scholars were equally capable of strictly scientific research, he pointed out that there were Western thinkers who believed that the history of religions should contribute to the reconstruction of cultural and religious life. Many students were motivated solely by pure love for the work and performed their studies according to the strict rules of science 'without asking whether the outcome of their investigation can serve the cultural or religious wellbeing of mankind'.[22] Others, however, felt that, not as a scholar, but as a man of science and as a citizen, it was right for them to share in the struggle for the preservation of the moral and religious values of humanity. Bleeker, whilst adopting a mediating approach and stressing the scientific nature of the study of religions, concluded: 'I think we can hardly withdraw from taking into account the express wish that the study of the history of religions should give its contribution to the clarification of present religious questions.'[23] He then mentioned four questions: 'What is true religion?'; the need for a survey of different types of religion; the value of religion for the present and the future, and the idea of sympathy and tolerance.

In the ensuing discussion, Professor Zwi Werblowsky submitted a short paper containing 'the basic minimum conditions for the study of the history of religions'. A variety of scholars had signified their general agreement with the statement. The first point rejected the distinction between Occidental and Oriental. 'There are *Religionswissenschaftler* in the East as there are "intuitionists" in the West.'[24] Secondly, *Religionswissenshaft* is seen as a branch of the Humanities. 'It is an anthropological discipline, studying religious phenomena as a creation, feature and aspect of human culture – the discussion of the absolute value of religion is excluded by definition, although it may have its legitimate place in other completely independent disciplines such as, e.g., theology and philosophy of religion.[25] Thirdly, the statement that 'the value of religious phenomena can be understood only if we keep in mind that religion is ultimately a realization of a transcendent truth' is rejected. Fourthly, it is said: 'The study of religions need not seek for justification outside itself so long as it remains embedded in a culture pattern that allows for every quest of historical truth as its own *raison d'être*. Whatever the subsequent use made by the individual scholar of his special knowledge, and whatever the analyzable sociological functions of scientific activity in any specific cultural and historical situation, the ethos of our studies is in themselves.'[26] Finally, it is stated, 'There may or may not be room for organizations in which students of religion join with others in order to contribute their share towards the promotion of certain ideals – national, international, political, social, spiritual and otherwise. But this is a matter of individual ideology and commitment, and must under no circumstances be allowed to influence or colour the character of IAHR.'[27]

Although the discussion revealed differences of emphasis, the general thrust of Professor Werblowsky's paper was accepted. Summarizing the discussion, Professor Bleeker ended by saying, 'We should make a clear distinction between our scientific work and the Ecumenical movement or the World Congress of Faiths – we are only a congress for scientific study of the history of religions. It is our duty to spread our light to people who do not know properly what religion is. But our task is not conversion to faith whatsoever, but simply enlightening.'[28]

The debates within IAHR from Tokyo to Marburg made clear the distinction between the academic study of religions and both theology on the one hand and the promotion of interfaith understanding on the other. In his scientific work, the student of religions should hold his personal beliefs in suspension and not confuse his study, which is an end in itself, with other causes, however worthy. Those concerned with interfaith organizations often did not fully appreciate the nature of the academic discipline. This, especially in the fifties and sixties, led to misunderstanding and suspicion. Many scholars kept aloof from interfaith bodies for fear that they would be placed in a false position or that their scholarly reputation would be jeopardized. This seriously weakened interfaith organizations, which also, at that time, lacked the support of religious leaders, afraid that their orthodoxy might be compromised. As a result interfaith gatherings often lacked the depth and scholarship that would have been beneficial.

In recent years, the position has changed considerably. The phenomenological approach to the study of religions has encouraged students to take more interest in believers' self-understanding of their faiths. One of the aims of the Open University's *Man's Religious Quest* study programme was 'to encourage the student to enter sympathetically into the thought-world of others and to appreciate what their religious beliefs and practices mean for them'.[29] In the churches, the theology of religions has become a subject attracting great interest. The interfaith organizations now give more weight to religious differences and do not presuppose a unity, which some scholars found difficult to accept. As a result, many distinguished scholars now speak at inter-religious gatherings and some have accepted leadership roles in interfaith organizations. Interestingly, the Open University course includes a unit on 'Inter-Religious Encounter', which itself has a paragraph on 'the urgency of global understanding'.[30]

Questions about methodology have, nonetheless, continued to be discussed at meetings of IAHR. Dr Terry Thomas, in his report on the Rome Congress in 1990, said that there were several papers on this by Dutch scholars and 'that the tempo of the debate was maintained right up to the final plenary session of the Congress'.[31]

The late sixties and seventies saw a great burgeoning of the study of religions. This was partly because of student choice, especially in North America. Partly it resulted from the recognition in the USA that a state university could teach religion in a plural way and from government support for the expansion of non-European studies. Certain African states have also recognized the need to have a balance in religious studies.[32]

The growing interest in the study of religions has been a worldwide phenomenon. This is now reflected in the activities and the broadening membership of IAHR. The 1985 Congress, for example, was held in Sydney, Australia. Apart from Japan, however, IAHR has until recently been dominated by 'western countries'. At the Rome Congress, where several new members were welcomed, it was clear that this had begun to change. Chinese participants had been at the three previous congresses. Prior to the 1990 congress, the Chinese Association for the Study of Religions had been restructured and at Rome was welcomed into membership. Other new member associations included the Indonesian Society for the Comparative Study of Religion, the Asociacion Latinoamericana papa los estudios de las Religiones, the Soviet Union's Sovietskaya Assatsiatsiya Istorikov Religii and the Czechoslovak Association for the Study of Religion.[33]

The broadening membership has raised questions about the official languages of IAHR congresses. IAHR's prestigious journal, *Numen* is published in English, French, German and Italian. At Rome, Dr Michael Pye, the Secretary General proposed that at congresses the official languages should be English, French and the language of the country or city in which the meeting was taking place. Thus at the next Congress, to be held in Mexico in 1995, the third language would be Spanish.

Increasingly IAHR is fulfilling its original intention to be a 'world-wide' organization. It seems likely that in future more attention will be paid to gender studies and more opportunity be given to younger scholars to participate.

The Universities

Whilst the academic study of religions does not itself carry implications about the relation of religions to each other, the great increase of knowledge for which it has been responsible has done much to foster awareness of and interest in other religions. The situation in each country is different. In India, the study of religions is usually part of the study of philosophy. In America, many colleges now have large departments for the study of religions. In Europe, the dominant position of theology has sometimes made it difficult to develop departments for the study of world religions. A comprehensive account of the position in Britain is given in a recent book of essays, in honour of Professor Geoffrey Parrinder, a pioneer in this field, entitled *Turning Points in Religious Studies*.[34]

In Britain, initial developments owed much to H. N. Spalding. Through his beneficence, Spalding, who believed that a study of world religions was vital for mankind's future, exercised an important influence. He and his wife gave Oxford University a Chair of Eastern Religion and Ethics, Lectureships in Chinese Philosophy and Religion and in Eastern Orthodox Culture, an Advisorship in Eastern Art, and four temporary Senior Research Fellowships in Indian History and Religion, as well as a wildlife and plant sanctuary on the Cherwell. He also founded and nurtured the School of Eastern Religious Studies at Durham and gave books to libraries across the world. With Dr Radhakrishnan and a group of people, internationally eminent in church and state and learning, he helped in 1951, to found, at Oxford, a Union for the Study of the Great Religions.

H. N. Spalding had various objectives in promoting the study of religions. He believed that knowledge and understanding would encourage tolerance. Secondly, he believed that every great civilization had been inspired by the possession of a spiritual content shared by all its members. Europeans, even if ignorant of the Bible and the classics, were subconsciously moulded by the legacy of Hellenized Rome and Christianized Judaism. Recent specialization was destroying this shared heritage, whilst the technological unity of the world required a broader base for any new shared spiritual culture. The belief of the founders of the Union for the

Study of the Great Religions was that 'just as European civilization achieved unity in diversity on a basis of Christianity and Hellenism, so a world culture could be built up and a world renaissance made possible if educational institutions throughout the world were inspired by a common study of the spirit of man as reflected in his approach to God. The great cultures and religions of East and West – of the Far East, India, Islam, ancient Greece and Palestine, Slav, Latin and Nordic Europe, and North and Latin America – should be impartially studied and compared in their independence, integrity and fruitful diversity'.[35]

Spalding's third objective was the 'restoration of faith in humanity and of happiness in living', which required the exercise of self-control.[36]

Through his trusts, much, in a quiet way, has been achieved. The first two holders of the Spalding Chair at Oxford, Dr Radhakrishnan and Dr Zaehner, exercised wide influence through their writings. The Spalding Trust has subsidized books, libraries, lectureships, and individual scholars. It has encouraged various new projects such as the Shap Working Party. The Union for the Study of Great Religions, although it seldom met as a body, had distinguished members.[37] For many years, it circulated a periodic report on current developments and a half yearly compilation of notes on a wide range of books – the work of Archimandrite Lev Gillet, a scholar with an amazing width of knowledge, who for a time was Secretary of the World Congress of Faiths. The Union was also responsible for the conception and implementation of the periodical *Religious Studies*. Gradually the study of world religions has spread in British universities. Particular mention may be made of the Lancaster Centre for the Study of Religion, built up by Professor Ninian Smart and others, and of the influence of Professor E. G. Parrinder at King's College, London.

The Union for the Study of Great Religions, through its then chairman, Sir Richard Livingstone, played a part in the setting up of the Center for the Study of World Religions at Harvard University, Cambridge, Massachusetts. There is a small residential centre, where scholars and students and their families, drawn from many religious traditions, can live in close contact. The centre is linked to Harvard Divinity school. The emphasis has been on the study of the living faith of members of the world religions. The influence of the centre has been very considerable.

The development of the Faculty for Comparative Study of Religions (FVG) at Antwerp also deserves to be mentioned. This has resulted from the self-sacrificing efforts of Rev. Christiaan Vonck. In the seventies, he came in touch with the World Congress of Faiths. At first, efforts were made to establish a Belgian branch of WCF, but soon Christiaan Vonck decided to concentrate on establishing a university department. As a protestant clergyman in a country where the Roman Catholic Church is dominant and where schools of theology are well established in the universities, the task was not easy. The first efforts were voluntary, but the department gained royal recognition and now is housed in a castle, which belongs to the Ministry of Education. The number of students, some from abroad, has gradually risen.[38]

Study Centres

Besides the welcome growth in university departments which specialize in the teaching of world religions, often with accompanying study centres, there are a variety of other institutions which encourage the study of religions. The Christian Institute for the Study of Religion and Society at Bangalore, India (CISRS) was established in 1957 as an autonomous institution, having ecumenical relations with a number of churches and organizations. Its particular aim was to help Christians in India establish vital contact with other religious communities in the country and to see how they could share more fully in nation building. The pioneering work of its first director, Dr Paul Devanandan, had a wide influence, especially through the World Council of Churches – an influence continued by others, such as Dr M. M. Thomas and Dr Stanley Samartha, who have also been associated with the centre. There is also an important Catholic institution for the study of world religions at Dharmaram Pontifical Institute in Bangalore. Institutes similar to those at Bangalore have been established at a number of places, for example at Rawlpindi and in the Punjab, Sri Lanka, Thailand and elsewhere. The Ecumenical Institute at Tantur, near Jerusalem, has also been an important centre for Christian scholars to enter into dialogue with Jews and to a lesser extent, with Muslims.[39]

The Selly Oak Colleges, Birmingham, England, have also become the home for several study centres. The Centre for the Study of Islam and Christian-Muslim relations was established in 1975. In the 1983, with the appointment of Rabbi Dr Norman Solomon as Jewish lecturer, steps were initiated to start the Centre for the Study of Judaism and Jewish-Christian Relations, which has now been set up. The Multifaith Centre, led by Sister Mary Hall, and the Centre for New Religious Movements, founded by Dr Harold W. Turner, have also both had a considerable international influence.

Schools and Colleges

The importance of encouraging tolerance and inter-religious understanding at a young age has been increasingly recognized. Provision for religious education varies from country to country. In many countries there are 'religious' schools, in which one faith or denomination has a dominant influence. Some of these have recognized the need for their pupils to be aware of other religions. Some also may have a large number of pupils of faiths other than that of those responsible for the school or college. In India, for example, Christian colleges have for many years debated the provisions that should be made for the religious development of students who are not Christian. In some countries religious education is provided in state schools, in other countries it is not allowed.

World Interfaith Colleges

An exciting project is the plan for some World Interfaith Colleges. In the early sixties, the United World College Movement started a number of international schools at which children from many countries would study and live together. Little thought was given initially to providing for these young people's religious development. The Atlantic College in Wales arranged, annually, a week's interfaith conference and, regularly, invited visiting speakers from different religions and other colleges made similar provision. Marks McAvity, who taught at the Lester B. Pearson College of the Pacific for several years, however, became increasingly concerned to see how the interfaith potential of such colleges could be developed. It became clear that a new movement was necessary, as the United World Colleges were not founded with a religious or interfaith intention. Since 1988, Marks McAvity has been full time project director of The World Interfaith Colleges Association and has travelled widely to gain support for the idea. Considerable progress has been made with plans for the first college.[40]

SHAP

What the Spalding Trust and the Union for the Study of Great Religions have done for scholars and universities, the Shap Working Party has sought to do for teachers and schools. Its task has been to provide adequate material for teachers of world religions. At a conference held at Shap, in the Lake District in 1969, a working party was set up with the intention:

1. To identify the practical problems at various educational levels involved in teaching about world religions.
2. To study and provide relevant syllabus material.

3. To generate new ideas, and to explore the possibilities of future conferences and in-service training courses for teachers.
4. To act as a clearing house for information on visual aids, books, conferences or working parties on related topics.[41]

Since its formation, the Shap Working Party has done much to fulfil its aims.[42] It is interesting that, although many of its leaders commend the wider significance of the study of world religions for its bearing on good community relations and the search for religious truth, nothing to this effect is included in the aims of the Working Party.

SCIFDE

The agreed terms of reference of the Standing Conference on Inter-Faith Dialogue in Education, which John Prickett did so much to create, are also non-committal, although dialogue has been seen as not just communicating information but also as a growing in truth.[43] The Selly Oak Conference in 1974 agreed that 'essential ingredients for meaningful dialogue are honesty and integrity and a "wanting to know", so that it becomes not merely a question of communication, though of course it is that, but something that involves discovering truths about ourselves, and that involves an openness that puts those of us who participate at risk. It does this because we are asked to face up to, amongst other things, the question of truth and the recognition of incompatibles – dialogue can provide us with deeper insights into our own faiths – it has a social value and implications both for the world community and for world peace'.[44] Here the significance of dialogue for international and interfaith understanding is recognized as well as its importance in the quest for religious truth.

Conclusion

Clearly the motives for studying world religions are varied. At one extreme is disinterested scientific study – 'Truth for truth's sake' – at the other such study is encouraged in the belief that it will foster human unity and the search for religious truth. Implicit in the views of those who have this latter hope is the belief that world religions have much in common. In between, are those who see the value of knowing what others believe, as this can help mutual understanding between religious communities, but who do not wish to compromise the truth claims of their own faith. The attitude to the study of religions therefore reflects a person's or organization's view of the relation of religions. Confusion is sometimes caused because these underlying premises are not examined.

Whatever the motivation, this century has seen an enormous increase in information about world religions. In many countries, such information is readily available and people can quite easily acquire a basic knowledge of the beliefs of other religious traditions. Ignorance, which may be a cause of prejudice, is, even so, still widespread. Interfaith bodies, therefore, have a continuing task of providing accurate information. Yet, increasingly, this work is being done by the religions themselves, or by the growing academic study of the subject. This means that interfaith bodies can concentrate on their particular and specific tasks, especially in helping members of one religious community to meet and get to know those of other communities.

· PART VII ·

Towards 1993

'to give thanks for the growth of the interfaith movement . . . and to renew our efforts to remove all prejudice and discrimination, to end violence and injustice and to remove poverty . . .'

· 33 ·

Towards 1993

By this stage the reader may well ask 'Why are there so many interfaith organizations?'. Partly it is history, partly it is because each serves a particular constituency or has a special emphasis to its work. Yet, if we dream of a convergence of all religions, it is natural to hope that there may be a growing partnership of interfaith organizations.

Ammerdown, 1985

It was with this hope that I suggested a meeting of representatives of international interfaith organizations. Eventually, through the efforts of the World Congress of Faiths, this was held at the Ammerdown Conference Centre near Bath in England in April 1985. It was not as representative as had been hoped, being dominated by Europeans and Americans. This was partly because no funds were available to subsidize travel for participants from Asia. Even so, the major international interfaith organizations participated. IARF, the Temple of Understanding, WCF, WCRP, World Thanksgiving, ICCJ and the Week of Prayer for World Peace were represented. A number of national groups and study centres also took part, including The Antwerp Faculty for Comparative Study of Religions, The Centre for the Study of Islam and Christian Muslim Relations at Selly Oak, Birmingham, the British Council of Churches Committee for Relations with People of Other Faiths, Interreligio from the Netherlands and L'Union des Croyants' from France. Dr Wesley Ariarajah, Director of the Sub-Unit on Dialogue at the World Council of Churches attended, although a member of the Vatican Secretariat for Non-Christians was prevented at the last moment from coming.

The Council for the World's Religions and the Global Congress of the

World's Religions, which are both sponsored by the Unification Church, were also present. This led to considerable discussion about the definition of an interfaith organization. The majority view was that a body which received all its funding from one source was not an interfaith organization. Like the WCC Sub-Unit, CWR and the Global Congress, it was felt, should be regarded as the interfaith dialogue department of a particular religious body. This was not a judgment on the quality or value of the work, but on the constitution of the body. It must be said, however, that this decision was coloured by hostility in some quarters to the Unification Church and the feeling that to be seen to co-operate with it would alienate others who were still hesitant about interfaith work. Whilst both the 'four' interfaith organizations and the Council of World Religions have been careful to avoid competition or hostility – indeed personal relationships are good – this issue has not yet been satisfactorily resolved. In general the 'four' organizations now accept that their members are free as individuals to decide whether or not to participate in events organized by bodies which are sponsored by the Unification Church, although in some bodies hostility has been expressed to those who have participated. None of the four international interfaith organizations felt able to co-sponsor events with the Council for the World's Religions or the Global Congress for the World's Religions.

Ammerdown, which is run by an ecumenical community of which the Sisters of Sion form a part, is a retreat as well as a conference centre. The discussions were deliberately set in the context of quiet, meditation and prayer. Time was given to building personal relations, which are vital in all interfaith work. Quite a lot of time was also spent in describing the work of the organizations represented.

An opening paper was given by Dr John Taylor of WCRP. Admitting that the group was 'heavily European, even British, and predominantly Christian',[1] he counselled a proper modesty. He stressed that the 'experience of interfaith work shows that our respective faiths are strengthened rather than weakened in this enterprise . . . Our interfaith work can become a corrective to the failures of religion and an effective rejoinder to the accusations that religion brings only division and bitterness to the crises of the contemporary world.'[2] He acknowledged the contribution made by groups which have an explicitly inter-religious vocation, such as the Bahá'ís, but stressed that interfaith work could not just be left to enthusiasts, but should become the 'commitment of all people of good faith'.[3] John Taylor insisted that interfaith dialogue 'should not deteriorate into a pact of religious people over against irreligious people'.[4] The respect that dialogue encouraged should extend to secular neighbours.

Dr Taylor recognized that the diversity of organizations was partly because they varied in their motivation. 'For some it may be the conviction that truth is one, for others that humanity is one, for others that peace and justice are for all, for yet others that the local or international community must be reconciled.'[5] Compared to the number of confessional organizations, the number of multifaith organizations remained extremely small.

Dr Taylor mentioned the need for better communications between the organizations represented. He raised the possibility that various organizations might co-operate in marking the centenary of the Chicago World's Parliament of Religions. He mentioned too the possibility of 'an on-going conciliar structure where regular consultation and decision-making . . . would be undertaken'.[6]

Most of the weekend was spent in group discussions, which reported to plenary meetings. Some of this discussion was about the nature of dialogue, the relationship between religions and the aspirations of interfaith organizations. The workshops were more specific. One of them hoped that the various events held to commemorate the Chicago World's Parliament of Religions might be linked and that the year 'could provide an opportunity to touch people more widely with the spirit of interfaith dialogue'.[7]

A World Council of Religions

In a rather euphoric mood, the conference warmed to the suggestion of trying to create a 'World Council of Religions', 'to bring together people of all religions to overcome religious sectarianism, to work for peace, and to link individuals and organizations which are working for interfaith understanding'.[8]

The Very Rev. James Parks Morton, President of the Temple of Understanding, John Taylor of WCRP and I were asked to pursue this. We met in New York in the summer of 1985 and explored a first tentative model. We suggested that a future 'World Council of Faiths' might draw on the various distinctive emphases of existing bodies. Its task would be, first, to encourage understanding by working to remove ignorance and prejudice and promoting education and dialogue. Secondly, it would strive for human rights and dignity, by working for religious liberty, freedom of conscience and responsible stewardship of the earth's resources. Thirdly it would contribute to peace-building, between religions, in local communities and at the UN.

We discussed possible representation and how to ensure the participation of religious leaders and local involvement. We even began to cost the project. It was hoped that the idea might be discussed at a second international meeting in Japan in 1986. To many, however, the idea was threatening. It threatened the independence of interfaith organizations, who sometimes reflect the jealousies of the world religions. There was great reluctance to create a 'super body'. Subsequent co-operative work has therefore been shared between the four organizations and all links have been only consultative. Religious leaders also seemed even more threatened by the suggestion that they actually did something together, rather than talk about it. The idea of a Council was perhaps too Western and organized a model. There was not then the groundswell of confidence and co-operation which is gradually being developed. Yet the dream, I think, remains, and may well be back on the agenda after 1993.

Continuing Consultation

Following Ammerdown, however, communication between interfaith organizations increased. James Morton, John Taylor and I, joined by Rev. Kazuyoshi Tanaka of Rissho Kosei Kai met in London in October 1985. We talked further about the proposed meeting in Japan. By early 1986 it was clear that we were not ready for such a meeting and plans for it were abandoned. In June 1986, on the occasion of Dr Robert Runcie's Sir Francis Younghusband Lecture, given to mark the fiftieth anniversary of the World Congress of Faiths, James Morton, John Taylor and I met briefly. William Stansmore, of the Temple of Understanding, and some Executive members of the WCF also joined us for part of the discussion. We agreed that a meeting for a few staff members of IARF, the Temple of Understanding, WCF and WCRP should be held in London in November of that year.

Before that meeting, the Assisi World Day of Prayer for Peace had taken place in October. To this, the WCF, the Temple of Understanding, IARF, World Thanksgiving and WCRP were invited to be present, although only WCRP was a full participant. WCRP had given considerable help in preparations for the day. The following day, the organizations were asked to the meeting that Cardinal Arinze, President of the Vatican Secretariat for Non-Christians, arranged for 'non-Christian' participants and to a separate meeting with the interfaith organizations. The whole event gave renewed impetus to the interfaith movement and to the desire of the interfaith organizations to work together more closely.

The November meeting was attended by representatives of WCF, by Dr John Taylor and Rev. Yasuo N. Katsuyama for WCRP, William Stansmore and Dr Kusimita Priscilla Pedersen for the Temple, Dr Roy Smith, for IARF and Canon Gordon Wilson for the Week of Prayer for World Peace. There was a report on the Assisi Day of Prayer and reports on the programmes and plans of the participating organizations. Rev. Yasuo Katsuyama described the plans for a Day of Prayer to be held at Mount Hiei, near Kyoto in Japan in August 1987. Dr Pedersen outlined plans for the Global Forum on Human Survival. Discussion then turned to a framework for future co-operation. It was agreed that it was not the time to take further the discussion about a possible World Council of Faiths. It was felt that co-operation would need to continue on an *ad hoc* basis, making use of staff time and resources of existing organizations. 'There was general agreement that it would be inappropriate to invite the Council for World Religions/Assembly of World Religions, organizations sponsored by the Unification Church, to be brought within the present *ad hoc* consultative framework of organizations which drew their constituency and support from a range of religious groupings.'[9] It was agreed to try to hold a second international conference at Ammerdown in April 1988. There was also discussion of the best way to mark the centenary in 1993 of the World's Parliament of Religions. The feeling was that a range of different events might be most appropriate, linked perhaps by 'the adoption of a common symbol or theme'.

In the summer of 1987, representatives of some interfaith organizations, on their way to the IARF Congress in San Francisco, met in Dallas at the invitation of Peter Stewart of World Thanksgiving.

Ammerdown, April 1988

In April 1988 a second meeting of international interfaith organizations was held, again at Ammerdown. Rev. Diether Gehrmann and Mr Koichi Saito represented IARF, Dr Pederson, Rev. Dan Anderson, Judith Hollister, Winifred McCulloch and Fr Luis Dolan and James Morton – all of whom had been at the Global Forum on Human Survival – represented the Temple of Understanding. Janice Dolley, Brian Pearce, Professor Keith Ward, Mary Braybrooke and I represented WCF and Dr John Taylor, Rev. Yasuo N. Katsuyama and Very Rev. John Gatu from Kenya represented WCRP. Fr Albert Nambiaparambil from India, Rev. Christiaan Vonck from Antwerp, Dr Wesley Ariarajah from the WCC, Dr John Berthrong of the United Church of Canada, Sister Jayanti of Brahma Kumaris, Mrs Detiger of the Tiger Trust and Ruth Weyl of the International Council of Christians and Jews and a few observers also participated.

The Friday evening was mainly occupied with personal introductions and brief comments. Fr Albert Nambiaparambil said a new world community is emerging, but that it will be expressed first through small local groups. He warned of the dangers of increasing fundamentalism.

Christiaan Vonck stressed the importance of our shared vision and Professor Seshagiri Rao said that our activities have to be local, but our understanding global.

On the Saturday morning groups described their present work and future projects. Quite a lot of time was taken up considering relations with the Global Forum on Human Survival, which had just held its first meeting at Oxford. It was made clear that this was a multireligious body rather than an interfaith organization.

The main outcome was a call for 'world wide celebration of the centenary of the World's Parliament of Religions'. At the concluding session, the following statement was adopted: 'The Ammerdown meeting encourages The International Association of Religious Freedom, the Temple of Understanding, the World Congress of Faiths and the World Conference of Religion and Peace to stimulate and initiate participation in the planning process for the global celebration of the 1993 centenary of the 1893 World's Parliament of Religions, held in Chicago. This could mean a wide range of celebration on every continent as well as one or more focal points of celebration. Further these initiating organizations should, at the earliest possible moment, seek the active participation and support of all globally concerned organizations, groups, faith communities, confessional families and individuals in the planning process (including representation of the religious, political, academic, artistic, and journalistic life of humankind). The 1993 Centenary should seek to celebrate the century of growing awareness of our shared global humanity through the broadest possible forms of participation, and while celebrating this centenary we encourage a vision to ensure just and peaceful co-operation and creativity among all people of the world.'[10]

It was agreed to submit to the Executive, Board or Council of the 'four' organizations a proposal for a joint congress. It was made clear that no 'new institutional interfaith superstructure' was envisaged.[11] It was suggested that the central theme for 1993 'should be forward looking and address the existential issues of the world which call for an action response from the world religions, secular organizations and political powers'.[12] Encouragement was given to developing interfaith networks, similar to the recently established British Interfaith Network. The Temple of Understanding agreed to try to do this in North America. It was also suggested that the interfaith organizations should strengthen their activity at the UN and seek to do more in terms of social service.

Plans to Mark 1993 as 'A Year of Inter-religious Understanding and Co-operation

By the following January, all four organizations had agreed at Council or

Board or Executive meetings to accept the responsibility entrusted to them by the Ammerdown meeting. Representatives of the four organizations therefore met in Melbourne on 30 January 1989, following the WCRP Assembly. They were joined by a number of others, who stayed on after the WCRP Assembly, who were interested in the project. Considerable discussion centred on the possibility and nature of a joint gathering and on the choice of a suitable venue. It was agreed to consider the feasibility of holding the joint gathering in either India or Japan. Time was also devoted to seeing how best participation in the centenary could be encouraged in different parts of the world. I agreed, through the WCF, to try to co-ordinate the various activities. There was a preliminary discussion of the text of a leaflet about the centenary.

Representatives of the four organizations, together with Rev. Tatsuo Miyake of the Konko Church of Izuo, Mr Masuo Nezu and Mr Keichi Akagawa of Rissho Kosei-kai and Mr Yuji Inokuma of Tsubaki Grand Shrine, met again at the IARF offices in Frankfurt on 10 April 1989. After considerable discussion it seemed that Bangalore, India would be the most suitable site and a date in August 1993 was suggested. A draft of a leaflet to promote 1993 as a Year of Inter-religious Understanding and Co-operation was agreed.[13] There was a review of information about other events being planned, especially in Chicago and Vancouver.

The next meeting was again at Frankfurt in November 1989. The meeting was now called 'The International Interfaith Organizations Co-ordinating Committee' (IIOCC), although as the Melbourne meeting was the first, this was actually the third meeting of the committee. David and Celia Storey, who run a New Awareness Centre at Chichester, England, volunteered to become secretaries of the committee and to take on the work of co-ordination. This offer was gladly accepted. Some progress had been made on plans for Bangalore. It was agreed that the theme should be 'Inter-religious Co-operation in the Twenty First Century'. It was suggested that a few people should be invited to write vision papers. These were to be circulated so that those coming to Bangalore could share the response of their communities to these vision papers. It was also agreed that besides the conference in Bangalore, there should be a major celebration in New Delhi, at which religious leaders would be invited to speak and which would make known to the world the achievements of the interfaith movement.

The committee met again in New York in June 1990. This was at the invitation of the Temple of Understanding and this enabled members of the committee to share their hopes and plans with members of the Temple's Board of Directors. Other interested guests were invited to the meeting.

It was also the first time that the committee met representatives of the Chicago and Vancouver groups. Ron Kidd, at that time the administrator of the Council for a Parliament of the World's Religions, spoke of the plans for Chicago. A major gathering is being planned in the city and already there is a widely based committee. An inaugural programme for the Council was held in November 1989 and an imaginative programme to prepare for 1993 is being arranged. The actual event in 1993 is expected to involve thousands of people. 'Thematic congresses will address critical world issues, seeking fresh approaches to problems of vital concern – poverty, racism, ecology and world peace.'[14] The plans for Vancouver presented by Dr Wayne Nelles of the Global Interfaith Network are equally ambitious. Over three thousand people are expected to participate on the theme 'Religion, Culture and Values in the Global Village: Understanding, Co-operation and New Directions for Our Common Future'.[15] In both cases, whilst especially in Chicago recalling the events of 1893, the emphasis will be on religions' contribution to major issues of the day. The Bangalore gathering will be more modest in scope and size. The emphasis will be upon discussion between participants, rather than on addresses to plenary gatherings. The discussions will be in a context of prayer and meditation. The theme will be 'Interfaith Co-operation in the Twenty-first Century: Our Vision'. The focus, therefore will be on the future possibilities and responsibilities of interfaith co-operation rather than on the tasks of religion *per se*. A major public gathering will be held in Delhi as a climax to the centennial celebration.

The International Interfaith Organizations Co-ordinating Committee has since met in Chichester in November 1990, in Southampton in July 1991 and in Bangalore in October 1991, following the World Conference of Religions, which was held in Cochin and organized by Fr Albert Namiaparambil.

Whilst the four organizations have started planning their focal event for 1993, they have also been encouraging members of all religions to plan appropriate ways to help mark 1993 as a Year of Inter-religious Understanding and Co-operation. Responses have been received from many parts of the world, including Japan, Korea, East and West Europe, Nigeria and Kenya, Latin America, North America and Australasia. There are, therefore, contacts in every continent. The planning process for 1993 has already brought the interfaith organizations closer together, with the possibility of discovering other areas of co-operation. The Temple of Understanding and WCF already jointly sponsor the journal *World Faiths Insight*. IARF is exploring the possibility of setting up an International Interfaith Centre, perhaps in Oxford, and in this wants to work with other interfaith organizations.

Whilst the hope is that the Year will encourage people of different religions to meet and overcome intolerance and bitterness, it will also challenge all involved in the interfaith movement to think about the way to develop further inter-religious co-operation and to create the necessary structures for this. Beyond that, the Year will point to the day when together people of all religions will most effectively tackle the scourges of war, poverty and injustice as well as the threat to humankind's common home. The hope is summed up in a message of support received from Baptists in the Soviet Union: 'Together with you, we believe that survival of life on this planet depends upon our realizing our oneness.'[16]

· PART VIII ·

Conclusions

'Through the night of doubt and sorrow
Onward goes the pilgrim band.'

· 34 ·

Conclusions

The interaction of people of different faiths has increased enormously in the last century. Partly, this is for technological reasons. Far more people travel to other countries, whilst television gives us easy access to information about other cultures. Large numbers of people have been uprooted from one country to another, either as refugees or immigrants.

This human interaction, which may be very personal as in the case of marriages between people of different faiths, has been accompanied by a growing desire to know about other people's religion and way of life. The study of religions has become more common in colleges and schools, whilst books about world religions are now plentiful. By contrast, one hundred and fifty years ago, very few of the religious classics of Asia had been translated into European languages and often Asians themselves were unfamiliar with their scriptures. At the same time, partly through the missionary efforts of the churches, some knowledge of Christian teaching is widespread. There are also Christian communities, often very small, in most countries of Asia and now Muslim, Sikh, Hindu and Buddhist centres are to be found throughout Europe and America.

Too often, the interaction is negative, hostile and violent. The recent revival of religious enthusiasm in some areas of the world has been accompanied by an increase in religious extremism and intolerance. In parts of the Muslim world, for example, the revival of Islam has led to the persecution of Bahá'ís and other religious minorities. Many minority groups, in countries across the world, feel that they suffer from discrimination. Religious differences also continue to enflame other causes of division, for example in the Punjab, in Israel and the West Bank, in Northern Ireland and in Sri Lanka.

Yet the ever-growing interaction of people of different religions has also been accompanied by the growing desire that this should be friendly and creative. I have been astonished, in my research, to discover how many groups in so many different places are seeking inter-religious understanding and co-operation. Only the larger groups have been mentioned above and not all of them. They are matched by numerous local groups and by the efforts of people of goodwill, who belong to no particular interfaith organization. I think of ministers of religion who proclaim their faith without adverse comments on the beliefs of others, or of teachers who treat with proper respect the different religions of their pupils, or television producers who convey with integrity the beliefs and practices of people of another faith, or of all who work for good community relations or who support the great variety of bodies which work for peace, justice, international understanding and the relief of human need. These efforts seldom attract media reports, but they need to be set in the balance when there are much-publicized accounts of inter-religious conflict.

Meanings of Dialogue

The wide range of such efforts point to the considerable variety of what may be described, rather generally, as inter-religious dialogue. Professor Diana Eck, who is Moderator of the World Council of Churches' Sub-Unit for Dialogue, has distinguished six forms of dialogue. The first is parliamentary style dialogue. She traces this back to the 1893 World's Parliament of Religions and sees it carried forward by the international interfaith organizations, although, as we have seen, their way of working is now very different from the approach of the World's Parliament. Secondly, there is institutional dialogue, such as the regular meetings between representatives of the Vatican and The International Jewish Committee for Inter-religious Consultation. Thirdly, there is theological dialogue, which takes seriously the questions and challenges posed by people of other faiths. Fourthly, dialogue in community or the dialogue of life is the search for good relationships in ordinary life. Fifthly, spiritual dialogue is the attempt to learn from other traditions of prayer and meditation. Lastly, there is inner dialogue, which is 'that conversation that goes on within ourselves in any other form of dialogue'.[1]

There are various levels of dialogue and it is a process of growth. An initial requirement is an openness to and acceptance of the other. It takes time to build trust and to deepen relationships. This is why some continuity in a dialogue group is helpful and why patience and time are necessary – all of which are particularly difficult to ensure at an international level. Too easily, we find ourselves imposing our presuppositions on the conversation. Christians, for example, often assume that Muslims really adopt a critical attitude to the Qur'an similar to that common amongst Christians in their reading of the Bible. We have to learn to enter another world that may seem alien and which has different presuppositions. We have to allow our deepest convictions to be questioned. Some Buddhists, for example, will question deeply held Christian assumptions about God and the self. It is important for those venturing into dialogue to be secure in their own faith. They need to beware of becoming marginalized in or alienated from their own religious tradition. Dialogue needs also to be of equals, that is to say of those with similar levels of scholarship and study.

At its deepest dialogue will raise questions of truth. Rabbi Dr Norman Solomon, Director of the Centre for the Study of Judaism and Jewish/ Christian Relations at Selly Oak, Birmingham, said in his inaugural lecture, 'Dialogue admits of degrees: there is dialogue which is of value though it does not reach deep. Much of the dialogue between Jews and Christians is a matter of simply learning to be nice to each other, trying a little to understand what the other is doing, co-operating in social endeavour . . . Many ordinary Jews or Christians lack the skills necessary to engage in a deeper, theological dialogue, and are rightly wary of setting their faith at risk in a confusing enterprise. Yet the heart of dialogue is in talk together of theologians of both faiths, for it is they whose concern is with the meaning of life at its deepest level and it is they who translate from the doctrinal formula to the underlying reality.'[2]

Dialogue does not necessarily produce agreement and, if it is a search for truth, there is no desire for easy compromise. Sometimes it makes clearer where essential differences lie, exposing the various presuppositions or view of the world with which partners in dialogue are operating. Sometimes it can be painful. The American Jewish writer, Dr Eugene Borrowitz has said, 'Only by directly confronting our deepest differences can we come to know one another fully. Despite risks, inter-religious discussion needs at times to be inter-religious debate. That is one way it shows its conviction that truth is ultimately one.'[3]

The Distinctive Character of Interfaith Organizations

With the growth of dialogue, the vocation of interfaith organizations needs to be distinguished, on the one hand from bodies which may be described as 'universalist movements for spiritual unity'[4] and, on the other hand, from the agencies for inter-religious relations of a particular religion, such as the Pontifical Council for Inter-Religious Dialogue. The work of interfaith organizations needs also to be distinguished from centres and bodies devoted to the academic study of religions.

The interfaith organizations all accept the multiplicity and particularity of the world religions. As Dr Francis Clark puts it in his *Interfaith Directory*, 'the majority of those who are involved in the world-wide interfaith movement . . . see the rich multiformity of the world's religious traditions as a positive value to be treasured and developed, and take it as a basic datum in their quest for inter-religious understanding and co-operation'.[5] It has been repeatedly said that no one participating in the organizations is expected to compromise their own faith commitment – the only requirement is that a person should show the same respect to the faiths of other people as he or she would hope that others would show to his or her religion. Members of interfaith organizations hold a variety of views about the relationship of religions to each other. The question of the relationship of religions to each other is very much a matter of debate within several of the world religions.

The 'universalist movements for spiritual unity', by contrast, are likely to presuppose or to proclaim a particular view of the relationship of religions. Because of their fear that members of the major religions will call them syncretistic, interfaith organizations have kept rather aloof from universalist movements. If, however, the distinction is acknowledged, there could in the future be a closer co-operation in some areas of work between interfaith and universalist bodies. It is perhaps particularly important that interfaith organizations enter into greater dialogue with New Age movements and also the so-called 'new religions'. It is understandable that whilst the interfaith organizations were themselves viewed with suspicion by the major religious communities, they were careful not to increase that suspicion by keeping company with 'strange bed-fellows'. Now that the major interfaith organizations have an established record of achievement and a proven integrity, they may feel greater confidence in entering into dialogue with New Age and universalist groups, not least because of the gap between those who share these spiritual aspirations and many members of more traditional religious communities.

If interfaith organizations respect the integrity of the world religions, equally they do not offer a preferential position to any one religious group. This is why they are all concerned to ensure a broad range of representation, drawn from many faiths, on their controlling body and to ensure that their funding comes from a variety of sources. This also distinguishes them from agencies for inter-religious relations of a particular religious community. Such agencies have to reconcile their search for good relations with other religious groups with their traditional claims to an exclusive or privileged knowledge of truth. For such agencies and their parent religions, questions of the relationship of dialogue and mission and of the truth claims of their religion are very important. Certainly members of these agencies may enter into the fullest and most open dialogue with people of other faiths, but they have to interpret their position to their fellow believers. Members of interfaith organizations, who are themselves believers, have, of course, the same questions with which to wrestle and the same task of interpretation. Yet this is not the responsibility of the interfaith organizations themselves. As the religions have seen the importance of dialogue, the number of their agencies for dialogue have increased.

In recent years, there has been growing partnership between the interfaith organizations and these agencies, as both recognize their particular tasks. In preparation for the World Day of Prayer for Peace at Assisi, the Vatican Secretariat for Non-Christians enlisted the help of WCRP, so that those of other faiths would feel that the invitation to participate had no hidden implications. Similarly, it is the interfaith organizations which rightly can sponsor The Year of Inter-religious Understanding and Co-operation, although the support of the agencies for dialogue will be vital.

Differences of Emphasis in Interfaith Work

Amongst the interfaith organizations themselves, differences of emphasis can be recognized. There are those which have concentrated on building up understanding and friendship and those who feel that such understanding will grow as people of different religions co-operate in tackling the urgent problems of the world. The latter have been less concerned to discuss the theoretical relationship of religions to each other.

Those interfaith organizations, such as WCF and the Temple of Understanding, which have seen the building up of a fellowship of faiths as their primary task have grappled with the question of the relationship of religions. They tend to assume a pluralist position, in which the independent validity of the world religions is acknowledged. No one religion is assumed to be superior. Rather, it is assumed that each has a contribution to make to the fuller awareness of truth. For some, the pluralist position is based on an 'impelling awareness of the historico-cultural limitation of all knowledge and religious beliefs, and the difficulty, if not impossibility, of judging the truth claims of another culture or religion on the basis of one's own'.[6] Such a view was particularly associated, in a previous generation, with the German theologian Ernst Troeltsch[7] and today with the British theologian and philosopher John Hick. Others put the emphasis on the infinity and ineffability of the Divine Mystery, to which all religions point. This is a view that echoes the 'neti-neti' tradition of Hinduism. The Divine transcends our human thought and language and this involves a recognition of the relativity of all religious language and symbols. This 'forbids any one religion from having the "only" or "final" word'.[8] Dr Radhakrishnan was an eloquent exponent of this position, which has also been expounded by Professor Wilfred Cantwell Smith of Harvard University. For Professor Raimon Panikkar, pluralism implies a pluralism of truth. For others, such as R. E. Whitson,[9] there is the suggestion that through dialogue there may be a growing convergence of religions in deeper understanding of the Divine – and this is one reason for seeing the interfaith movement as a 'pilgrimage of hope'.

The other hope that inspires the interfaith movement is that together people of all faiths may work for peace and justice and the protection of the environment. 'Economic, political, and especially nuclear liberation is too big a job for any one nation, or culture, or religion', writes Paul Knitter of Xavier University, Cincinnati, 'A worldwide liberation movement needs a worldwide interreligious dialogue.'[10] This emphasis has characterized WCRP and also organizations, which are multi-religious in character, which campaign on specific issues, such as the Global Forum or the World Wide Fund for Nature.

One Interfaith Organization?

Would it be helpful, for the various interfaith organizations to come together in one body? Such a suggestion was made at the first Ammerdown Conference as they began to get to know each other better, but on fuller acquaintance, there has come the recognition that each has its own constituency and its own special vocation. Yet, easily, the organizations could become competitive for resources. Already certain world religious leaders are in great demand to attend international inter-religious conferences. Rather than creating one organization, it may be more valuable to strengthen the mechanisms for co-ordination and co-opera-tion, both between interfaith organizations themselves and between such organizations and the agencies for dialogue of the religious communities. Planning for the Year of Inter-religious Understanding and Co-operation in 1993 is already an occasion for greater liaison. More permanent and effective structures for co-ordination will be necessary in the future. The interfaith networks established in the United Kingdom and in North America may provide models.

What Has Been Achieved?

As of all efforts to change attitudes, it is hard to estimate what has been achieved in one hundred years of the Interfaith Movement. There has been an ever widening circle of those involved in interfaith encounter. As it is a personal journey, each individual has to make the discoveries for herself or himself. Dialogue, therefore, involves a continuing process of learning and re-education. This suggests that the struggle against prejudice and intolerance is also a continuing process. At one time, I hoped that tolerance would gradually spread as people of different faiths got to know each other better. It seems, however, that certain forms of religious experience and loyalty breed intolerance, which too easily is exploited by political leaders, and that constant vigilance is necessary to curb religious extremism. Tolerance itself has its own limits and the search for inter-religious co-operation means opposition to those who use religion to bolster fanaticism and to those who use religion as a cloak for power, prejudice and injustice.

Those who have entered deeply into dialogue all speak of the personal enrichment, both in terms of new friendships and of a deeper appreciation of other faiths and of their own. Many have had to sense a feeling of alienation within their own religious community. Today, however, the religious communities have begun to appreciate the importance of inter-religious dialogue and are encouraging their adherents to take part in it. This, one hopes, will bring to the religious communities the enrichment that individuals have already discovered.

In terms of the struggle for peace and a world community, the interfaith movement has done much to break down prejudice, both by encouraging personal meeting and by public education. The skills necessary to make effective contributions to conflict resolution have yet to be adequately developed. Together members of all religions need to give increasing attention to the search for shared moral values, which undergird human rights, and which can give an ethical basis to the emerging world society.[11]

When he addressed the Global Forum on Human Survival in Moscow in 1990, President Mikhail Gorbachev acknowledged that it was the alarm voiced by some scientists, which was taken up by some members of the public and then by the media, which had forced the politicians to take notice and to act. The beginnings of change lie with a few visionary individuals and a creative minority. An example of this is the way that the suggestion of international arbitration to settle disputes, made in some small peace groups in the middle of the last century, has been adopted by the nations. The prayer and work for peace in the eighties of this century seems to have created a new international atmosphere to which the politicians have responded. Increasingly members of all religions speak of the need for understanding and co-operation, rather than of the conquest of the world by a single religion. Change is possible and it is made possible by the vision and creative energies of dedicated people, but continuing vigilance is necessary to ensure that changes for the better are not eroded.

The Interfaith movement has been a creative energy, building friendship between people of different religions and enabling them to work together for a better world. Its hopes are far from realized. It has been said that the next century will be a spiritual century or it will not be. Interfaith pilgrims need still to discover for themselves that the One God of many names is a Lover of all nations and they need to share that discovery with others so that we all may know, in our hearts, in our homes, in our nations and in our world, the 'peace of God's will, the peace of our need'.[12]

APPENDIX

The Nairobi Assembly of the
World Council of Churches

The different attitudes to dialogue came to the fore at the World Council of Churches 1975 Assembly at Nairobi in the debates of Section III on 'Seeking Community'.

The commission was chaired by Metropolitan Paulos Gregorios (Paul Verghese) and had some two hundred and fifty members, although attendance was erratic. The commission divided into three sub-sections on Faiths, Cultures and Ideologies. When the report was presented to the Assembly, it was attacked by several speakers who though it would be understood as spiritual compromise or rejection of the church's missionary obligations. The attack was led by Dr Per Lönning of the Church of Norway, and Bishop Michael of the Russian Orthodox Church. Metropolitan Paulos Gregorios offered to draft a supplementary page to cover the points made; but Dr Lönning felt that the objections were so serious that the Assembly should see a revised version before voting. By a large majority, the report was referred back to the section for reconsideration.

Although this vote showed that a number of delegates were unhappy about dialogue, it was also an expression of frustration at conference procedures by some who felt that real decisions were not made by the Assembly but by the World Council of Churches' 'managers'. In any case, the Sub-Unit on Dialogue had been a focus of attack by those evangelicals, who for some time had been critical of developments in the World Council of Churches. Feeling that the World Council of Churches had stressed social action at the expense of proclamation of the Gospel, they saw the interest in dialogue as a further betrayal of the church's missionary obligation. It was this cumulative criticism that was voiced by Dr Per Lönning. The debate was dominated by opponents and Asian speakers were not called, although twelve more people had indicated their wish to contribute.

The revised text of the section report has added to it a Preamble, which deserves to be quoted in full:

1. We are all agreed that the *skandalon* (stumbling block) of the gospel will always be with us. While we do seek wider community with people of other faiths, cultures and ideologies, we do not think there will ever be a time in history when the tension will be resolved between belief in Jesus Christ and unbelief. It is a tension that divides the Church from the world. It is a tension which also goes through each Christian disciple, as each is unable to say that his or her faith in Jesus Christ is perfect.
2. We should also make a proper distinction between the division created by the judging Word of God and the division caused by sin.
3. We are all agreed that the Great Commission of Jesus Christ which asks us to go out into all the world and make disciples of all nations, and to baptize them in the Triune Name, should not be abandoned or betrayed, disobeyed or compromised, neither should it be misused. Dialogue is both a matter of hearing and understanding the faith of others and also of witnessing to the gospel of Jesus Christ.
4. We are all opposed to any form of syncretism, incipient, nascent, or developed, if we mean by syncretism conscious or unconscious human attempts to create a new religion composed of elements taken from different religions.
5. We view the future of the Church's mission as full of hope, for it is not upon human efforts that our hope is based, but upon the power and promise of God.[1]

The introduction begins by affirming that the Christian Gospel creates community, but it is recognized that there is an urgent desire to seek a wider community. 'Whether we like it or not, we find ourselves thrown in with all humanity in a common search for peace and justice.' Such a wider community must be sought 'without compromising the *skandalon* of the gospel'. All agreed that they were linked to others as 'fellow-creatures of God – although in a fallen creation, sin and unbelief divide. Many of us believe and some witness to the actual experience of a common ground far beyond our common humanity. They have found that Christ sets them free to explore a community under God with men and women of other faiths. We believe that in this, as in all matters, the gifts are different. Some seem to be called to bold pioneering, adventures and risks beyond the confines of present ecclesiastical and theological structures. Others acknowledge an equally exacting calling to deepen the time-honoured understanding of the community that is ours in Christ.'[2]

The section on Faith and the Search for Community suggests that the term 'wider ecumenism' should be avoided and 'inter-religious' used instead, although the 'wider community is one of people with people, not of religions with religions or systems with systems'.[3] Paragraph 16 asked whether there was a theological basis on which Christians should seek community with their neighbours of other faiths and convictions, and mentioned several answers. 'Many stressed that all people have been created by God in his image and that God loves all humanity. Many believed that in a world broken by sin it is the incarnation of God in Jesus Christ which provides the basis for the restoration of the creation to wholeness. Others would seek this basis for community in the trinitarian understanding of God. Still others find theological meaning in the fact that history has removed and is removing geographical and cultural barriers which once kept us isolated and so is moving us towards one interdependent humanity. In all this discussion we encountered the question of a possible double basis for our search for community. Christians have a specifically theological basis for such a search. Is there also a common basis which should be mutually acceptable to people of differing faiths and ideologies? Considerable difficulty was experienced about this and no agreed conclusion reached. It would appear, however, that in practice in particular situations men and women of various cultures, faiths, and ideologies can enter into community together, although their own understanding of their motivations will vary.'[4]

'The question was discussed', paragraph 17 continues, 'whether we can posit that Jesus Christ is at work among people of other faiths. Here opinions differed. Some stated as their conviction that Jesus Christ as Saviour is not present in other religions, although they accepted the idea of a natural knowledge of God. Others acknowledged the presence of *logoi spermatikoi* (scattered seeds of truth) in other religions but stressed that only in Jesus Christ do we receive fullness of truth and life. Others gave first-hand testimony that their own faith in Jesus Christ had been greatly deepened and strengthened through encountering him in dialogue with those of other faiths. The point was also made that the Spirit works among people outside Israel and outside the Church, and that this Spirit is one with the Father and with the Son.'[5]

The next paragraph recognizes that one can only talk about each specific religion, not religions in general, and that the influence of Jesus may act as a ferment beyond the Christian church.

Many in the section stressed the importance of dialogue. 'It should not be seen as an alternative for mission and it should not compromise our faith.'[6] The variety of situations and the nature of the partners affect the way dialogue is understood and undertaken. 'Depending on the partners and the situation, a dialogue might sometimes start with common concerns in society and ways of working together in tackling problems: sometimes theological issues would be the basis for dialogue. Very often these are interrelated.'[7] 'The terms "spirituality" and "sharing"', the report continues, 'need clarification in the context of dialogue. "Sharing in spirituality" need not mean entering into common worship. For some, it implies seeking to understand with empathy the dimensions of worship, devotion and meditation in the religious tradition and practice of the partners.'[8]

The sections on 'Cultures and the Search for Identity', 'Ideologies and the Search for Community' and 'Recommendations to the Churches', do not make any fresh contribution to the discussion of dialogue.

The whole report is indecisive and describes various views within the section, because clearly there was not a common mind. Dialogue is not rejected nor is it endorsed: but the impression given is that it is subservient to the church's evangelistic task. The primary community is the Christian church and the search for a wider community is based on a common humanity rather than any 'religious' link. There is no suggestion that the saving power of God may extend beyond the Church.

When the revised text was presented to the Assembly, Principal Russel Chandran, of the Church of South India, said that the report was weak and uncommitted and the new preamble made it still more cautious. He therefore felt bound on behalf of many others to ask for a more definite endorsement of the dialogue approach.

In this debate not only the first-hand experience of those who have lived and moved with people of other faiths but also the deeper theological understanding of the gospel, Jesus Christ, the Holy Spirit, the doctrine of the Trinity and the meaning of revelation led many to modify or abandon the Kraemerian approach and to adopt the approach of dialogue. It was this development which led to the establishment of the World Council of Churches' Secretariat on Dialogue following the Uppsala Assembly. The second Vatican Council also led the Roman Catholic Church to establish a secretariat for relations with other faiths . . .

This development is not simply the consequence of human considerations of tolerance, religious harmony, and peace. On the contrary, it is deeply rooted in our confession of Jesus Christ as Lord and Saviour and our commitment to the Trinitarian faith.

The theology of creation affirms the presence and work of God in all cultures. Our confession of Christ as Lord is an affirmation that he is Lord, not only of Christians but of all peoples. He is the Logos who holds all things together. He is the light which lightens everyone. It is in him all things and all peoples are to be united. We also need to acknowledge that we have not yet fathomed the depths of the unsearchable riches of Christ and our knowledge of him must never be absolutized or identified with the fullness of the reality of Christ. It is the Holy Spirit who leads us into all truth. He does this by interpreting Christ to us and by helping us to learn from one another's experience of Christ. In a genuine sense, our knowledge and experience of Christ is enriched by the response of the people of other faiths. Witnessing to Christ is, therefore, a two-way movement of mutual learning and enrichment.

The Church which evangelizes is also evangelized in the sense that its knowledge and experience of Jesus Christ and his gospel is deepened by the response of those to whom the gospel is proclaimed . . .

We would like our brethren who are concerned about the commitment to the great commission of our Lord and the dangers of syncretism to be willing to listen to the testimony and insights of those who have more intimate knowledge of other faiths and are in no way less committed to Jesus Christ and his mission.[9]

Dr Lynn A. de Silva, a Methodist from Sri Lanka, who was Director of a Study Centre, also stressed the value of dialogue.

1. Dialogue does not in any way diminish full and loyal commitment to one's own faith, but rather enriches and strengthens it. Many have borne testimony to this fact.
2. Dialogue, far from being a temptation to syncretism, is a safeguard against it, because in dialogue we get to know one another's faith in depth. One's own faith is tested and refined and sharpened thereby. The real test of faith is faiths-in-relation.
3. Dialogue is a creative interaction which liberates a person from a close or cloistered system to which he happens to belong by accident of birth, and elevates him to spiritual freedom, giving him a vision of wider dimensions of spiritual life by his sharing in the spirituality of others.
4. Dialogue is urgent and essential for us in Asia in order to repudiate the arrogance, aggression and negativism of our evangelistic crusades which have obscured the gospel and caricatured Christianity as an aggressive and militant religion . . .
5. Dialogue is essential to dispel the negative attitude we have to people

of other faiths, which makes proclamation ineffective and irrelevant.[10]

Other criticisms of the report as both too cautious and incautious were raised, but the motion to commend the report to the churches for study and appropriate action was carried.

Notes

PART I

1. The World's Parliament of Religions · I

1. The official record is *The World's Parliament of Religions*, ed. John Henry Barrows, The Parliament Publishing Co, Chicago 1893. Page references are to this work.

2. Emil Hirsch, 'The Spiritual Results of the World's Fair', *Reform Advocate*, 11 November 1893, p.202.

3. F. Max Müller, 'The Real Significance of the Parliament of Religions', *Arena* 11, December 1894, pp.1–2.

4. Charles W. Wendte, *The Wider Fellowship*, Beacon Press, Boston 1927, II, p. 553.

5. This refers to a reported remark of George T. Candlin, a missionary to China, *The Christian Intelligencer* 64, 4.10.93, p.11.

6. Joseph M. Kitagawa, 'The World's Parliament of Religions and its Legacy', The 1983 John Nuveen Lecture, University of Chicago Divinity School 1983, p.2.

7. Richard Hughes Seager, *The World's Parliament of Religions, Chicago, Illinois 1893: America's Coming of Age*, Harvard University Doctoral Thesis, Harvard University, Cambridge, Massachusetts 1986.

8. Ibid, pp.78–9.

9. The bill is printed in full in US Statutes at Large, 26:62–66. See Kenten Druyvesteyn, *The World's Parliament of Religions*, an unpublished doctoral thesis for Chicago University, Chicago, Illinois 1976, p.10.

10. Charles Carroll Bonney, 'A World's Congress at the World's Fair: A Symposium', *Statesman* 6, October 1889, p.1.

11. Druyvesteyn, p. 17. Much of this account is drawn from his first chapter.

12. Seager (n.7), p.10.

13. Membership as recorded by Barrows (p.6) was Rev. L. P. Mercer (Swedenborgian), J. W. Plummer (Society of Friends), Rev. J. Berger (German Methodist Church), Rev. John Z. Torgersen (Norwegian Lutheran Church), Rev. M. Ranseen (Swedish Lutheran Church), Rt Rev. Charles Edward Cheney (Reformed Episcopal Church), Rev. Jenkin Lloyd Jones (Unitarian), Rev. Dr A. Canfield (St Paul's Universalist Church), Dr E. G. Hirsch (Sinai Temple), Rev. Dr Frank M. Bristol (Methodist), Rev. William M. Lawrence (Second Baptist Church of Chicago), Rev. Dr F. A. Noble (Union Park Congregational Church), Rt Rev. William E. McLaren (Protestant Episcopal Bishop), Most Rev. P. A. Feehan (Archbishop of the Catholic Church), Rev. David Swing (Central Church of Chicago), Rev. John Henry Barrows (First Presbyterian Church, Chairman).

14. The proposed objects, agreed in 1892, are the clearest statement of the aims:

1. To bring together in conference for the first time in history the leading representatives of the great historic religions of the world.

2. To show man, in the most impressive way, what and how many important truths the various religions hold and teach in common.

3. To promote and deepen the spirit of human brotherhood among religious men of diverse faiths, through friendly conference and mutual good understanding, while not seeking to foster the temper of indifferentism, and not striving to achieve any formal and outward unity.

4. To set forth, by those most competent to speak, what are deemed the important distinctive truths held and taught by each religion and by the various chief branches of Christendom.

5. To indicate the impregnable foundations of Theism and the reasons for man's faith in immortality, and thus to unite and strengthen the forces which are adverse to a materialistic philosophy of the universe.

6. To secure from leading scholars (representing the Brahman, Buddhist, Confucian, Parsee, Mohammedan, Jewish and other faiths, and from representatives of the various churches of Christendom) full and accurate statements of the spiritual and other effects of the religions which they hold, upon the Literature, Art, Commerce, Government, Domestic and Social Life of the peoples among whom these faiths have prevailed.

7. To enquire what light each religion has afforded, or may afford, to the other religions of the world.

8. To set forth, for permanent record to be published to the world, an accurate and authoritative account of the present condition and outlook of religion among the leading nations of the earth.

9. To discover from competent men, what light religion has to throw on the great problems of the present age, especially on important questions connected with Temperance, Labour, Education, Wealth and Poverty.

10. To bring the nations of the earth into a more friendly fellowship in the hope of securing permanent international peace. (Barrows, p.18).

15. There were three main Swedenborgian churches: General Conference of the New Church, The General Convention of the New Jerusalem in the USA and The General Church of the New Jerusalem.

16. C. C. Bonney 'The Genesis of the World's Religious Congresses of 1893', *New Church Review* 1, January 1894, pp.73–78 passim.

17. Ibid. The information about Swedenborg is drawn from relevant articles in the Encyclopaedia Britanica.

18. This is quoted by Druyvesteyn (n.9) from a preliminary publication of the Department of Religion which survives only in an 1892 edition.

19. Ibid.

20. Bonney, 'Genesis' (n.16), p.83.

21. Druyvesteyn (n.9), p. 24.

22. Kitagawa (n.6), p.8.

23. Seager (n.7), p.234.

24. J. H. Barrows, *Christianity: The World-Religion*, A. C. McClurg, Chicago, 1897, pp.26–36 and p.201. Quoted by Seager (n.7), p.237.

25. J. H. Barrows, *A World Pilgrimage*, ed. Mary Eleanor Barrows, A. C. McClurg,

Chicago 1897, quoted by Seager, p.238.

26. J. H. Barrows, *The Christian Conquest of Asia*, Charles Scribner's Sons, New York 1899, quoted by Seager, p. 239.

27. J. N. Farquhar, *The Crown of Hinduism*, Calcutta 1913, Oxford 1919.

28. Kitagawa (n.6), p.10.

29. Quoted by Seager (n.7), p. 235.

30. Kitagawa (n.6), p.9.

31. Ibid.

32. In *Unity*, Chicago, 26 September 1918, p. 286, quoted by Thomas E. Graham, 'The Feet of the World's Parliament of Religions: Jenkin Lloyd Jones', in a paper presented to the American Academy of Religions in 1990, on which I draw for much of this information.

33. Jenkin Lloyd Jones, 'The Creedless Church', a sermon preached on 12 June 1891, in the Jenkin Lloyd Jones Collection of Meadville/Lombard Theological School, Chicago, Sermon File 615.

34. Quoted by Albion Small in *Unity*, 12 December 1918, p. 193.

35. Letter of Barrows to Jones, 6 April 1894. Joseph Regenstein Library, University of Chicago, Jenkin Lloyd Jones Papers, Box 1, file 11.

36. Thomas Graham, 'Jenkin Lloyd Jones and the World's Columbian Exposition of 1893', Association for Liberal Religious Studies, Collegium Proceedings, 1, 1979, 62–81, quoted by Seager, p.96.

37. 'Books on the Parliament', *Unity* 32, January 1894, 274–5, quoted by Seager, p.96.

38. Jenkin Lloyd Jones, 'The Parliament's Challenge to the Unitarians', *Unity*, 32, Jan 1894, pp.306–7, quoted by Seager, p.205–6. His address at the closing session is reported by Barrows on p. 177.

2. The World's Parliament of Religions · II

1. Hans Küng, 'No peace in the World without Peace among Religions', *World Faiths Insight*, New Series 21, February 1989, p.14.

2. A phrase I think first used by Canon Peter Schneider in, for example, *Ends and Odds*, No. 22, March 1980, p.1.

3. See below pp. 259ff.

4. Druyvesteyn (I,n.9), p.53.

5. L. P. Mercer, *Review of the World's Religious Congresses of the World's Congress Auxiliary of the World's Columbian Exposition, Chicago, 1893*, Rand, McNally and Co, Chicago 1893, quoted by Druyvesteyn, p. 55.

6. Clay Lancaster, *The Incredible World's Parliament of Religions*, Centaur, Fontwell, Sussex 1987, p.27.

3. The World's Parliament of Religions · III

1. Seager (I, n.7), p. 87.

2. Ibid, p.43.

3. P. J. Muldoon, 'Sermon of Welcome' in Jay P. Dolan (ed.), *The World's Columbian Catholic Congresses and Educational Exhibit*, 1893, reprint, Arno Press, New York 1978, pp.10–13, quoted by Seager, p. 43. Note the use of 'Third World'.

4. Ibid,p.16, Seager,p.44.

5. Ibid, p.17.

6. John Keane, 'The World's Parliament of Religions', *Boston Pilot*, 14.10.1893, p.4, quoted by Seager, p.197.

7. Seager, p. 198, who cites Patrick Henry Ahern's *The Life of John J. Keane, Educator and Archbishop 1839–1918*, Bruce Publishing Co, Milwaukee 1954, pp.147–149 and Ahern's *The Catholic University of America, 1887–1896*, Catholic University Press, Washington, DC, 1948, pp.142–3.

8. 'Editorial Notes', *Reform Advocate*, 22.7.1893, 421, quoted by Seager, p.45.

9. Frederick Douglas and Ida Wells, *The Reason Why the Coloured American Is Not in the World's Columbian Exposition*, n.p. 1893, pp.3–4, quoted by Seager, p.47.

10. Seager, p.50.

11. See Kitagawa (I, n.6), p.7.

12. *Speeches and Writings of Swami Vivekananda*, Madras, n.d., p.31.

13. See *Life of Swami Vivekananda*, Advaita Ashrama, Calcutta 1960, p.267. See Hal French, 'The Impact of Swami Vivekananda on the World Parliament', *World Faiths Insight*, Summer 1991.

14. Anantanand Rambachan, 'Swami Vivekananda: A Hindu Model for Interreligious Dialogue' in *Inter-Religious Dialogue: Voices From a New Frontier*, ed. M. Darrol Bryant and Frank Flinn, New Era Books, Paragon House, New York 1989.

15. See my *Together to the Truth*, CLS, Madras 1971, p. 101.

16. See George M. Williams, 'Swami Vivekananda: From the Apostle of Hinduism to Vedanta to the Religion Eternal, the Unity of All Religions', paper to the American Academy of Religions, 1990.

17. Druyvesteyn, p.91.

18. Charles Little, 'The Parliament of Religions', *Methodist Review*, 76, March 1894, p.211.

19. Seager, p.184.

20. Seager, pp. 158–9 and pp. 163–8 and see below p. 268.

21. Seager, p. 189–90 and see below p. 297.

22. Druyvesteyn, p. 87.

23. Donald H. Bishop, 'Religious Confrontation, A Case Study: The 1893 Parliament of Religions', *Numen* 16, April 1969, pp.63–76. Bishop's use of inclusion is different to that made familiar by Alan Race in *Christians and Religious Pluralism*, SCM Press 1984.

24. *The American Advocate of Peace*, October 1893, p.229.

25. *Proceedings of the 26th Annual Meeting of The Free Religious Association of America*, FRA, Boston, 1894, p.2, quoted by Bishop.

26. See p.30 above.

27. Lancaster (II, n.6) lists alphabetically all who gave talks, pp. 225–240.

4. The World's Parliament of Religions : Conclusions

1. Druyvesteyn (I,n.9), p. 272.

2. Kitagawa (I, n.6), pp.10–11.

3. See above, pp.28–30.

4. Lancaster (II, n.6), p. 215.

5. Ibid, p. 216.

6. Chicago *Tribune*, 17.9.1893, p. 1., quoted by Seager (I, n.7), p. 273.

7. Chicago *Tribune*, 24.9.1893, p.12., quoted by Seager, p. 275.

8. Seager, p. 274.

9. Sidney E. Ahlstrom, *The American Protestant Encounter with World Religions*, (II Impact in America), The Brewer Lectures on Comparative Religions, Beloit College, Beloit, Wisconsin, 15–17 October 1962, n.p., n.d., quoted by Druyvesteyn, (I, n.9) p.275.

10. Henry Nash Smith (ed.), *Popular Culture and Industrialism, 1865–1890*, Doubleday, Anchor Books, Garden City, N.Y., 1967, p.xvii., quoted by Druyvesteyn, p.275.

11. Druyvesteyn, p. 276.

12. M. Braybrooke, *Together to the Truth*, (III, n.13) p. 101.

13. Kitagawa (I, n.6), p.12.

PART II

5. Is There a Unity of Faiths?

1. See my *Together to the Truth*, CLS Madras 1971, pp.98–100.

2. Ibid, p.101 and see above p. 33.

3. Sarvepalli Radhakrishnan, *Eastern Religions and Western Thought*, Oxford 1939, pp.viii-ix. See also for a general discussion of Radhakrishnan's thoughts about an emerging world religious consciousness the article 'Radhakrishnan and the Development of a Global Paradigm of Meaning' by David M. Brookman in *World Faiths Insight*, New Series 23, October 1989, pp. 33–43.

4. Sarvepalli Radhakrishnan, *Religion and Society*, Kamala Lectures, Allen and Unwin 1947, p.55.

5. Sarvepalli Radhakrishnan, *Religion in a Changing World*, Allen and Unwin 1967, p. 133.

6. Sarvepalli Radhakrishnan, 'Fragments of a Confession' in *The Philosophy of Sarvepalli Radhakrishnan*, ed., A. Schilpp, Tudor Publishing Co., New York 1952, p.62.

6. The International Association for Religious Freedom · I

1. Charles William Wendte, *The Wider Fellowship, Memories, Friendships and Endeavours for Religious Unity, 1844–1927*, Beacon Press, Boston 1927, Vol I, p.15. See also for the history of IARF until about 1972, Elke Schlinck-Lazarraga, *Wiedergeburt Schopferischer Religion im Weltbund fur Religiose Freiheit*, (Renaissance of Creative Religion in the International Association for Religious Freedom) n.d. (about 1975), n.p. Elke Schlinck-Lazarraga's history is very comprehensive and gives details of the papers presented at the various congresses etc. The address of IARF is Dreieichstrasse 59, D–6000 Frankfurt 70, Germany.

2. Wendte I, p. 16.

3. Wendte I, p. 1.

4. Wendte I, p. 115.

5. Wendte I, p. 148.

6. Wendte II, p. 285.

7. Wendte II, p. 354, see also Elke Schlinck-Lazarraga, n.1, p. 79.

8. Quoted from *An Historical Sketch* by S. van der Woude in *The IARF Its Vision and Work*, ed. Percival F. Brundage, W. Gaade NV, Delft, Holland 1955, p.7.

9. Jabez T. Sunderland, 'Two World Parliaments of Religion' in *World Fellowship of Faiths*, ed. Charles Frederick Weller, Liveright, New York, 1935, 2nd ed., 1938, pp.512–23.

10. Wendte II, p. 192.

11. Wendte II, p. 287.

12. Wendte II, p. 330.

13. June Bell 'Encounter with Change' in *IARF, The Twentieth Congress*, Boston, IARF Information Service 67/68 Spring 1970, p.29.

14. *IARF Newsletter*, 1976, 1, p.1.

15. They were the Deutsche Unitarier Religionsgemeinschaft; the German branch of the World Congress of Faiths, known as Arbeitsgemeinschaft fur religiose und weltanschauliche Begegnung; an Algerian group called Union des Croyants and a Japanese Shinto group called the Konko Kyo Izuo Church.

16. Diether Gehrmann, 'The IARF, a World Community of Religions for Service and Peace', *Echoes of Peace*, Rissho Kosei-kai, Tokyo, Vol.3, No.2, May 1984.

17. Quoted by Diether Gehrmann, 'The IARF, a World Community of Religions for Service and Peace', in *Dharma World*, Rissho Kosei-kai, Tokyo, August 1984, p.30.

18. Ibid, p.30.

19. *Dharma World*. (n.17), p.32.

20. H. Faber, 'Europeans in Boston', in *The Twentieth Congress*, (n.13) p.13.

7. The International Association for Religious Freedom · II

1. Quoted by Elke Schlinck-Lazarraga, *Wiedergeburt*, p.178.

2. *IARF Newsletter*, 1979, 2; 1985, 2; 1989, 1.

3. *Manifesto on the World Community*, IARF, 1975.

4. Keynote addresses were given by Professor L. Leertouwere, from Leiden University, on 'Tribal Religions in the Tide of Religion' and by Rev. K. Dasgupta, from the Brahmo Samaj, Calcutta on 'The East West Vision'.

5. 1981 Declaration.

6. 1984 Declaration, p.3.

7. It was addressed by Rev. William Schulz, President of the Unitarian Universalist Association, Rev. Motoyuki Naganuma, Chairman of Rissho Kosei-kai, Maya Angelou, an author from the USA, Professor Sam Keen, an American psychologist, Professor Masahiro Mori, a Japanese scientist, and Professors John Cobb and Clare Fischer, theologians from the USA.

8. 1987 Declaration, p.1.

9. *IARF Newsletter*, 1987,2.

10. Ibid.

11. Conference resolution.

12. Address by Robert Traer, *World Faiths Insight*, New Series 26, Autumn 1990, p.26. and in *Religions Co-operating for One World*, IARF, 1991, pp. 315–17.

13. Ibid.

14. Ibid.

15. Gehrmann (I, n.7), p.5.

8. The World Congress of Faiths: The Beginnings

1. The standard biography of Sir Francis Younghusband is by George Seaver, published by John Murray in 1952, on which this account of his life is based. The quotation is from G. Seaver, *Francis Younghusband*, p. 14. The address of WCF is 28 Powis Gardens, London W11 1JG. For a short history of WCF see Marcus Braybrooke, *Faiths in Fellowship*, WCF 1976 and Heather McConnell, *A Venture of Faith for All Faiths*, WCF 1986.

2. Seaver (n.1), pp. 97 ff.

3. Francis Younghusband, *Vital Religion*, John Murray 1940, pp. 3–4.

4. Ibid, p.6.

5. Seaver, (n.1), quoted on p. 275.

6. The titles of his other religious books are: *The Gleam, The Reign of God, Life in the Stars, The Living Universe, Modern Mystics, The Sum of Things* and *Vital Religion*.

7. *Vital Religion*, n.3., p.7.

8. Ibid, p.5.

9. Ibid, p.31.

10. Ibid, p.17.

11. Quoted in A. Peacock's *Fellowship Through Religion*, WCF, London 1956, pp. 12–13.

12. In *Religions of Empire*, ed. William Loftus Hare, pp. 18–19. See below pp. 281–2.

13. Peacock (n. 11), p. 11.

14. *World Fellowship*, ed. Charles Frederick Weller, Liveright, New York 1935. See below pp. 114–16.

15. See below, pp. 124ff.

16. *Faiths and Fellowship*, The Proceedings of the World Congress of Faiths, held in London July 3–17, 1936, ed. A. Douglas Millard, published for WCF by J. M. Watkins, London 1937, p. 131.

17. Ibid, p. 224.

18. Ibid, p. 422.

19. Ibid, p. 309.

20. Ibid, p. 9.

21. *Vital Religion* (n. 3), p. 93.

9. The History of the World Congress of Faiths

1. The Oxford and Cambridge Conferences. There are brief reports in G. Seaver, *Francis Younghusband*, John Murray 1952.

2. Quoted by A. Peacock, *Fellowship Through Religion*, WCF, London 1956, pp. 12–13.

3. Quoted by G. Seaver, (n.1) p. 371.

4. Erik Palmstierna, *The World's Crisis and Faith*, John Lane, Bodley Head 1941, p. 24.

5. Ibid, p. 24.

6. Peacock (n.2), p.27.

7. Plutarch, *De Fraterno Amore*, 19. For Barth and Kraemer see further below p. 185.

8. Reginald Sorensen, *I Believe in Man*, The Lindsey Press 1970, passim, but especially p. 114.

9. Ibid, p.120.

10. Ibid, p. 54.

11. Reginald Sorensen, Conference Sermon in *World Faiths*, No. 77, Autumn 1969, p. 19.

12. Ibid, p. 20.

13. Ibid, p. 18.

14. George Appleton, 'Faiths in Fellowship', *World Faiths*, No 101, Spring 1977, p. 3.

15. Ibid, pp. 4–5.

16. Edward Carpenter, 'A Pluralist Society', The St Paul's Lecture, 1975.

17. Yehudi Menuhin, *World Faiths*, No. 101, Spring 1977, p.2.

18. Ursula King, 'Exploring Convergence: The Contribution of World Faiths', *World Faiths*, No. 106, Autumn 1978, pp. 1–16.

19. R. Panikkar, *World Faiths Insight*, New Series 26, October 1990, p.7.

20. *World Faiths Insight*, New Series 27, February 1991, p. 29.

21. Dr Yaqub Zaki, *World Faiths Insight*, New Series 23, Oct 1989, p.10.

22. R. Panikkar (n.19), p.11.

23. Seshagiri Rao, *World Faiths Insight*, January 1983, New Series 6, p. 10.

24. Zaki Badawi, *World Faiths Insight*, June 1986, New Series 13, p. 3.

25. Ibid, p. 11.

26. Norman Solomon, *World Faiths Insight*, February 1986, New Series 12, p. 25.

27. Ibid, p.25.

28. R. Runcie, *World Faiths Insight*, October 1986, New Series 14, p.3.

29. Ibid, pp. 10–11.

30. Ibid, p. 12.

31. Ibid, p. 14.

32. M. Vajiragnana, *World Faiths Insight*, October 1989, New Series 23, p. 32.

10. The Work of the World Congress of Faiths

1. *World Faiths*, Nos. 101 and 102, Spring and Summer 1977.

2. *World Faiths*, No. 110, Spring 1980.

3. *World Faiths*, No. 107, Spring 1979.

4. *World Faiths Insight*, New Series 16, June 1987.

5. Ibid and *World Faiths Insight*, New Series 17, October 1987.

6. *World Faiths Insight*, New Series 21, February 1989.

7. *World Faiths Insight*, New Series 22, June 1989.

8. *World Faiths Insight*, New Series 23, October 1989.

9. *World Faiths Insight*, New Series 24, February 1990.

10. *World Faiths Insight*, New Series 5, Summer 1982.

11. *World Faiths Insight*, New Series 2, Spring 1981, pp. 24–7.

12. *World Faiths*, No. 90, 1973.

13. *World Faiths*, No. 97, 1975.

14. See below pp. 88–9 Bernice Joachim describes the first Ammerdown weekend in *World Faiths*, No. 99, Summer 1976, pp. 22–4. For the First St Alban's Congress see *World Faiths Insight*, New Series 1, Autumn 1980, pp. 25–9.

15. *World Faiths Insight*, New Series 8, January 1984, p. 33 and *World Faiths Insight*, New Series 24, February 1990, p. 27.

16. *World Faiths Insight*, New Series 26, October 1990, pp. 27–28.

17. Will Hayes, *Every Nation Kneeling*, published by the Order of Great Companions, 1954.

18. *World Faiths*, No. 91, 1974, pp. 15–17.

19. Marcus Braybrooke (ed.), *Inter-Faith Worship*, Galliard 1974.

20. The Report of the Archbishops' Consultants is in *Ends and Odds*, No. 22, March 1980. The BCC Report is *Can We Pray Together?*, BCC 1983. See also my article on the subject in *A New Dictionary of Liturgy and Worship*, ed. J. G. Davies, SCM Press and Westminster Press 1986, pp. 284–286.

21. In 1966 the Commonwealth Day Act of Witness was held at St Martin-in-the-Fields, but then, because of some protests, it was moved to a secular building, the Guildhall, in the city of London. It is now held annually at Westminster Abbey and is usually attended by the Queen and the Duke of Edinburgh or senior members of the Royal Family.

22. *Forum*, No. 14, Sept 1952.

23. *World Faiths*, No. 99, Summer 1976. Fr Murray Rogers' talk is reproduced in this issue.

24. John M. Hull, *School Worship: An Obituary*, SCM Press 1975.

25. *World Faiths*, No. 48, March 1961, pp. 15–17.

26. *World Faiths*, No. 73, 1968, p. 24.

27. Bernard Cousins, *Introducing Children to World Religions*, CCJ 1965.

28. *World Faiths*, No. 62, March 1965, p. 11.

29. Statement on RE in *World Faiths*, No. 81, 1970, p. 20.

30. Ibid.

31. Ibid.

32. *World Faiths*, No. 86, 1972.

33. The addresses given in the *Interfaith Network Handbook* 1989 for The Hon. Secretary of SHAP is 70, Brisbane Rd, Ilford, Essex, IG1 4SL; for the Standing Conference on Interfaith Dialogue in Education it is 88a Brondesbury Villas, Kilburn, London NW6 6AD and for the Religious Education Council it is Hatfield Polytechnic, Wall Hall Campus, Aldenham, Watford WD2 8AT. See below pp. 291–2.

34. *Interfaith News*, No. 18, October 1988, article by Dr Brian Gates, pp.1ff.

35. The account of Interreligio is based on a summary of a booklet *Interreligion – Respect for the Other One*, by Dr R. Boeke in *World Faiths*, No. 105, Summer 1978.

36. L'Union des Croyants. Information based on leaflets and correspondence from the sixties and seventies in my possession. I have had no contact with the group since the early eighties. Dr Ursula King, describes Teilhard de Chardin's thinking about convergence and his links with L'Union des Croyants in her Younghusband Lecture, *World Faiths*, No. 106, Autumn 1978, pp. 6–8.

37. The Faculty for the Comparative Study of Religions (FVG), 164, B–2610, Antwerp, Belgium See also *World Faiths Insight*, New Series 25, June 1990, p. 27. See below pp. 289–90.

38. Dr Ahamed Kabeer, 71 C, Jaihind Puram 1st St, Madurai 11, India (1989 Address).

39. Bernice Joachim, 'Religions of India Tour', *World Faiths*, No. 107, Spring 1979, pp. 31–34.; 'Pilgrimage to Israel', *World Faiths*, No. 111, Summer 1980, p. 15; Joan and Bill Steiner 'WCF North India Tour', *World Faiths Insight*, New Series 3, 1981, pp.20–22 and Mary Braybrooke 'First Impressions of India', pp. 23–24.

40. Memorandum 26.6.78.

41. The *Handbook*, Introduction. The address of the Inter Faith Network (UK) is 5–7 Tavistock Place, London WC1H 9SS.

42. Ibid.

43. Paul Weller in *Discernment*, British Council of Churches Vol. 3 No. 2 Autumn 1988, pp. 30–34.

44. WCF leaflet, 1989, backcover.

45. Baron Palmstierna, quoted by George Seaver, *Francis Younghusband*, John Murray 1952, p. 343. Sir Francis' own prayer, adopted by the Congress, is 'May the Spirit of Fellowship quicken within us and abound among all people'.

11. The Temple of Understanding · I

1. *Six Days of Hope*, Leaflet of the Temple of Understanding, n.d. column 2. There is a long interview with Judith Hollister in *Hoka Hay*, Summer Issue 1989, Austin, Texas, USA, and an article by Robert Wallace, 'Judith Hollister and Her Wonderful Obsession' in *Life*, December, 1964. The address of the Temple of Understanding is at the Cathedral of St John the Divine, 1047 Amsterdam Avenue at 112th Street, New York, NY 10025, USA.

2. *Six Days of Hope*, n.1., column 4.

3. Some of this information is derived from private letters to me from Mrs Hollister.

4. Leaflet '*To build a house*', Temple of Understanding 1972; Leaflet '*It is better to light a candle*', Temple of Understanding, Oct 1974 and Minutes of the Board, 11.12.1986.

5. *The Temple of Understanding Newsletter*, Spring 1968, p.2.

6. *The World Religions Speak*, ed. Finley R. Dunne, Jr, World Academy of Art and Science, N. V. Publishers, The Hague 1970, contains the papers. The declaration is on pp. 208–9.

7. *World Faiths*, No. 80, Summer 1970, p. 15. A summary of Dr Eugene Carson Blake's paper is on pp. 1–3. See also the *Temple of Understanding Newsletter*, Spring 1970, p.2.

8. *Temple of Understanding Newsletter*, Summer 1971, p.1.

9. Fr J. Mason, SJ, in *The Bulletin of the Vatican Secretariat for Non-Christians*, quoted in the *Temple of Understanding Newsletter*, Fall 1972, p.4.

10. *Temple of Understanding Newsletter*, Spring 1974, pp. 1–2.

11. Ibid. and private correspondence with John Gillooly and conference papers.

12. *Temple of Understanding Newsletter*, Spring 1976, p.1.

13. Ibid., p.2.

14. Ibid., p.3.

15. Ibid., p.5.

16. Ibid.

17. Ibid., pp. 5–6.

18. Ibid., p.7.

19. Ibid.

20. Ibid.

12. The Temple of Understanding · II

1. Edward J. Bednar, *Nonviolence for the 1980s in the Footsteps of King and Gandhi*, unpublished paper 28.1.83, and *Reverence for Life*, Temple of Understanding, 1983.

2. The wording of the draft 'Declaration of Principles for a Global Spirituality', as printed in the *Temple of Understanding Newsletter*, Summer 1983, p.2 was:

1. The awareness of an **ultimate mystery** which gives life and meaning and is at the centre of creation.

2. The value of ceremony and **worship** to give thanks, to celebrate community, and to affirm the reality of oneness and unconditional love.

3. The importance of **spiritual exercises**, prayer, meditation, fasting, contemplation, to serve as links between human life and the universe.

4. The need for an inner '**change of heart**' to bring about the outer changes of peace, justice and human solidarity.

5. A commitment to **simplicity**, non-attachment, and dedicated service for the alleviation of suffering in the world.

6. A resolution to think and act with **reverence** for life and the recognition of the interdependence of all life.

7. Respect for '**the other person**', for the rights of religious diversity and the peaceful coexistence of different religious communities.

8. **Nonviolence** as a rule of life in the conduct of all personal, social, economic and political relationships.

9. The **renunciation of force** – whether by authority, threat, propoganda, or violence – to impose one's will upon another.

10. A belief in the **convergence** of the human race at a point of spiritual unity.

3. Letters to me from S. William Stansmore of 9.12.83 and 20.2.84.

4. Printed on the back cover of the programme for Spiritual Summit VI, 1984 and inside the backcover of Issues of *World Faiths Insight* for 1985.

5. Programme for Spiritual Summit VI and *Temple of Understanding Newsletter*, Spring 1985.

6. Letter to me from Dr Pedersen, 13.1.86 and draft.

7. *Temple of Understanding Newsletter*, Summer 1986, also *Shared Vision*, the newsletter of The Global Forum and Anuradha Vittachi, *Earth Conference One*, New Science Library, Shambhala, Boston and Shaftesbury 1989.

8. Marcus Braybrooke 'We are all in the same boat', *World Faiths Insight*, New Series 25, June 1990, pp. 22–4. and *Shared Vision*, Vol. 4, No. 7, 1990. The Moscow Declaration is printed on p. 16.

9. *Shared Vision*, Vol.4, No.7, 1990, p. 15.

10. Minutes of the Temple of Understanding, 23.6.88.

11. *North America Interfaith Network 1987*, ed. Daniel L. Anderson, Temple of Understanding, New York 1987.

12. *Network*, Newsletter of the North America Interfaith Network, Vol. 1, No.1, June 1988, and William Robbins, 'From Wichita to the World, A Vision', *New York Times*, 2.11.88.

13. North America Interfaith Conference Programme.

14. Finley P. Dunne, *The World Religions Speak* (I, n.6), p xii.

15. Thomas Merton in *The World Religions Speak* (I n.6), p.81.

13. World Fellowship, World Thanksgiving and World Interfaith Association

1. The record of the 1933 conference is *World Fellowship: Addresses and Messages by leading spokesmen of all Faiths Races and Countries*, ed. Charles Frederick Weller, Liveright,

New York 1935. Information about the development of World Fellowship may be found in an article by Gail Kelley in *The Boston Sunday Globe*, 23.7.89, p. 29. Further details from Rev. Dr C. Shmauch, RR 2, Box 53, North Conway NH 03860, USA.

2. Charles Weller, 'History and Fundamentals of the World Fellowship of Faiths' in Weller (n.1), p. 536.

3. Dr Herman Neander, 'World Progress Waits for Religious Unity', in Weller, p.509. Neander quotes from an article by Rudolf Otto in *The Hibbert Journal*, July 1931.

4. Ibid., p.505.

5. Weller, p.535.

6. Ibid., pp.v–vi.

7. See Francis Clark (ed.), *Interfaith Directory*, New Era Books, International Religious Foundation, New York 1987, pp. 45–6.

8. K. L. Seshagiri Rao, 'Thanks-Giving Square', *World Faiths Insight*, New Series 25, June 1990,pp. 2–7. Further details from the Centre for World Thanksgiving, PO Box 1777, Dallas, Texas 75221, USA.

9. Muhammad Abdul-Rauf, *The Concept of Thanksgiving in Islam*, Thanksgiving Press 1982. Cyclostyled copies of various talks and the pamphlet by Ven. Dr Henepola Gunaratana, *The Place of Thankfulness in Buddhism* have also been produced by the Centre.

10. The information is based on a brochure of the World Interfaith Association and conversations with Dr Fisher. The address is 304 Avenue Louise, 1050, Brussels, Belgium.

11. Words of Fr Marcel Dubois on the election of Dr Fisher as Honorary President of the Interfaith Association in Jerusalem.

PART III

14. 1914–1964

1. See Henry O. Thompson, *World Religions in War and Peace*, McFarland Jefferson, NC 1988 and John Ferguson, *War and Peace in the World's Religions*, Oxford University Press, New York 1978.

2. A. C. F. Beales, *The History of Peace*, Dial Press, New York 1931.

3. Charles S. Macfarland, *Pioneers for Peace Through Religion, Based on the records of The Church Peace Union*, (Introduction by Arthur J. Brown), Flemming H. Revell Co., New York 1946, p.26.

4. Ibid., pp. 28–30.

5. Ibid., p.163.

6. Ibid., p.164.

7. Ibid., p.165.

8. Ibid., p.165.

9. Ibid., p. 167.

10. *World Religions and World Peace*, ed. Homer A. Jack, Beacon Press, Boston 1968, p. 204.

11. Macfarland (n.3), p. 173.

12. Quoted by Homer A. Jack, p.204 from *The Japan National Conference for International Peace Through Religion*, Tokyo 1931.

13. Macfarland (n.3), p.182.

14. Ibid., pp. 224 ff.

15. G. Seaver, *Francis Younghusband*, John Murray 1952, p.371 and see p. 79 above.
16. Macfarland (n.3), p. 241.

15. Towards the World Conference on Religion and Peace

1. *Religion and Peace: Papers from the National Inter-religious Conference on Peace*, ed. Homer A. Jack, Bobbs-Merrill, Indianapolis, 1966, p. ix. Much of the material in this chapter is based on this book. Dr Homer A. Jack is preparing a full history of WCRP.
2. Ibid., p.xiv.
3. Appendix B, p.125–131, lists the officers and participants.
4. Ibid., p.39.
5. Ibid., p.39–43.
6. Ibid., p.89.
7. Ibid., p.92.
8. A note on prepositions: this is the most commonly used name, although the legal name was World Conference of Religion for Peace. See the Newsletter, *Religion for Peace*, November 1974, p. 3. In that year, the name of the newsletter was changed from *Beyond Kyoto* to *Religion for Peace*.
9. Ibid., p. 6.
10. The report of the conference is *World Religions and World Peace*, ed. Homer A. Jack, Beacon Press 1968. The account of the preparations is given by Dana McLean Greeley in his introduction. This quotation is on p. xii.
11. *Religion and Peace* (n.1), p.22.
12. Ibid., p.43.
13. Ibid., Quoted on p. 76.
14. Ibid., pp. xv-xvi.
15. Ibid., pp. 163–5.
16. This account is based on *Religion for Peace, Proceedings of the Kyoto Conference on Religion and Peace*, ed. Homer A. Jack, Gandhi Peace Foundation, New Delhi and Bharatiya Bhavan, Bombay. The introduction tells the story of the preparations and of the conference itself.
17. At Louvain, in 1974, where the same procedure was adopted, there was considerable criticism of this, because those present felt they were an uninvolved audience watching others pray rather than themselves participating. Judging from the texts of the prayers, it seems that at least some of those who led them at Kyoto tried to involve those present. The Christian prayers, for example, allowed for a congregational response. A difficulty at both conferences was the presence of film crews and photographers, which created a restless atmosphere.
18. *Religion for Peace*, (n.16), p. 10.

16. The WCRP Assemblies

1. *Religion for Peace, Proceedings of the Kyoto Conference on Religion and Peace*, ed. Homer A. Jack, Gandhi Peace Foundation, New Delhi and Bharatiya Bhavan, Bombay, pp.118–19.
2. Ibid., p. 99.
3. Ibid., p. 107.
4. Ibid., pp. 108–9.

5. Ibid., p. 109.
6. Ibid., p. 144.
7. Ibid., pp ix-xii.
8. Ibid., p.190.
9. Ibid., p.21.
10. Ibid., p.23.
11. Ibid., p.149.
12. Ibid., p.149.
13. Ibid., p.150.
14. Angelo Fernandes, 'Religion and the Quality of Life', in *World Religion/World Peace*, ed. Homer A. Jack, WCRP, New York 1979, p. 19.
15. Ibid., p.23.
16. Ibid., p.23.
17. Thich Nhat Hahn, 'I Walk on Thorns' in *World Religion/World Peace* (n. 14), p.3.
18. Ibid., p.4.
19. *Religion for Peace*, November 1974, p.4.
20. *World Religion/World Peace* (n.14), pp. i-ii.
21. Ibid., p.ii.
22. Ibid., p.iii.
23. Ibid., p.vi.
24. *Religion in the Struggle for World Community*, ed. Homer A. Jack, World Conference on Religion and Peace, New York, 1980, p. 42.
25. Ibid., pp. 42–3.
26. Ibid., p.43.
27. Ibid., p.44.
28. Ibid., pp.45–6.
29. Ibid., p.53.
30. Ibid., p.53.
31. Ibid., p.54.
32. Ibid., pp.57–66.
33. Ibid., p.67.
34. Ibid., p.123.
35. Ibid., p.iv.
36. Ibid., p.vi.
37. Ibid., p.xxi.
38. Ibid., p. xxi.
39. Ibid., p. xxi.
40. Ibid., p. xxi.
41. Ibid., p.xxii.
42. Ibid., p.30.
43. *Religions for Human Dignity and World Peace*, ed. John B. Taylor and Günther Gebhardt, World Conference on Religion and Peace, Geneva 1986, p. ix.
44. Ibid., p.8.
45. Ibid., p.17.
46. Ibid., p.23.
47. Ibid., p.31.
48. Ibid., p.33.
49. Ibid., p.37.

50. Ibid., p.ii.

51. Ibid., p.iii.

52. Ibid., p.x.

53. David Penhman, Cyclostyled text, p.1.

54. Charles Willie, Cyclostyled text, p.6.

55. *Melbourne Declaration*, WCRP, Geneva 1989, p.1.

56. Ibid., p.1.

57. Ibid., p.1.

58. Ibid., p.2.

59. Ibid., p.2.

60. Ibid., pp.2–4.

61. Ibid., p.4.

62. Robert Runcie in an address to the general Synod of the Church of England on 9.7.1989, quoted in *Common Ground*, CCJ, London 1989, 2.

17. WCRP's Achievements

(The address of WCRP is 14 Chemin Auguste-Vilbert, CH-1218, Grand Sacconex, Geneva, Switzerland.)

1. *Disarmament, Development and Human Rights. The Findings of WCRP I*, WCRP 1970, p. 47.

2. *Religion for Peace*, WCRP, December 1982, March 1983, October 1983.

3. From reports presented at WCRP V.

4. *Religion for Peace*, July 1982.

5. *Religion for Peace*, October 1985.

6. *Religion for Peace*, October 1977.

7. *Religion for Peace*, July 1977 and June 1981.

8. *World Faiths Insight*, New Series 27, February 1991, p.29.

9. *Religion for Peace*, July 1976.

10. *Religion for Peace*, December 1986.

11. *Religion for Peace*, July 1977.

12. *Religions for Human Dignity and World Peace*, WCRP 1986, p. xii.

13. *Religion in the Struggle for World Community*, WCRP 1980, p. xxi.

14. *Religion and Peace*, January 1988.

15. *Common Ground*, CCJ, Spring 1990, p.6.

16. See my *Together to the Truth*, CLS, Madras 1971.

18. Other Peace Groups

1. See above pp. 136–38ff.

2. See Mark Shepard, *Gandhi Today*, Seven Locks Press, Washington DC 1987.

3. Quoted by Henry O. Thompson, *World Religions in War and Peace*, McFarland, Jefferson, NC, 1988, p. 71.

4. See above p. 123.

5. Richard Deats, 'The Rebel Passion; Seventy Five Years of the Fellowship of Reconciliation', *Fellowship*, Jan./Feb. 1990. See also the lecture 'Peace' by Jo Vallentine, a Senator for Western Australia (cyclostyled copy).

6. Alfred Hassler, 'The Fellowship's Statement of Purpose, 1930–65' in *Fellowship*, Supplement 1965.

7. See Thompson, (n.3) p. 71 from Hal W. French and S. Arvind Sharma, *Religious Ferment in Modern India*, St Martin's, NY, 1981, pp. 146–7.

8. *Religion and Peace*, WCRP, No.52, December 1988/January 1989, p.4.

9. Week of Prayer for World Peace, Kent House, Rutland Gardens, London SW7.

10. *World Faiths Insight*, New Series 4, Winter 1981/2, p.23.

11. The World Day of Prayer for Peace. See *World Faiths Insight*, WCF, New Series 15, February 1987, pp. 1–8. See also below pp. 280–1.

12. One Million Minutes for Peace and, more recently, Global Co-operation for a Better World are inspired by the Brahma Kumaris Movement, of which the headquarters is at Mt Abu in India. People of many traditions have participated. The International Co-ordinating Office is at 28 Baker Street, London W1M 4DF.

13. Freedom, Justice and Peace Society, 150 Werimus Lane, Hillsdale, New Jersey 07642, USA.

14. The United Nations Environment Programme, 2 UN Plaza, New York, NY 10017, USA.

15. See the WCRP Report by Dr Homer Jack, No. M.5.

16. *British Weekly and Christian Record*, No.4959, 14 May 1982, p.1.

17. *World Faiths Insight* New Series 23, October 1989, pp. 21–23.

18. UN Colloquium Against Apartheid.

19. *Religions and the Death Penalty and Arguments for Human Rights From the World's Religions*, Amnesty International 1989.

20. *World Faiths Insight*, WCF, New Series 23, October 1989, pp. 21–3.

21. *Earth Conference*, by Anuradha Vittachi, New Science Library, Shambhala, Boston and Shaftesbury, 1989 gives a picture of the Oxford Conference. There are numerous articles in journals. *Hinduism Today*, Hanamaulu, Hawaii 96715, Vol. 12, 3, March 1990 gives a good account of the Moscow Conference. The address of the Global Forum is 304 East 45th Street, 12th Floor, New York NY 10017, USA. See above pp.119–121.

22. C. Longley, *The Times*, 25 November 1989.

23. Ibid.

24. Ibid.

PART IV

19. Bilateral Conversations

1. See below Part V.

2. Tarek Mitri, 'Christian-Muslim Relations: Apprehensions and Possible Convergences' in *The Challenge of Dialogue*, WCC, Geneva 1989.

20. The International Council of Christians and Jews (ICCJ)

1. *Anti-Semitism in the World Today*, Church of Scotland Board of World Mission and Unity 1985, Appendix, p.68

2. W. W. Simpson, *Where Two Faiths Meet*, CCJ 1955, p.4 and pp 15–16.

3. W. W. Simpson and Ruth Weyl, *The International Council of Christians and Jews (ICCJ)*, ICCJ Heppenheim 1988, p.16. I am much endebted to this valuable study.

W. W. Simpson's original history was written in 1979 and a revised edition appeared in 1982.

4. *Where Two Faiths Meet* (n.2), p.15.

5. Ibid., pp. 15–16.

6. *ICCJ*, (n.3), p.15.

7. *Where Two Faiths Meet* (n.2), 15–16.

8. *ICCJ* (n.3), p.159.

9. *In Spirit and in Truth, Aspects of Judaism and Christianity*, ed. G. A. Yates for the Society of Jews and Christians. Hodder and Stoughton 1934. The Christians who took part were liberal scholars such as Oliver Quick, B. H. Streeter, W. R. Matthews, C. C. M. Webb, Charles Raven and John Oman. The Jews too were Liberal or Reform and included Rabbi Mattuck, Rabbi Reinhart, Claude Montefiore, Lily Montagu and Herbert Loewe.

10. Ibid., p. xii.

11. W. W. Simpson, 'Retro-Circum-Prospect', *Common Ground*, Council of Christians and Jews, XXVIII, (CCJ) 3, Autumn 1974, p.5.

12. *Where Two Faiths Meet* (n.2), p.16. also W. W. Simpson, 'Jewish Christian Relations Since the Inception of the Council of Christians and Jews', a paper read to the Jewish Historical Society on 17.3.82, *Transactions of the Jewish Historical Society of England*, Vol. XXVIII.

13. The South African Society of Jews and Christians came into existence in the thirties. In 1939 it started to publish the journal, *Common Sense*. This was intended primarily 'to combat anti-semitism and to foster better understanding and good will between the Jewish community and its Christian neighbours', but it soon became clear that anti-semitism could not be isolated from other forms of prejudice and from the economic and social problems of society. *Common Sense* therefore developed into a journal devoted to 'the combatting of all forms of racial and group prejudice, the promotion of interfaith and intercultural education and the fostering of constructive thinking on South Africa's major problems'. After a time the publication of this journal became the society's main work, but eventually it had to cease publication because of lack of support and because of hostility to its purpose. See *Common Ground*, CCJ IX, 2, March 1955, p.18.

14. Participants came from Australia, Britain, Canada, Czechoslovakia, Denmark, France, Germany, the Netherlands, Palestine (as it then was), South Africa, Sweden, Switzerland and USA.

15. *ICCJ* (n.3), p.23.

16. The six commissions were on: (*a*) Group Tensions, (*b*) Fundamental Postulates of Christianity and Judaism in Relation to Human Order, (*c*) Religious Freedom, (*d*) Justice and its claims, (*e*) Mutual Responsibility in the Community and (*f*) Education and Training for Responsible Citizenship.

17. Quoted in *ICCJ* (n.3), p. 23. The Findings of Commission 2 on 'Fundamental Postulates of Christianity and Judaism in Relation to Human Order' are quoted on pp.81–2.

18. Ibid., p.24.

19. Jules Isaac, *Jésus et Israel*, 1946, ET *Jesus and Israel*, Rinehart and Winston, New York 1971.

20. The ten points of Seelisberg are quoted in *ICCJ* (n.3), pp. 85–6 and in various pamphlets. Many church statements are to be found in Helga Croner, *Stepping Stones to Further Jewish-Christian Relations*, and *More Stepping Stones to Jewish-Christian Relations*,

Stimulus Books 1977 and 1985, and in *The Theology of the Churches and the Jewish People*, ed. Allan Brockway, WCC 1988. I summarize many of these in my *Time to Meet*, SCM Press and Trinity Press International 1990, Part I.

21. *ICCJ* (n.3), p.27.

22. Ibid., pp. 28–9.

23. Hendrik Kraemer, *The Christian Message in a Non-Christian World*, Lutterworth 1938.

24. *ICCJ* (n.3), p.30, where an extract from Archbishop Heenan's address is quoted. Heenan, soon afterwards, was appointed Cardinal. See also my *Children of One God*, Vallentine Mitchell 1991, pp. 33–41.

25. Ibid., p.32.

26. Ibid., p.35.

27. The *ICCJ Guidelines on the Protrayal of Jews and Judaism in Education and Teaching Material* is printed as Appendix III to *ICCJ* (n.3), pp.87–96 and the *Guidelines on the Teaching of History* is Appendix IV, pp.97–109.

28. *CCJ Newsletter*, Autumn 1984.

29. *CCJ Newsletter*, Summer 1985.

30. See my 'Reconciliation Between Jews and Christians Through Common Prayer', which was an article in the journal *From the Martin Buber House* (1986, pp.49–52), about joint prayer.

31. *ICCJ* (n.3), p.60.

32. *ICCJ News*, No.3, Winter 1988/89, p.1.

33. See above, pp. 183–5. and n.20.

34. See my *Time to Meet* (n.20), pp.38–9 and Alexandre Safron, *Resisting the Storm, 1940–47, Memoirs*, ed. Jean Ancel, Yad Vashem, Jerusalem 1987, pp. 260–61.

35. *ICCJ* (n.3), p.64.

36. *ICCJ News* (n.31).

37. *Common Ground*, CCJ, 1989 No. 2, p.15.

38. See above p.190 and n.28.

39. In 1990 Member organizations were: Australia, The Council of Christians and Jews; Austria, Aktion gegen den Antisemitismus; Belgium, Contacts Interconfessionels; Brazil, Conselho de Fraternidade Cristao-Judaica; Canada, Canadian Council of Christians and Jews; Federal Republic of Germany, Geselleschaften fur christlich-judische Zusammenarbeit – Deutscher Koordinierungsrat; France, Amitie Judeo-Chretienne de France; Great Britain, The Council of Christians and Jews; Ireland, Irish Council of Christians and Jews; Israel, The Israel Interfaith Association; Italy, Federazione delle Amicizie Ebraico-Cristiane in Italia; Luxembourg, Comitie Interconfessionel Luxembourgeois; The Netherlands, Overlegorgaan van Joden en Christenen in Nederland (OJEC); Spain, Centro de Estudios Judeo-Cristianos; Sweden, Samarbetsradet for Judar och Kristna; Switzerland, Christlich-Judische Arbeitsgemeinschaft in der Schweiz; USA, National Conference of Christians and Jews; Uruguay, Confraternidad Judeo-Cristiana del Uruguay; Venezuela, Comite de Relaciones entre Iglesias y Sinagogas. Secretariat is ICCJ, Martin Buber House, Werlestrasse 2, Postfach 305, 6148 Heppenheim, FR Germany.

40. *Common Ground*, CCJ, 1990 No.1, p.4.

21. Official Conversations

1. See above p.178.

2. *Christian-Jewish Relations*, Vol. 19, No. 3, Institute of Jewish Affairs, London, June 1986, p.3.

3. See Geoffrey Wigoder, *Jewish-Christian Relations since the Second World War*, Manchester University Press, Manchester 1990, pp.51–4. For Hermann Cohen see *Die Religion der Vernuft aus den Quellen des Judentums*, 1919 also *Reason and Hope, Selections from the Writings of Hermann Cohen*, ET Eva Jospe 1971. For Franz Rosenzweig, *Der Stern der Erlosung*, 1921, ET *The Star of Redemption*, 1971. Martin Buber's *Ich und Du* was published in 1923. For Claude G. Montefiore see *Judaism and St Paul*, 1914, *The Synoptic Gospels* (2 vols), 1927. For Joseph Klausner, *Jesus of Nazareth*, ET, New York 1927; *From Jesus to Paul*, ET 1942.

4. *Judaism*, Winter 1971, p.95. Quoted by Wigoder, (n.3), p.62.

5. Ibid., p. 100. Quoted by Wigoder, p.63.

6. *Fifteen Years of Catholic-Jewish Dialogue*, 1970–1985, Selected papers. Libreria Editrice Vaticana & Libreria Editrice Lateranense, Rome 1988, p.31.

7. Ibid., p.32.

8. Ibid., p.37.

9. Ibid., p.30.

10. See below, pp.206–9.

11. Pope John Paul II in *Fifteen years of Catholic-Jewish Dialogue* (n.6), p.322.

12. Ibid.

13. Wigoder (n.3), p.82.

14. See below p. 263.

15. *Fifteen Years of Catholic-Jewish Dialogue* (n.6), p. 1–2.

16. T. Federici, 'Study Outline on the Mission and Witness of the Church', in *More Stepping Stones to Jewish-Christian Relations*, ed. Helga Croner, Stimulus Books, Paulist Press 1985, pp. 37–55.

17. *Fifteen Years of Catholic-Jewish Dialogue* (n.6), p. xix.

18. *Common Ground*, 1991, 1, p.32.

19. *More Stepping Stones to Jewish-Christian Relations*, ed. Helga Croner, Stimulus Books, Paulist Press 1977, pp. 1–2.

20. Gerhard Riegner in *Fifteen Years of Catholic-Jewish Dialogue* (n.6), pp. 277–8.

21. Ibid, p. 278.

22. *The Times*, 18 March 1989.

23. Wigoder (n.3), p.100.

24. *Jewish-Christian Dialogue*, IJCIC and WCC, Geneva, 1975, p.9.

25. Helga Croner (ed.), *Stepping Stones*, Stimulus Books 1977, pp. 69–72.

26. Ibid., pp. 72–3.

27. *The World Council of Churches Consultation on the Church and the Jewish People: Sigtuna, Sweden, 30 Oct–4 Nov, 1988, Report*, WCC Geneva 1989.

28. Marc Ellis in the *Tablet*, June 1990, suggests that Christian-Jewish dialogue should be suspended because of Israeli treatment of the Palestinians.

22. Israel

1. Ezra Spicehandler 'Is Dialogue Possible in Jerusalem?', *World Faiths*, WCF, Spring 1977, No. 101, p.13.

2. Dr Jacobus Schoneveld, 'Towards a New Jewish-Christian Understanding in Israel', *Judaism*, 86, vol.22, No.2, p.206.

3. Fr Marcel Dubois in *Inter-Faith Dialogue in Israel*. Retrospect and Prospect. An interfaith symposium held in May 1973. Published by *Immanuel*, The Ecumenical Theological Research Fraternity, Jerusalem, as a special supplement in 1973, p. 23.

4. Geoffrey Wigoder, *Jewish-Christian Relations since the Second World War*, Manchester University Press, Manchester 1990, p.126.

5. Dubois (n.3), p.13.

6. Spicehandler (n.1), p.13.

7. Professor Zwi Werblowsky in *Inter-Faith Dialogue in Israel* (n.3), p.33.

8. Fr Elias Chacour in *Inter-Faith Dialogue in Israel* (n.3), p. 25. See also Nain Stifan Ateek, *Justice and Only Justice*, Orbis Books, New York 1989.

9. *Ten Years of the Ecumenical Fraternity. Retrospect and Prospect*, a talk by J. Schoneveld. Cyclostyled 1976, p.1.

10. Spicehandler (n.1), pp.13–14.

11. Wigoder (n.4), p.129.

12. Dr Goldstein, *Judaism* (n.2), p.204.

13. Z. Werblowsky (n.7), p.33.

14. J. Schoneveld, 'Dialogue with Jews', *Immanuel*, No.6, Spring 1976, p.68. See also *Judaism* (n.2), p.206.

15. *Christian News from Israel*, XXIII, Spring 1973, p.243.

16. *Neve Shalom*, Cyclostyled leaflet, n.d.

17. *Common Ground*, CCJ, 1989, No.2, p.23.

18. Uriel Tal, 'The New Pattern in Jewish Christian Dialogue', *Immanuel*, No.1, Summer 1972, p.54.

19. Shemaryahu Talmon, *Interfaith Dialogue in Israel* (n.3), p.10.

20. Ibid., p.11.

21. D. Hartman, *Immanuel*, No.5, p.98.

22. Wigoder (n.4), p.139.

The address of the Interreligious Co-ordinating Council in Israel is POB 7855, Jerusalem.

23. Christians and Jews: Conclusions

1. *The World Council of Churches Consultation on the Church and the Jewish People: Sigtuna, Sweden, 30 Oct–4 Nov, 1988, Report*, WCC Geneva, 1989, p.14.

2. Quoted by G. Wigoder, *Jewish-Christian Relations Since the Second World War*, Manchester University Press, Manchester 1990, p.141.

3. For example, G. Wigoder's book (n.2); *The Theology of the Churches and the Jewish People* ed. Allan Brockway, WCC, Geneva 1989. From WCC; Gerhard Reigner's; Fifteen years of Catholic-Jewish Dialogue; and my *Time to Meet*, SCM Press and Trinity Press International 1990.

4. Allan Brockway in *The Theology of the Churches and the Jewish People* (n.3), p.186.

5. Wigoder (n.2), p.139.

6. Ibid., p.140.

7. Johnathan Sacks, 'Living Together: The Interfaith Imperative', *Common Ground*, 1990, No.1, p.12.

24. Christians and Muslims

1. *Meeting in Faith, Twenty Years of Christian-Muslim Conversations*, sponsored by the World Council of Churches, compiled by Stuart E. Brown, WCC Publications, Geneva

1989 contains reports of the meetings. The documents relating to the earlier meetings are also to be found in *Christians Meeting Muslims*, WCC, Geneva 1977. The reference here is to *Meeting in Faith*, p.3.

2. Ibid., p.3.
3. Ibid., p.5.
4. See below p.256.
5. *Meeting in Faith*, (n.1), p. 23.
6. Ibid., p. 26. See also *Alive to God*, compiled by Kenneth Cragg, Oxford University Press 1970.
7. See p.256.
8. *Meeting in Faith*, (n.1) p.50.
9. Ibid., p.52.
10. Ibid., p.53.
11. Ibid., p.64.
12. Ibid., p.67.
13. See below p.258 and appendix pp. 317–22.
14. *Meeting in Faith*, (n.1), p. 74–86.
15. Ibid., p. 83.
16. Ibid., p.ix.
17. Ibid., p.102.
18. Ibid., p. 105.
19. Ibid., p. 106.
20. Ibid., p. 106.
21. Ibid., p ix.
22. *The Challenge of Dialogue: Papers from the Meeting of the Dialogue Working group, Casablanca, Morocco, June 1989*, WCC, Geneva 1989, p. 65.
23. Ibid., p.66.
24. Ibid., p. 66.
25. Ibid., p. 67.
26. Ibid., p. 69.
27. See below pp. 247–253.
28. Michael L. Fitzgerald, 'Twenty-Five Years of Dialogue: The Pontifical Council for Inter-Religious Dialogue', *Islamochristiana*, 15, Rome 1989, gives a full account of these journeys and of the delegations received in Rome.
29. *The Bulletin of the Secretariat for Non-Christians*, XI/I, 31, Rome 1976, p. 10.
30. Ibid., p. 21.
31. p.13 and Michael L. Fitzgerald, 'Twenty-Five Years of Dialogue' (n. 28), p. 110.
32. *The Bulletin of the Secretariat for Non-Christians*, XI/I, 31 (n.29), p. 13.
33. Michael L. Fitzgerald, 'Twenty-Five Years of Dialogue' (n.28), p. 116.
34. Ibid., p. 118.
35. Ibid., p. 113, note 15. *The Guidelines or Orientations pour un dialogue entre Chretiens et Musulmans* were edited by Maurice Borrmans, Cerf, Paris 1981.
36. *Chiesa e Islam*, Cittadel Vaticano 1981.
37. The addresses may be obtained from The UK Interfaith Network.
38. See for example David Brown's *A New Threshold*, British Council of Churches 1976.
39. See *JCM Newsletter*, for July 1972, February 1973, July 1973 and June 1974 and articles by Lionel Blue in *The Journal of Ecumenical Studies*, Vol. 10, No.1, 1973 and in

European Judaism, Winter 1974–5. The proceedings of the London Conference in 1972 were published under the title *The Faith of Our Fathers – The Fate of Our Children*.

40. Quoted in *The Bulletin of the Secretariat for Non-Christians*, 41–42, 1979, p.106.

41. *Christians Meeting Muslims* (n.1), Foreword.

42. Ibid.

43. Mr A. K. Brohi in an address to an International Seminar on Muslim Communities in Non-Muslim States, held in London in July 1978, reported in the Times, 25 July 1978, p. 6. See also, Dr Yaqub Zaki on 'Is Dialogue Possible?' in 'Hans Küng: A Different Muslim Response', *World Faiths Insight*, New Series 23, October 1989, pp. 9–12.

25. Dialogue with Hindus

1. Swami Vivekananda, *Selection from Swami Vivkananda*, The Ramakrishna Society, Calcutta 1957, pp. 17–18. For a fuller discussion of Christian-Hindu dialogue see my *The Undiscovered Christ*, CLS Madras 1973; M. M. Thomas, *The Acknowledged Christ of the Indian Renaissance*, SCM Press 1969 and S. J. Samartha, *The Hindu Response to the Unbound Christ*, CISRS, Bangalore and CLS, Madras 1974.

2. See above, pp. 45–46.

3. W. Miller, *The Madras Christian College*, Edinburgh 1905, p.8.

4. Kaj Baago, *Pioneers of Indigenous Christianity*, CLS, Madras 1969, p. 75.

5. M. Gandhi, *Satyagraha in South Africa*, S. Ganesan, Madras 1928, p. 165, quoted by Nirmal Minz, *Mahatma Gandhi and Hindu-Christian Dialogue*, CLS Madras 1970.

6. Quoted by Minz, p. 51 from M. Gandhi, *All Religions Are True*, p. 228.

7. Ibid., p. 26, quoted by Minz, p. 52.

8. Quoted by Minz, p. 55 from M. Gandhi, *The Story of My Experiment with Truth*, Ahmedabad 1927, p. 343.

9. Quoted by Minz, p. 56 from M. Gandhi, *The Way to Communal Harmony*, p. 406.

10. M. Gandhi, *The Message of Jesus Christ*, Ahmedabad, 1940, pp. 28ff.

11. 'The Aims and Basis of the all-Kerala Inter-Religious Student Fellowship', printed as an appendix in *The Witness of S. K. George*, by T. K. Thomas, CLS, Madras 1970, pp. 149–150.

12. Ibid.

13. S. K. George, *Gandhi's Challenge to Christianity*, Ahmedabad 1960, p. 47. The book was written during the year he spent in 1938 at Manchester College, Oxford, at the invitation of the General Assembly of Unitarians.

14. Ibid., pp. 38–40.

15. The office is at 52 Green Meadow Rd, Birmingham B 29 4DE.

16. This is recounted by S. K. George in the *Fellowship of the Friends of Truth Quarterly*, Vol. V, No. 1 and reprinted in *The Witness of S. K. George*, (n. 11). I am also grateful for material supplied by the secretary, Ruth Richardson. See also *Quaker Encounters*, Vol.3, 'Whispers of Truth' by John Ormerod Greenwood, Sessions of York 1978, pp.232–33.

17. The original statement says, 'The Fellowship of the Friends of Truth is alive to the urgent need in the world today of bringing together people of different faiths in common endeavour to realize the good life for all through the way of truth and love. It attempts to do this on the basis: (1) of reverence for all religions, implying thereby a frank acceptance of the fact of variety in men's growing apprehension of truth; (2) of silent worship; (3) of united brotherly action on non-violent lines'. Only one alteration has been made to this original statement. The word 'meditation' has been added after 'silent worship'.

18. See above, pp. 136–8.

19. Mark Shepherd, *Gandhi Today*, Seven Locks Press, Washington D.C. 1987.

20. P. Chenchiah in *The Pilgrim*, reprinted in *The Theology of Chenchiah*, ed. D. A. Thangasamy, CISRS, Bangalore 1966, 181.

21. Ibid., p. 183.

22. Ibid., p. 192–3.

23. H. Kraemer, *The Christian Message in a Non-Christian World*, Lutterworth 1938, p. 302. See above p. 185.

24. The Christian Institute for the Study of Religion and Society, PO Box 4600, 17 Millers Rd, Bangalore 560046, India.

25. *Christian Revelation and World Religions*, ed. Joseph Neuner, Burns and Oates 1967. See also *Religious Hinduism* by Jesuit Scholars, St Paul Publications, Allahabad 1964, based on articles that appeared from 1957–9.

26. Abhishiktananda, *Hindu-Christian Meeting Point*, Institute of Indian Culture, Bombay and CISRS, Bangalore, 1969, p. 4. See the other books by Abhishiktananda.

27. Sister Vandana, *Gurus, Ashrams and Christians*, Darton, Longman & Todd 1978 and Bede Griffiths, *Christian Ashram*, Darton, Longman & Todd 1966, *The Marriage of East and West*, Collins 1982 and other writings.

28. This information is based on private letters from Fr Albert Nambiaparambil and from Sangam, the newsletter of WFIRC.

29. See below p. 116.

26. Meetings with Buddhists, Sikhs and Traditional Believers

1. *Bulletin of the Secretariat for Non Christians*, 41/2, 1979, p. 93.

2. *The Challenge of Dialogue*, Papers from the Meeting of the Dialogue Working Group, Casablanca, Morocco, WCC, Geneva 1989, p. 95. See also the Editorial in the Supplement to *Dialogue*, published by the Ecumenical Institute for Study and Dialogue, Colombo, New Series Vol. IX, nos 1–3, Jan.-Dec .1982.

3. Ibid., p. 98. Some of the papers have been published in Buddhist-Christian Studies, ed. David Chappell at the University of Hawaii. See also John H. Berthrong, 'Buddhist-Christian Theological Encounter', *The Catholic World*, May/June 1990, Vol.233, No.1395, pp.122–6.

4. *The Challenge of Dialogue* (n.2), p. 101. A newsletter is published by The Society for Buddhist-Christian Studies. This is available from Professor Donald W. Mitchell, Dept of Philosophy, Purdue University, West Lafayette, IN 47907, USA.

5. See his article in *World Faiths Insight*, New Series 27, February 1991.

6. William Johnston, *The Inner Eye of Love*, Collins 1978; *The Mirror Mind*, Collins 1981; Aelred Graham, *Zen Catholicism*, Collins 1964; Douglas V. Steere, *Mutual Irradiation: A Quaker View of Ecumenism*, Pendle Hill Pamphlet 175, 1971.

7. *The Challenge of Dialogue* (n.2), p. 85.

8. Patiala Conference Papers, Patiala University, Punjab, India.

9. See *The Sikh Bulletin*, West Sussex Institute of Higher Education.

27. Religions Engage in Dialogue

1. In a letter to me, dated 26.7.90. Prot No. 30444.

28. The Pontifical Council for Inter-religious Dialogue

1. See my *Time to Meet*, SCM Press 1990, pp. 13–16.

2. 'Declaration on the Relationship of the Church to Non-Christian Religions' in *The Documents of Vatican II*, ed. W. M. Abbott SJ, Geoffrey Chapman 1966, p. 660.

3. Ibid., p. 661.

4. Ibid., p. 662.

5. Ibid., p. 662–3.

6. Pope Paul VI, 'Discourse to the Sacred College', 23.6.64, *Acta Apostolica Sedis*, Vol.56, p. 584.

7. *Bulletin of the Secretariat for Non-Christians*, 4.3.67, p. 29.

8. Ibid., p. 33.

9. Ibid., p. 33.

10. Ibid., p. 35.

11. Ibid., p. 37.

12. Ibid., p. 38.

13. Ibid., p. 39.

14. Ibid., pp.39–40.

15. Ibid., p. 31.

16. Cardinal Francis Arinze, 'The Christian Commitment to Interreligious Dialogue', *L'Osservatore Romano*, 17.7.89 – N.29, Para 2.

17. Ibid., para 3.

18. Ibid., para 4.

19. Ibid., para 8.

20. Ibid., para 9.

21. Ibid., para 12.

22. Ibid., para 11.

23. This account is based on Msgr Pietro Rossano 'The Secretariat for Non-Christian Religions from the beginnings to the present day: history, ideas, problems', *Bulletin* 1979–XIV/2–3, 41–42. pp. 88–109 and Michael L. Fitzgerald 'Twenty-Five Years of Dialogue: The Pontifical Council for Inter-Religious Dialogue', *Islamochristiana* 15, Rome 1989, pp. 109–120.

24. *Islamochristiana* 15, p. 110.

25. *Islamochristiana* 15, p. 113.

26. *Islamochristiana* 15, p. 109, quoting from Cardinal Arinze in *The Bulletin*, 69 (1988) p. 185.

27. Bulletin 56 (1984).

28. Cardinal Francis Arinze, 'The Christian Commitment to Interreligious Dialogue' (n.16), Para 17 and *World Faiths Insight*, New Series 15, February 1987, pp. 1–6.

29. *World Faiths Insight*, New Series 15, February 1987, p.2.

30. Cardinal Francis Arinze, 'The Christian Commitment to Interreligious Dialogue' (n.16), Para 18.

29. The World Council of Churches

1. Marlin van Elderen 'The Challenge of Dialogue' *One World*', No 148, Aug/Sep 1989, Geneva, reproduced in *The Challenge of Dialogue*, WCC, Geneva 1989, p. 7.

2. *The International Review of Mission*, 1970, pp. 173ff. See also S. J. Samartha

'Dialogue as a Continuing Christian Concern', *Ecumenical Review*, XXIII, p. 128. Samartha refers to the following meetings, amongst others, Christian-Hindu at Kottayam, India, October 1962; Christian-Muslim, Birmingham, Jan, 1968; Christian-Buddhist-Confucian, Seoul, Korea, October 1967.

3. S. J. Samartha 'The World Council of Churches and Men of Other Faiths and Ideologies', *Ecumenical Review* XXII, p. 192.

4. Quoted by S. J. Samartha, op. cit., from *Minutes of the Central Committee of the WCC*, Geneva 1969, p. 29.

5. *Ecumenical Review* XXIII, p. 134.

6. S. J. Samartha, 'Dialogue: Significant Issues in the Continuing Debate', *Ecumenical Review*, XXIV, p.328, 1972.

7. *Study Encounter*, Vol.X,3, WCC, Geneva 1974.

8. Samuel Ryan, SJ, 'The Ultimate Blasphemy', *The International Review of Mission*, LXV, No.257, Jan. 1976, p. 131. See also S. J.Samartha in *World Faiths*, No.100, 1976, pp. 33ff. and Rabbi Arnold Wolf, who was one of the non-Christian observers, in *Common Ground*, Summer 1976.

9. Samuel Ryan (n.8), p. 132.

10. Ibid., p.133.

11. 'Dialogue in Community'. Text of the statement of the Chiang Mai Consultation (cyclostyled). Para 19, p. 10. See also S. J. Samartha, 'Dialogue in Community, A Pause for reflection' and 'Dialogue in Community, A Step Forward'. Both cyclostyled from WCC, Geneva.

12. 'Dialogue in Community', Para 19, p. 10.

13. S. J. Samartha, 'Dialogue in Community, A Step Forward', n.11, p. 5.

14. 'Dialogue in Community', Para 9, p. 6.

15. S. J. Samartha, 'Dialogue in Community, A Pause for reflection' and 'Dialogue in Community, A Step Forward', p. 1.

16. See Gwen Cashmore's report of Chiang Mai in *World Faiths*, No.103, 1977, p.27.

17. Quoted by S. Wesley Ariarajah, 'Religious Plurality and its Challenge to Christian Theology', *World Faiths Insight*, New Series 19, June 1988. pp. 6–7 from Arvind P. Nirmal. 'Redefining the Economy of Salvation', *The Indian Journal of Theology* XXX, 34, July-December 1981, p. 214

18. Quoted by S. Wesley Ariarajah, (n. 17) from *Monthly Letter on Evangelism*, WCC, p. 1.

19. Quoted by S. Wesley Ariarajah, (n. 17) from Emilio Castro, Editorial for issue on 'Dialogue an Ecumenical Concern', *Ecumenical Review*, XXXVII, 4, October 1985, pp. 384–5.

20. Marlin van Elderen (n.1), p.9.

21. Ibid., p.8.

22. *Current Dialogue*, 18, June 1990, WCC, p. 4.

23. Ibid., p. 5.

24. Ibid., p. 7.

25. *Current Dialogue* 20, July 1991, pp. 34–7 and *Common Ground* 1991, No. 2, pp. 45–6.

26. Marlin van Elderen (n.1), p. 15.

27. Ibid., p. 18.

28. See for example 'Jews, Christians and Muslims: The Way of Dialogue', in *The*

Truth Shall Make You Free. The Lambeth Conference 1988, Church House Publishing 1989, Appendix.

30. Other Religions' Initiatives

1. Nikkyo Niwano, *A Buddhist Approach to Peace*, Kosei Publishing Co., Tokyo 1977, p.67. The book has an appendix outlining some of Rev. Nikkyo Niwano's activities.
2. Sulak Svaraksa, 'Global Problem-Solving: A Buddhist Perspective'. An unpublished lecture given at the Consultation on 'World Religions Responding to Global Threats', sponsored by UN University of Peace, Costa Rica in March 1991.
3. See above pp. 237–8.
4. Carl T. Jackson in the article on 'Theosophy' in the *Encyclopaedia Britannica*, 15th Edition, 1977, Macropaedia, 18, p. 276.
5. *Selections from the Writings of the Bāb*, Bahá'í Publishing Trust, 1976 p. 56.
6. Firuz Kazemzadeh in the article on The Bahá'í Faith in the *Encyclopaedia Britannica*, 15th edition, 1977, Macropaedia 2, p.588, quoting Bahá'u'lláh.
7. H. M. Balyuzi, *Abdu'l-Bahá*, George Ronald 1971, p. 141.
8. *Gleanings From the Writings of Bahá'u'lláh*, Bahá'í Publishing Trust 1949, p.95.
9. *Abdu'l-Baha in London*, Bahá'í Publishing Trust, 1982 p.35.
10. Ibid.
11. *Religions of the Empire*, ed. William Loftus Hare, Duckworth 1925, pp.304–325.
12. *Bahá'í World* Vol.VII (1936/38), published by National Spiritual Assembly of the United States, pp 634–645.
13. *Gleanings From the Writings of Bahá'u'lláh* (n.6), p. 215.

31. The Unification Church

1. Rev. Sun Myung Moon, *The Divine Principle*, The Holy Spirit Association for the Unification of World Christianity, Fifth edition 1977, p. 108.
2. From Rev. Moon's Founder's Address at the Fourth International Conference on God: The Contemporary Discussion, Seoul, Korea, 11.8.84, quoted in 1985 Assembly of the World's Religions Programme.
3. Warren Lewis (ed.) *Towards A Global Congress of World Religions*, Rose of Sharon Press, New York 1978, p. 28.
4. Ibid.
5. Ibid., p.29.
6. Ibid., pp. 29–30.
7. Global Congress of the World's Religions leaflet, 1980.
8. *Assembly of the World's Religions 1985*, A Report by M. Darrol Bryant, John Maniatis and Tyler Hendricks, A New Era Book, International Religious Foundation, Paragon House, New York 1986, p. xvii.
9. Programme for the 1990 Assembly.
10. *The Council for the World's Religions*, pamphlet (n.d.) p. 2–8.
11. The Impressive list of the conferences arranged by CWR is as follows:

1985: Intra-Religious Buddhist Conference at Chiang Mai, Thailand; Vedanta, Its Unity and Variety, Pune, India; Unity and Plurality in Judaism Today,

Hertenstein, Switzerland; The Future of Ecumenical Co-operation, Bad Neuheim, West Germany; Promoting Understanding in the Islamic World, Istanbul, Turkey.

1986: Religious Harmony: Problems and Possibilities, Bangalore, India; The World-wide Interfaith Movement: Present Situation and Future Prospects, Bad Neuheim, West Germany; Buddhist Dialogue, Chiang Mai, Thailand; Intra-Jewish Dialogue, Vitznau, Switzerland; Promoting Understanding and Unity in the Islamic World, Istanbul, Turkey; Bhakti, Its Experiences and Expressions, Varanasi, India; The Way Forward in Christian Ecumenism, San Diego, California.

1987: Intra-Buddhist, Colombo, Sri Lanka; Intra-Christian, Eibsee, West Germany; Interfaith, Vancouver, Canada; Intra-African, Nairobi, Kenya; Intra-Jewish, Kiamesha Lake, New York; Intra-Muslim, Casablanca, Morocco.

1988: Mid-East Interfaith, Toledo, Spain; Intra-Christian, Istanbul, Turkey; Hindu-Sikh, Srinagar, India; Intra-Jewish, Stansstad, Switzerland.

1989: Intra-Muslim, Istanbul, Turkey; Intra-Christian, Moscow, USSR; Intra-Jewish, Toledo, Spain; Nigerian Regional, Ile-Ife, Nigeria.

1990: 'Places of Worship in Multi-Faith India', New Delhi, India.

The address of the Council For the World's Religions is JAF Box 2347, New York, NY 10116, USA.

12. Francis Clark (ed.) *Interfaith Directory*, A New Era Book, International Religious Foundation, New York 1987.

13. *IRF Newsletter*, New York, Vol. 6, No. 1, Spring 1991, p.2.

14. See relevant sections of *Investigation of Korean-American Relations*, US Government Printing Office, Washington, D.C., 1978. The Unificationist reply is in *Our Response*, New York, The Holy Spirit Association for the Unification of World Christianity, New York 1979. See also Eileen Barker, *The Making of a Moonie: Brainwashing or Choice?* Blackwell, Oxford 1984.

15. From a CWR leaflet circulated to interested colleagues and others engaged in inter-religious activity.

32 Studying and Teaching World Religions

1. W. W. Simpson, *Where Two Faiths Meet*, CCJ 1955, p. 16.

2. *What is the Inter-Religious Organization?* Statement of aims on back cover of *Is Religion Necessary?*, Inter-Religious Organization, Singapore 1974.

3. William Loftus Hare (ed.), *Religions of the Empire*, Duckworth 1925, p.3.

4. Despite the intention of the organizers, Sir Francis Younghusband, in his opening address, voiced the hope that the religions of the world could work together for peace.

5. Hare (n.3.), p.4.

6. Ibid., p.3.

7. Dr Yaqub Zaki in *World Faiths Insight* New Series 23, October 1989, p. 12 and passim and Ven. M. Vajiragnana, pp. 28ff.

8. *Actes du Premier Congres International d'Histoire des Religions*, Paris 1901, Ernest Leroux, Paris 1901. From the circular of 12.5.1899, quoted on p. iii.

9. C. J. Bleeker, *The History of Religions, 1950–75*, University of Lancaster, n.d., p.2.

10. Ibid., p.3.

11. Ibid., p.4.

12. Eric J. Sharpe, *Comparative Religion: A History*, Duckworth 1975.

13. *Proceedings of the Ninth International Congress for the History of Religions, Tokyo, 1958*, Maruzen, Tokyo 1960, p. vi.

14. Sharpe (n.12), p. 271. See also C. J. Bleeker, 'The Future Task of the History of Religions', *Numen* VII, 1960, p. 221.

15. *Proceedings* (n.13), pp. 7–2.

16. Marcus Braybrooke, *Faiths in Fellowship*, WCF 1976 and see above p. 115.

17. *Proceedings* (n.13), pp.12–13.

18. Ibid., p.18.

19. Ibid., p.19.

20. Ibid., p.21.

21. R. J. Zwi Werblowsky, *The Hibbert Journal*, Vol.LVIII, October to July 1960, p.34.

22. Bleeker (n.14), p.226.

23. Ibid., p.232.

24. Annemarie Schimmel, 'Summary of the Discussion', *Numen* VII, 1960, p. 236.

25. Ibid., p. 237.

26. Ibid., p. 237.

27. Ibid., p. 237.

28. Ibid., p. 239.

29. 'Seekers and Scholars', Unit 1 of *Man's Religious Quest'*, The Open University, 1977, p.6.

30. 'Inter-Religious Encounter', Units 29–30.

31. Terry Thomas in the *BASR Bulletin*, No.62, Nov. 1990. See also *Marburg Revisited: Institutions and Strategies in the Study of Religion*, ed. Michael Pye, Diagonal-Verlag, Marburg 1989, especially 'History or mythistory in the study of religion? The problem of demarcation' by Don Wiebe.

32. Eric J. Sharpe in the *BASR Bulletin*, No.47, Nov. 1985.

33. Michael Pye in the *BASR Bulletin*, No.62, Nov. 1990.

34. *Turning Points in Religious Studies*, ed. Ursula King, T&T Clark 1990.

35. *Union for the Study of the Great Religions*, leaflet, June 1954, p.1. See also the obituary of H. N. Spalding (1877–1953) by K. D. D. Henderson in *The Oxford Magazine* for 21.1.1954 and the article by the same author 'The Work of the Spalding Trust and the Union for the Study of the Great Religions' in *World Faiths*, No.79, Spring 1970, pp. 1–6.

36. *World Faiths* (n.35), p.3.

37. Members included A. C. Bouquet, Bishop Bell, William Ernest Hocking, Lord Samuel, Wilfred Cantwell Smith and D. T. Suzuki. The original co-ordinating committee consisted of Sir Richard Livingstone, Charles Raven, Arthur Arberry, K. J. Spalding and T. W. Thackers.

38. The address is FVG, 164, B–2610, Antwerp, Belgium.

39. For the addresses see *Interfaith Directory*, ed. F. Clark, International Religious Foundation, New York 1987.

40. World Interfaith Colleges, PO Box 7348, Station 'D' Victoria, BC, Canada V8B 5B7.

41. John R. Hinnels (ed.) *Comparative Religion in Education*, Oriel Press, Newcastle-upon-Tyne 1970, p. 109.

42. For example, a handbook for teachers is regularly produced and conferences are arranged.

43. The terms of reference agreed at the first meeting of The Standing Conference on Inter-Faith Dialogue in Education, held at 23 Norfolk Square, London on 6.12.73, were 'It shall be the function of the Standing Conference to convene, or encourage the convening, of national and regional interfaith conferences concerned with education in school and community, including Religious Education, and to circulate or publish reports of the proceedings or findings of those conferences'. For the address of SHAP and SCIFDE, see above n. 33 on p. 331.

44. John Prickett, 'World Religions, Humanists and Religious Education', *World Faiths*, No. 94, 1974, pp. 24–25. John Prickett has edited several books in The Living Faiths series, published by Lutterworth: *Initiation Rites*, 1978; *Marriage and the Family*, 1985; *Death*, 1980.

33. Towards 1993

1. John B. Taylor, 'Conference of International Interfaith Organizations', *World Faiths Insight*, New Series 12, February 1986, p.4.

2. Ibid., p.5.

3. Ibid., p.6.

4. Ibid., p.6.

5. Ibid., p.8.

6. Ibid., p.10.

7. Conference report, unpublished, p.7.

8. *Interfaith News*, WCF, Summer 1985, p.1. See also David Edwards, *The Futures of Christianity*, Hodder & Stoughton 1987, pp. 270ff. and the review of this book by William Stansmore in *World Faiths Insight*, New Series 23, October 1989.

9. Minutes of Meeting, 10.11.86, p. 8.

10. Minutes of Ammerdown Conference, 15–17.4.88, p.1.

11. Ibid., p.3.

12. Ibid., p.3.

13. The text of the leaflet is:

1993: A Year of Interreligious Understanding and Co-operation

This is an invitation to you to join in a worldwide celebration of the unity of the human family. It is a chance to give thanks that with the wonderful variety of different races, colours, languages, religions and customs, we belong to one family. It is an occasion to renew our efforts to ensure fullness of life for all members of that family.

Many people believe that the survival of life on this planet depends upon our realising our oneness. For a just and peaceful world, we must replace competition with co-operation. We can only tackle the problems of war, poverty, homelessness and the environment, if we think and act on a global scale.

Often rivalry between religions has made matters worse: but all the great faiths inspire love and respect for other people. Nearly one hundred years ago, people of many religions came together in the hope that religions would 'no longer make war on each other, but on the giant evils that afflict humankind'. They met in Chicago, USA, in 1893, for the World's Parliament of Religions, at which Swami Vivekananda proclaimed his message of 'universal acceptance'. It was discovered that people could be loyal to their own beliefs, whilst appreciative of the beliefs of others.

Since then many local interfaith groups and some national bodies for interreligious co-operation have come into being. Four main organizations, The International Association for Religious Freedom, the Temple of Understanding, the World Congress of Faiths and the World Conference on Religion and Peace seek to link interfaith co-operation worldwide. Their members hope to share in common celebration in India in August 1993 and will take part in other events being planned around the world.

We encourage you to share in celebrating one hundred years of the interfaith movement and to start planning now. We hope that all places of worship will arrange special celebrations and that schools and youth organizations will plan educational programmes so that 1993 becomes a real Year of Interreligious Understanding and Co-operation.

1993 is a chance to give thanks for the growth of the interfaith movement and the progress made in religious co-operation, shown, for example, at the World Days of Prayer for Peace which have been held at Assisi, Italy at Mt Hiei, Japan and at Melbourne, Australia. 1993 is also a time to renew our efforts to remove all prejudice and discrimination, whatever its cause, to end violence and injustice and to remove poverty, so that all members of the human family enjoy a worthwhile life.

(Further details from David and Celia Storey, Rawmere, Rew Lane, Chichester, West Sussex, PO19 4BH.)

14. Leaflet of the Council for a Parliament of the World's Religions, Chicago, n.d.
15. Circular letter and enclosures from Dr Wayne Nelles, 17.5.90.
16. Telegram from Rev. A. Stoian, 26.3.90.

34. Conclusions

1. Diana L. Eck, 'What Do We mean by "Dialogue"', *Current Dialogue*, WCC, Geneva 1987, pp.5ff.

2. Norman Solomon, 'Jewish/Christian Dialogue. The State of the Art', *Studies in Jewish/Christian Relations*, No. 1, Selly Oak, Birmingham 1984, p. 8.

3. Eugene R. Borrowitz, *Contemporary Christologies: A Jewish Response*, Paulist Press 1980, p.19.

4. Francis Clark (ed.), *Interfaith Directory*, New Era, New York 1987, p. viii.

5. Ibid., p. v.

6. Paul Knitter, 'Preface' to *The Myth of Christian Uniqueness*, ed. John Hick and Paul F. Knitter, SCM Press and Orbis Books 1988, p. ix.

7. E. Troeltsch, 'The Place of Christianity Among the World Religions' in *Christian Thought*, 1923. See my *Together to the Truth*, CLS, Madras 1971, pp. 112–13.

8. Knitter (n.6), p. x.

9. Robert Edward Whitson, *The Coming Convergence of World Religions*, Newman Press, Westminster, Md 1971.

10. Knitter (n.6), p. xi.

11. See for example *The Ethics of World Religions and Human Rights*, ed. Hans Küng and Jürgen Moltmann, SCM Press 1990, my chapter, 'Seeking Community' in *Belonging to Britain*, ed. Roger Hooker, The Council of Churches of Britain and Ireland 1991,

R. Traer *Faith in Human Rights*, Georgetown University Press, Washington D.C. 1990 and Hans Küng, *Global Responsibility*, SCM Press and Crossroad Publishing, New York 1991.

12. I echo the prayer, 'O God of many names' by George Appleton, used by the Week of Prayer for World Peace. I recognize, of course, that some Buddhists and other are uneasy with the use of the term 'God'.

Appendix

1.*Breaking Barriers: The Nairobi Assembly of the World Council of Churches*, ed. David M. Paton, SPCK 1976, pp. 73–74.

2. Ibid., p.75.
3. Ibid., p.75.
4. Ibid., p.76.
5. Ibid., p.76.
6. Para 20, p. 77.
7. Para 22, p. 77.
8. Para 23, pp. 77–8.
9. Quoted by Paton, pp. 71–2.
10. Ibid., pp. 72–3.

Index of Names

Blavatsky, Madame, 31, 266
Bleeker, Prof C. J., 285–6
Blomfield, Lady, 268
Blue, Rabbi Lionel, 225
Boardman, Rev. George Dana, 25
Boeke, Dr Rudolph, 87
Boesak, Rev. D. Allan, 160
Bold, Geoffrey, 83
Bonney, Charles Caroll, 7–42 passim, 122
Bool Chand, Dr, 136
Borhi, A. K., 227
Bornkamm, Dr Günther, 40
Borrowitz, Rabbi Dr E., 311
Bousset, Wilhelm, 48
Braybrooke, Mary, 100, 301
Brickner, Rabbi Balfour, 131
Bristol, Dr F., 25
Brockway, Rev. Dr Allan, 214
Brohi, Mr A. K., 148, 151, 274
Brown, Lester, 57
Brown, Dr Stuart, 221
Browne, Prof E. G., 268
Brundtland, Mrs, Gro Harlem, 109
Bryant, Dr M. Darrol, 274, 276
Buber, Martin, 188, 209
Buddha, Gotama, 16, 19, 21, 31, 35, 41, 68, 268
Buddhadasa Kirthisinghe, 265
Buddhadasa, Ven Bhikkhu, 265
Bunker, Mrs Ellsworth, 95
Buren, Dr Paul van, 189
Burrell, David, 36
Burt, Bishop John, 136
Bush, President George, 117
Butler, R. A. (Lord), 183

Calvin, John, 98
Camara, Dom Helder, 108, 142–3
Candlin, Rev. George, 25
Cardinal, Fr Edward, 182
Carnegie, Andrew, 123
Carpenter, J. Estlin, 34, 37, 49
Carpenter, Lilian, 75
Carpenter, Very Rev. Dr Edward, 74–5, 84, 168, 186
Carter, Mrs, 148
Carter, President Jimmy, 148, 151, 155
Carter, Rev. Stewart Henry, 55, 181
Caspar, Fr R., 252
Castro, Dr Emilio, 260
Ceresole, Paul, 166
Chacour, Fr Elias, 208
Chakravarty, Dr Amiya, 98

Chakravati, Prof C. N., 22
Chandra, Dr Frank, 81
Chandran, Dr R., 320
Chapin, Rev. Augusta, 22, 25–6
Chardin, Fr Teilhard de, 87
Charyar, Nara Sima, 32
Chenchiah, P., 234
Chidananda, Swami, 148, 151
Chinmoy, Sri, 100, 108
Chitrabhanu, Master, 100–1
Choudry, Punyabrata Roy, 61
Chouraqui, Dr Andre, 152
Clark, Dr Francis, 276, 311
Clinchy, Rev. Everett R., 179, 182, 185
Cobb, Professor John, 240
Coggan, Rt Rev. Lord, Donald, 189
Cohen, Professor Hermann, 195
Columbus, Christopher, 8
Combermere, Viscount, Michael, 77
Confucius, 22, 31, 35
Cook, Joseph, 27–8
Cooke, Cardinal, 147
Corrigan, Bishop Daniel, 131
Coulson, Rev. R. G., 72
Cousins, Bernard, 86
Cousins, Dr Ewart, 101
Cox, Prof Harvey, 99
Cracknell, Rev. Kenneth, 88, 245
Cumont, Franz, 40
Curzon, Lord, 64, 72
Cuttat, Jacques Albert, 236

D'vivedi, Manilal N., 23
Dalai Lama, HH, 64, 84, 95, 106, 108–9, 117–8, 162, 252, 264
Damianos, Archbishop, 106
Dard, Moulvri, A. R., 67
Das Gupta, Kedarnath, 114
Dasgupta, Surendranath, 67
Davies, Rev. Tyssul, 83
de Madariage, Prof, Salvadore, 126
de Silva, Dr Lynn A., 321
Dearlove, Olive, 74, 90
Deissman, Adolf, 40
Dennis, James, 27
Detiger, Mrs E., 301
Dev, Mohun, 32
Devanandan, Dr Paul, 290
Dewey, Peter, 82, 89
Dharmapala, Anagarika, 16, 19, 22, 23, 30–1, 34, 41–2
Din, Rabbi Dovid, 274

Index of Organizations